THE COLUMBIA GUIDE TO

The Cold War

THE COLUMBIA GUIDES TO AMERICAN HISTORY AND CULTURES

About the Author

Michael Kort is professor of social science in the College of General Studies at Boston University. He is the author of *The Soviet Colossus: History and Aftermath*, 4th edition (1996) and coauthor of *Modernization and Revolution in China*, revised edition (1997). He received his Ph.D. in Russian history from New York University in 1973.

THE COLUMBIA GUIDE TO

The Cold War

Michael Kort

COLUMBIA UNIVERSITY PRESS

NEW YORK

Columbia University Press
Publishers Since 1893
New York   Chichester, West Sussex
Copyright © 1998 Columbia University Press

Library of Congress Cataloging-in-Publication Data
Kort, Michael, 1944–
The Columbia guide to the Cold War / Michael Kort.
p.   cm. — (The Columbia guides to American history and cultures)
Includes index.
ISBN 0–231–10772–2
1. United States—Foreign relations—1945–1989. 2. United States—
History—1945– 3. Cold War. I. Title. II. Series.
E744.K696   1998
973.9—dc21   98–7154

Casebound editions of Columbia University Press books are printed
on permanent and durable acid-free paper.
Printed in the United States of America
c 10 9 8 7 6 5 4 3 2 1

In memory of Jack M. Chvat

CONTENTS

ACKNOWLEDGMENTS

I owe a great debt to John Zawacki, who for many years has provided an extraordinary learning experience on the Cold War not only for his students at Boston University's College of General Studies but also for his colleagues. I am grateful to James Warren, my editor at Columbia University Press and himself a serious student of the Cold War, for conceiving this project, encouraging me to undertake it, and providing invaluable help from beginning to end. Gregory McNamee was a superb copyeditor and source of many valuable suggestions for improving the text. I will always owe my parents, Paula and the late Victor Kort, more gratitude than I can ever express. Finally, I owe a special thanks to my daughters, Tamara and Eleza, and to my wife, Carol, for making sure I did not allow this or any other project to obscure my appreciation for what really matters in life.

ACKNOWLEDGMENTS

INTRODUCTION

This guide is intended to introduce students to the vast body of materials available on the causes, progression, and conclusion of the Cold War, as well as to the issues the Cold War has raised in the scholarly community. It is designed to be a flexible reference and teaching tool that can be profitably used by both high-school and undergraduate students.

The guide is divided into four parts. Part I is a narrative essay. It provides an overview of the Cold War and some commentary on the issues that have engaged and divided students of the Cold War since it began. Bibliographical references in both the text and endnotes introduce the reader to books and articles that deal with these issues.

The narrative essay is divided into six chapters. The first reviews the debates and discussions among scholars over who was to blame for the Cold War. It divides these scholars into three main categories, according to their general point of view: traditionalists, revisionists, and postrevisionists. The next five chapters form a chronological survey of the Cold War: its beginning (1945–1953), the period from Stalin's death to the Cuban Missile Crisis (1953–1962), the Vietnam War and détente (1962–1975), the so-called New Cold War (1975–1984), and the end of the Cold War (1985–1990). These chapters, which are subdivided topically, also suggest questions the student of the Cold War might ask in order better to understand why events proceeded as they did, such as: How did Soviet and American relations in Europe conflict in the first months of the postwar era? What drew the United States into Vietnam? What factors led to the unraveling of détente? This format allows the reader to get a broad overview by reading entire narrative or to focus directly on a time period or issue of particular interest.

It is important to understand that the narrative essay is only a starting point. It covers only a fraction of the issues that are part of the Cold War debate, and mentions only a few selected works. However, it should give the reader a good sense of the debates that surround the origins and waging of the Cold War and an indication of where to look to broaden one's knowledge and perspective.

Part II is an A-to-Z encyclopedia. It includes a variety list of topics that are central to understanding the Cold War. The reader can turn to a very specific topic such as Stalin or the Marshall Plan, or to a more general topic such as "Doctrines," which covers a series of policies ranging from the official Truman Doctrine to the unofficial Sinatra Doctrine. The former, announced before Congress, was a central fixture at the beginning of the Cold War, whereas the latter, despite lacking any official standing, was pivotal in ending the Cold War. Readers will notice that some of the people, events, and other topics discussed in the narrative essay are highlighted; this indicates they also are included in the encyclopedia, so one can turn there for additional information. In addition, the encyclopedia includes many entries that are not covered in the narrative.

Part III is a concise chronology. Although it briefly mentions what may be called a prehistory of the Cold War, the chronology begins in 1945 with the Yalta Conference and ends in 1991 with the dissolution of the Soviet Union. The chronology includes the major events of the Cold War as well as many background events that may not be mentioned in the overview. It should be used in conjunction with and as a supplement to the narrative essay and the encyclopedia.

Part IV, the longest part of this volume, is a guide to resources on the Cold War. It includes concise descriptions of books, articles, websites, journals, primary source collections, and much more. It is the place to which the reader can go to learn more about the subjects covered or mentioned in the first three parts of this volume. Each entry is annotated to give an sense of the material covered and, often, to indicate the author's or producer's point of view. Because of the many types of materials it covers, the resources part of this volume includes its own introduction.

THE COLUMBIA GUIDE TO

The Cold War

PART I

Narrative Overview

CHAPTER ONE

The Cold War and Its Historians

The Cold War was the defining event of the second half of the twentieth century. It began as the guns of World War II, the most destructive war in human history, had barely fallen silent. It continued through a number of phases of varying intensity until the late 1980s and finally was formally declared over in 1990. The Cold War involved many nations and two major alliance systems. It spread from its point of origin in Europe to Asia, Africa, and even Latin America and divided not only Europe but also much of the world into two hostile camps. Yet through it all the Cold War had two main combatants: the United States and the Soviet Union.

The term "cold war" was first used to apply to the developing post–World War II Soviet-American confrontation by the journalist Walter Lippmann, whose book *The Cold War* appeared in 1947. However, the term has a much older lineage. It appears to have been first used by a Spanish political commentator named Don Juan Manuel, who in the fourteenth century wrote, "War that is very strong and very hot ends with either death or peace, whereas cold war neither brings peace nor gives honor to the one who makes it." In the 1890s the German socialist thinker Eduard Bernstein, writing of the contemporary arms race in Europe, suggested that it had created a "cold war," one in which there "is no shooting, but there is bleeding." And just two years before Lippmann popularized the term, the prescient British author and journalist George Orwell, contemplating a world living in the shadow of nuclear war, warned of a "peace that is no peace," which he called a permanent "cold war."[1]

The Cold War was multidimensional. In one sense, it was a geopolitical conflict that arose from the aftermath of World War II, which had left Germany and Japan defeated and occupied, gravely weakened Great Britain and France, and turned the United States and the Soviet Union into the world's dominant powers. In this respect the Cold War was a traditional power struggle between the two greatest military giants of the age, whose command of massive nuclear arsenals gave them destructive power that exponentially exceeded that of any other states in history. So great was their command of destructive technology that a new term, "superpower," had to be coined to describe these military giants.

The Cold War, however, was at its core an ideological conflict, a struggle between two economic and social systems and radically different ways of life, totalitarian communism and democratic capitalism, represented, respectively, by the Soviet Union and the United States. In this sense, the roots of the Cold War stretch back to the Bolshevik Revolution of 1917 in Russia. It was this ideological core, the conflict between two ways of life in which each side, at least initially, saw the other as an illegitimate regime, that gave the Cold War what historian Arthur Schlesinger Jr. has called its "religious intensity."[2]

Of course, in practice this black-and-white dichotomy of totalitarian communism and democratic capitalism was colored in multiple shades of gray. Both superpowers sought allies and proxies when and where they could find them, basing their decisions to render support on criteria of realpolitik that had nothing to do with promoting democracy or communism. Often this meant that the United States supported dictatorships in various parts of the world whose policies most Americans found repugnant. For its part, the Soviet Union frequently forged working relationships with non-Communist regimes that happened to be at odds with the United States or one or more of its allies. Still, these concessions to realpolitik abroad, no less than the deviations from principle that marked day-to-day life at home, did not negate the profound differences between the two competing ways of life, one based on Western democratic and free market traditions and the other on Russian autocratic and Marxist legacies, whose respective symbolic capitals were Washington and Moscow.

The Cold War also took on an apocalyptic dimension because of atomic weapons, another legacy of World War II. The existence of atomic weapons was what made the superpowers "super" and distinguished their rivalry from earlier ones. Their nuclear arsenals gave each of them, as physicist Robert Oppenheimer, quoting the *Bhagavad-Gita*, put it, the terrifying potential to be the "destroyer of worlds." At the same time, these arsenals forced the superpowers to operate within strict limits, lest they cross the threshold of nuclear warfare and inevitably seal their mutual doom.

A massive worldwide conflict spanning almost half a century, the Cold War was laced with ironies. It began without a formal declaration—indeed, historians still debate its precise starting date—and ended with a suddenness that amazed virtually everyone. In the course of four and a half decades the Cold War was peppered with shooting ("hot") wars, often between Soviet and American proxies, including three bitter conflicts—in Korea, Vietnam, and Afghanistan—that among them claimed over 100,000 American and at least 15,000 Soviet lives. Altogether, the small and not-so-small hot wars, some the outgrowths of the superpower conflict and others the result of extraneous local disputes, that flared in various parts of the world outside Europe during the Cold War took, according to one estimate, over 20 million lives.[3] Yet aside from a few idiosyncratic incidents—most notably the clandestine (though not insignificant) combat activities of Soviet pilots in Korea and antiaircraft gunners in Korea and Vietnam—the United States and the Soviet Union never fired a shot in anger at each other. In fact, for the entire history of the Cold War the two superpowers were legally at peace. They had normal diplomatic relations, competed on friendly terms alongside each other in international sporting events, and exchanged visits by cultural, scholarly, and artistic individuals and groups. Their leaders met in a series of irregularly spaced "summit" meetings in usually unsuccessful attempts to improve relations and ease international tensions. In Europe, where the Cold War began and where it finally ended, and where the superpowers had their closest allies, hundreds of thousands of troops, and large arsenals of **nuclear weapons**, their soldiers never clashed on a battlefield. The greatest arms race in history, which gave each nuclear superpower the ability to destroy the world many times over, ended not with the dreaded unprecedented bang, but with an unanticipated proverbial whimper, and significant arms limitation treaties already in place.

Meanwhile, the apocalyptic power of their nuclear arsenals restrained rather than emboldened both superpowers. This technologically imposed restraint was inherently fragile and tenuous, as the **Cuban Missile Crisis** of 1962 so terrifyingly demonstrated. Still, restraint born of nuclear weapons contributed to the creation of a workable and reasonably predictable, albeit tense, international order. It helped prevent serious crises from escalating into the general war that would have destroyed civilization, confounding the predictions of distinguished observers who were understandably pessimistic about humanity's ability to survive the combination of its newly developed destructive capacity and ancient penchant for violent conflict. All were unduly despairing, from the physics genius Albert Einstein, who wrote in the 1950s that "unless we are able, in the near future, to abolish the fear of mutual aggression, we are doomed"; to strategist Herman Kahn, who predicted in the 1960s that "we are not going to reach the year 2000—and maybe not the year 1965—without a cataclysm"; to political scientist Hans Morgenthau, who warned in the 1970s that "the world is moving ineluctably towards a third world war—a strategic nuclear war."[4] Instead of bringing on the end of

the world as feared, the Cold War, at least as far as the two leading protagonists and their main allies were concerned, ushered in an era of tense stability and nuclear standoff that John Lewis Gaddis, one of the foremost historians of that struggle, has called the "Long Peace."[5] Although some might
argue the many local wars that racked the **Third World** between 1945 and
1990 preclude calling that era a "long peace," the fact remains that at center
stage, where the superpowers stood and the potential for destruction was im-
measurably greater than anywhere else, the guns remained silent from beginning to end.

SCHOLARS DEBATE THE COLD WAR

Most scholars and expert observers agree that World War II set the stage for the
American-Soviet confrontation and, hence, for the Cold War. They concur
that the United States and the Soviet Union, heirs to vastly different historical
and cultural traditions and practitioners of radically divergent ways of life, were
uneasy allies during the war. Several disputes and misunderstandings between
1941 and 1945 produced suspicion and mistrust that made it extremely difficult
for them to establish a genuine peace once the fighting was over. By destroying the power of Germany and Japan and sharply reducing that of Britain and
France, the war left it to the United States and the Soviet Union to determine
the shape of the postwar order. Yet by war's end each power saw the other
through a glass darkly as a mortal threat: The United States viewed the Soviet
Union as an expansionist power driven by its Communist ideology of world
revolution and led by a ruthless and brutal dictator; the Soviet Union in turn
viewed the United States as the fountainhead of international capitalism determined to strangle the Soviet system. Putting together a stable and peaceful
postwar order from these incompatible and ill-fitting pieces promised to be
very difficult at best.

It is at this point that students of the Cold War begin to disagree. Although
any specific event related to the Cold War may provoke its own particular debate (Was the **Truman Doctrine** the proper response to the situation in
Greece in 1947? Should **United Nations** forces have crossed the 38th parallel
in Korea? Did President **John F. Kennedy** overreact to the presence of Soviet
missiles in Cuba? Should the United States have committed hundreds of
thousands of soldiers to preserve the government of South Vietnam?), the fundamental fault line in debates over the Cold War is about who was responsible for it, or how it began, in the first place.

Scholars and expert observers have answered this question in many ways, but their approaches and conclusions generally place most of them into three broad categories: traditionalists, revisionists, and postrevisionists. The "traditionalists," who received that name because most of the early books on the Cold War were by American and British historians who took this approach, cited Soviet expansion in Europe as the cause of the conflict. The "revisionists," so named because they pointedly disagreed with the traditionalists, generally blamed United States economic expansion and policies in support of that expansion for the outbreak of the Cold War. The revisionists in turn were challenged by the postrevisionists, who tended to shift the blame back toward the Soviet Union, although not as totally as the traditionalists.

It should be stressed that these categories are extremely wide-ranging and that each includes a great variety of scholars and works. Some of the historians, political scientists, and other specialists who have written about the Cold War do not fit neatly into any category. They may be placed in one category or another depending on who is doing the categorizing, what factors are being stressed, or what book or article by that particular historian is being considered. In addition, although the traditional, revisionist, and postrevisionist schools are sometimes viewed as following each other chronologically (the revisionists "revised" the traditionalists, and were in turn revised by the postrevisionists), in fact the three schools overlapped in time. Thus the first major revisionist tract, William Appleman Williams's *The Tragedy of American Diplomacy*, appeared in 1959, eleven years before Herbert Feis's *From Trust to Terror: The Onset of the Cold War, 1945–1950*, a classic statement of the traditionalist case. As for postrevisionism, John Lewis Gaddis's *The United States and the Origins of the Cold War, 1941–1947*, appeared in 1972, at about the same time as many influential revisionist works. Since the 1970s all three tendencies have been well represented as books continue to pour off the presses. Finally, it should be noted that although the aforementioned categories are the most widely accepted, some commentators have suggested alternate systems of categorizing Cold War scholarship.[6]

Traditionalists

The traditionalist school (also called the "orthodox" school) dominated the scholarly discussion of the Cold War during the 1940s and 1950s. Traditionalist scholars generally supported the basic thrust of American postwar policy, known as "containment," and the official defense of that policy, such as the analysis offered by **George F. Kennan** in his 1947 *Foreign Affairs* article "Sources of Soviet Conduct." These scholars blamed the Cold War on Soviet expansionism in Europe, which they saw as motivated by either Communist ideology, traditional Russian great-power foreign policy goals, or, most often, a combination of the two. Soviet expansion was made possible by World War II, which by devastating large parts of Europe and destroying German power had created a power vacuum into which the Soviet Union could move. Traditionalists often cited Soviet policy in Poland as a key factor in initiating the Cold War. **Joseph Stalin**, they said, violated the Yalta agreements by forbidding free elections and installing a puppet Communist regime. Soviet expansion into eastern and central Europe not only violated the principle of self-determination, supposedly one of the cornerstones of the Allied war effort against Nazi Germany, but also created a threat to Western Europe, where physical destruction and psychological demoralization had created fertile ground for Communist subversion.

It was not only the Soviet Union's policy in Europe, but its aggressive actions in the Near East during 1945 and 1946 vis-à-vis Iran and Turkey, that provided a clear picture of its menacing intentions. Therefore, the traditionalists maintained, the United States was responding to a palpable threat and genuine need when it intervened in European affairs, beginning with the **Truman Doctrine** and **Marshall Plan**. In fact, the United States had to overcome its historical reluctance to get involved in European affairs before it finally took decisive, and urgently necessary, measures to check Soviet expansion in 1947 and 1948 with the Truman Doctrine and Marshall Plan. Thus the United States was forced to intervene in European affairs to prevent a single aggressive power from dominating the continent, much as it did by entering World War II. The major difference was that during the war the menacing power was Nazi Germany and in the postwar era it was Soviet Russia.

Their basic areas of agreement notwithstanding, traditionalist scholars often differed regarding the most important cause of Soviet postwar expansionism. Thus Herbert Feis (*From Trust to Terror*, 1970) and André Fontaine (*History of the Cold War from the October Revolution to the Korean War*, 1968) stressed the role of Communist ideology, whereas Hans J. Morgenthau (*In Defense of National Interest: A Critical Examination of American Foreign Policy*, 1951) and Norman Graebner (*Cold War Diplomacy: American Foreign Policy 1945–1950*, 1962) focused on traditional Russian great power goals and national interests. Morgenthau, Graebner, and others who shared their point of view—including, within a few years after he wrote "Sources of Soviet Conduct," George Kennan—often are classified in a distinct school of thought called "realism," which is an analytical approach drawn from the field of political science. Realists saw the Soviet threat as more limited than did other traditionalists, and urged a more restrained and less global American response than the policy Washington followed after 1947. In effect, realists wanted to "contain" the American policy of "containment" by limiting it to circumstances where they found a direct threat to American national interests. However, given the basic thrust of their analysis, which viewed Soviet conduct as the prime cause of the Cold War, the realists also legitimately can be placed in the traditionalist camp.

Traditionalists of all stripes agreed about the existence of a Soviet postwar threat to Europe in general and Western Europe in particular. They therefore saw a threat to American security, and ultimately affirmed the necessity and validity of a strong American response. In short, traditionalists maintained that the Soviet Union was the prime mover in initiating the Cold War and that the United States had no choice but to wage it in order to protect Western Europe and to preserve the freedom of the Western world. As Arthur Schlesinger Jr. put it in summarizing the traditionalist position, "The most rational of American policies could hardly have averted the Cold War."[7]

Although the 1940s and 1950s are sometimes considered the heyday of traditionalism, many of the most important traditionalist works were written later. Arthur Schlesinger Jr. published his article "Origins of the Cold War," which was written in response to early revisionist criticism, in the journal *Foreign Affairs* in October 1967. And as noted before, Herbert Feis's *From Trust to Terror* was published in 1970, while important works supporting the traditionalist outlook have appeared throughout the 1980s and 1990s.

Revisionists

It has been pointed out many times that every American war since the War of 1812 has had its "revisionists," observers who concluded after the fighting ended that the official explanation for the war was wanting and that the national interest did not require that war be waged. This was true even of World War II. After the war a number of historians accused President Franklin D. Roosevelt of deliberately exaggerating and thereby misleading the American people about the extent of the threat posed by Germany and Japan. According to these historians, the president pursued a foreign policy he knew would lead to war. Roosevelt's critics included the distinguished historian Charles A. Beard. Nonetheless, Beard and his supporters ultimately found little acceptance among most scholars, in large part because their critiques of American prewar policies relied excessively on far-fetched conspiracy theories and on the highly dubious assertion that Japan, and especially Germany, did not represent a serious threat to American security.

The revisionist school that developed over the issue of the Cold War has proved to be far more durable than that associated with World War II.[8] Revisionists strongly disagreed with the traditionalists about the Soviet threat. They insisted that in 1945 the Soviet Union, badly damaged by the fighting and having suffered huge population losses, was far weaker than the United States and in no position to threaten the West. The military, technological, and economic strength of the United States simply was overwhelming. Notwithstanding Stalin's brutality at home, Soviet policy in central and eastern Europe and elsewhere was cautious and defensive. Stalin wanted to rebuild his devastated country, make sure he had friendly regimes along the Soviet Union's western borders, and prevent once and for all a resurgence of German power. These were all legitimate objectives, the revisionists maintained, for a country in the Soviet Union's circumstances.

Why, then, did the United States react so strongly against Soviet gains after World War II? The main culprit, the revisionists generally argued, was American capitalism and its insatiable demand for new markets and additional raw materials, which had turned the United States into an expansionist power. The first notable revisionist scholar to make this case was William Appleman Williams in *The Tragedy of American Diplomacy*. Williams blamed the Cold War on the American "Open Door" economic policy, which dated from the late nineteenth century. According to Williams, when the United States resisted Soviet influence in eastern Europe so that it could penetrate the region economically, it caused an understandable Soviet reaction, sparking a chain reaction that resulted in the Cold War. Williams was not nearly as critical of the United States as later revisionists. Thus for Williams, the "tragedy of American diplomacy is not that it is evil, but that it denies and subverts American ideas and ideals."[9] Two years later, D. F. Fleming seconded Williams's critique. In *The Cold War and Its Origins*, Fleming specifically blamed President **Harry Truman** for ending Roosevelt's policy of cooperation with the Soviets and turning to confrontation, thereby beginning the Cold War.

Williams's views were echoed and expanded by his students of the "Wisconsin School" (Williams taught at the University of Wisconsin), such as Walter LaFeber, Lloyd C. Gardner, and Thomas J. McCormick. The Wisconsin School in turn helped launch the radical "New Left" school of historiography. The New Left revisionists, strongly influenced both by Marxism and the **Viet-**

nam War, sharpened and hardened the critique of the United States and its foreign policy. Marxism was important because it provided an analytical framework that its practitioners claimed was useful in critiquing not only American foreign policy but also the American capitalist system. The Vietnam War was important because it aroused widespread opposition among Americans and suggested to many that if the United States followed the wrong policy in Vietnam, it could have done the same thing after World War II and provoked the Cold War.

New Left revisionist themes included the assertion that the Cold War began because American economic expansionism, supposedly the inevitable product of American capitalism, forced the Soviet Union to take defensive measures to protect its legitimate interests. American expansionism in turn fit the classic Marxist concept of imperialism, which posited that powerful capitalist states engage in economic exploitation abroad to enable a flawed and unjust economic system at home to survive. Overall, New Left revisionists criticized American foreign policy for opposing economic reform in Europe and for being imperialistic and counterrevolutionary elsewhere in the world.

One of the first New Left indictments of United States policy was David Horowitz's *Free World Colossus*, published in 1965. Two years later, Walter LaFeber published *America, Russia, and the Cold War, 1945–1966*, which became a standard revisionist text as it was updated through seven editions that eventually covered the entire Cold War. Gabriel Kolko, ultimately one of the most prolific of the New Left revisionists, published *The Politics of War* in 1968. Using a strict Marxist analysis, Kolko maintained that the Cold War's origins lay in America's quest for global economic dominance. However, many revisionist scholars writing in the 1970s took a more moderate tone than Kolko and other New Left historians. Stephen E. Ambrose, whose *Rise to Globalism: American Foreign Policy, 1938–1970* appeared in 1971, and Thomas Paterson, whose *Soviet-American Confrontation: Postwar Reconstruction and the Origins of the Cold War* appeared in 1973, were among the prominent moderate revisionist historians.

For a time the sheer volume of revisionist works seemed to dominate the Cold War debate, despite criticism from traditionalists that revisionists ignored Soviet aggressiveness, failed to consider the totalitarian nature of the Soviet regime and the role of **Joseph Stalin**, affirmed conclusions about Soviet intentions without access to Soviet archives and relevant documents, and were at times sloppy in their use of sources. In any event, by the early 1970s a new group of historians already was challenging the revisionists. Although much of their work was either contemporaneous with or even preceded revisionist scholarly output (for the revisionists, undaunted, continued to write), these critics of revisionism were called postrevisionists.

Postrevisionism

Postrevisionism made its first clear-cut appearance in 1972 when John Lewis Gaddis published his highly acclaimed study, *The United States and the Origins of the Cold War, 1941–1947*. Other notable postrevisionists were Vojtech Mastny (*Russia's Road to Cold War: Diplomacy, Warfare, and the Politics of Communism*, 1979), Bruce Kuniholm (*The Origins of the Cold War in the Near East: Great Power Conflict and Diplomacy in Iran, Turkey, and Greece*, 1979), and William Taubman (*Stalin's American Policy: From Entente to Détente to Cold War*, 1982). Postrevisionism, as its name implies, was in many ways a reaction to what its practitioners saw as the excesses of revisionism. In particular, postrevisionists rejected the revisionist condemnation of American postwar foreign policy and that school's single-minded focus on economic determinism (the capitalist quest for markets and raw materials) as the prime mover behind that policy. At the same time, many postrevisionists also had differences with traditionalism. They objected to what they saw as the traditionalists' overly moralistic critique of Soviet policies in Eastern Europe, their readiness to blame the Soviet Union exclusively for the Cold War, and a tendency to overstate the degree to which Soviet policies were grounded in Communist ideology.

Postrevisionists generally viewed the genesis of the Cold War in geopolitical terms. They were less concerned with placing blame on either the Soviet Union or the United States than were the traditionalists or the revisionists. Postrevisionists instead focused on the geopolitical vacuums that resulted from World War II, especially in Eastern Europe, and saw both the United States and the Soviet Union motivated by security interests rather than expansionism. Postrevisionists also tended to find that both the Soviet Union and the United States contributed to the outbreak of the Cold War; however, they nonetheless still tilted noticeably toward the traditionalists in finding the Soviet Union primarily responsible for the Cold War. According to the general postrevisionist scenario, it may well have been the case that after 1945 the Soviet Union was acting out of security interests and had limited objectives, and that Stalin was not an out-of-control megalomaniac. But it was also true that Soviet advances in Eastern Europe were dramatically expansionist when compared to the prewar, and even the 1941, state of affairs. It was therefore legitimate to conclude that Soviet expansion was a threat to the European balance of power that required an American response.

Critics of postrevisionism pointed out that this analysis was suspiciously similar to the traditionalist wine, albeit in new bottle and under a new name. Interestingly, a number of European historians joined the debate in support of the postrevisionist point of view. One, the Norwegian scholar Geir Lundestad, pointed out that in the years immediately after World War II Western European leaders urgently wanted the United States to play a active role in European affairs to provide an essential counterweight to Soviet power. If the United States established an "empire" of sorts in Europe, it was, said Lundestad, an "empire by invitation."[10]

Furthermore, the postrevisionist interpretation of evidence that emerged after the mid-1970s nudged some of its advocates closer to the traditionalist camp. Prominent among those shifting their positions was John Lewis Gaddis, whose views, particularly his analysis of Stalin's intentions, were influenced by the work of scholars like Vojtech Mastny, Robert Tucker, Alan Bullock, and the Russian historian Dmitri Volkogonov.[11] Thus in his 1994 article "The Tragedy of Cold War History" Gaddis noted the fundamental similarities between fascism and Marxism-Leninism and between Stalin and Hitler, concluding that it is "quite difficult . . . to see how there could have been any long-term basis for coexistence—for 'getting along'—with either of these fundamentally evil dictators." Gaddis also criticized historians who failed to distinguish between dictatorial and democratic regimes while evaluating their international policies—drawing a sharp line between the "Wilsonian" vision and that of "Lenin, Stalin, Hitler, Mao, and their imitators"—and praised the United States for its decisive postwar role in "resistance to authoritarianism."[12]

How Has the New Evidence From Soviet or Eastern European Archives Affected the Debate Over the Cold War?

In recent years new evidence has emerged from both Soviet and Eastern European archives and from other sources, such as the publication of the memoirs of Soviet Foreign Minister **Viacheslav Molotov**, that points to the Soviet Union as the main instigator of the Cold War. For example, it was with unapologetic pride that Molotov told an interviewer, "My task as minister of foreign affairs was to expand the borders of the fatherland as much as possible. And it seems that Stalin and I coped with this task quite well."[13] Molotov's memoirs and archival evidence indicate strongly that the Soviets were not simply acting defensively in Europe; instead, they pushed forward until they encountered American resistance in a policy historian Peter Stavrakis has called "prudent expansionism."[14] There also is growing evidence that Stalin had serious hopes that the Communist parties in one or more Western Europe countries, especially France and Italy, would be able to exploit the postwar chaos and economic hardship and take power. Some of the new sources also support the traditionalists who argued that Stalin and other Soviet leaders viewed the world through a Marxist-Leninist prism. As for the appropriateness of the Western response in the immediate postwar era, the new evidence lends credence to the view that the main restraint on Stalin's outward probes was the Soviet dictator's fear of American power. Two Russian scholars, Vladislav Zubok and Constantine Pleshakov, on the basis of their study of recently declassified Soviet archival material, have concluded that rather than being too assertive immediately after the end of World War II, "the West was not firm enough, it did not check Stalin's imperial expansion."[15]

Other recently unearthed evidence conclusively demonstrates that Stalin both assisted and approved the North Korean invasion of South Korea in 1950, having made the decision to strike when he became convinced the United States would not respond. In contrast to what Western historians previously believed, Stalin also provided extensive assistance to the Chinese Communist Party led by **Mao Zedong** during the Chinese civil war. New evidence from the Soviet archives also demonstrates the extent to which Communist parties in Western countries, including the United States, spied for the Soviet Union. Perhaps the most important Soviet espionage coup was its penetration during World War II of the Manhattan Project, the top-secret American program to build an atomic bomb, which enabled the Soviets to explode their first nuclear weapon in 1949, well ahead of Western expectations.

Much of this evidence appears to strengthen the traditionalist and postrevisionist interpretations of the early Cold War years at the expense of the revisionist view. However, it is important to remember that far more remains hidden in the Soviet and Eastern European archives than has been revealed. In addition, not all scholars are convinced that what has recently emerged is decisive. Thus Melvin Leffler's recent study *A Preponderance of Power: National Security, the Truman Administration, and the Cold War* (1992) reaffirms the revisionist argument that an expansive concept of security that emerged during the 1940s led the United States to challenge vital Soviet security interests in Eastern Europe and thereby cause the Cold War.

Although this overview is intended to provide a useful framework for understanding the debate over the Cold War, it is essential to keep in mind that no brief summary can possibly capture the innumerable nuances and shades that exist within all three of the tendencies discussed.[16] It is also true that there are scholars who do not fall within any of these categories, no matter how loosely they are defined, and that the debate still goes on as new evidence becomes available. This means that it is up to each student of the Cold War to examine the evidence and arguments closely before drawing conclusions about a conflict that did so much to shape the world in which we live.

CHAPTER TWO

The Cold War Begins: 1945–1953

By January 1945 World War II was almost over in Europe. The Grand Alliance, that odd and ungainly coupling of the United States, Great Britain, and over twenty other democratic countries with the totalitarian Soviet Union, had held together since 1941 and was on the verge of defeating Nazi Germany; the final surrender clearly was only months away. The alliance had survived a variety of deep-seated fears, suspicions, and recriminations that grew out of both prewar and wartime events and disputes. Prior to the war, these included the Western intervention on the anti-Bolshevik side in the Russian civil war, the American refusal to recognize the Soviet regime until 1933, and the Nazi-Soviet pact of August 1939 that freed Hitler to attack Poland and ignite World War II. Between September 1939, when the war began, and June 1941, the Soviet Union's occupation of eastern Poland, its attack on Finland, its annexation of the Baltic states (Lithuania, Latvia, and Estonia), and its extensive economic ties with Germany that helped supply the Nazi war machine all alienated Moscow from the Western powers. Once the Soviet Union and the United States respectively joined the war against Germany in mid- and late 1941, the Grand Alliance remained under constant strain, troubled by Western fears during 1942 and 1943 that Stalin might make a separate peace with Germany, Soviet bitterness over the West's failure to mount a "Second Front" in Europe before June 1944, the revelation in 1943 that the Soviets had murdered thousands of Polish officers three years earlier, and other problems.

The alliance held and won the war. Yet serious differences growing out of fundamentally different social systems and views of the world remained unresolved, and ultimately turned out to be irresolvable. Washington, London, and the other Western capitals were the headquarters of democratic societies with free-enterprise economic systems. At least when it came to Europe, the Western democracies believed in self-determination. They wanted to see that doctrine applied in Eastern Europe, particularly in Poland, no less than in the western part of the continent. Moscow, formerly the core of the old Russian empire, was the fountainhead of totalitarian Communism. Its leaders not only had no interest in national self-determination but also were determined that in Eastern Europe, and especially in Poland, neither national self-determination nor other Western concerns, such as access to markets and raw materials, would be allowed to stand in the way of Soviet geopolitical and security concerns.

The Grand Alliance had been solidified to some extent by the generally positive first meeting of the leaders of its "Big Three"—Franklin Roosevelt of the United States, Joseph Stalin of the Soviet Union, and **Winston Churchill** of Great Britain—at Teheran in late 1943. Yet as 1945 dawned there was deep concern in Washington and London. The American and British armies had not yet reached the Rhine, but Soviet forces already had overrun much of Eastern Europe and were rapidly advancing westward. These advances, even as they were welcome steps toward Germany's final defeat, also raised the specter of Soviet control of much of Eastern Europe and the very real possibility, as Churchill told Roosevelt, that "the end of this war may prove to be more disappointing than was the last."

These fears were not new: they echoed concerns in the West about Russian power that extended back well over a century to the time when the army of Tsar Alexander I reached Paris during the Napoleonic Wars. They took on a new and potent ideological dimension after the Bolshevik Revolution of November 1917 and the establishment of the Soviet regime, with its commitment to spreading revolutionary Marxism abroad. By early 1945, the Western powers were at loggerheads with Moscow's strategic objectives. From the Kremlin's perspective, the disasters that had befallen the Soviet Union after its invasion by Germany in June 1941 meant that future Soviet security could best be guaranteed by extending its sphere of influence as far westward into Europe as possible.

It was to head off the dangerous expansion of Soviet power and to set the basis for a postwar peace made durable by Big Three cooperation that the British and Americans invited the Soviets to a second conference. The **Yalta Conference** took place from February 4–11, 1945, at the Soviet Black Sea resort town of Yalta.

YALTA, HIROSHIMA, AND THE END OF WORLD WAR II

Could Roosevelt Have Negotiated a Better Deal at Yalta?

The Yalta Conference, held in the former summer home of Russia's last tsar amid war wreckage that littered the surrounding countryside of the Crimean

Peninsula, was graced by unusually warm and sunny weather for that time of year. It produced significant agreements the Americans and British wanted. The Soviets agreed to enter the war against Japan within three months after Germany's surrender and to compromise on voting and membership issues in a projected new international organization, the United Nations. The Yalta participants also agreed to divide Germany into four occupation zones (one each for the Big Three and one for France) and to create a temporary Polish-Soviet border called the Curzon Line, which closely followed the ethnic frontier in the region between Poles on one hand and Belarusians and Ukrainians on the other. However, on the key issue of who would control Poland, the conference produced far less favorable results for the West. Roosevelt and Churchill accepted vague language about the composition of a future Polish government—it was to be expanded from the Communist-dominated regime the Soviets had set up in January—and Stalin's promise of "free and unfettered" elections in the near future. The language was so vague that Admiral Thomas D. Leahy, Roosevelt's Chief of Staff, complained to the president, "This is so elastic that the Russians can stretch it all the way from Yalta to Washington without breaking it."[1]

When Poland quickly fell under Communist control in the wake of Yalta, the agreements came under bitter criticism in the United States. Roosevelt was accused of giving the Soviets too much, and especially of betraying Poland and selling it out to Soviet domination. Yet it appears that Roosevelt was justified when he told Leahy that given the circumstances he could do no better for Poland. The reality on the ground was that the Soviets already controlled most of Poland and British and American forces were far away and struggling against strong German resistance. As Churchill pointed out with his usual pragmatism, with hundreds of German divisions still in the field it was a very poor time to pick a quarrel with the Soviet Union. Stalin was determined to exploit his military position to control Poland, through which the Germans had invaded his country twice in a generation, and Western needs in the Far East and goals for the postwar world left him in a position to do just that. The United States, still months away from a successful test of the atomic bomb, desperately wanted Soviet help in what was expected to be a difficult and very costly effort to defeat Japan. The Western Allies also still hoped for Soviet cooperation in establishing a durable peace once the fighting finally ended. If Roosevelt can be faulted for Yalta-related actions, it is because he hid the unpalatable but unavoidable facts about Poland from the American people and their elected representatives in Congress when he returned home.

The Use of the Atomic Bomb Against Japan

On August 6, 1945, the United States dropped an atomic bomb on the Japanese city of Hiroshima. In an instant the bomb killed over 80,000 people and destroyed 80 percent of the city. Three days later a second atomic bomb leveled the city of Nagasaki, killing an additional 60,000 people. On August 14 the Japanese accepted Allied surrender terms as announced in the Potsdam Declaration of July 26, subject to the proviso that their emperor would remain on his throne. The formal surrender in Tokyo Harbor took place on September 2, 1945, on the United States battleship *Missouri*, finally putting an end to World War II.

The use of the atomic bomb against Japan ultimately ignited one of the most intense of the many historical controversies that surround the Cold War. President Harry Truman maintained he made the decision to use the bomb to shorten the war and save American lives. Despite a few critics, in the years immediately following the war the prevailing consensus among historians supported the president's decision and accepted his explanation for it. Traditionalist historians generally argued that the Japanese were not prepared to surrender prior to the bomb's use and that an invasion of Japan, scheduled to take place in two stages—the first in November 1945 with an assault on the southern island of Kyushu and the second in March 1946 with a landing near Tokyo—would have cost hundreds of thousands of lives. (The United States lost about 400,000 dead in the entire war.) Herbert Feis, in *Japan Subdued: The Atomic Bomb and the End of the War in the Pacific* (1961), took a somewhat different tack, arguing that the Japanese probably would have surrendered by late 1945 without the use of the bomb, but at the time Truman was convinced that his decision would save thousands of American lives and end the war in the shortest possible time.

During the 1960s this view was challenged by revisionist historians. The most strident attack on Truman came from historian Gar Alperovitz, whose book *Atomic Diplomacy: Hiroshima and Potsdam, the Use of the Atomic Bomb, and the American Confrontation with Soviet Power*, appeared in 1965. Alperovitz insisted that Truman knew that the atomic bomb was not necessary to force Japan's surrender and that it was used for "atomic diplomacy," that is, to intimidate the Soviet Union and make Stalin more pliable in postwar negotiations. Put another way, Alperovitz insisted that the use of the atomic bomb was not a necessary step to end World War II but the opening salvo of the Cold War.

Although revisionist historians generally accepted large chunks of the atomic diplomacy thesis, many did not go as far as Alperovitz. For example, Gabriel

Kolko, in *The Politics of War: The World and United States Foreign Policy, 1943–1945*, actually rejected much of the atomic diplomacy thesis. Some revisionists who found more validity in the thesis nonetheless argued that "atomic diplomacy" was a secondary rather than a primary factor in the bomb's use against Japan. Thus Martin Sherwin (*A World Destroyed: The Atomic Bomb and the Grand Alliance*, 1975), maintained that American policy makers never seriously questioned whether the bomb would be used once it became available. In other words, bureaucratic momentum—that is, the continued acceptance of a long-standing decision to use a weapon that had been built by mobilizing vast scientific talent and at enormous cost to win the war—played a key role in the ultimate decision to use the atomic bomb against Japan. Revisionists also cited the hatred for the Japanese and the desire for revenge after the bombing of Pearl Harbor. At the same time, some revisionists who minimized or rejected the significance of atomic diplomacy were critical of Truman for other reasons. Barton Bernstein ("A Postwar Myth: Five Hundred Thousand U.S. Lives Saved," *Bulletin of Atomic Scientists* 42, 1986), argued that Truman, to justify the use of the atomic bomb, drastically inflated the casualty estimates for the invasion of Japan. Bernstein's lower figures in turn were challenged by traditionalist-minded historians such as Robert James Maddox (*Weapons of Victory: The Hiroshima Decision Fifty Years Later*, 1995), who pointed out that there were many casualty estimates being made in 1945 and that several, including those in July based on the latest intelligence about Japanese troop movements, were significantly higher than those cited by Bernstein.

The revisionist argument in its various forms elicited a sharp response and produced a vigorous debate. Critics of the revisionist case insisted that there is no solid evidence that the United States and its allies could have brought about a Japanese surrender by diplomatic means, and considerable evidence suggesting that without the use of atomic weapons a costly invasion of Japan would have been necessary. During mid-1945 the Japanese were reinforcing their troops at the expected point of the Allied invasion, which is why American analysts raised their casualty estimates. Japan's diplomatic approaches to the Soviet Union were designed to end the war on terms that would have been totally unacceptable to the Allies. Not even the fire bombing of Tokyo in March 1945, which took more lives than the bombing of Hiroshima several months later, could force a Japanese surrender. Japan's hard-line military leaders, who controlled the government, bitterly opposed any surrender prior to August 6, and even after the bombing of both Hiroshima *and* Nagasaki the government remained deadlocked over whether to surrender until Emperor Hirohito intervened and tipped the scales for peace.

There is also convincing evidence that Truman's primary motive for using atomic weapons against Japan was to shorten the war and save American lives. This imperative took on increasing urgency in the face of the ferocity of Japanese resistance and high American losses in battle after battle. The extremely heavy American losses at the battle of Okinawa, which finally ended in June 1945 and was the last major battle prior to the planned invasion of Japan, appalled Truman and his top advisors. Nor by August 1945 was there much sympathy in the United States for the Japanese, who had bombed Pearl Harbor and committed many atrocities in countries they had overrun. There is, in addition, at least one point on which many revisionists and nonrevisionists agree. The effort to build an atomic bomb, originally undertaken because of fears that Germany would build a bomb, had begun in August 1942 and cost the immense sum of $2 billion. American leaders had assumed that when the atomic bomb was ready it would be used. A reversal of that assumption would have required a fundamental reconsideration of American policy, something that was most unlikely in the hectic days of mid-1945 after almost four years of bloody war.

Any attempt to use the atomic bomb to intimidate the Soviet Union in negotiations that took place after the war ended therefore would appear unrelated to the decision Harry Truman made about bombing Japan in July 1945. Critics of the "atomic diplomacy" thesis add that there is scant evidence of such an attempt.

THE ORIGINS AND EVOLUTION OF CONTAINMENT, 1945–1949

In the 1830s, the French aristocrat and political commentator Alexis de Tocqueville noted the following about two huge countries, one on Europe's eastern fringe and the other directly west across the Atlantic Ocean:

> There are on earth today two great people, who, from different points of departure, seem to be advancing toward the same end. They are the Russians and the Anglo-Americans.
>
> Both have grown great in obscurity; and while the attention of mankind was occupied elsewhere they have suddenly taken their places in the first rank among the nations, and the world has learned, almost at the same time, both of their birth and of their greatness.
>
> All the other peoples appear to have attained approximately their natural limits, and have nothing left but to preserve their positions; but these two are growing; all the others have stopped or continue only by

violated a wartime treaty. It took a sharply worded American message to bring about a Soviet withdrawal a few months later. In February, the same month a Soviet atom-spy ring based in Canada was exposed, Stalin gave a highly publicized hard-line speech in Moscow. The Soviet dictator stated that Communism and capitalism were "incompatible" and that the Soviet Union therefore had to begin a military buildup. That was enough to convince some pessimists that the Soviets were preparing for war; Supreme Court Justice William O. Douglas said the speech was a declaration of World War III. Actually, the only war that took place was a war of words. The next salvo in that verbal war came from Winston Churchill, who had been voted out of office the previous July. At Truman's invitation, in March Churchill came to Fulton, Missouri, where, with the American president approvingly sitting behind him on the speaker's platform, he issued an eloquent and dire warning about Soviet expansionism:

> A shadow has fallen upon the scenes so lately lighted by Allied victory. . . . From Stettin in the Baltic to Trieste in the Adriatic, an iron curtain has descended across the Continent. Behind that line lie all the capitals of the ancient states of Central and Eastern Europe. Warsaw, Berlin, Prague, Vienna, Budapest, Belgrade, Bucharest, and Sophia, all these famous cities . . . lie in what I must call the Soviet sphere, and all are subject in one form or another . . . to a high and, in many cases, increasing measure of control from Moscow. . . . This is certainly not the liberated Europe we sought to build up. Nor is it one which contains the essentials of a permanent peace.[5]

Thus, as Walter LaFeber observed, "by early 1946 Stalin and Churchill issued their declarations of Cold War."[6]

In August came a second Soviet probe outside Europe when Stalin demanded from Turkey that it grant the Soviet Union joint control of the Dardanelles linking the Black and Mediterranean seas. This demand immediately produced a serious U.S.-Soviet confrontation. President Truman ordered American naval warships to the region, at which point the Soviets backed down. Meanwhile, two American proposals to the United Nations for the international control of atomic weapons died from fatal doses of Soviet-American mistrust; civil wars between conservative governments and Communist guerrillas broke out in Greece and China; Communist parties flourished and belonged to coalition governments in France and Italy; and constant disputes caused tension between Western and Soviet occupation administrations in Germany.

George F. Kennan's Long Telegram of 1946

Late in February, two weeks after Stalin's menacing speech, a sixteen-page telegram arrived in Washington from the American embassy in Moscow. It was from George F. Kennan, the State Department's leading expert on Russia. According to Kennan, the Soviets, driven by Russia's traditional sense of permanent insecurity and their fiercely anticapitalist Marxist-Leninist outlook, were irrevocably hostile to the West. The Soviet regime was a brutal dictatorship—"a police regime par excellence, reared in the dim half world of tsarist police intrigue, accustomed to think primarily in terms of police power." It needed foreign enemies to justify its harsh rule. Kennan warned that the Soviet Union would continue its expansionist policies and attempt to undermine the capitalist states of Western Europe, all of which would be a serious threat to the security of the United States. While avoiding specific policy proposals, Kennan noted that Soviet power "Impervious to the logic of reason . . . is highly sensitive to the logic of force." He added that despite its malevolent nature, the Soviet Union remained weaker than the West which, provided it maintained "cohesion, firmness and vigor," could influence Soviet behavior.[7]

The Long Telegram quickly made the rounds among top administration officials. Kennan's analysis seemed to confirm what Truman and his advisors were seeing and to validate the tougher stance the administration was taking toward the Soviets. Nor was Kennan alone in his opinions. In a series of telegrams sent just one month later to London, Frank Roberts, an expert on Russia serving in Britain's Moscow embassy, expressed the same gloomy outlook. Ironically, in September the Soviet Union's ambassador to Washington, Nikolai Novikov, sent his own long telegram to Moscow. Following the classic Marxist-Leninist analysis discussed by Kennan, Novikov postulated an American drive for world dominance and warned that the United States was preparing for war against the Soviet Union. Taken together, the telegrams were a statement that diplomacy between the two sides had reached a dangerous impasse.

The Truman Doctrine and the Marshall Plan

In February 1947 a disturbing note arrived in Washington from the British government. It informed Truman and his new Secretary of State, **George Marshall**, that the British could no longer afford to support the conservative Greek government in its struggle against Communist guerrillas. Great

Britain, the only country that had fought the Germans from the very beginning to the bitter end of both World War I and World War II, was exhausted. The British also said they could no longer afford to supply financial aid to Turkey.

Truman and Marshall believed that without outside support the Greek government would fall to the insurgents. It was a corrupt regime that had limited public support. Its main virtue from the West's point of view was its staunch anti-Communism. However, in Truman's view, much more was at stake than a tottering anti-Communist regime. Washington feared that a Communist victory in Greece would allow Soviet power to expand into the Mediterranean region. This could destabilize both France and Italy, whose Communist parties were very strong and might be able to come to power legally via elections. It would threaten the vital sea routes to the oil-rich Middle East and destabilize both Turkey and Iran, both of which bordered on the Soviet Union and formed a "northern tier" protecting the rest of the Middle East. In short, the Truman administration was convinced that the collapse of Greece had implications far beyond its borders that were vital for American security.

There is one irony to this analysis. The main outside support for the Greek Communists was coming from Communist-controlled Yugoslavia, not the Soviet Union. In fact, Stalin had been urging Yugoslavia's leader, Marshall **Josip Broz Tito,** to stop helping the Greeks because Stalin feared provoking a strong Western reaction. However, Truman was not aware of this and assumed the Soviets were behind the trouble in Greece.

The problem was how to respond. Demobilization had left the United States with a skeleton force of troops in Europe, mostly inexperienced draftees. The defense budget had been cut to the bone. There was little inclination in the Republican-controlled Congress to spend additional money, especially if that meant raising taxes, to meet what the President might maintain were new and urgent needs. The American public, just settling down to peacetime life after a long war, was reverting to its traditional isolationism and was simply not interested in foreign affairs or problems in faraway Europe.

This public indifference helps explain Truman's speech to Congress, in which he asked for $400 million to aid Greece and Turkey. The rhetoric was broad and stark. Greece and Turkey were only the tip of the iceberg. Truman stressed that the real issue was the struggle between free and totalitarian societies. No democratic country, including the United States, could be secure in a world dominated by the latter. That is why the national interest demanded that the United States "support free peoples who are resisting attempted subjugation by armed minorities or outside pressures." This commitment became known as the Truman Doctrine.

Actually, although American aid helped turn the tide against the Communists in Greece by 1948, the Truman Doctrine initially amounted to much less than it seemed. Although Truman's wording in theory implied the potential for a worldwide anti-Communist commitment, in practice his program provided only piecemeal and limited assistance for two countries on the fringe of Europe. There were no funds, nor was there a coherent strategy, to provide any meaningful support for the major countries of Western Europe, the key area of American concern abroad. Only additional and dramatically larger commitments could give a viable shape and structure to a new American policy that ultimately would be known as "containment."

Although the Truman Doctrine garnered broad national support, it also had its critics, such as Secretary of Commerce Henry Wallace, who believed that the President's hard line was an overreaction and likely to worsen relations with the Soviet Union. Wallace also pointed out that contrary to the Truman Doctrine's goal of defending so-called free peoples, neither Greece nor Turkey had democratic governments. The debate was continued by historians in the years to come, with revisionists generally echoing and expanding on Wallace's criticisms and traditionalists and postrevisionists tending to support Truman's policy, if not always his rhetoric.

In any event, commitments implicit in the Truman Doctrine soon became clearer. The Truman administration quickly found itself facing increasingly serious difficulties abroad, especially in Europe. The problem was that despite two years of peace and extensive American loans, the countries of Western Europe were not recovering from the devastation of the war. The harsh winter of 1946–47 had crippled the British economy, leaving millions unemployed, cold, and hungry. Conditions were no better in France or Italy, and far worse in Germany, where economic hardship was driving people to desperation. The demoralization in Western Europe was creating ideal conditions for Communist propaganda; in France the Communist Party was winning one-fourth of the vote, in Italy one-third. In addition, Europe could no longer afford to buy American products, which boded ill for the nation's economy.

The Truman administration's response was the European Recovery Program, better known as the Marshall Plan. Marshall announced the plan during a speech at Harvard University early in June of 1947. He called for the United States to give, not loan, the nations of Europe $28 billion for economic recovery. It was an astounding sum, twice the annual United States defense budget at the time. At first Congress balked, even though Truman lowered

Marshall's initial request to $17 billion. It took the Soviet-sponsored coup in Czechoslovakia in February 1948, which overthrew that country's democratic government and replaced it with a Communist dictatorship, to highlight the growing Soviet threat to Western Europe. Within a matter of weeks Britain, France, and the Benelux countries (Belgium, the Netherlands, and Luxembourg) signed a defensive military treaty called the Brussels Pact. At the end of March, Congress passed the Marshall Plan.

Over the next three years the United States provided more than $12 billion in economic aid to Western Europe. Along with funds for reconstruction and other purposes, the Marshall Plan encouraged economic cooperation among the recipients. By 1952, Western Europe had completed an economic recovery that was little short of miraculous. Because the European nations spent some of their aid for necessary goods in the United States (they were required to do so by Marshall Plan regulations), and because Europe's economic recovery increased the ability of its people to purchase additional American products, the Marshall Plan also benefited the United States. Although a number of economic historians, particularly Europeans, have pointed out that the first Marshall Plan aid did not reach Europe until mid-1948, by which time a European recovery had in fact already begun, it seems fair to say that the Marshall Plan played a central role in checking the growth of Communist influence in Western Europe and was the most successful American foreign policy program of the Cold War.

Winston Churchill called the Marshall Plan the "most unsordid act in history." Although they have not gone quite that far, most other commentators on the Cold War have applauded the Marshall Plan for both its intent and its success. A number of New Left historians, however, following the lead of William Appleman Williams, have taken a more jaundiced view of the Marshall Plan. For example, Gabriel and Joyce Kolko view the Marshall Plan as a tool for accomplishing several self-interested American foreign policy goals, including "suffocating internal radicalism" in Western Europe and fostering American "expansionism."[8]

Even before Congress approved the Marshall Plan, the evolving United States policy toward the Soviet Union was given a name. Writing in the journal *Foreign Affairs* under the pseudonym "X" (which fooled few people for very long), George F. Kennan repeated the arguments he made in his Long Telegram. He also added a general policy recommendation: "In these circumstances it is clear that the main element of any United States policy toward the Soviet Union must be that of a long-term, patient but firm and vigilant containment of Russian expansive tendencies." Kennan further suggested that bottling up the Soviet Union over time ultimately would lead to "either the break-up or the gradual mellowing of Soviet power."[9]

In his article Kennan provided no specific suggestions for how to carry out containment; later he voiced strong disagreements with how it was being implemented. What in fact happened over the next few years was that containment took shape in an ad hoc fashion as the Truman administration crafted individual policies to meet successive crises. As historian Walter Miscamble has noted, "the containment doctrine . . . did not dictate the policies determined from 1947 to 1950 but rather the policies gave form and meaning to the doctrine."[10]

The Berlin Blockade and NATO

The Marshall Plan was a blow to Stalin's overall foreign policy strategy. The Soviet Union wanted to see Western Europe remain economically weak and in crisis, inasmuch as a weak Europe strengthened the Soviet position on the continent. The Marshall Plan clearly was a massive American commitment to prevent that from happening. But there was more. A primary goal of Soviet foreign policy was to keep Germany weak. Yet the Western powers, led by the United States, were well aware that there could be no general European economic recovery without a German recovery. They took steps to combine their three zones into a unified and anti-Communist state whose economic recovery was one of the prime goals of the Marshall Plan. Simultaneously Britain, with American encouragement, had organized the Brussels Pact, whose main purpose was self-defense against the Soviet Union. Furthermore, Stalin was quarreling with Yugoslavia's Marshall Tito, who, unlike other Communist leaders in the Soviet satellite states of Eastern Europe, had come to power without his help and therefore was an independent force. In June 1948 that quarrel led to a split in the Communist world, and Yugoslavia in effect defected from the Communist bloc and became one of the first avowedly neutral states in the intensifying Cold War.

Stalin reacted in several ways. To prevent any further erosion of his Eastern European empire, he tightened his grip on the other states of Eastern Europe through a series of purges. Farther west, Stalin ordered the French and Italian Communist parties to foment strikes to undermine the economies of those countries. The Soviet dictator's main target, and therefore the scene of his strongest countermove, was Germany. Stalin was convinced that the United States was the main source of his troubles. He especially did not want to see Germany—and the Western allies controlled the industrial heartland and therefore the most important part of that country—cast its lot with the Americans and the West. If he could demonstrate to the Europeans that the United States would not stand firm under real pressure, the Germans might decide to rely less on the United States and cut the best deal they could with the Soviet Union. Discrediting American resolve might also weaken Western Europe's transatlantic ties.

Stalin's tool was the Berlin Blockade. Its purpose was to force the United States, Britain, and France out of the city. The Western powers were especially vulnerable there because **Berlin**, and with it their occupation zones in the city, was entirely surrounded by Soviet-controlled territory. On June 24, 1948, the Soviets banned all overland and river traffic to Berlin. They technically were within their rights, insofar as the Potsdam agreements did not guarantee the Western powers surface access routes to their zones in Berlin. Truman's response nonetheless was unequivocal: "We are going to stay, period," he told his advisors. The question was how to do so without risking war by using force to reach the Western-controlled zones of the city. The answer was the remarkable Berlin Airlift, which for eleven months supplied 2.5 million people with all of their needs, from coal, blankets, and machinery to eggs, dried milk, and medicine. Unwilling to risk war by interfering with the West's massive air armada, and seeing the Western powers increasingly coming together, Stalin finally lifted the blockade on May 12, 1949.

By blockading Berlin Stalin unintentionally helped create another problem for the Soviet Union: the **North Atlantic Treaty Organization (NATO)**. On April 4, 1949, while negotiations were underway to end the Berlin Blockade, the United States, Britain, France, Canada, and eight other nations signed the treaty that brought NATO into existence. Its members pledged to provided each other "continuous self-help and mutual aid" and affirmed that an attack against one "shall be considered an attack against them all." Within a few years NATO had fifteen members, including West Germany (the Federal Republic of Germany), which was formally set up as an independent state just days before the Berlin Blockade officially ended.

NATO was a landmark in more ways than one. It was a devastating defeat for Soviet policy in Europe. Moscow furiously denounced it as anti-Soviet and aggressive and an attempt "to intimidate the states which do not agree to obey the dictates of the Anglo-American grouping of Powers that lay claim to world domination."[11] NATO marked the first time that the United States entered a military alliance in peacetime. It promoted European integration, at least on the western half of the continent. Its very existence was a major step in the institutionalization of the Cold War. And it signaled Europe's unnatural division into a capitalist west and a Communist east that would last for four decades.

THE SOVIET ATOMIC BOMB, THE FALL OF CHINA, AND NSC 68

Two other events in 1949 played major roles in shaping the Cold War. On August 29 the Soviet Union tested its first atomic bomb, a development that shocked Washington and the rest of the country. (In fact, information from nuclear spy Klaus Fuchs probably speeded up the development of a Soviet bomb by one to two years.) Suddenly the monopoly the United States had enjoyed in atomic weaponry was over, years before prognosticators had expected. Meanwhile another huge bomb, this one political, was going off in China as Communist forces were completing their victory in a three-year civil war in which the United States had invested $3 billion in support of the anti-Communist Nationalist forces. On October 1, Communist Party leader Mao Zedong announced the founding of the People's Republic of China (PRC).

Truman's response was to order a reevaluation of the United States defense posture in January 1950. At the same time, after a meeting that lasted only seven minutes, Truman ordered a speedup of research on thermonuclear weapons, or hydrogen bombs, which potentially were far more powerful than atomic bombs. Truman acted despite criticism by J. Robert Oppenheimer, the supervisor of the original American atomic bomb project, and other like-minded people who feared that such a decision would lead to a disastrous arms race and quite possibly an apocalyptic nuclear war. In retrospect, Truman made the correct decision, since the Soviet Union began priority research on a thermonuclear bomb in late 1949, only a few months after testing its first atomic bomb.

A few months after requesting the defense evaluation, Truman got his answer in the form of a document known as NSC 68 (National Security Council Paper Number 68). Its main author was **Paul Nitze**, who would participate in many high-level policy decisions during the course of the Cold War. NSC 68 warned that the Soviet Union was relentlessly expansionist and predicted that the future would bring "an indefinite period of tension and danger." The United States had to take a global view of its security needs and be prepared to respond to Soviet or Communist expansion anywhere in the world. In other words, containment should become a global policy. Because the Soviets now had atomic weapons, the United States must build up its conventional warfare capability. One advantage of increased conventional military strength was that it would lessen America's reliance on nuclear weapons and reduce the chance of nuclear war. The down side was that it would be very expensive. The State Department estimated that the NSC 68 recommendations would cost at least

$35 and perhaps as much as $50 billion, compared to about $15 billion that Truman was planning to spend on defense in the coming years.

It was anybody's guess how the administration could convince Congress to foot that huge bill. However, on the Korean peninsula thousands of miles away from Washington events were about to unfold that made most of the NSC 68 recommendations a reality.

THE KOREAN WAR

Korea was one of the first victims of the Cold War. The country had endured repressive Japanese rule between 1910 and 1945. At the end of World War II it was divided—supposedly temporarily—at the 38th parallel, with Soviet forces in the north and American forces in the south. However, the Soviets thwarted reunification by installing a Communist dictatorship headed by **Kim Il-Sung**. In the south, American-sponsored elections in 1948 led to the election of **Syngman Rhee**, whose main virtue was his staunch anti-Communism rather than any commitment to democracy, and American troops left Korea the next year. Perhaps the sharpest scholarly critic of the American presence in Korea is New Left historian Bruce Cumings, who argues that to understand the **Korean War** one must consider American policy in South Korea beginning in 1945, including the U.S. role in suppressing leftist dissidents.[12]

On June 24, 1950, Kim's Soviet-equipped army invaded South Korea. In contrast to what was widely accepted for many years, Kim did not act without Soviet knowledge. As historians Sergei N. Goncharov, John W. Lewis, and Xue Litai point out, recently released Soviet archives show that the invasion was "preplanned, blessed, and directly assisted by Stalin and his generals, and reluctantly backed by Mao at Stalin's insistence."[13] Neither the North Koreans nor Stalin believed the United States would intervene, in part because American officials had made public statements that left Korea outside the U.S. defense perimeter in Asia. Stalin and the North Koreans were wrong. President Truman saw the invasion as a direct threat to Japan and a test of American resolve to defend its interests in Asia. The American response, under the auspices of the United Nations, was swift and forceful. By the fall of 1950 United Nations troops had defeated the North Koreans. At that point, urged on by General **Douglas MacArthur**, the commander of UN forces in Korea, Truman decided to cross the 38th parallel and reunify Korea under non-Communist control. That decision led to disaster when it brought the PRC into the war. After the Chinese drove UN forces southward with heavy losses, the fighting stabilized near the 38th parallel, dragging on until an armistice finally was signed in July 1953.

The Korean War has been called "The Forgotten War" because it has been overshadowed in the history books by World War II, which preceded it by only a few years, and the Vietnam War, which loomed so large because it lasted so long and deeply divided the American people. Yet the impact of the Korean War is not easily forgotten or ignored. The war claimed over 54,000 American lives, 1 million Chinese lives, and approximately 3.5 million Korean lives, North and South. It left the peninsula divided and devastated. American relations with the People's Republic of China, which were bad to begin with, were poisoned for a generation, in particular because the United States decided to defend the remnants of the Nationalist government, which had taken refuge on the island of Formosa, 110 miles off the Chinese coast. The war also led to an American military buildup along the lines suggested by NSC 68, which was formally adopted in September 1950. Finally, the Korean War contributed significantly to the anti-Communist hysteria in the United States.

THE COLD WAR AT HOME

How Did the Cold War Affect the Tone and Tenor of American Politics and Culture?

The Cold War caused confusion and anxiety in the United States. Many Americans found it difficult to understand why the United States, having triumphed so completely in World War II, was unable to assert itself more successfully in peacetime. There was particular anxiety about Soviet spying, which certainly took place and did real damage to the United States, but which also became the grist for unwarranted rumors and fear mongering. The postwar era also produced its demagogues who were prepared to exploit and fan public fears for their own purposes or advancement. All these factors contributed to the so-called Red Scare that began in the late 1940s and reached its zenith in the early 1950s.

Beginning in the late 1940s, many areas of American political and cultural life were disrupted by efforts to ferret out Communists who supposedly had infiltrated this country's institutions. One government body particularly active in hunting for allegedly underground Communists was the House Un-American Activities Committee (HUAC). It searched for Communists in

Washington, in America's schools and universities, and in many other places. The committee became best known for its investigation of Hollywood and the movie industry. As a result of its activities, ten screenwriters and directors who refused to cooperate with HUAC went to prison. Hundreds of others in the entertainment business were blacklisted and had their careers ruined because of their political views. Thousands of Americans had their constitutional rights violated and lost their jobs because they held unpopular views or dared to criticize the excesses taking place. The committee ignored criticism that it was violating the rights of American citizens, even when the critics included President Truman himself, who at one point called HUAC the "most un-American thing in America."

Politicians faced the danger of being branded "soft on Communism." It was to avoid this label and quell the growing public obsession with Communist subversion that President Truman in 1947 instituted a loyalty program designed to ensure there were no Communists in the United States government. However, the anti-Communist frenzy received a boost in 1948 when Alger Hiss, a former State Department official who had advised President Roosevelt at Yalta, was accused of having been a Communist spy in the 1930s. Hiss denied the charges before HUAC, but soon became tangled in a web of his own lies and in 1950 was convicted of perjury and sent to prison.

The peak of the Red Scare is associated with the career of Senator **Joseph McCarthy**. McCarthy began his anti-Communist crusade in 1950 with wild accusations, which he never could prove, about Communists in the State Department. His recklessness, cruelty, and false accusations gave the English language a new word — "McCarthyism" — which means engaging in vicious and irresponsible attacks on people and, without evidence, slandering them because of their political views. McCarthy finally overreached himself in 1954 when he attacked the United States Army for supposedly harboring Communists. Millions of Americans saw his disgraceful behavior first hand when Congressional hearings on his charges were broadcast live on the latest sensational new gadget in their homes: television. After the Senate censured McCarthy that same year, the anti-Communist hysteria in the United States gradually receded.

However, the impact of anti-Communist crusading on American culture was felt long after the passing of McCarthy. Much of what Americans saw on television or in the movies preached a strident and unreasoned anti-Communist message. The message often was repeated in the most widely read newspapers and magazines such as *Time, The Reader's Digest,* and *The New York Daily News*. It reached down to organizations such as the Boy Scouts and into the schools, where children engaged in senseless drills supposedly to help them survive a nuclear attack. And it functioned as a virulent form of political correctness that imposed a conformity on viewpoints that both ordinary people and public figures could openly express. One of the sad ironies of the early Cold War era was that while the United States was waging the Cold War abroad to preserve its freedoms, it permitted fear and uncertainty to undermine those very freedoms at home.

CHAPTER THREE

From the Thaw to the Brink: 1953–1962

On January 20, Harry Truman was succeeded as President of the United States by **Dwight David Eisenhower**, the enormously popular former general who had been supreme commander of Allied forces in Europe during World War II. Less than two months later, Joseph Stalin died. He was followed by a so-called collective leadership with Georgi Malenkov as prime minister, which in reality was a fig leaf for a poorly concealed power struggle eventually won by **Nikita Khrushchev**. In contrast to the United States, where the transition took place openly and smoothly according to law, the Soviet transfer of power took several years. Khrushchev emerged as number one in 1955 and retained his position in a second round of struggle in 1957, by which time Eisenhower was in his second term. By 1958, Khrushchev held the twin posts of first secretary of the Communist Party and prime minister of the Soviet Union.

Stalin's death immediately produced better conditions inside the Soviet Union. His policy of rule by terror finally was brought to an end, and new economic policies over time significantly raised the Soviet standard of living. Stalin's successors also instituted reforms that prevented any future leader from exercising Stalin's absolute power. The dead tyrant's personal dictatorship evolved into a dictatorship of the Communist Party leadership. At the same time, during 1953 the new leadership's political uncertainty and domestic agenda made it seek reduced tensions with the United States and its allies, even as East Berlin was rocked by anti-Communist riots that had to be quelled by Soviet tanks. The result, at least in the short run, was a thaw in the Cold War.

THE THAW: 1953–1955

How Did Cold War Tensions Ease After Stalin's Death?

The first major crisis to be resolved was the dangerous and costly Korean War. Negotiations to end the fighting began in 1951 but became stuck on the issue of repatriation of Chinese and North Korean prisoners who did not want to return home. The PRC insisted that they be returned against their will, which the United States refused to do. The changing of the guard in Moscow, combined with increased military pressure and privately transmitted threats from an impatient Eisenhower, who had promised the American electorate he would end the war, brought about an armistice on American terms. The armistice—there has never been a peace treaty—left Korea divided at approximately the same place as before the war with two hostile states separated by a narrow demilitarized zone.

Another Asian war far to the south ended in 1954. Since 1946 the French had been fighting to keep control of their colony in Vietnam. They were opposed by a formidable Communist-dominated movement with broad nationalist appeal called the Vietminh, led by a skillful Moscow-trained politician, **Ho Chi Minh**. The United States had been aiding the French since 1950 in the increasingly futile struggle and by 1954 was paying most of the financial cost of the war. After French forces were defeated at the Battle of Dienbienphu in May 1954, a multinational conference that included delegations from the United States, the Soviet Union, the PRC, France, and Britain produced the Geneva Accords. The settlement was possible because it served, at least for the moment, the interests of the major non-Vietnamese powers involved in the conflict: the French wanted to get out of Vietnam while saving face; the Soviets had more urgent priorities in Europe; the Chinese, unenthusiastic about a strong united Vietnam on their southern border, were pleased to see the country divided; the British, convinced that Communist gains in Indochina did not threaten the rest of Southeast Asia, wanted the war ended; and the United States was not prepared to act alone to prevent Communist control of the northern half of Vietnam. The main losers at Geneva, ironically, were Ho and the Vietminh, who bitterly resented the settlement that they believed denied them what they had won on the battlefield.

The Geneva Accords, which the United States did not sign but promised not to disturb, called for the French to leave Vietnam. The country temporarily was divided at the 17th parallel, with the Vietminh in control of the north and the French and their Vietnamese supporters in the south, pending elections scheduled for 1956. However, the elections never were held, largely because neither the PRC nor the United States, for their own reasons—the PRC did not want a united Vietnam, the United States did not want a Communist Vietnam—wanted to see Vietnam united under Ho's control. After deciding early in 1954 not to intervene militarily to save the French, the United States reversed its course and started propping up the anti-Communist but also dictatorial government of Ngo Dinh Diem in South Vietnam. Eisen-hower's rationale became famous as the "domino" theory: "You have a row of dominos, you knock over the first one, and what will happen to the last one is the certainty that it will go over very quickly," he explained.[1] In other words, according to Eisenhower, if South Vietnam was allowed to fall to the Com-munists, the other countries of Southeast Asia would follow. Containment, having reached northeast Asia in 1950, was now firmly established in South-east Asia, with fateful results. What the United States had once considered a "French problem" over the next decade became an enormous and costly American problem.

During 1955 the main effects of the thaw were felt in Europe. Austria, which like Germany was divided into four occupation zones in 1945, was reunified when the Soviet Union agreed to withdraw from its zone in return for Austria's neutrality in the Cold War. The Soviets also withdrew from a naval base they had occupied in Finland. All this helped lead to the first postwar summit meet-ing in Geneva attended by the leaders of the United States, the Soviet Union, Great Britain, and France. However, the so-called Spirit of Geneva that per-vaded the conference proved to be ephemeral and failed to produce concrete results. More long-lasting were East/West economic, scientific, and cultural exchanges, which were resumed in 1955 after a lapse of almost a decade. Among the many Soviet citizens who participated in these exchanges was Alexander Yakovlev, who thirty years later was one of the main architects of **Mikhail Gorbachev's** policy of reform known as perestroika.

A number of books written in the 1980s praised Eisenhower for his modera-tion and restraint. As biographer Stephen E. Ambrose has noted, Eisenhower himself made a strong case for his foreign policy when he boasted that "the United States never lost a soldier or a foot of ground in my administration. We kept the peace."[2] However, Corel Bell (*Negotiating From Strength: A Study in the Politics of Power*, 1963) and other historians have suggested that the chang-ing of the guard in the Soviet Union created an opportunity to settle important Cold War issues that Eisenhower and Secretary of State **John Foster Dulles** failed to exploit. Soviet specialist Adam Ulam (*Expansion and Coexistence: A History of Soviet Foreign Policy, 1917–1967*, 1968) has pointed out that as early as 1952 the Soviet Union had indicated a willingness to accept a united, rearmed, but strictly neutral Germany, and that offer seems to have stood through 1953. By July 1955, when the summit meeting finally took place, the Soviet attitude toward Germany had changed and the "thaw" already was coming to an end.[3]

One sign of the vanishing thaw was West Germany's admission to NATO in May. A few days later, the Soviet Union announced the formation of a rival alliance, the **Warsaw Pact**, made up of itself and its Eastern European satellites. These two alliances would face each other across the **Iron Curtain** fault line for more than three decades.

THE "NEW LOOK" AND PEACEFUL COEXISTENCE

During the 1952 presidential campaign, the Republicans had attacked Truman and the Democrats for their failures vis-à-vis the Soviet Union and Communism and for spending too much on their futile efforts in the bargain. There even was vague talk about "liberation" of Eastern Europe, although in reality that was little more than campaign rhetoric. In fact, the Eisenhower administration, like every Cold War administration, continued the policy of containment. But under Eisenhower the job was done less expensively than under Truman. The new president was concerned that excessive government spending fueled by a runaway defense budget could bankrupt the country. During 1954 and 1955, Eisenhower therefore cut Truman's projected defense budgets from about $41 billion to $31 billion.

This was done by getting, as the slogan went, "more bang for the buck." Instead of maintaining a huge standing army, the United States under the Republican "New Look" policy relied more on nuclear weapons for containment. The United States would threaten the Soviet Union with "massive retaliation" with nuclear weapons if the latter became too aggressive. To make the threat believable, the United States would engage in what Dulles called "brinkmanship": going to the brink of war. Another way to make the threat believable was to develop small nuclear weapons designed for battlefield use. Cutting costs was facilitated by setting up alliances such as the Southeast Asia Treaty Organization (**SEATO**). These alliances enabled the United States to use foreign troops, which were cheaper to maintain than American troops, to man the containment barricades.

In practice, the Eisenhower administration was far more cautious than its rhetoric implied. "Liberation," which might have set off World War III, never was a policy option. Eisenhower bluntly told this to South Korea's Syngman Rhee in 1954 and demonstrated it by his inaction in 1956 when Hungary revolted unsuccessfully against Communist rule. Furthermore, as the Soviet Union developed its own nuclear arsenal, brinkmanship became much too risky a gamble. If it had any use at all it was against the PRC, at the time a non-nuclear power. According to Secretary of State Dulles it was used to make the Chinese back down in Korea in 1953 and during a crisis in the Formosa Straits in 1955, when Beijing was pressured to end its artillery bombardment of two small Nationalist islands (Quemoy and Matsu) just off the Chinese coast. As for Dulles himself, although his public advocacy for brinkmanship and strident anti-Communism have exposed him to criticism, historians who have examined his career closely have concluded that Dulles, far from being one-dimensional, was in fact a sophisticated analyst of the Soviet Union and the rest of the Communist world.[4]

If brinkmanship in practice exaggerated American militancy, Nikita Khrushchev's policy of "peaceful coexistence," announced in 1956, was less pacific than it sounded. To be sure, recognizing full well that a nuclear exchange would be catastrophic, Khrushchev rejected the established Soviet doctrine of an inevitable war between the Communist and capitalist worlds. His policy of "peaceful" coexistence, however, meant only that the two systems would henceforth compete by political and economic means short of war. The inevitable result still would be a global Communist victory. Khrushchev also openly expanded the area of competition to include Asia and Africa, where the old European colonial empires were in the process of dissolution and where his anti-Western sentiments were widespread. He even carried the competition to Latin America, previously the exclusive preserve of the United States. Overall, then, Khrushchev's conception and practice of "peaceful coexistence" did as much to raise Cold War tensions as to lower them, and in fact brought them to their terrifying pinnacle during the Cuban Missile Crisis in 1962.

HUNGARY AND SUEZ

By 1956 the thaw in the Cold War was over, as crises in two different parts of the world brought trouble for both of the superpowers. Both crises involved nationalism, a force of dramatically growing power throughout the world that bowed to neither Communist nor capitalist ideology. The Soviets ran afoul of nationalist sentiment in Eastern Europe, while the United States was stung by rising Third World nationalism in the Middle East.

The Soviet Union's crisis, as had Russia's so often before 1917, began in Poland, which despite over a century of domination had never accepted Russian or Soviet/Communist rule. The trouble erupted in the wake of Khrushchev's "secret speech" to the 20th Congress of the Communist Party of the Soviet Union in February. The speech, in which Khrushchev denounced Stalin for a variety of crimes, soon lost its veil of secrecy and raised hopes for real change throughout the Soviet bloc. That hope helped ignite riots in

Poland in June in which workers demanded improved living conditions and the end of Communist rule. The Soviets finally calmed the waters in October by accepting the rise to power of **Wladyslaw Gomulka**, a Communist who had been imprisoned under Stalin. Gomulka demanded and received a measure of autonomy in managing Poland's internal affairs. However, just as the calm was being restored in Poland, matters careened completely out of control in Hungary. There the new reformist leadership under Imre Nagy announced the end of one-party rule, Hungary's resignation from the Warsaw Pact, and its intention to become a neutral nation in the Cold War. The Kremlin responded by sending tanks and troops into Hungary, in turn sparking a full-fledged rebellion. More than 20,000 Hungarians died and 200,000 fled to the West before the Soviets crushed the **Hungarian Revolution**.

While the Soviet Union was engaged in Eastern Europe, warfare erupted in the Middle East that caused problems for the United States. Two separate disputes and several conflicting ambitions rubbed together to ignite that crisis. Great Britain and France, both close American allies, were infuriated when the nationalist-minded Egyptian regime of **Gamal Abdul Nasser** seized control of the Suez Canal from its British owners. Nasser planned to use the canal's revenues to help build a great dam on the Nile River to provide hydroelectricity and water for irrigation. He also planned to make himself the leader of the Arab world. To that end he had been sponsoring terrorist raids for years into neighboring Israel. Nasser mounted the attacks from Egypt's Sinai Peninsula and from the Gaza Strip, a sliver of land along the Mediterranean coast that had fallen to Egyptian troops in the unsuccessful Arab war to destroy Israel in 1948–49. By 1956 the Israelis were determined to stop the attacks, which had cost them hundreds of civilian lives. This imperative brought Israel together with France and Britain and late in October the three countries attacked Egypt.

In a rare display of unanimity, the United States and the Soviet Union both reacted angrily to the British/French/Israeli attack, although for completely different reasons. The Soviets used the attack to condemn the three countries involved, stand as an opponent of Western imperialism, and ingratiate themselves to the Egyptians and the rest of the oil-rich Arab world. Once the crisis was over they would build Nasser's Aswan Dam and further increase their influence in the Arab world. The United States was angry because its NATO allies had acted without its consent and because the entire enterprise had damaged America's relations with the Arab world.

American pressure forced a relatively quick withdrawal, but not without severely straining relations between the United States and its allies. The standing of Britain and France as great powers continued to decline, while Soviet prestige in the Arab world grew. In response to these developments, in 1957 the United States announced the Eisenhower Doctrine, a commitment to use military force if necessary to contain Communism in the Middle East. In 1958 the Eisenhower Doctrine was put into practice when U.S. warships were sent into the eastern Mediterranean to protect King Hussein of Jordan from Syrian threats, in effect containing the Syrians rather than the Soviets. That year Eisenhower also sent fourteen thousand marines to Lebanon to prop up that country's weak pro-Western regime.

SPUTNIK AND THE ARMS RACE

On October 4, 1957, the Soviet Union stunned the United States and its allies by launching the world's first artificial satellite, Sputnik I. The launching was more than a scientific triumph in the technology of space exploration; it was a demonstration of Soviet progress in developing long-range rockets—intercontinental ballistic missiles (ICBMs)—that could be launched in the Soviet Union and carry nuclear warheads three thousand miles or more to obliterate American cities. Sputnik came on the heels of the development of thermonuclear weapons equal to millions of tons of TNT, as opposed to thousands of tons for atomic bombs, that both superpowers successfully tested in the first half of the decade. It therefore caused great concern in Washington—one foreign diplomat compared its influence to the bombing of Pearl Harbor—and euphoria in Moscow and Beijing, where there were growing numbers of believers in Mao Zedong's recent claim, "The East Wind Prevails over the West Wind."

Sputnik not only marked the beginning of the space race, with the Soviet Union initially in the lead—the well-publicized American failures at the time led some people to refer to U.S. satellites as "flopniks"—but it also accelerated the already well-established nuclear arms race. The Eisenhower administration responded to Sputnik and public concern by speeding up the American missile research program. But the president refused to be stampeded into an expensive military buildup. Thanks to intelligence provided by U-2 spy planes, ultramodern aircraft that flew too high for Soviet interceptors to shoot down, Eisenhower was well aware that Khrushchev's claim about the Soviet Union turning out missiles "like sausages" was empty boasting. In fact, the Soviets were waiting for a second generation of more reliable missiles to build an ICBM force. The United States, with its modern bomber force and soon-to-be-commissioned nuclear submarines armed with medium-range missiles, remained by far the more powerful nuclear power. There never was, as Eisenhower's critics charged, a "missile gap" threatening American security. Nonetheless, the administration established the National Aeronautics and Space Administration (NASA), which in 1969 landed the first man on the moon. Sputnik and subsequent Soviet space triumphs also led to American educational reforms. Efforts were made to have American high school students study more science and math. Improvements in science and math education in public schools were aided by the National Defense Education Act (1958). That program also provided money to help college and graduate students.

Meanwhile, the nuclear arms race accelerated over the next decade as both superpowers developed new ballistic missiles capable of delivering nuclear warheads far more accurately. The warning time each country had of a missile attack shrank to a scant thirty minutes, while the ominous cloud cast by a potential nuclear war grew longer.

THE COLD WAR IN THE THIRD WORLD

Why Did the Cold War Expand to the Third World?

In the 1950s the world was divided into three uneven and unequal parts: the United States and its industrialized and generally democratic allies, the Soviet bloc of Communist nations, and most of the countries of Asia, Africa, and Latin America. Those countries in the last group, or "Third World" (now often called the "developing world"), held the great majority of the world's population, but were unindustrialized and poor. The People's Republic of China occupied a unique position. Its Communist regime and alliance with the Soviet Union made it a part of the Soviet bloc, at least as far as the United States and its allies were concerned. At the same time, China was just beginning to industrialize and therefore could be considered part of the Third World.

One reason the Third World became a Cold War arena is that it was an enormous area in a state of flux. The old European colonial empires in Asia and Africa began disintegrating in the decade after World War II. Between 1946 and 1960 thirty-seven countries achieved independence. In territories where the colonial powers were resisting independence they often faced guerrilla uprisings. Other factors also brought the Cold War to the Third World.

Many of the newly independent nations were important sources of valuable raw materials for the United States and the industrialized nations of the West. Other countries, because of their location, were considered strategically important by American and Soviet policymakers; the United States in particular needed military bases abroad as part of its containment policy.

The Third World provided Stalin's successors with an irresistible opportunity to expand Soviet influence at the expense of the United States and its European allies. In 1955, the year twenty-nine mostly Asian and African countries met in Bandung, Indonesia, to support the idea of nonalignment or neutralism in the Cold War, Soviet leader Nikita Khrushchev, accompanied by prime minister Nikolai Bulganin, smilingly strode onto the Third World stage by touring several Asian countries. Khrushchev's most important stop was in India, independent since 1947 and the world's most populous country after the PRC. Over the next few years the Soviets established a good relationship with India, led by **Jawaharal Nehru**, a firm advocate of nonalignment, and with Egypt, the most powerful Arab state. They also developed friendly relations with Indonesia, whose President Sukarno was another forceful advocate of nonalignment. Elsewhere the Soviets supported rebellions, or what they called "wars of national liberation," often with radical or Communist leanings, against the colonial powers or native regimes, often dictatorial, backed by the United States.

Many Third World leaders, resentful after decades of Western colonial domination and wary of Soviet-style socialism, agreed with Nasser's assertion, "We will not be subjected, either by West or East." This did not sit well with the United States, and especially with Secretary of State Dulles, who called neutralism "obsolete" and "short-sighted" as well as usually "immoral." His outspoken criticism often made the job of American diplomats more difficult.

The Soviet Union's growing activities and influence in the Third World alarmed the United States from the start. America countered by offering economic and military aid to non-Communist Third World regimes. Whether they were democratic or authoritarian was considerably less important than their anti-Communist credentials. American foreign aid, which during the 1940s and early 1950s went largely to Europe, was redirected. By the 1960s it flowed mainly to Third World countries. The United States also sponsored alliances with pro-Western Third World countries. In the Middle East, the United States helped found the Central Treaty Organization (CENTO) in 1959. Its other members were Britain, Pakistan, Turkey, and Iran. (CENTO, itself the successor to the defunct Baghdad Pact, collapsed in 1979 when a revolution in Iran brought anti-American Islamic fundamentalists to power in Iran.) Containment in Asia was consigned to the Southeast Asia Treaty Organization (SEATO).

Along with the United States, Britain, and France, SEATO members included Australia, New Zealand, the Philippines, Pakistan, and Thailand. Supposedly an Asian version of NATO, SEATO never received its own military forces or command structure. It limped along ineffectually until it was disbanded in 1976.

Far more controversial was direct American intervention in Third World countries. These secret projects, known in the intelligence community as "covert ops," were handled by the Central Intelligence Agency (CIA), which during the 1950s was headed by the legendary World War II spy Allen Dulles, brother of the Secretary of State. Two "covert ops" of note took place early in the Cold War, the first in Iran and the second in Guatemala. Iran became a major concern for the Eisenhower administration because of Prime Minister Mohammed Mossadegh, who had come to power in 1951 and promptly nationalized the British-owned Anglo-Iranian oil company. He also allied himself with a pro-Communist political party and pushed aside Iran's pro-Western monarch, the Shah. In 1953 the CIA staged a coup that restored the Shah to power and landed Mossadegh first in prison and then in exile. The Guatemala coup was organized in 1954 after that country's legally elected president, a leftist politician named Jacobo Arbenz, seized land owned by the United Fruit Company, a U.S. corporation, and distributed it to landless native peasants. Organizing the coup and driving Arbenz from power proved to be a relatively simple matter, after which the United States installed its own choice as Guatemala's president.

Not all U.S. interventions went so smoothly. In 1961, the American-sponsored attempt to overthrow **Fidel Castro** in Cuba ended as an embarrassing fiasco. In addition, direct intervention aroused considerable resentment against the United States in many countries. CIA plotting in the newly independent Congo in the early 1960s angered nationalists throughout Africa. Closer to home, after the assassination of long-time dictator Rafael Trujillo in 1961, the United States worked to prevent local leftist political forces, even of the non-Communist variety, from taking power in the Dominican Republic. This effort culminated in 1965 when President Lyndon B. Johnson sent over twenty thousand marines to the Dominican Republic to keep its conservative government in power. He then announced the Johnson Doctrine, which stated that the United States would not permit another Communist regime to take power in the Western Hemisphere. The American invasion thwarted leftist forces in the Dominican Republic, but only at the expense of U.S. prestige in Latin America. Critics of the American invasion at home and abroad pointed out that it violated the charter of the Organization of American States, which specifically prohibited intervention in the affairs of another country.

In the long run, direct intervention had serious disadvantages. In the case of Guatemala, the 1953 operation brought to power one of the most repressive regimes in Latin America. In Iran, the overthrow of Mossadegh came back to haunt the United States when the Shah was overthrown in 1979 by Islamic fundamentalists who were far more anti-American than the former prime minister. These and other "covert ops" almost certainly cost more in bad public relations than they were worth. Even when they succeeded in the short run, they made the United States more enemies than reliable friends, especially when once-secret activities were made public.

Overall, for much of the Cold War the United States stumbled in its dealings with the Third World. With few exceptions—in particular South Korea and Taiwan—American foreign aid did little to improve conditions in Asia, Africa, and Latin America. Corrupt regimes resting on narrow social bases generally were unreliable or unstable allies and U.S. support for them generated widespread enmity. Direct intervention produced a few short-term successes, but by making it seem easy they eventually helped lead the United States to its disastrous intervention in Vietnam. The United States did succeed in establishing its influence while keeping the Soviets at bay in the oil-rich Persian Gulf region, but lost a valuable ally when the Shah of Iran, notwithstanding his enormous arsenal of modern American weapons, was deposed.

If the United States could take any satisfaction from its expensive and frustrating relationship with the Third World during the Cold War, it was that over the long haul the Soviet Union, despite early apparent successes, in the end failed as badly, or worse, than its capitalist rival. Cuba, ninety miles from Florida, defected to the Communist camp after 1959, but the People's Republic of China, cheek-by-jowl with the Soviet Union along a four-thousand-mile-long border, split with Moscow in the 1960s. Iran turned against the United States after the fall of the Shah, but Egypt turned away from the Soviet Union a few years after the death of Nasser. The United States wasted its dollars by lavishing aid on right-wing dictatorships, but the Soviets wasted their rubles on left-wing dictatorships. And although United States was weakened by its unsuccessful war in Vietnam, the Soviet Union was undermined even worse by its military failure in Afghanistan.

FROM EISENHOWER TO KENNEDY

The last years of the Eisenhower administration saw a number of crises that frustrated attempts to improve Soviet-American relations. The most positive event was Nikita Khrushchev's trip to the United States in September 1959, the first such visit by a Russian or Soviet leader. Notwithstanding some rough moments, the down-to-earth, peasant-born Khrushchev made a generally favorable impression on the American people. He was at his best when touring an Iowa farm or visiting with workers at a Pittsburgh steel factory. The Soviet leader also left a positive final impression with a genuinely warm farewell speech to the American people on nationwide television, which he began in English with the words, "Good evening, American friends" and ended with, "Good luck, American friends." However, Khrushchev's visit as a whole failed to produce progress on key issues, including the arms race.

Khrushchev's visit was sandwiched between problems. Aside from the 1958 crisis over West Berlin, a projected Eisenhower-Khrushchev summit meeting in Paris in May 1960 was aborted after the Soviets finally succeeded in shooting down a U-2 spy plane. When Eisenhower refused to apologize for the reconnaissance flights, a furious Khrushchev walked out of the conference. He followed up his angry words in Paris with a stormy visit to the United Nations General Assembly in New York City in September. Khrushchev used the occasion as the stage for one of his most embarrassing public performances. The Soviet leader attacked both the UN and its General Secretary, the widely respected **Dag Hammarskjöld**, and also rudely interrupted a speech he did not like by pounding his desk with a shoe. Khrushchev completed his New York visit by meeting with and extolling the virtues of Cuban Communist dictator Fidel Castro, also in town for the UN meeting, a tactic that did little to endear him in Washington.

Beginning in 1961, Khrushchev found himself dealing with a new American president, John F. Kennedy. Kennedy had criticized the Eisenhower administration for relying too heavily on nuclear weapons to implement containment. He pointed out that there were few crises that could possibly justify the use, or even the threat to use, nuclear weapons. Eisenhower's overreliance on nuclear weapons to deter the Soviet Union therefore left the United States without the proper means to respond to the kind of crises that regularly occurred worldwide. Kennedy replaced Eisenhower's "New Look" with a policy he called "flexible response." It called for strengthening conventional forces to meet any kind of challenge as well as building a wide variety of nuclear weapons. Kennedy claimed that his flexible response policy lessened the chance of nuclear war because it gave the United States a greater variety of options for any given problem without having to threaten the use of nuclear weapons.

BERLIN AND THE BERLIN WALL

It turned out that one of the first major crises Kennedy faced found him without an effective response. It occurred in Berlin.

Berlin was a trouble spot from the very beginning of the Cold War. The problem was the existence of the enclave of West Berlin, technically still under Allied occupation, deep within the Soviet satellite state of East Germany. Because Berlin itself was not physically divided, East Germans, especially young people, began using it as an escape hatch to the West. Eventually about three million East Germans took the Berlin route to freedom. They came first to East Berlin and then crossed over unmolested to the Western sector. This steady flow and the prosperity of West Berlin, which contrasted so dramatically with the drabness of East Berlin, frustrated and angered the Soviet Union and its East German clients. In 1958 Khrushchev provoked the most serious tension over Berlin since 1948–49 when he made a series of demands designed to force the United States, Britain, and France out of the city. Eisenhower held fast and weathered that storm.

In 1961, with the stream of East Germans escaping via Berlin reaching a torrent, the Soviets built the Berlin Wall. The construction of the wall embarrassed the new Kennedy administration, which had no legal grounds to prevent it, but it was a far greater embarrassment to the Soviets and East Germany, whose Communist systems were being so decisively rejected by the German people. At the same time, the Berlin Wall actually brought some stability to the city. Berlin remained a symbol of the Cold War, but ceased being a source of recurring superpower crises.

CUBA AND THE MISSILE CRISIS OF 1962

Cuba became a factor in the Cold War in 1959, during the Eisenhower administration, when a revolutionary movement led by Fidel Castro overthrew a corrupt dictatorial regime with close ties to the United States. American interests owned a large chunk of Cuba's economy, including valuable real estate and tourist hotels. Although the Soviets played no role in Castro's coming to power, and in fact knew very little about him, by 1960 it was clear that Castro was a Communist. His regime was seizing property owned by U.S. citizens and the Soviets were moving in with a trade agreement and aid for their newfound ally. That same year President Eisenhower approved a CIA plan to overthrow Castro by sending U.S.-backed Cuban exiles to invade the island. At the same time, the CIA was hatching several unsuccessful attempts to murder Castro. On January 3, just weeks before leaving office, Eisenhower broke diplomatic relations with Cuba.

When he became president, Kennedy inherited the invasion plan. It was launched in April 1961 with disastrous results. Landing at the Bay of Pigs, the entire invasion force of 1,500 was captured or killed. Kennedy was furious and deeply embarrassed. His mood did not improve in June when he had a get-acquainted meeting with Khrushchev in Vienna. The young American president came away convinced that Khrushchev believed he could be pushed around. As he told an advisor, Arthur Schlesinger reports in *A Thousand Days*, "If Khrushchev wants to rub my nose in the dirt, it's all over. That son of a bitch won't pay any attention to words. He has to see you move."[5]

In the wake of the Bay of Pigs fiasco the United States continued CIA activities to undermine the Castro regime, violating international law in the process. Meanwhile, in Moscow Nikita Khrushchev also had his eyes on Cuba. By 1962, a "missile gap" did in fact exist, but it was the Soviets who lagged behind in the ICBM race. Under pressure from powerful forces within the Soviet establishment to improve the country's military posture vis-à-vis the United States, and, secondarily, determined to protect the Castro regime from a second U.S. invasion, Khrushchev hatched a plan of his own for Cuba. In spite of Kennedy's warning about supplying "offensive" missiles to Cuba, Khrushchev, having received Castro's approval, decided to install intermediate-range (IRBM) and medium-range (MRBM) ballistic missiles on the island. Because Cuba lies only ninety miles from Florida, the Soviet Union could threaten a large part of the eastern United States with its missiles. This would plug the Soviet Union's "missile gap" until ICBMs were available, help protect Castro, and repay the United States in kind for stationing missiles right along the Soviet border in Turkey.

Kennedy's sharp reaction to the discovery of missiles by a United States U-2 spy plane on October 14 began the Cuban Missile Crisis. He placed a blockade around Cuba and demanded that the Soviets remove their nuclear missiles. For almost two weeks the world stood on the brink of nuclear war. In the end, the Soviets, facing the full might of the American nuclear arsenal, backed down, ending the crisis. The most important terms in the settlement called for the Soviets to remove the missiles in return for an end to the blockade and a public American pledge not to invade Cuba.

The Cuban Missile Crisis was the closest the world has ever come to nuclear war. It seems fair to say that both sides acted recklessly: Khrushchev by placing missiles in Cuba, without even considering how the Americans would react and what he would do if the Soviets were caught in the act, and Kennedy by not approaching the Soviets privately and allowing them the far easier option of a nonpublic retreat. There is an enormous amount of scholarly literature on the Cuban Missile Crisis that debates every aspect of the event. Among the most enlightening books by a participant on the American side is *Reflections in the Cuban Missile Crisis* (1987), by Raymond Garthoff. A good summary of the Soviet viewpoint is provided in *Soviet Views on the Cuban Missile Crisis: Myth and Reality in Foreign Policy Analysis* (1982), edited by Ronald R. Pope. *On the Brink: Americans and Soviets Reexamine the Cuban Missile Crisis* (1989), edited by James G. Blight and David A. Welch, includes the edited transcripts of two international conferences on the crisis in which American and Soviet participants in the crisis revealed a wealth of new information about the most dangerous two weeks in human history.

In the wake of the crisis both sides drew back and moved to improve relations. In 1963 a "hotline" telephone line was established between the White House and the Kremlin. The two superpowers also signed a partial nuclear test ban treaty banning atmospheric tests. However, Kennedy and Khrushchev would be unable to do more to calm Cold War tensions. Kennedy was assassinated on November 22, 1963. Khrushchev, severely weakened at home because of the Soviet retreat in Cuba, was removed from power by the Communist Party leadership in October 1964.

THE SINO-SOVIET SPLIT

The Cold War took on a new coloring in 1949 when the Communists won the civil war in China and established the PRC. The defection to the Communist side of the world's largest country appeared to herald a great victory for the Soviet Union. It fueled the Red Scare and McCarthyism in the United States as critics of the Truman administration accused it of "losing China," as if that enormous, distant, and ancient country were America's to lose. The founding of the PRC was followed in February 1950 by the Sino-Soviet Treaty of Friendship, Alliance, and Mutual Assistance, which caused further anxiety and recriminations in the United States.

However, behind the Communist façade of friendship were old national rivalries and bitter political disputes about who should be the leader of world Communism. These disputes grew increasingly serious by the late 1950s, especially in the wake of China's Great Leap Forward program that began in 1958. In launching his utopian lunge toward full-fledged Communism, Chinese leader Mao Zedong in effect challenged the Soviet Union for leadership in the Communist world. That challenge produced economic chaos in China and caused a famine that took an estimated thirty million lives. Another source of Sino-Soviet tension was Mao's cavalier attitude toward nuclear war, which deeply unnerved Khrushchev. By 1960, the **Sino-Soviet split** was out in the open and soon the two countries had heavily fortified their four-thousand-mile-long border. In 1969 they fought a deadly full-scale battle using heavy weapons along the Ussuri River in the Far East. The Sino-Soviet split changed the complexion of the Cold War as much as the original Communist victory in China, but this time in favor of the United States. It created opportunities for American diplomacy that the **Nixon** administration exploited with great skill in the 1970s, and therefore helped pave the way for the détente of that era.

CHAPTER FOUR

Vietnam and Détente: 1962–1975

Some historians have divided the Cold War into two main phases separated approximately by the year 1962. The Cold War's first phase was a bipolar and highly ideological struggle, albeit short of war, during which the antagonism between the two superpowers often approached levels generally seen only during wartime. Over time the superpower confrontation mellowed, taking on the nature of a multipolar permanent truce. The two sides, while continuing to avoid direct military conflict, also in effect accepted each other's legitimacy and spheres of influence, as well as the idea that nuclear weapons were unusable since they would lead to mutual destruction.[1] While the transition from the first to the second phase of the Cold War was gradual and involved many steps, three events stand out as crucial catalysts: the building of the Berlin Wall in August 1961, the Cuban Missile Crisis of October 1962, and the Sino-Soviet split, which became unmistakably clear by 1962. The Berlin Wall largely defused the Berlin issue by apparently making the division of Germany permanent. The Cuban Missile Crisis demonstrated with terrifying clarity the dangers of nuclear brinkmanship and the necessity of controlling the arms race. The Sino-Soviet split decisively ended the bipolar era and opened the door for nations other than the superpowers to influence Cold War developments. The post-1962 Cold War context thus allowed two apparently contradictory events to unfold side-by-side: the long and costly **Vietnam War**, in which American troops fought Soviet-backed North Vietnamese and Vietcong forces; and the improvement, or détente, in Soviet-American relations that produced the first limits on the nuclear arms race.

THE VIETNAM WAR

The struggle for control of Vietnam lasted for three decades. It included two wars: the first between the French and the Vietminh (1946–1954) and the second (early 1960s–1975) between the United States and South Vietnam on one side and North Vietnam and the National Liberation Front (NLF) on the other, with the North Vietnamese and the NLF backed by the Soviet Union and China. During that thirty-year period five American presidents tried to prevent the victory of Communism in Vietnam: Truman, Eisenhower, Kennedy, Johnson, and Nixon. Each president from Truman to Johnson increased America's stake and the role American forces played on the ground in that small southeast Asian country. Truman relied mainly on American money and equipment to keep the French in the field against the Vietminh under Ho Chi Minh. Eisenhower continued to back the French until their final defeat in 1954; thereafter his administration sent American money and advisors to prop up the unpopular and corrupt regime of Ngo Dinh Diem in South Vietnam. When Kennedy became president fewer than a thousand U.S. advisors were in Vietnam; at his death in November 1963 there were about sixteen thousand. Johnson sent the first American combat units to Vietnam in 1965 and raised the total number of American troops there to more than half a million. Nixon, who over the course of four years reduced America's role in the ground war by gradually withdrawing combat troops from Vietnam, escalated the air war against Communist forces in both South and North Vietnam and expanded the ground fighting into neighboring Laos and Cambodia. By then the war in Vietnam had divided the people of the United States more than any conflict since the Civil War.

Historians and Vietnam

The Vietnam War has produced a vast scholarly literature. Historians have debated, often with great intensity, every aspect of that struggle, including how the United States was drawn into Vietnam and why the war was lost. George Herring (*America's Longest War: The United States and Vietnam, 1950–1975*, 1979) and Stanley Karnow (*Vietnam: A History*, 1983) have produced two of the most balanced accounts of that controversial war. In explaining America's entry into the war and its ultimate defeat, Herring suggests that the United States erred by viewing the conflict through the prism of containment. It turned what might have remained a local struggle into a major international conflict. In doing so, the United States "placed itself at the mercy of local forces," with itself on the weaker, and eventually the losing, side. Karnow, who calls the Vietnam War "The War Nobody Won," offers a similar explanation. He also stresses the determination of the North Vietnamese, who "saw the war against the United States and South Vietnamese as the continuation of two thousand years of resistance to Chinese and later

French rule." This made them, as one U.S. general pointed out, "the best enemy we faced in our history."[2]

Among other volumes that blame misplaced anti-Communism, or what has been called "flawed containment," for dragging the United States into Vietnam are David Halberstam's *The Best and the Brightest* (1972) and Frances FitzGerald's *Fire in the Lake: Vietnamese and Americans in Vietnam* (1972). Fitzgerald also focuses on the war from the Vietnamese perspective. Many historians believe that United States could have won the war. Guenter Lewy used his access to previously classified documents to defend America's role in Vietnam. The problem, he asserts, is that the United States did not take the actions required, including forcing the South Vietnamese to make reforms, to win the war. Col. Harry Summers, in *On Strategy: A Clinical Analysis of the Vietnam War* (1982), blames America's political leaders for adopting a misdirected strategy that lost the war. A similar case is made by Phillip Davidson, who served as an intelligence officer in Vietnam, in *Vietnam at War: The History, 1946–1975*. A gripping introduction to the American military experience is Harold Moore and Joseph Galloway's *We Were Soldiers Once . . . and Young* (1992). Drawing on interviews with participants on both sides, the book chronicles the fighting in the Ia Drang Valley, the first major battle between American soldiers and North Vietnamese troops. A key point is the lessons each side learned. The North Vietnamese concluded, accurately, that they could counter American air power. The Americans concluded, erroneously, that they could wear down the North Vietnamese.

New Left historians, heavily influenced by Marxism, generally have focused on economic explanations and the phenomenon of imperialism to explain U.S. involvement in Vietnam. According to Marxist thinking, Western imperialism in the Third World is a result of capitalist countries requiring markets and raw materials to keep their economies going. Gabriel Kolko, in *Anatomy of a War: Vietnam, the United States, and the Modern Historical Experience* (1985), views the United States as the "major inheritor of the mantle of imperialism in modern history."[3] It therefore was driven to oppose revolutionary movements in the Third World, including in Vietnam. Thomas J. McCormick (*America's Half-Century: United States Foreign Policy in the Cold War and After*, 1995) offers a somewhat different version of the economic argument. He suggests that the United States viewed Southeast Asia as essential to the development of the Japanese economy, whose health was important to the world capitalist system. Lloyd C. Gardner has provided a detailed analysis from a New Left perspective of America's policies toward Vietnam prior to 1954 in *Approaching Vietnam: From World War II Through Dienbienphu* (1988).

What Drew the United States Into Vietnam?

Whatever their disagreements, most historians appear to agree that the logic of containment was an important factor that drew the United States into Vietnam. By the 1950s the dominant viewpoint in Washington was that the Communist world was monolithic and that any Communist movement anywhere, including any armed insurgency in the Third World, could be traced back to Moscow or Beijing. It was further assumed by most Washington policymakers that any Communist victory should be seen as an American defeat and damaging to the security of the United States. This was the logic John F. Kennedy accepted when he became president. According to a report he received from his top advisors shortly after taking office, the loss of South Vietnam would expose a much larger area to Communist subversion: "The loss of South Vietnam would make pointless any further discussion about the importance of Southeast Asia to the free world; we would have to face the near certainty that the remainder of Southeast Asia and Indonesia would move to a complete accommodation with Communism, if not formal incorporation with the Communist bloc."[4]

However, while it is true that the dominant approach to containment led the United States into Vietnam, it is not necessarily true that the Vietnam debacle was the inevitable outcome of containment. Indeed, from the very beginning there were debates about where containment should be applied and what means should be used to implement it. Among the vocal critics of America's involvement in Vietnam was George F. Kennan, whose dissent regarding the practice of containment went back to the Truman administration and who argued that Vietnam was not vital to U.S. interests. He and other critics rejected the domino theory, arguing that the countries of Southeast Asia were very different from each other and would not collapse in the wake of a Communist victory in Vietnam. There is evidence, admittedly scanty, that President Kennedy ultimately concluded that leaving Vietnam was not incompatible with his policies for pursuing containment. According to **Robert McNamara**, who served both Kennedy and Johnson as Secretary of Defense, just before Kennedy was assassinated he had decided to withdraw American troops from Vietnam after his presumed reelection in 1964. However, upon entering office President Kennedy not only believed that vital U.S. interests required preventing a Communist takeover of Vietnam, but he and his advisors also welcomed the challenge of battling the Communists in that particular Third World arena. Vietnam was to be a test of the Kennedy administration's policy of "flexible response." Among the advisors Kennedy sent to Vietnam were highly trained counterinsurgency Special Forces ("Green Beret") troops, whose job was to demonstrate that Communist guerrilla forces could be defeated at their own game. At the same time, Vietnam would also be the place to prove the viability of what the administration called "nation building," an omnibus term for economic, social, and political programs designed to foster prosperity along capitalist lines and give Third World countries an alternative to Communism.[5]

After Kennedy's assassination, the job of containing Communism in Vietnam fell to **Lyndon Johnson**, whose dilemmas in dealing with Vietnam have been carefully detailed in Larry Berman's *Planning a Tragedy: The Americanization of the War in Vietnam* (1982). Like Kennedy, Johnson firmly believed that one of the central lessons of World War II was that if democratic countries failed to stop aggression when it began, they ultimately would have to go to war under conditions less favorable than those they originally faced. As he put it in his usual graphic style, "If we don't stop the Reds in South Vietnam, tomorrow they will be in Hawaii, and next they will be in San Francisco."[6] Johnson changed the character of the war by escalating American involvement until U.S. soldiers were bearing the brunt of the fighting against the Communist forces. In other words, he turned the fighting in Vietnam into an American war. Yet even as fateful decisions were being made in 1965, there were highly placed advisors inside the Johnson administration warning against escalation, largely on the ground that the war was unwinnable. Perhaps the most forceful case against escalation came from Undersecretary of State George Ball, who told the president, "The decision you face now is crucial. Once large numbers of U.S. troops are committed to direct combat . . . [and] once we suffer large casualties, we will have started a well-nigh irreversible process. Our involvement will be so great that we cannot—without national humiliation—stop short of achieving our complete objectives. Of the two possibilities, I think humiliation would be more likely than achievement of our objectives—even after we have paid terrible costs."[7]

The costs were indeed terrible: over 58,000 dead, over $100 billion dollars spent, and bitter dissent that tore at the fabric of American society. And, in the end, America's objective of preventing a Communist victory in South Vietnam was not achieved.

Why Was the United States, Despite Increasing Escalation, Unable to Achieve Its Objectives in Vietnam?

Historians have cited many reasons for America's failure in Vietnam. The United States began in 1954 by backing a repressive regime without broad popular support in South Vietnam. Ngo Dinh Diem and his main supporters came from the class of Vietnamese who over several generations had served the French colonial powers. They adopted the language, culture, and Catholic religion of the French, and as a group they were out of touch with their country's largely peasant and Buddhist majority. As Diem's situation deteriorated, the United States found it impossible to get him to undertake necessary social reforms. In exasperation, the United States sanctioned a coup against Diem in early November 1963, although Kennedy and his advisors were shocked when the military officers who staged the coup murdered Diem and his brother Ngo Dinh Nhu. After Diem's fall South Vietnam saw a succession of American-backed governments, but none proved capable of winning popular support, or what Lyndon Johnson called the "hearts and minds" of the people.

By contrast, Ho Chi Minh, a committed Communist and a ruthless political practitioner by any standard, also had impeccable credentials as a nationalist. He had devoted his life to the struggle against French colonialism and was the leader of the Vietminh movement, which finally defeated the French and established the independent state of North Vietnam. When the North Vietnamese made their decision in 1959 to launch an armed revolt against the Diem regime in the south, the local Communist guerrillas, aided from the start by the North Vietnamese cadres, were able to don the Vietminh's mantle of nationalism as well as that of social reform against an unpopular and repressive government in Saigon backed by a foreign power, the United States. During the war the United States and South Vietnamese claimed that the National Liberation Front, the presumptive rebel umbrella group of Communists and non-Communists leading the insurgency, was controlled by the North Vietnamese. This was true enough; the North Vietnamese organized the NLF in 1960. It is also true that the NLF and North Vietnamese made extensive use of terror and murder in their campaign against the South Vietnamese government. Yet the NLF, bolstered by Saigon's repressive policies, enjoyed considerable support, even among many non-Communists. Its popular backing was broader and deeper than the limited social base of the various South Vietnamese regimes backed by the United States.

In reality, while the United States saw itself as struggling to contain Communism in South Vietnam, it was fighting against what the majority of Vietnamese saw as a nationalist struggle for independence. North Vietnam received massive material support from the Soviet Union and the PRC, as the United States claimed. But in fact it was independent of both Communist giants, who by the 1960s had become rivals, and was able to exploit the competition between them in Southeast Asia to its own advantage. The durability and tenacity of the North Vietnamese and NLF became increasingly evident as the United States escalated its involvement under President Johnson. The decision to send combat troops to South Vietnam took place in early 1965. American escalation was gradual, mainly because Johnson feared that massive escalation and the inevitable rise in casualties it would bring would undermine American support for the war. Johnson also hoped gradual escalation would enable him to avoid a congressional debate that might damage his domestic Great Society programs. Another objective was to avoid a confrontation with the Soviet Union or the PRC.

The trouble was that as the United States escalated, so did the North Vietnamese, who sent increasing numbers of soldiers and larger quantities of supplies to South Vietnam through a series of jungle paths called the Ho Chi Minh trail. This made it impossible for the United States to gain the battlefield advantage it needed in order to dictate peace on its terms, namely North Vietnam's acceptance of a non-Communist South Vietnam. Massive bombing of North Vietnam did enormous damage but never succeeded in raising the cost of the war beyond the point that the government of North Vietnam, a totalitarian Communist dictatorship that did not have to bow to public opinion, was willing to pay. From Hanoi's point of view, the struggle was for national independence. That cause already had claimed great sacrifices, too great to consider bending to American will. Nor did the North Vietnamese ever doubt that they could outlast the United States, whose vital interests lay elsewhere, and win the war.

Meanwhile, in the jungles and rice paddies of the south, the war was enormously frustrating for American soldiers. They were fighting, for the most part, an enemy that hid in the forests or among a local population that was often hostile to Americans. American troops could never be sure where the enemy was, and their casualties continued to mount without any clear signs that the war was being won.

Another factor hampering the American effort in Vietnam was domestic opposition to the war, which grew with the number of U.S. troops fighting in South Vietnam and their rising casualties. The intense media coverage, especially on television, brought the Vietnam War home to the American public far more than any previous war. The brutality of the fighting, the rising American casualties, and the seeming inability of the Johnson administration to verify its claims that the war was being won undermined American support for the war effort. The administration lost credibility with the American public as many of its claims about the situation in Vietnam were revealed to be at best half-truths and at worst outright distortions. The country was rocked by dissent, especially on college campuses. Some demonstrations in major cities, including Washington, drew tens and even hundreds of thousands of protestors. Among the books that chronicle and evaluate the antiwar movement are Charles DeBenedetti's *An American Ordeal: The Antiwar Movement of the Vietnam Era* (1990) and David Levy's *The Debate Over Vietnam* (1991). Levy claims that weariness was the key factor that turned an increasing percentage of the American people against the war. Melvin Small, in *Johnson, Nixon, and the Doves* (1988), suggests that even though the antiwar movement did not influence Johnson or Nixon, it did influence important opinionmakers and through them forced the government to start winding down the war.

When **Richard Nixon** took office in 1969, having promised in the campaign he had a secret plan to end the war, he reduced American casualties by gradually withdrawing American combat troops from South Vietnam. The American role in the fighting was gradually transferred to the presumably revamped and improved South Vietnamese army under a program known as Vietnamization. It was a sad comment on how much had gone wrong with the American effort that the Vietnam War had to be "Vietnamized" in the first place. Although Vietnamization did reduce American casualties, it also left the North Vietnamese in the position of having merely to wait until the Americans had left before launching their final push against the South. For a people who had resisted Chinese pressure on their country for a thousand years, fought the French from 1946 to 1954, and continued the struggle against the American-backed regimes in Saigon and the United States itself for more than a decade, that was not a difficult task.

Vietnamization was part of the Nixon-Kissinger plan to get the United States out of Vietnam with its credibility intact, so they could focus on their primary foreign policy objectives such as détente. However, they may well have undermined their efforts by expanding the war into Cambodia, a point made by Arnold R. Isaacs in *Without Honor: Defeat in Vietnam and Cambodia* (1983).

What Were the Results of the Vietnam War?

In 1975, six years after the death of Ho Chi Minh and two years after the last American combat troops left South Vietnam in 1973, the North Vietnamese, having violated the agreements under which American forces left South Vietnam, overran the country and took Saigon. (Several American measures to prop up the South Vietnamese military also violated the agreements.) The fiction that the NLF had any autonomy whatsoever was swept aside and Vietnam was unified under a dictatorship that ruled from Hanoi, the capital of North Vietnam. Communist forces also seized power in Laos and Cambodia, Vietnam's two smaller neighbors in the western part of Indochina.

However, the Communist victory and Vietnam's reunification did not bring peace to the region. Its Communist regimes, without a common enemy to unite them, allowed old ethnic rivalries to rise to the surface and began fighting among themselves. One serious problem for the Hanoi regime was the Communist Khmer Rouge government in Cambodia, which was unfriendly toward Vietnam and friendly to China, Vietnam's long-time nemesis. The Khmer Rouge, who were determined to rebuild their society from scratch, were fanatics on a scale that the world has rarely seen. In barely three years they killed at least one million people, and possibly many more, out of Cambodia's population of seven million. In 1978 Vietnam, acting for strategic rather than humanitarian interests, invaded Cambodia, ousted the Khmer Rouge, and installed a regime friendly to itself. The Vietnamese then became bogged down in a guerrilla struggle that lasted over a decade. Making matters worse, in 1979 China retaliated by attacking Vietnam and starting a short but ferocious war.

In terms of the global Cold War, the end of the Vietnam War revealed a more restrained United States and a more aggressive Soviet Union. Until the 1980s and the presidency of **Ronald Reagan** the United States was less willing to get involved in new Third World conflicts. This reluctance was referred to as the "Vietnam Syndrome," and its effects were magnified after the Watergate scandal drove Richard Nixon from office in August 1974. At a deeper level, the Vietnam War ended the foreign-policy consensus in the United States on containment that had existed since the late 1940s. It seemed that reacting to the specter of Communism wherever it appeared had led the United States into a costly failure. It also was clear that the Communist world was no longer monolithic. Indeed, by 1969 the Soviet Union and the PRC had fought along their heavily militarized border, and the Soviet Union had even secretly approached the United States about a preemptive strike to prevent China from developing nuclear weapons. And within a few years of the fall of Saigon, Vietnam had fought two wars, one against the Communist regime in Cambodia and the other against the one in China.

The Soviet leadership, peering at the world through its Marxist prism, mistakenly assumed that it was witnessing signs of permanent American decline. It took advantage of American inaction to help Marxist movements seize or hold power in several Third World countries, including Angola in Africa, Nicaragua in Central America, and Southern Yemen on the Arabian Peninsula.[8] The Soviets pushed this advantage to the hilt, until they eventually went beyond the limits of their capabilities by invading Afghanistan in 1979 and thereby plunging into what became their own Vietnam.

However, neither the United States nor the Soviet Union allowed the Vietnam War to derail the movement toward improved mutual relations, or détente. The superpowers had been edging away from the nuclear brink and toward stabilizing agreements since the shock of the Cuban Missile Crisis. They continued in that direction as Johnson succeeded Kennedy (November 1963) and Nixon succeeded Johnson (January 1969) in the White House and when **Leonid Brezhnev** succeeded Khrushchev (October 1964) in the Kremlin. Even as the Vietnam War raged, a series of agreements reduced the intensity of the Cold War and set the first, albeit incomplete, limits on the nuclear arms race. When it came to nuclear weapons, not even a shooting war could overcome the instinct for survival.

DÉTENTE

Détente dates from the mid-1960s, when the Vietnam War was at its height. In June 1967, President Johnson met with Soviet Premier Alexei Kosygin in Glassboro, New Jersey, to discuss starting negotiations to control the nuclear arms race, by far the most important issue in relations between the two superpowers. The rather unusual site for the talks reflected the tension at the time: Kosygin, who was in New York to attend a UN meeting, refused to come to Washington to talk to the president. Instead, the president would have to meet the Soviet leader halfway, which he did in Glassboro, a small college town in southern New Jersey. The negotiations the two men discussed were called the Strategic Arms Limitation Talks (SALT).

Neither the SALT talks nor détente progressed very far during the Johnson administration. After the Glassboro meeting, the Soviets agreed to begin the talks in September. These plans were interrupted in August, when the Soviet Union led a massive Warsaw Pact invasion of Czechoslovakia, where a new Communist leadership under Alexander Dubček was introducing radical democratic reforms. The idea of mixing genuine democracy with Communism horrified Moscow. The Brezhnev regime saw the Dubček reforms as a threat not only to Communist rule in Czechoslovakia, but also to Communist rule in the rest of Eastern Europe and the Soviet Union itself. The Warsaw Pact invasion, which employed both Soviet troops and soldiers from several other member nations, put an end to what the Czechs called "socialism with a human face." A month later, Moscow announced the Brezhnev Doctrine, under which the Soviet Union claimed the right to intervene to prevent a socialist country from returning to capitalism.

The Warsaw Pact invasion of Czechoslovakia led to cancellation of the SALT talks and stymied further improvements in Soviet-American relations. However, these setbacks proved temporary. The Soviets remained interested in arms negotiations and improved relations. Meanwhile, Richard Nixon's inauguration as president in January 1969 brought to the White House a new approach to foreign policy as formulated by Nixon and **Henry Kissinger**, the president's national security advisor and later his secretary of state.

Keith L. Nelson has provided a comprehensive analysis of the origins of détente in *The Making of Détente: Soviet-American Relations in the Shadow of Vietnam* (1995). Nelson suggests that the United States and the Soviet Union turned to détente for the same reason: neither superpower could afford to continue the Cold War struggle at its pre-détente level of intensity. Former American foreign policy official and historian David Garthoff discusses the entire history of détente in his huge (1147 pages) and detailed volume *Détente and Confrontation: American-Soviet Relations from Nixon to Reagan* (1985). Garthoff defends détente against critics such as Ronald Reagan who claimed it was a one-sided affair in favor of the Soviet Union. However, he criticizes both the American and Soviet governments for overselling détente's achievements to the public. Garthoff also argues that both sides broke the rules of détente while expecting the other side to obey them, thereby ultimately undermining détente itself. Another comprehensive overview is *Superpower Détente: A Reappraisal* (1988), by British scholars Mike Bowker and Phil Williams. They argue that détente was a realistic American response to difficult international circumstances and rising Soviet power. In considering the Soviet perspective, Bowker and Williams place a greater stress than does Garthoff on Soviet expansionism in the Third World during the détente era. They argue that Soviet expansionism undermined support for détente in the United States and thereby contributed to détente's collapse.

What Was the Rationale Behind the Nixon-Kissinger Foreign Policy Strategy?

The Nixon-Kissinger strategy was based on the idea that the original postwar bipolar world had changed in important ways by the late 1960s. First, neither the Soviet Union nor the United States, their military might notwithstanding, dominated the world as they had after World War II. New major power centers had arisen that could no longer be ignored. Western Europe and Japan were major economic powers and the People's Republic of China, the world's most populous country, had returned to the world stage as a formidable regional power in East Asia. Kissinger, a student of the European balance-of-power system of the nineteenth century, stressed that the world's problems could be managed only if the world's five great powers, as opposed to just its two military superpowers, recognized each other's legitimate interests and cooperated with each other. Kissinger also stressed that the United States simply did not have the power to determine the values or internal policies of other states, including Communist ones. The best America could do was to make every effort to create incentives that encouraged other countries to act in a responsible manner.

A second fundamental change was the strategic position of the Soviet Union. Since the Cuban Missile Crisis the Soviets had been engaged in a massive effort to match the United States, or achieve "parity," in long-range, or "strategic," nuclear weapons. These weapons included long-range bombers, ICBMs, and submarine-launched ballistic missiles (SLBMs). The Soviets had reached their goal about the time Nixon entered office in 1969, and they continued to add to their arsenal. Meanwhile, a simultaneous Soviet buildup of army and naval forces gave them a global military reach they had not had before. Nixon and Kissinger did not regard Soviet equality, or parity, with the United States as an unacceptable threat to American security. They accepted the doctrine of "sufficiency," which assumed that what each superpower needed was a nuclear arsenal large enough to guarantee that in the event of a nuclear war the other side would be destroyed. Any more than that served no purpose and was therefore a waste of money. The idea was that "mutually assured destruction" (MAD) would deter both sides from ever starting a nuclear war. However, the problem facing Nixon and Kissinger was that the Soviet buildup was unrelenting. Either a way had to be found to stop or slow the Soviet buildup, or the United States would face an increasingly expensive arms race that would not buy it security, but leave it under the shadow of ever more destructive Soviet nuclear weapons. Faced with these options, Nixon stated frankly in his inaugural address, "After a period of confrontation, we are entering an era of negotiation."[9]

A key element in the Nixon-Kissinger strategy was what Kissinger called "linkage," which meant solving two or more international issues by tying them together in a package deal. Washington would use inducements as well as pressures to get the Soviet Union to make concessions on issues important to the United States. It would create a situation where the Soviet Union would benefit by becoming more cooperative in solving international problems. In the language of containment, the Soviet Union would find it in its interests to practice "self-containment."

The Nixon-Kissinger strategy of linkage also applied to China. Kissinger had particular hopes that he could use linkage to get the Soviets and Chinese to stop aiding North Vietnam and thereby force a settlement that preserved the independence of South Vietnam. In the case of Moscow, a favorable economic deal would be an incentive to help end the war in Vietnam. Those hopes turned out to be in vain, in part because North Vietnam had its own agenda and, Soviet and Chinese aid notwithstanding, operated independently of the two Communist giants.

Why Was the Soviet Union Interested in Détente?

The Soviet Union had its own compelling reasons for preferring negotiation to confrontation. Although it had achieved military parity with the United States, its economy was under great strain from the costs of the military buildup and suffered from serious shortcomings in both the industrial and agricultural sectors. Faced with a stagnating standard of living that lagged far behind their capitalist rivals, the Soviets knew that only trade with the West would get them the technology they needed to solve their growing economic problems. Furthermore, like the United States, the Soviet Union feared a renewed arms race. The Soviets were especially concerned because weapons involving new and complex technologies were on the horizon, and it was in high technology that the United States held its greatest advantage in the arms race. One weapon was called the MIRV, or multiple independently targeted reentry vehicle. An MIRV was a missile with multiple warheads, each one directed against a different target. An MIRV warhead turned each individual guided missile (or launcher) into five, ten, even twenty weapons. At the other end of the new weapons spectrum were defensive antiballistic missiles (ABMs) designed to shoot down incoming missiles. These defensive weapons would be not only extremely difficult to develop, assuming that even was possible, but also enormously expensive to build and deploy.

The Soviets also wanted the West to go beyond its grudging acceptance of the reality of their Eastern European empire by recognizing that control as legitimate. This goal translated into the United States' accepting the Soviet Union as an equal in determining how the world should be ordered. Finally, on their eastern front, the Soviets were concerned about the growing power and undisguised hostility of the People's Republic of China, which was just emerging from the self-isolation imposed by its chaotic Cultural Revolution. They also were concerned that China's new realism in foreign affairs might lead to improved relations with the United States, a development that would increase American leverage on the Soviet Union.

What Role Did West Germany Play in the Development of Détente?

In 1969 **Willy Brandt**, the long-time mayor of West Berlin, led the Social Democratic party to victory in the German parliamentary elections. Unlike previous German leaders, Brandt believed it served the interests of the German people as a whole for West Germany to stop isolating East Germany and build ties with that Soviet satellite. This in turn required better ties with the Soviet Union and the rest of the Soviet bloc. To that end, between 1970 and 1972 Brandt negotiated treaties in which West Germany accepted the borders Stalin drew after World War II and by which the two German states normalized diplomatic relations. West Germany thus accepted Poland's and the Soviet Union's annexation of former eastern territories and the division of Germany into two states. In return, Brandt won a Soviet guarantee (in an agreement signed by the four occupying powers of the city) for permanent Western access to West Berlin and agreements that fostered the reunification of German families divided by the postwar borders. Brandt's policies played a significant role in reducing East-West tensions in Europe and thereby moved détente forward even as SALT negotiations between the United States and the Soviet Union, which finally began in Helsinki in November 1969, inched along at a snail's pace.

What Was the Significance of the SALT I Arms Control Treaty?

The SALT I treaty signed in May 1972 was the centerpiece of détente. (A second SALT treaty would be signed later by both powers but never ratified by either.) SALT I built on two other treaties: the 1963 partial nuclear test ban treaty and the Nuclear Nonproliferation Treaty of 1968. The former banned nuclear tests in the atmosphere and the latter limited the spread of nuclear weapons by pledging non-nuclear states that signed it not to acquire nuclear weapons in the future. However, until SALT II the superpowers never had accepted any restrictions on their nuclear arsenals.

SALT I had two parts. The first limited ABM installations to two per country, a figure so low as to render them useless. The agreement thereby gave both superpowers relief from having to build a missile defense, an effort that was at one time enormously expensive and technologically dubious. It also in effect formalized the acceptance of the MAD doctrine of deterrence, as both sides were leaving themselves defenseless against ballistic missile attack.

The second part of the 1972 SALT I agreement put numerical limits on ICBMs and SLBMs. The agreement allowed the Soviet Union a numerical advantage in both ICBMs and SLBMs, but the United States, far ahead in MIRV deployment, actually had more warheads. The United States also boasted a greater than 2:1 advantage in long-range bombers, a category not covered by the 1972 agreement.

Because the SALT I agreement did not ban MIRVS, or the development of new missiles and bombers, there is some justification for historian Stephen E. Ambrose's observation that the agreement was "about as meaningful as freezing the cavalry of European nations in 1938 but not the tanks."[10] Many critics in fact complained that SALT appeared to be a fig leaf for escalation of the nuclear arms race.

However, it also was true that SALT I was the first Soviet-American agreement that placed any limits at all on the arms race, and that made it an important precedent if not an ideal treaty. Furthermore, two years later, in November 1974, President **Gerald Ford** and Soviet leader Brezhnev signed an agreement at Vladivostok on the Soviet Union's Pacific shore that established an outline for a new proposed treaty, SALT II. The Vladivostok agreement placed an overall limit of 2,400 on the total number of ICBMs, SLBMs, and long-range bombers each nation could have in its arsenal. Of the missiles, only 1,320 could be tipped with MIRVs. SALT II had an odd history. The superpowers signed it in 1979. But although the agreement was never ratified and therefore never officially went into effect, both sides still adhered to it. All in all, the SALT treaties, were, as foreign policy analyst William Hyland points out, remarkable in that "the two deeply hostile superpowers agreed to restrict the very armaments they ultimately depended on for their basic security—a fundamental bargain that . . . lasted for almost twenty years," until superseded by the arms reduction agreements of the 1990s.[11]

What Role Did the People's Republic of China Play in the Nixon-Kissinger Strategy?

After the Communist victory in China in 1949, the United States refused to recognize the new regime. The United States also used its power to keep the Beijing regime out of the United Nations. China's seat in the General Assembly and the Security Council continued to be held by the Nationalist regime. That regime governed only the island of Taiwan, where it was sheltered by

American military might and bolstered by American economic aid. American policy, which made it impossible to deal constructively with China, dated from the anti-Communist hysteria of the late 1940s and early 1950s and the Korean War. By 1969 the American-Chinese relationship was ripe for change.

The PRC, far from being a Soviet ally or part of a world Communist monolith, was openly hostile toward the Soviet Union. The United States and the Chinese also shared a common fear: rising Soviet military power. President Nixon, who had made his first mark on American politics as a militant anti-Communist, now saw the international scene in a different light. To Nixon and Kissinger, normalized Chinese-American relations were part of their strategy for an international balance of power that would allow better management of the world's problems. It also would put pressure on the Soviet Union to moderate its behavior.

After a number of preliminary steps, including a secret Kissinger trip to Beijing in 1971, Richard Nixon arrived in China on an official state visit in February 1972. The scene at the Beijing airport was a far cry from what had occurred at the Geneva Conference in 1954, when Secretary of State Dulles refused to shake hands with Chinese Foreign Minister Zhou Enlai. This time, Zhou greeted a smiling Kissinger with the words, "Ah, old friend." As for Nixon, who had learned to eat with chopsticks before his arrival, he used a toast at a state dinner to quote none other than Mao Zedong by urging those gathered to "seize the day, seize the hour."

Zhou's and Nixon's friendly words notwithstanding, serious differences remained between the two powers, the most important being the status of Taiwan. Although the United States acceded to Beijing's replacing the Nationalist regime in the United Nations in 1972 (leaving Taiwan outside the organization) and in 1979 established full diplomatic relations with the PRC (while ending formal diplomatic ties with Taiwan), it continued to maintain close ties with Taiwan through other channels and made it clear that it would not allow Beijing to reunify China by force. Beijing was further frustrated by Taiwan's growing prosperity, progress toward democracy, and total lack of interest in "reunification." These factors caused a deep strain in U.S.-Chinese relations that outlasted the Cold War.

DÉTENTE AT ITS PEAK

Détente peaked in 1975, the year of the Helsinki Accords. The accords were the culmination of negotiations called the Conference on Security and Cooperation in Europe that began in Geneva in 1973. The Helsinki Accords initially appeared to be a great triumph for Soviet leader Leonid Brezhnev. The Western powers formally accepted the Soviet-imposed border changes at the end of World War II and agreed to increased trade that the Soviet Union badly needed to modernize its economy. In return, the Soviets and their satellites promised to respect human rights. At the time, that concession did not seem to be significant: the Communist Parties of the Soviet bloc were in firm control of their countries and the United States and its NATO allies did not appear inclined to let the human-rights issue interfere with détente.

There were two great ironies in all this, as yet unrecognized by the political leaders who engineered the Helsinki Accords. On the one hand, ongoing tensions and budding crises were well on their way toward undermining détente, which did not survive the decade. Far more important, however, the Soviet bloc agreement to adhere to human rights energized dissenters in Eastern Europe and the Soviet Union. Their activities, combined with the corrosive social and economic problems that were eroding the legitimacy of Communism, set loose forces of change that few observers thought existed. As a result, the Soviet bloc did not survive the 1980s. The Soviet Union itself barely made it into the 1990s before collapsing.

CHAPTER FIVE

The New Cold War: 1976–1984

The Cold War during the year 1975 resembled a deceptive ocean tide. There were visible waves of détente that seemed to be rising and working their way toward shore, the most dramatic being the meeting in space of Soviet and American spacecraft in July and the signing of the Helsinki Accords in August. At the same time, beneath the waves lurked a persistent undertow. It had been there since détente began, hardly a surprise given the legacy of a generation of Cold War. By 1975, however, its outward pull was intensifying. During the presidency of **Jimmy Carter** (1977–81) the tide of détente clearly was receding, and by the end of the decade it ran out entirely. By the first term of Ronald Reagan many observers were talking about a "New Cold War."

THE DECLINE OF DÉTENTE

Détente always rested on a shifting and therefore insecure foundation, as the 1973 Arab-Israeli war made clear. The war began when Egypt and Syria launched a surprise attack on Israel on the eve of Yom Kippur, the holiest day of the Jewish year. Both Syria and Egypt were Soviet clients and had been heavily armed by their patron, a consistent supporter of the Arabs in the Arab-Israeli conflict. Israel, the region's only democracy, was America's most reliable Middle Eastern friend.

The United States was angered and alarmed at Soviet conduct both prior to the war and during the three weeks of bitter fighting. The Soviets had failed to warn the United States about Arab plans, thereby, at least from the American point of view, violating the spirit of détente. The Egyptians and Syrians initially sent the stunned Israelis reeling backward. Meanwhile the Soviets openly urged other Arab states to join the war, reinforced Syria and Egypt with a massive sea and airlift of arms and supplies, blocked efforts to arrange a ceasefire, vigorously supported an Arab oil boycott against the United States, and urged Arab governments to withdraw their multibillion-dollar deposits from

Western banks. It was little wonder that a worried Kissinger warned, "Détente cannot survive irresponsibility in the Middle East."

The war soon led to a serious Soviet-American confrontation. It occurred after the Israelis turned the tide of battle and were on the verge of destroying the Egyptian forces along the Suez Canal. With the Egyptians in a panic, Soviet leader Brezhnev threatened to send military forces and intervene directly in the fighting. President Nixon, who already had approved an American arms airlift to resupply the Israelis, responded by putting U.S. military forces worldwide on alert. At this point the Soviets dropped their cease-fire conditions, which would have brought both Soviet and American troops into the region as peacekeepers. Instead, the superpowers agreed on cease-fire terms that included a UN emergency force to separate the combatants. The latest Arab-Israeli war, and Soviet-American confrontation, was over.

Détente suffered another setback in 1974. The problem began when Congress linked granting the Soviet Union most-favored-nation trade status to Moscow allowing more Jews to emigrate to Israel. The bill, written in part by legislators who were highly critical of détente, also set a low limit on credits the U.S would grant the Soviet Union to finance trade. The Soviets considered the bill an unwarranted intrusion into their internal affairs and yet another example of the United States refusing to treat their country as an equal. They responded by canceling a number of agreements, including the trade agreement the United States had linked to Jewish immigration.

What Factors Led to the Unraveling of Détente?

Although détente survived the 1973 Arab-Israeli war and the flap over trade and Jewish immigration, it ran into further trouble for a variety of interlocking reasons. Most fundamentally, the two sides had a different view of what détente meant. Nixon and Kissinger saw détente as a means of managing Soviet conduct. Détente would make it in the interest of the Soviet Union to exercise restraint and cooperate on a broad range of international issues. The Soviets viewed détente differently, in part because they saw it as the outcome of America's decline. They expected that the United States would have to accept the Soviet Union as an equal in influencing world affairs. The Soviets were therefore angered when Kissinger succeeded in excluding them from Arab-Israeli negotiations in the wake of the 1973 war. As for their own actions, the Soviets viewed détente as binding them only with regard to specific Soviet-American agreements, to which they were prepared to adhere, but not in areas those agreements did not specifically cover. In stark contrast to the American view, the Soviets did not consider themselves limited in their efforts to promote Marxist revolutions in the Third World. Beginning in 1975 the Soviets intensified their activities in Africa. They took advantage of American's post-Vietnam and post-Watergate reluctance to get involved in Third World struggles to help a Marxist faction win a three-cornered civil war in oil-rich Angola, adding insult to injury by flying in Cuban troops to tilt the balance decisively. Soviet-sponsored Cuban troops also helped to prop up a Marxist dictatorship in Ethiopia after revolutionaries seized power there in 1977.

Détente also was undermined by the continuing arms race, and especially by technological progress that rendered SALT I increasingly obsolete. Both sides took advantage of their right to modernize their nuclear forces and, using new MIRV technology, dramatically increased their stockpiles of strategic nuclear warheads. Modernization took several forms, all of them threatening to both sides. The United States continued its development of the new MX ICBM and Trident SLBM missiles. However, after taking office in 1977 Jimmy Carter cut the American defense budget. The Soviet buildup covered a broader range of weapons, both nuclear and conventional, and their military spending continued to increase.

The newer, more powerful, and more accurate strategic nuclear weapons raised new concerns in both Washington and Moscow. More accurate weapons could allow one side to launch a surprise attack, destroy most of the victim's nuclear weapons, and thereby circumvent MAD and win a nuclear war. Concern over a Soviet "first strike" arose during the Nixon administration and intensified during the 1970s when American intelligence discovered that the Soviets were targeting their highly accurate ICBMs on U.S. missile installations. This targeting differed from the traditional strategy of targeting the opponent's cities and industries. That approach left the attacker open to retaliation since an attack on civilian targets would not destroy the other side's missiles stored in hardened silos. It therefore left the MAD deterrent operative. Much of the American concern involved two huge new Soviet missiles, the SS-18, which carried ten warheads, and the SS-19, which carried six and was more accurate than the SS-18. The Soviets added to the general alarm about their intentions when they installed a new generation of mobile intermediate-range missiles (the SS-20) in Europe. These developments stimulated increased criticism of both SALT I and détente in the United States, where worries increased about a "window of vulnerability" in America's nuclear force deterrent. Meanwhile, the highly accurate and MIRV-tipped MX raised identical "first strike" anxieties in Moscow. By the time SALT I expired in 1977, both sides were much more heavily armed than ever before and détente had become dangerously frayed.

Jimmy Carter, Human Rights, and SALT II

Jimmy Carter came to the presidency determined to go beyond détente and end the Cold War once and for all. As diplomatic historian Gaddis Smith has pointed out in *Morality, Reason, and Power: American Diplomacy in the Carter Years* (1986), not since Woodrow Wilson had a president tried so hard to infuse moral concerns into American foreign policy. Carter was convinced that the time had come for the United States to overcome its "inordinate fear of communism" and focus less on its longstanding confrontation with the Soviet Union. In what the president called "a new world," there should be "a new American foreign policy—a policy based on constant decency in its values and on optimism in the nation's historical mission." The "soul" of that policy would be human rights, which Carter intended to support wherever they were being suppressed, regardless of whether the offending nation was a dictatorial American ally, a nonaligned Third World country, or the Soviet Union and its satellites. There has always been an idealistic thread in American foreign policy, and Carter found some support among both ordinary Americans and specialists. Thus Jerel A. Rosati (*The Carter Administration's Quest for Global Community: Beliefs and Their Impact on Behavior*, 1987) generally supports Carter's effort.[1] However, analysts also have criticized the emphasis on human rights as counterproductive, notwithstanding its good intentions. Joshua Muravchik (*The Uncertain Crusade: Jimmy Carter and the Dilemma of Human Rights Policy*, 1986) praises Carter administration "Country Reports" that publicized human rights violations across the world. However, he points out that major offenders that also happened to be powerful, such as the Soviet Union, China, and Saudi Arabia, escaped serious pressure. Carter's pressure to uphold human rights instead tended to be directed against small Latin American countries that happened to be U.S. allies.

As far as the obsession with Communism was concerned, Carter proposed to establish normal diplomatic relations not only with the PRC, which was a logical extension of the Nixon-Kissinger policy toward Beijing, but also with Cuba and Vietnam, the two small but respectively irritating (Cuba) and painful (Vietnam) Communist thorns long stuck in America's side. He also proposed to remove American troops from South Korea.

Carter enjoyed some significant foreign policy successes. In the face of conservative opposition at home, during 1977 he negotiated and won Senate approval of treaties that returned sovereignty of the Panama Canal Zone to Panama, signaling a major change in United States policy toward Latin America. The next year he brought Prime Minister Menachem Begin of Israel and President **Anwar Sadat** of Egypt to the United States where they negotiated and signed the Camp David Accords, the first major step in establishing peace between the two old enemies and the first break in the wall of Arab rejection of Israel's right to exist. In 1979, the United States and China established full diplomatic relations.

What Factors Undermined Carter's Foreign Policy?

Carter's optimism about a new world order and his focus on human rights in shaping foreign relations was premature. Although much of what went wrong may have been beyond his or anyone else's control, Carter also exhibited poor timing in choosing when to promote human rights. One major error occurred in 1977 when he strongly criticized the Soviet Union's harsh treatment of its human rights activists just before sending Brezhnev a new arms control proposal. The criticism angered the Soviet leadership and helped doom Carter's proposal. Overall, as Soviet specialist Adam Ulam points out in *Dangerous Relations: The Soviet Union in World Politics, 1970–1982* (1983), the Soviets were exasperated by what they considered Carter's posturing and inconsistency. In Foreign Minister **Andrei Gromyko's** blunt words, Carter's public statements about human rights "poisons the political climate. . . . We do not need any teachers when it comes to the internal affairs of our country."[2]

Carter's ability to deal with the Soviets, or with anything else, for that matter, was dealt a devastating blow by events in Iran. Warren Christopher (*American Hostages in Iran*, 1985), a deputy secretary of state during the crisis and later secretary of state during the first term of the Clinton administration, joined other American officials in defending Carter's handling of the crisis. However, Carter has been severely criticized by other observers. Michael Ledeen and William Lewis (*Debacle: The American Failure in Iran*, 1981) assert that the Carter administration was slow to understand the realities of the 1979 Iranian Islamic revolution. Gary Sick (*All Fall Down: America's Fateful Encounter With Iran*, 1985) criticizes Carter for allowing the crisis to dominate his administration.

Iran under the Shah was staunchly pro-American, a country Carter himself called an "island of stability" in the volatile Middle East. But in January 1979 bitterly anti-Western Islamic fundamentalist revolutionaries led by a cleric, the Ayatollah Khomeini, overthrew the Shah. In November, shortly after the terminally ill Shah was admitted to the United States for medical treatment, a large mob of fanatical Iranian students, violating all the traditional rules protecting diplomats, seized control of the United States embassy in Teheran and took its staff members hostage. For the next 444 days, as the Iranians proclaimed their hatred for the country they called the "Great Satan," Carter allowed himself and his administration to become hostage to the Iranian hostage crisis. He commented that he felt the same helplessness that a powerful person feels when his child is kidnapped. He made the mistake of allowing those feelings to be known publicly. While Carter visibly agonized over of the fate of the hostages, the United States looked like a weak and helpless giant as the Iranians mistreated the hostages and taunted the president. A humiliating failed rescue attempt in April 1980 only made the United States and its president look worse. Carter made the decision to attempt the rescue while his secretary of state, **Cyrus Vance**, was not in Washington. "Stunned and angry that such a momentous decision had been made in my absence," as he recalls in his memoir *Hard Choices*, Vance later resigned his position.[3] Not until the eve of Carter's leaving office in January 1981 did the Iranians agree to release the hostages. By then Carter's foreign policy, and his presidency, lay in ruins.

SALT II

When SALT I expired in October 1977, despite the lack of a new agreement and notwithstanding other tensions in their relations, the United States and the Soviet Union agreed to observe the limits of SALT I until a new agreement could be forged.

This development was a measure of both superpowers' desire to keep the nuclear arms race from spinning completely out of control. Negotiations meanwhile inched along for more than two years until the SALT II treaty was signed by Carter and Brezhnev in Vienna in June 1979. SALT II was extremely complicated. Its main features were a limit on all strategic nuclear launchers (missiles and heavy bombers)—2,400 until 1981 and 2,250 thereafter—and a limit on the number of missiles that could be converted into MIRVs. The treaty did not mention some very important weapons. They included the Soviet supersonic Backfire bomber, much feared by American military strategists, and the newly developed American cruise missiles, which are subsonic missiles that fly close to the ground and are therefore extremely difficult to detect. The limits set by SALT II were so high that, like SALT I, the new agreement in reality allowed both sides to increase their stockpiles of strategic nuclear weapons. Nonetheless, SALT II was severely criticized in the United States for allegedly allowing the Soviet Union unacceptable advantages. In the end, SALT II was never ratified by either superpower and therefore never officially went into effect. Yet once again the imperative of avoiding the total collapse of nuclear arms control made its weight felt. Both the United States and the Soviet Union for the most part adhered to the terms of SALT II until it officially expired in 1985. They even continued to observe its terms thereafter until improved U.S.-Soviet relations finally produced a genuine arms reduction agreement several years later. Not even Ronald Reagan, a vigorous critic of SALT II before becoming president in 1981 and the architect of a massive American military buildup during his first term, was prepared to dispense with SALT II until he had negotiated something far better.

The Soviet Invasion of Afghanistan

In an effort to shore up Congressional support for SALT II in 1979, Carter asked for funds to deploy the new MX missile. He also agreed with America's NATO allies to install new and extremely accurate Pershing II intermediate missiles and cruise missiles in Europe in response to the Soviet deployment of SS-20s.[4] However, Carter's standing in the area of defense, never very strong, especially with critics of détente, suffered a severe blow in the summer when he announced that the Soviet Union had secretly and illegally deployed a combat brigade in Cuba. To the president's great embarrassment it turned out that the brigade had been there since 1962, and was permitted under the agreement that had ended the Cuban Missile Crisis. Not only did Carter antagonize the Soviets with the latest American fiasco involving Cuba, but he looked foolish and incompetent at home.

With SALT II in trouble and détente on the ropes, the Soviet Union in one swoop inadvertently killed both of them. In 1978 pro-Soviet revolutionaries had overthrown the government of Afghanistan and established a Communist regime. The regime was unpopular from the start in that conservative and Islamic country and by 1979 was on the verge of collapsing. In December 1979 Soviet troops invaded Afghanistan and installed a new Communist leadership that Moscow calculated would be more effective. Although the initial assault, carried out by elite forces, was successful, the invasion turned into Soviet disaster. Local Afghan forces soon had Soviet forces entangled in a costly and futile guerrilla war that not even 100,000 Soviet troops were able to end.

Brezhnev and his colleagues considered their invasion defensive. They calculated that they were saving a friendly Marxist regime threatened by both American and Chinese subversion. In addition, the Soviets feared that Islamic fundamentalism, which already had led to the overthrow of the Shah in Iran, would spread via Afghanistan to millions of Muslims living in the Soviet Union. From the Soviet point of view, the invasion of Afghanistan was consistent with the Brezhnev Doctrine, which affirmed the Soviet Union's right to intervene outside its borders to prevent the fall of Communist regimes.

The United States and other countries did not see things that way. The invasion of Afghanistan was the first time Soviet troops had been sent into action outside the Soviet bloc since World War II, and that unnerved leaders in capitals from Washington to Beijing. Beginning in early 1980 President Carter announced a series of measures to punish the Soviets. He withdrew the SALT II treaty from consideration by the Senate, restricted American grain sales to the Soviets, and cut off high-technology sales. Having made the charge that the Soviet advance into Afghanistan posed a threat to the Persian Gulf region, the president also announced the Carter Doctrine: the United States would use force if necessary to protect its access to the oil resources of the Persian Gulf. He also authorized a series of military measures that included increased defense spending, a new rapid deployment force to defend the Middle East, and Presidential Directive 59 (PD-59), under which more American missiles were targeted on their Soviet counterparts. Carter's retargeting inevitably raised fears in Moscow that the United States was moving away from accepting MAD and toward adopting a first strike strategy. Adding insult to injury, Carter pulled the United States out of the 1980 Olympic games scheduled to be held in Moscow. (Four years later, the Soviets returned the favor by boycotting the Los Angeles Olympics.)

Having entered the White House with grand plans to transcend longstanding American fears about Communism and to end the Cold War, by 1980 Carter was increasingly preoccupied with what he called Soviet expansionism. Defeated in the 1980 elections by Ronald Reagan, Carter left office with Soviet-American relations at their lowest ebb in years.

RONALD REAGAN AND THE NEW COLD WAR

During the presidential campaign of 1980 Ronald Reagan's campaign speeches echoed the doubts many Americans felt about both the Soviet Union and détente. Some of his speeches sounded as if they had been transported, perfectly frozen and preserved, from the frigid 1950s. As he told one audience, "Let's not delude ourselves. The Soviet Union underlies all the unrest that's going on. If they weren't engaged in this game of dominoes, there wouldn't be any hot spots in the world."[5] Three years later Reagan succinctly summed up his view of the Soviet Union when he called it an "evil empire." Meanwhile, inside the evil empire the old-guard Soviet leadership was dying off. Brezhnev, increasingly enfeebled during his last years in office, died in November 1982. His two elderly and sickly successors, Yuri Andropov and Constantin Chernenko, each died after barely a year in office. As the Soviet gerontocracy expired Reagan watched from afar, becoming the first American president since Stalin's death to spend a term in office without meeting a Soviet leader face-to-face. During that term Soviet-American relations chilled to the point that observers spoke of what they called a new Cold War, or "Cold War II."

The Reagan Military Buildup

Ronald Reagan entered the White House determined to seize the initiative in the competition for international influence from the Soviet Union. He believed this possible because, as Russian historian Richard Pipes pointed out in the journal *Foreign Affairs*, he was convinced that "the Soviet Union was not strong, but weak, that its power rested on terror at home and blackmail abroad, and that, being in the profoundest sense unnatural, it did not have long to live."[6] At the same time, Reagan believed that the Soviet Union's growing military might was a threat to American security. His administration responded by launching the largest American military buildup of the Cold War. Additional billions went to both conventional and nuclear arms and to all the service branches.

Reagan was not dissuaded by officials in Moscow who complained about his open hostility toward their country. Nor was he moved by critics at home who warned about the lack of attention to domestic pressing social problems, wasteful spending on unnecessary weapons, and dangerously high budget deficits that threatened to undermine the health of the American economy. He disagreed with critics such as George F. Kennan, who in an article called "On Nuclear War" urged drastic cuts in nuclear weapons by both superpowers.[7] Reagan also did not seem disturbed by comments from members of his administration about the possibility of fighting and winning a nuclear war. Perhaps the most controversial statement came from a defense department official who noted that "if there are enough shovels to go around" people could survive a nuclear war. "It's the dirt that does it," the official added. "With a little bit of dirt, just about anybody could survive a nuclear war."[8] In some areas Reagan simply picked up where Carter left off. Thus despite Soviet attempts at intimidation and widespread antinuclear demonstrations in Europe, but with the strong support of America's NATO allies, the United States went ahead with the installation of new missiles on European soil to counter the SS-20s already deployed by the Soviets.

Star Wars

Reagan brought to the White House a new approach to arms control. Instead of SALT, or limiting nuclear arms to what turned out to be a higher level that already existed, he proposed START, or Strategic Arms Reduction Talks. These talks got under way in 1982 but made little progress.[9] The next year Reagan announced what became his most controversial nuclear arms project: the Strategic Defense Initiative (SDI), or, as skeptics immediately named it, Star Wars. The idea was to use new, and unproven, technology in a system based in space to defend against a nuclear attack. Critics quickly pointed out that SDI, even if it worked, would be fantastically expensive. Numerous experts in the field warned that SDI, no matter how much was spent on it, could never do the job Reagan proposed. A few days after Reagan made his announcement, Jerome Weisner, a former presidential scientific advisor and president of the Massachusetts Institute of Technology, observed that "there are 10,000 or more nuclear weapons on each side. A defense system that would knock out 90 or 95 percent would be a miracle—and the remaining 5 or 10 percent would be enough to totally destroy civilization."[10] Other critics argued that deploying SDI would violate the limits of the 1972 Soviet-American antiballistic missile agreement, an argument the president challenged. Not surprisingly, the Soviets also strongly criticized SDI. They clearly feared another expensive round in an arms race they could ill afford and that would be based on technology in which they trailed the United States. Soviet leader Yuri Andropov warned that the project was "not just irresponsible. It is insane."[11] The SDI proposal also met with little enthusiasm among America's NATO allies.

The Reagan Doctrine

Another key aspect of Reagan's approach to dealing with the Soviet Union was known as the Reagan Doctrine. According to this latest, and last, American Cold War doctrine, the United States would actively use military force and other means to undermine Marxist regimes in the Third World. This would further stretch Soviet resources, which already were spread very thin. While a variety of anti-Communist forces received aid, the three main targets of the Reagan Doctrine were Grenada, Afghanistan, and Nicaragua. In Grenada, an American invasion in 1983, officially launched to prevent Soviet/Cuban military use of the island and to protect hundreds of Americans attending medical school there from local violence, overthrew a Marxist regime that had itself recently seized power by toppling another Marxist faction. In Afghanistan, Muslim rebels, aided by U.S.-supplied weapons, were tying down and bleeding a Soviet occupation force of 100,000 troops. In Nicaragua, a Marxist-dominated movement called the Sandinistas had come to power in 1979 after overthrowing a corrupt but pro-American dictatorship. Notwithstanding economic aid sent by the Carter administration, the Sandinistas soon allied with Cuba and the Soviet Union. They also tried to export their revolution to neighboring El Salvador, where another pro-American dictatorship ruled. The Cuban/Soviet involvement in Nicaragua infuriated the Reagan administration, which armed and otherwise aided a guerrilla rebellion by anti-Sandinista forces collectively known as the Contras. Many Americans opposed that policy, in part because some elements of the Contras were identified with the pre-Sandinista dictatorship, and eventually Congress banned further help to the rebels. Among the many critical historical accounts of Reagan's policy in Nicaragua is E. Bradford Burns's *The War in Nicaragua: The Reagan Doctrine and the Politics of Nostalgia* (1987). An account that supports Reagan's contention of a Soviet threat to Latin America is Timothy Ashby's *The Bear in the Back Yard: Moscow's Caribbean Strategy* (1987).

Blocked by Congress from openly supporting the Contras, the administration turned to illegal methods of supporting them. The plan became public during Reagan's second term and turned into a scandal called the Iran-Contra affair that seriously weakened the Reagan presidency. The workings of the Reagan White House during Iran-Contra are chronicled by journalists Paul Schieffer and Gary Paul Gates in *The Acting President* (1989). Profits from secret arms sales to Iran, supposedly an enemy of the United States, were funneled illegally to support the Contras. Although the Contras still were unable to overthrow the Sandinistas, American political and economic pressure continued under Reagan and his successor, **George Bush**. It ultimately weakened the regime to the point that the Sandinistas agreed to free elections in 1990. Their defeat, just as the Cold War was winding down, ended Marxist rule in Nicaragua.

The Final Frost

A number of other factors contributed to worsening Soviet-American relations during Reagan's first term in office. In Poland, resistance to Communist rule in 1980 gave birth to a trade union called Solidarity, the first independent trade union in any Communist country. A year later the Polish regime, backed and pressured by Moscow, dispersed Solidarity and arrested its leaders. In September 1983 Soviet defense forces shot down a Korean Air Lines 747 jet when it strayed over Soviet territory, killing all 269 people aboard. The KAL affair raised serious doubts about both Soviet intentions and the technological competence of its defense forces, which seemed unable to distinguish civilian and military aircraft. Then during 1983 and 1984 the Soviets walked out of three sets of arms control negotiations: talks on reducing strategic nuclear weapons, on intermediate-range nuclear weapons, and on conventional forces in Europe. For the first time since the 1960s the superpowers were not even discussing how to control the arms race. The New Cold War seemed to be frozen solidly in place. But by 1985 new and warmer winds were blowing from Moscow. What lay ahead this time was not simply a thaw, but a historic meltdown and the end of the Cold War.

CHAPTER SIX

The End of the Cold War: 1985–1990

The end of the Cold War, although not provoking the intense controversy surrounding its origins, has produced its own debates. There is no general agreement about precisely when the Cold War ended, although the signing of the Charter of Paris in November 1990 provides a logical marker for its termination, in the same way the Yalta Conference of February 1945 marks the beginning of the struggle. There is sharp disagreement about what role the United States military buildup under Ronald Reagan, and in particular his Strategic Defense Initiative proposal, played in bringing an end to the Cold War. Experts such as Samuel F. Wells contend that the Reagan administration hastened the end of the Cold War by confronting the Soviet Union with a new arms race that its leadership knew it could not afford. Raymond L. Garthoff concurs with analysts who give the lion's share of the credit for the end of the Cold War to Soviet leader **Mikhail Gorbachev**.[1] In a similar vein, there is even a debate about who won the Cold War. There is no doubt that the Soviet Union, which collapsed shortly after the Cold War ended, was the most decisive loser. But what about the United States? The end of the Cold War and the subsequent collapse of the Soviet Union left the United States as the world's only political and military superpower. At the same time, the United States paid a tremendous economic and social price in waging and winning the Cold War. Therefore, a case can be made that, like the Soviet Union, America ended up a loser. The real winners in this scenario were Germany and Japan, losers in World War II, who during the Cold War, protected by the American nuclear umbrella, focused their energies and resources on building civilian industries and infrastructure and emerged from that era with healthier economies than that of their superpower protector.

GORBACHEV, PERESTROIKA, AND THE COLD WAR

Why Did Gorbachev Initiate a Fundamental Change in the Foreign Policy of the Soviet Union?

Mikhail Gorbachev assumed his post as General Secretary of the Communist Party of the Soviet Union determined to change his country's priorities in order to cope with long-neglected and increasingly serious problems. At home, the Soviet economy, largely unreformed since Stalin's day, had stagnated. The cumbersome and inefficient central planning system was unable to incorporate the technological advances that were revolutionizing the economies of the West. The Soviet standard of living therefore continued to lag far behind that of Western Europe and the United States. Social problems such as rampant alcoholism and growing drug use were getting worse, as was the corruption that pervaded Soviet life. Many of the Soviet educated elite were increasingly restive, fed up with intolerable censorship and interference in their lives and frustrated by their country's inability to provide for its people the way Western countries provided for theirs. The country's political leadership—old, enfeebled, and unable to cope with the nation's problems—was an embarrassment.

At the same time, Soviet foreign policy since the 1960s was a demonstrable failure. Brezhnev's military buildup had provoked an even more formidable buildup by the United States. The Soviet quest for absolute security through military might had solidified the NATO alliance and driven the Soviet Union's neighbors in Asia—most importantly Communist China and Japan—closer to the United States. Meanwhile, Eastern Europe was doing anything but providing the Soviet Union with security. The region had become a chronic economic burden and unending source of irritation because of continued popular rejection, despite the passage of four decades, of the Soviet-imposed Communist regimes. In addition, propping up Third World Communist regimes in Asia, Africa, and Central America was another expensive enterprise whose returns were meager by any reasonable standard. By far the most painful Soviet Third World problem was in Afghanistan, where the long and expensive guerrilla war already had cost thousands of Soviet lives and undermined the prestige of its supposedly formidable military machine. In short, the Soviet Union had to contend with much more than its old nemesis of capitalist encirclement. It faced a new set of problems associated with Communist states—from Eastern Europe to Afghanistan to China—that political scientist Seweryn Bialer dubbed "communist encirclement."[2]

Gorbachev's policy for overhauling the Soviet economy was called *pere-stroika* (restructuring), a term that also applied to his policies as a whole. However, implementing perestroika at home required enormous resources. This in turn required a new Soviet foreign policy that would reduce tensions with the United States and its allies and thereby permit the Soviet Union to divert resources from military to civilian needs. With an economy less than half the size of the United States, the Soviet Union could no longer compete with the United States in the Cold War arms race and have any hope of solving its economic difficulties and other domestic problems. The Soviet military was consuming about 25 percent of the country's gross domestic product, versus about 6 percent in the United States. Its best scientists and engineers and its most efficient factories served military rather than civilian demands. The excessive military burden explains why, as early as 1983, the same year as Ronald Reagan was denouncing the "evil empire" and Soviet-American relations were hitting rock bottom, a rising Mikhail Gorbachev was opposing increased military spending. Once he was in power, what he called "new thinking" revolutionized Soviet foreign policy with breathtaking speed.

New thinking postulated a fundamental change in the Soviet Union's relationship with the West. Under Lenin and Stalin the assumption was that the capitalist and Communist worlds would decide their struggle for world supremacy by war. Although "peaceful coexistence" became the official Soviet policy in the 1950s, that new wrinkle, though decidedly less dangerous than the original Leninist formulation, still assumed an economic and political competition between the two systems, which Communism, of course, naturally would win. Gorbachev, with the aid of **Eduard Shevardnadze**, who replaced the venerable Andrei Gromyko as Soviet foreign minister in 1985, was determined to put Soviet-Western relations on an entirely new footing. He would seek a relationship aimed at ending the Cold War and terminating the exhausting and futile competition between capitalism and communism. Ideological competition with the West would yield to normal interstate relations. Rather than seek security through an endless effort to win an unwinnable arms race, the Soviet Union would guarantee its security through arms control approaches and other measures that provided the West with an equal measure of security. The end of the arms race would give Gorbachev the resources he desperately needed to restructure the Soviet economy and deal with other pressing social issues at home. It also would leave the former Cold War protagonists free to cooperate in solving problems that threatened them all, such as the damaged global environment. Gorbachev explained his outlook in his book, *Perestroika: New Thinking for Our Country and the World* (1987):

The time is ripe for abandoning views on foreign policy which are influenced by an imperial standpoint. Neither the Soviet Union nor the United States is able to force its will on others. . . . From the point of view of long-term, bit-time politics, no one will be able to subordinate others. That is why only one thing—relations of equity—remains. All of us must realize this. Along with the . . . realities of nuclear weapons, ecology, the scientific and technological revolution, and information systems, this also obliges us to respect one another and everybody.[3]

What Role Did the Reagan and Bush Administrations Play in Ending the Cold War?

The Reagan and Bush administrations, as well as America's NATO allies, in essence responded to changes that emanated initially from Moscow and the Soviet bloc. To the surprise of many, Gorbachev found a willing negotiating partner in Ronald Reagan, the same man whose military buildup and militant anti-Soviet rhetoric had so antagonized and unnerved earlier Kremlin leaders. Influenced by advisors such as Secretary of State **George Shultz**, Reagan apparently was satisfied by the end of his first term that the United States was positioned to "negotiate from strength." American policy toward the Soviet Union therefore was changing, and the administration was sending signals about its readiness to negotiate arms control agreements. Thus, in September 1984, before the end of Reagan's first term and before Gorbachev came to power, Soviet Foreign Minister Andrei Gromyko was invited to the White House to discuss reviving arms control discussions. The resumption of talks was officially announced after a meeting in Geneva between Gromyko and Shultz. After a false start at the rushed and poorly prepared summit between Reagan and Gorbachev at Reykjavik, Iceland in October 1986, which foundered on Reagan's refusal to abandon SDI and ended as the worst summit failure of the Cold War, arms reduction negotiations were put firmly on the fast track. In December 1987 the two sides negotiated a treaty that eliminated all intermediate-range nuclear weapons in Europe. Although the resulting Intermediate Nuclear Forces treaty (INF) covered only a small fraction of each side's nuclear arsenal, it was nonetheless a crucial breakthrough because it both reduced the size of those arsenals and eliminated an entire category of nuclear missiles. Meanwhile, the START talks made rapid progress and were well on their way to completion when Reagan was succeeded by George Bush in January 1989. A month later Gorbachev delivered on a promise he made in February 1988, which had been greeted with considerable skepticism, when the last Soviet troops left Afghanistan.

George Bush's role in ending the Cold War was different from Reagan's, mainly because of the growing instability in the Soviet Union during his term that led to its collapse at the end of 1991. Bush's most significant accomplishment was to balance timely support for Gorbachev with a steady but restrained focus on Western interests as the Soviet Union staggered from crisis to crisis and finally to disintegration. As historian Thomas Powers has pointed out, "Bush's policy of accommodation, understanding, and circumspection was well suited to the Soviet Union's last two years of life."[4] The Bush administration thereby played a key role in assuring that the collapse of Communism in Eastern Europe and the Soviet Union during 1989–91 took place peacefully, a remarkable development in that the process could easily have taken a disastrously violent course. In the aftermath of that historic change, the Bush administration pushed major arms-control negotiations to successful conclusions.

1989: *The Year of the People*

The Cold War began as a result of Soviet expansion into Eastern Europe and the imposition of Communist regimes on the countries of the region; its termination required that the Soviet satellites receive the right to self-determination. By 1989 the process of reform in the Soviet Union had gone farther than anyone had expected. In addition to perestroika, the changes included the elimination of totalitarian controls on information and communication, or *glasnost*, and the democratization of Soviet political life, or *democratizatsia*. What Gorbachev found out was that he could not, as he apparently first intended, administer small, controlled doses of freedom to Soviet society from his Kremlin office. To his surprise the Soviet people reacted to each dose by incessantly demanding more and within a few years the process of reform took on a life of its own and bolted from Gorbachev's control.

The ferment of reform meanwhile was spreading throughout Eastern Europe. Gorbachev was unwilling to shoulder the cost of further propping up unpopular satellite regimes, which the struggling Soviet Union could not afford. He also was well aware that continuing to do so would destroy his policy of normalizing relations with the West. That is why in 1989 he warned the regimes of Eastern Europe that they would have to introduce reforms or risk being swept away. Gorbachev hoped that they could revitalize socialism in Eastern Europe. Instead, beginning in mid-year in Poland and Hungary, the Communist regimes began to splinter and collapse. It was at this point that Gorbachev faced a historic choice: use force to save Communism in Eastern Europe, and destroy both his new foreign policy and his reform program at home in the process, or accept the demise of the regimes Stalin had imposed over four decades earlier. Gorbachev, to his great credit, chose the second course. During the summer of 1989 he publicly repudiated the Brezhnev Doctrine under which the Soviet Union had maintained the right to intervene abroad to save Communist regimes. In effect it was replaced by what one Soviet official dubbed the "Sinatra Doctrine": henceforth the Eastern European states would "do it their way." By the end of the year the continental Communist collapse had swept from Poland and Hungary to East Germany, Bulgaria, Czechoslovakia, and Romania. The symbolic climax occurred on November 9, when the crumbling Communist regime in East Germany, in a last futile attempt to survive, opened the Berlin Wall. Tens of thousands of Germans from east and west celebrated freedom around and on the hated structure that for twenty-eight years had stood for oppression, the division of Europe, and the Cold War itself. As 1990 dawned, the only former Eastern European satellite still under Communist rule was tiny and isolated Albania, an ultra hard-line, lone-wolf state whose leadership had broken with the Soviet Union back in the 1960s.

THE COLD WAR ENDS

By 1989 announcements from some quarters, ranging from the *New York Times* to Mikhail Gorbachev, were heralding the end of the Cold War. Something approaching an official declaration took place in 1990. During that year several agreements helped close the book on the Cold War, beginning with Soviet commitments to Hungary and Czechoslovakia to withdraw its troops from those two former satellites. In June, Gorbachev came to Washington for a summit meeting with George Bush in which the two leaders signed agreements dealing with both chemical and nuclear weapons. Perhaps most significantly, during the fall of 1990 the question of German unification was resolved. The settlement took place on Western, and especially German, terms, not Soviet ones. There was, in fact, no great enthusiasm in the West for immediate German reunification, but both Western hesitancy and Soviet opposition were unable to derail the blitzkrieg diplomatic campaign launched by German chancellor **Helmut Kohl**, who lavished assurances about Germany's peaceful intentions on leaders from Washington to Moscow. After holding out for a while, Gorbachev accepted both German reunification and its membership in NATO. In return he received limits on the size of the German army, German's renunciation of nuclear, chemical, and biological weapons, a guarantee that NATO troops would not be stationed on the territory of the former East Germany, and billions of dollars of desperately needed aid. Germany's official reunification took place on October 3, erasing yet another of the most indelible marks of the Cold War. Twelve days later Mikhail Gorbachev was awarded the Nobel Peace Prize for 1990, an honor he richly deserved.

On November 21, 1990, the United States, the Soviet Union, and thirty other nations signed the Charter of Paris, a document designed to regulate their relations in the post–Cold War era. The charter included a nonaggression pact between NATO and the soon-to-be-dissolved Warsaw Pact. After signing the charter, President George Bush provided a low-key, semiofficial epitaph to the long, bitter, and costly struggle that had dominated world affairs since 1945 when he said, "We have closed a chapter in history. The Cold War is over."

That point was underscored by a major arms agreement reducing conventional forces in Europe, the Conventional Forces in Europe (CFE) treaty, signed in Paris two days earlier. The Cold War's passing was further demonstrated in early 1991 by Soviet acquiescence to Operation Desert Storm. In that American-led military campaign, a coalition of nations drove Iraq, which had invaded Kuwait in August 1990, from its small oil-rich neighbor. The signing in July of the START I treaty, which called for major cuts in the superpowers' nuclear arsenals, was an important step out of the Cold War's long nuclear shadow.

What Factors Decided and Ultimately Ended the Cold War?

The policy of containment and what it did or did not achieve remains a matter of debate among historians of the Cold War. Revisionist historians continue to view it as an overreaction to Soviet activities which, they believe, were not a threat to American security. Revisionists see containment as a policy that inevitably led the United States to prop up undemocratic regimes throughout the world and to a series of harmful blunders, the worst of which was the quagmire of Vietnam.

However, although at times the United States did overreact and, as containment became global in scope, failed to distinguish between vital and secondary interests, the case for containment as being both necessary and successful appears to be quite solid. There is substantial evidence that immediately after World War II a real threat existed to Western Europe, and hence to democratic political systems and America's vital national interests. The Soviet Union was not simply another authoritarian regime; it was a totalitarian society led by Joseph Stalin, a paranoid and ruthless dictator who viewed the Communist and capitalist worlds as irreconcilable enemies. Documentable Soviet expansionist designs, combined with weakness and demoralization in Western Europe, could have led to Communist takeovers and therefore destroyed democracy in countries like France and Italy, even without direct Soviet intervention. Containment restored the shattered balance of power in Europe and within a short time enabled the democratic societies of the West to recover. As historians John Spanier and Steven W. Hook have put it, after the defeat of Nazi Germany in World War II, containment facilitated the "defeat of the second totalitarian challenge to Western-style democracy" in the twentieth century.[5] Over the long run and despite excesses and blunders that were a part of containment, the policy also forced a change in Soviet society that in fact led to its dissolution, much as George F. Kennan predicted back in 1947.

The role of nuclear weapons in determining the shape and duration of the Cold War is another issue that divides historians. Richard Ned Lebow and Janice Gross Stein argue that the Soviet and American policies of deterrence based on nuclear weapons "provoked the type of behavior it was designed to prevent" and in fact "likely prolonged the Cold War."[6] However, there is a persuasive case nuclear weapons, whose use by the superpowers would have destroyed civilization, preserved the peace until the Cold War could be resolved. John Lewis Gaddis has written that "what we wound up doing with nuclear weapons was buying time." Arthur Schlesinger has observed that nuclear weapons were the "reason the Cold War never exploded into a hot war" and therefore suggested with a touch of irony that "the Nobel peace prize should have gone to the atomic bomb." Along the same lines, Thomas Powers answered the question of who "won" the Cold War by observing, "The bomb won."[7]

If it can be persuasively argued that the awesome power of atomic weapons kept the Cold War within limits, another type of power without any physical qualities whatsoever played a pivotal role in tilting the scales toward the West: the power of ideas. Since 1985 it has become increasingly clear just how important American support for the ideas of democracy, freedom, and human rights was to dissidents living behind the Iron Curtain, who listened to American broadcasts on the Voice of America and Radio Liberty and took heart from the Helsinki Accords. The accords in particular served as morale boosters for dissident organizations such as Charter 77 in Czechoslovakia, Solidarity in Poland, and human rights groups in the Soviet Union, where the accords served, in Martin Walker's words, as "the West's secret weapon, a time bomb planted in the heart of the Soviet empire."[8] In short, during the course of the

Cold War the United States provided crucial support for advocates of democracy on both sides of the Iron Curtain.

The Cold War finally ended when the Soviet Union became economically exhausted by the burdens of keeping up with the far richer and more efficient United States and its allies. Yet it has often been pointed out that even an exhausted Soviet Union probably would have continued the struggle if its post-Brezhnev leadership had remained within the traditional Soviet mold. Thus, along with economic exhaustion, the advent of Mikhail Gorbachev and his path-breaking policy of perestroika was another necessary factor in ending the Cold War.

What Were the Costs of the Cold War?

Losers, winners, and even nonparticipants all paid a heavy price for the Cold War. The burden of the Cold War severely weakened the Soviet Union and prepared the way for its demise in December 1991. The United States, the supposedly victorious superpower, also paid dearly for the Cold War. It forced America to pour resources into the military that were needed for civilian uses. As its civilian infrastructure deteriorated from lack of long-term support, during the 1980s the United States was transformed by its massive budget and balance of payment deficits from the world's largest creditor into the world's largest debtor nation. By 1990 the United States was paying almost a quarter of a trillion dollars interest annually on its skyrocketing national debt. About 15 percent of that money went to foreign bond holders, the majority of whom were Japanese. Many of America's leading high-tech companies focused their resources and scientific expertise on military rather than civilian industrial applications. These factors help explain the difficulty the U.S. companies had by the Cold War's close in competing with German and Japanese industrial firms in civilian industrial markets worldwide, including those in the United States itself.

The Cold War's decades-long unbroken string of huge military budgets promoted what President Eisenhower in his 1961 farewell address called the "military-industrial complex," an interlocking network made up of the federal military establishment and companies producing arms and other defense-related products, all with an interest in maintaining or increasing military expenditures. Eisenhower worried that the military-industrial complex could distort the American economy and undermine the country's economic health. The Cold War certainly distorted the federal government. By the time the Cold War finally ended, as Ernest R. May has noted, the Pentagon was "the crest of a mountainous defense establishment, which employs two-thirds of the nearly five million persons who work for the U.S. government." This establishment, which includes branches concerned with national security, intelligence, foreign affairs, and other agencies designed to enlist broad sectors of American society in what May calls the "global diplomatic-military contest with a hostile, secretive, heavily armed rival superpower," appears, he argues, poorly suited to meeting the challenges the United States faces in the post-Cold War era.[9] In fact, the origins of what some historians call the "national security state" date from World War I. World War II accelerated its development exponentially. But it was the Cold War that made it an integral and enormous part of American life during what at least officially was peacetime.

The American way of life suffered in other ways as the country focused so much of its energy on the Cold War. The United States became a more violent society with a burgeoning prison population. The government's failure to tell the truth about its conduct of the Vietnam War made many Americans cynical about what public officials told them. The Watergate scandal widened a breach between the American people and their government that, for many, did not close in subsequent decades. Yet it is also true that as the Cold War ended the influence of American culture worldwide was greater than ever before. American blue jeans, rock & roll, and fast-food outlets seemed to be everywhere. Potentially much more important, as historian Warren I. Cohen has pointed out, was the heightened international "concern for human rights, the hope for governments that rule by law—governments of the people, for the people, by the people—and the illusions about the miracles that a market economy will bring."[10]

Beyond the borders of the Cold War participants, the costs of that struggle also could be measured in the neglect of serious and worsening problems, from environmental deterioration to ethnic conflicts that wreaked havoc in many regions, including in some of the world's poorest countries. The end of the Cold War created the opportunity to devote more time and resources to those problems, but by itself did not assure that the necessary commitment would be mustered to combat them.

NOTES

CHAPTER ONE

1. Quoted in David Reynolds, "Introduction," in David Reynolds, ed., *The Origins of the Cold War in Europe: International Perspectives* (New Haven and London: Yale University Press, 1994), pp. 1, 234.
2. Arthur Schlesinger, Jr., "Some Lessons from the Cold War," in Michael J. Hogan, ed., *The End of the Cold War: Its Meaning and Implications* (New York: Cambridge University Press, 1992), p. 61.
3. See Walter LaFeber, *America, Russia, and the Cold War, 1945–1992*, 7th ed. (New York: McGraw Hill, 1993), p. 355.
4. Quoted in John Muller, "Quiet Cataclysm: Some Afterthoughts on World War III," in Hogan, ed., *The End of the Cold War*, p. 43.
5. See John Lewis Gaddis, *The Long Peace: Inquiries Into the History of the Cold War* (New York: Oxford University Press, 1987).
6. For example, Kenneth Thompson, in *Cold War Theories* vol. 1, *World Polarization, 1943–1953* (Baton Rouge: Louisiana State University Press, 1981), uses the categories orthodox, "hard" and "cold" revisionist, and "interpreter-critic," the last of which includes people like Walter Lippmann and George Kennan. Jerald A. Combs, in *American Diplomatic History: Two Centuries of Changing Interpretations* (Berkeley: University of California Press, 1983), refers to "hard" and "soft" or "restrained" realists, as well as "moderate" and "radical" revisionists. Michael H. Hunt ("The Long Crisis in Diplomatic History: Coming to Closure," in Michael J. Hogan, ed., *America and the World: The Historiography of American Foreign Relations Since 1941* [New York: Cambridge University Press, 1995], pp. 93–126) divides the contending points of view into "realists," "progressives," and "internationalists," the last category being a rather broad and diffuse tent that encompasses a variety of Marxist and non-Marxist commentators.
7. Arthur Schlesinger, Jr., *The Crisis of Confidence: Ideas, Power, and Violence in America Today* (New York: Houghton Mifflin, 1969), p. 144.
8. Cold War revisionism criticized American foreign policy from a liberal or radical perspective. However, the earliest revisionist tendency dealing with the origins of the Cold War criticized American postwar foreign policy from a conservative perspective. Writers such as William Henry Chamberlin (*Beyond Containment*, 1953)

and Anthony Kubek (*How the Far East Was Lost*, 1963) accused both Roosevelt and Truman of failing to take strong enough measures against the Soviet Union and Communism. This point of view did not gain wide acceptance, at least in the academic circles that produced most of the books on the Cold War. As a result, when one speaks of Cold War "revisionism" one is speaking of critics of American foreign policy from the political left.

9. William Appleman Williams, *The Tragedy of American Diplomacy*, 2d revised and enlarged ed. (New York: Dell, 1973), p. 291.

10. See Geir Lundestad, "Empire by Invitation? The United States and Western Europe, 1945–1952," *Journal of Peace Research* 23 (September 1986): 263–77.

11. See Vojtech Mastny, *Russia's Road to the Cold War: Diplomacy, Warfare, and the Politics of Communism, 1941–1945* (New York: Columbia University Press, 1979); Robert C. Tucker, *Stalin in Power: The Revolution From Above, 1928–1941* (New York: Norton, 1990); Alan Bullock, *Hitler and Stalin: Parallel Lives* (New York: Random House, 1992); Dmitri Volkogonov, *Stalin: Triumph and Tragedy* (New York: Grove Weidenfeld, 1994).

12. John Lewis Gaddis, "The Tragedy of Cold War History: Reflections on Revisionism," *Foreign Affairs* 73:1 (Jan./Feb. 1994): 149–50.

13. Quoted in Steven Merritt Miner, "Revelations, Secrets, Gossip, and Lies: Sifting Warily Through the Soviet Archives," *The New York Times Book Review*, May 14, 1995, p. 21.

14. Peter Stavrakis, *Moscow and Greek Communism, 1944–1949* (Ithaca: Cornell University Press, 1989), pp. 5, 214.

15. Vladislav Zubok and Constantine Pleshakov, "The Soviet Union," in Reynolds, ed., *The Origins of the Cold War in Europe*, p. 60.

16. For example, the revisionist tendency in Cold War historiography has produced a number of subschools, including "world systems" theory, "corporatism," and, most recently, "cultural studies." All are rooted in Marxist theory, although cultural studies also draws from a variety of disciplines and recent intellectual currents that have become fashionable in certain academic circles. All also have been the focus of debate.

World systems theory, whose practitioners include Bruce Cumings and Thomas J. McCormick, views the world as made up of a core of powerful capitalist states that attempt to dominate less developed regions on the periphery. (See Thomas J. McCormick, "World Systems," in Michael J. Hogan and Thomas G. Paterson, eds., *Explaining the History of American Foreign Relations* [New York: Cambridge University Press, 1991], pp. 89–98.) Among the critics of this theory are Melvyn P. Leffler and John Lewis Gaddis, both of whom consider it far too narrow to explain a complex world.

Corporatism examines foreign policy with reference to organized economic power blocs and their relationship with the state. Historians identified with this point of view include McCormick and Michael J. Hogan. (See Michael J. Hogan, "Corporatism," *Explaining the History of American Foreign Relations*, pp. 226–36.)

Gaddis is among those who have criticized corporatism for overemphasizing the domestic roots of U.S. foreign policy and neglecting the external geopolitical pressures and security interests that also shaped that policy, a flaw he attributes to New Left historiography in general.

Cultural studies, which has little to do with traditional cultural history, is probably the most controversial of this trio, mainly because of its reliance on the postmodernist theories about discourse and meaning associated with European thinkers like Michel Foucault and Jacques Derrida. (See Anders Stephanson, "Commentary: Considerations on Culture and Theory," *Diplomatic History* 18 (Winter 1994): 107–19.) These theories are so controversial because they deny the possibility of objective truth and thereby challenge established rules of evidence that have long formed the basis of historical scholarship. They have met therefore with sharp criticism both within the historical profession and in other disciplines. Melvyn P. Leffler has strongly criticized cultural studies for focusing on "culture, language, and rhetoric" at the expense of "questions of causation and agency," which he maintains are vital to understanding the foreign policies of nations. (Melvyn P. Leffler, "Presidential Address: New Approaches, Old Interpretations, and Prospective Reconfigurations," *Diplomatic History* 19 [Spring 1995]: 180.) Bruce Kuklick has criticized cultural studies on related grounds, objecting that its emphasis on theory is "no substitute for empirical research." (Bruce Kuklick, "Commentary: Confessions of an Intransigent Revisionist About Cultural Studies, *Diplomatic History* 18 [Winter 1994]: 122.) For an overview of cultural studies see Akira Iriye, "Culture and International History," *Explaining the History of American Foreign Relations*, pp. 214–25.

CHAPTER TWO

1. William J. Leahy, *I Was There* (New York: Whittlesley House, 1950), pp. 315–16.
2. Quoted in Louis J. Halle, *The Cold War as History* (New York: Harper & Row, 1967), p. 10.
3. Quoted in Stephen E. Ambrose, *Rise to Globalism: American Foreign Policy Since 1938*, 7th revised ed. (New York: Penguin, 1993), p. 59.
4. Quoted in John Lewis Gaddis, *The United States and the Origin of the Cold War, 1941–1947* (New York: Columbia University Press, 1973), p. 289.
5. *Congressional Record*, 78th Congress, Second Session, 1946, pp. A 1145–47.
6. Walter LaFeber, *America, Russia, and the Cold War, 1945–1992*, 7th ed. (New York: McGraw-Hill, 1993), p. 38.
7. "The Kennan 'Long Telegram,'" in Kenneth M. Jensen, ed., *The Origins of the Cold War: The Novikov, Kennan, and Roberts "Long Telegrams" of 1946* (Washington, D.C.: 1991), pp. 27–28.
8. Joyce Kolko and Gabriel Kolko, *The Limits of Power: The World and United States Foreign Policy, 1945–1954* (New York: Harper & Row, 1972), p. 357.

9. "Sources of Soviet Conduct," *Foreign Affairs* (July 1947): 575, 582.

10. Walter Miscamble, "The Foreign Policy of the Truman Administration: A Post–Cold War Appraisal," *Presidential Studies Quarterly* XXIV:3 (Summer 1994): 483.

11. Quoted in Alvin Z. Rubinstein, *Soviet Foreign Policy Since World War II: Imperial and Global*, 2d ed. (Boston: Little, Brown, 1985), p. 64.

12. See Bruce Cumings, *The Origins of the Korean War*, vol. 1, *Liberation and the Emergence of Separate Regimes, 1945–1947* (Princeton: Princeton University Press, 1981) and vol. 2, *The Roaring of the Cataract, 1947–1950* (Princeton: Princeton University Press, 1990).

13. Sergei N. Goncharov, John W. Lewis, and Xue Litai, *Uncertain Partners: Stalin, Mao, and the Korean War* (Stanford: Stanford University Press, 1993), p. 213.

CHAPTER THREE

1. News Conference, April 7, 1954, *Public Papers of the Presidents, Dwight D. Eisenhower, 1954* (Washington, D.C.: U.S. Government Printing Office, 1960), pp. 282–83.

2. Quoted in Stephen E. Ambrose, *Eisenhower*, vol. 2, *The President* (New York: Simon & Schuster, 1984), p. 626. See also Fred I. Greenstein, *The Hidden-Hand Presidency: Eisenhower as Leader* (New York: Basic Books, 1982) and Robert A. Divine, *Eisenhower and the Cold War* (New York: Oxford University Press, 1981).

3. See also Townsend Hoopes, *The Devil and John Foster Dulles* (Boston: Little, Brown, 1973); Raymond L. Garthoff, *Assessing the Adversary: Estimates by the Eisenhower Administration of Soviet Intentions and Capabilities* (Washington, D.C.: Brookings Institution, 1991); and McGeorge Bundy, *Danger and Survival: Choices About the Bomb in the First Fifty Years* (New York: Random House, 1988).

4. See Michael A. Guhin, *John Foster Dulles: A Statesman and His Times* (New York: Columbia University Press, 1972); Ronald W. Preussen, *John Foster Dulles: The Road to Power* (New York: Free Press, 1982); Richard H. Immerman, ed., *John Foster Dulles and the Diplomacy of Cold War* (Princeton: Princeton University Press, 1990). See also the chapter on "The Unexpected John Foster Dulles" in John Lewis Gaddis, *The United States and the End of the Cold War: Implications, Reconsiderations, Provocations* (New York: Oxford University Press, 1992).

5. Arthur M. Schlesinger, *A Thousand Days: John F. Kennedy in the White House* (Boston: Houghton Mifflin, 1965), p. 391.

CHAPTER FOUR

1. See Anders Stephanson, "The Big Two," in David Reynolds, ed., *The Origins of the Cold War in Europe*, pp. 24–25, and Vladislav Zubok and Constantine Pleshakov, *Inside the Kremlin's Cold War: From Stalin to Khrushchev* (Cambridge: Harvard University Press, 1996), p. 7.

2. See George Herring, *America's Longest War: The United States and Vietnam,*

PART II

The Cold War A to Z

Acheson, Dean Gooderham (1893–1971), U.S. secretary of state (1949–53) and one of the primary architects of the policy of containment.

The son of a clergyman who rose to become Episcopal bishop of Connecticut, Acheson was a graduate of Yale University and Harvard Law School. After serving in the navy during World War I, he was the private secretary to Supreme Court Associate Justice Louis Brandeis and a successful lawyer in private practice. He briefly served as undersecretary of the treasury in 1933 before a disagreement with President Franklin Roosevelt resulted in his resignation. Between 1941 and 1945 he served as assistant secretary of state and in 1945 as undersecretary of state, the second highest post in the State Department. In that capacity he was a strong advocate and formulator of policies that later came to be called the Truman Doctrine and the Marshall Plan. Convinced that the Soviet Union would soon develop atomic weapons, Acheson also advocated an attempt to establish international control of those weapons through the United Nations. President Truman asked Acheson and David E. Lilienthal, the head of the Tennessee Valley Authority, to draw up a such a plan. It was presented to the United Nations Atomic Energy Commission, with significant revisions reflecting a harder line toward the Soviet Union, by Bernard Baruch (the Baruch Plan) and promptly rejected by the Soviets.

Acheson was appointed secretary of state, succeeding George Marshall, in January 1949. Under his direction the policy of containment of Communist expansion through foreign economic and military aid was developed. He played a central role in establishing the North Atlantic Treaty Organization and a security pact with Australia and New Zealand. Although he was considered a hard-liner in dealing with the Soviet Union in Europe, his attempts to disassociate the United States from the Nationalist Chinese regime on Taiwan, which had just lost the civil war for control of mainland China, subjected him to relentless and often vicious attack from conservatives in both political parties, but especially from Senator Joseph McCarthy. Acheson vainly tried to defend State Department diplomats who were the objects of similar attacks and also stood by Alger Hiss, which further opened him up to personal attacks and criticism regarding his handling of the loyalty and security policy of the State Department. With the outbreak of the Korean War, Acheson supported the extension of containment to Asia and the military defense of South Korea. The intervention of Communist China late in 1950, which resulted in United Nations troops once again being pushed south of the 38th parallel, intensified the conservative attacks on the Truman-Acheson policy of refusing to expand the war to Chinese territory and returning to the original UN goal of restoring the former border between North and South Korea at that parallel. After leaving government service in 1953, Acheson subsequently served as an advisor to President Kennedy during the Cuban Missile Crisis—advocating an immediate air strike against Soviet missile bases, advice that Kennedy rejected—and to President Johnson during the Vietnam War in 1968, at which point Acheson, once a supporter of the war, concluded that it was unwinnable and that the United States should withdraw. Acheson was the author of several books, including the Pulitzer Prize-winning *Present at the Creation* (1969).

Adenauer, Konrad (1876–1967), first chancellor of the Federal Republic of Germany, architect of West Germany's postwar political rehabilitation, economic recovery, and integration into the Western alliance system.

The son of a civil servant, a lawyer, and a member of the conservative Catholic Center party, Adenauer became mayor of Cologne and served in that post until 1933 when his strong anti-Nazi views led to his dismissal from office. He remained in Germany during the Nazi era and was twice arrested, but managed to survive the war. In 1945 he became the co-founder of the conservative Christian Democratic Union political party and was its president from 1946 to 1966. Adenauer led the party to a very narrow victory in the elections of August 1949 and then was elected chancellor at age seventy-three by the new parliament, the Bundestag, by one vote. He was reelected in 1953, 1957, and 1961, and also served as his country's foreign minister from 1951 to 1955.

A strong anti-Communist who viewed the Soviet Union as the major threat to Germany, *der Alte* (the old man), as he was known, saw the solution to the Federal Republic's problems in European integration and its alliance with the West. He firmly opposed any plans for reunification that might compromise those commitments. While serving as his government's foreign minister, Adenauer negotiated the German peace treaty with the Western allies (1952) and obtained recognition of West Germany's full independence and led Germany into NATO in 1955, the same year he negotiated an agreement that established diplomatic relations with the Soviet Union. West Germany's membership in NATO was an important step in strengthening that alliance. The year 1955 also saw the final success of Adenauer's diplomatic efforts to keep the economically important Saar region a part of Germany (France had hoped to annex it) when the local population voted in a referendum to reunite with the Federal Republic. As part of his effort to rehabilitate Germany's reputation in the wake of World War II and the Holocaust, Adenauer promoted reconciliation between Germany and France and agreed that West Germany would pay reparations to the state of Israel, where the majority of Holocaust survivors found refuge after 1945.

In 1957 Adenauer led Germany into the European Economic Community (EEC). He also initiated the process, along with France's Charles de Gaulle, that ultimately produced the Franco-German Friendship Treaty of 1963, Adenauer's last year in office. After a series of political troubles that began in 1961, Adenauer resigned from office in 1963 and was succeeded by his economics minister Ludwig Erhard. He is recognized as the indispensable patriarch in West Germany's postwar rehabilitation and economic recovery.

Attlee, Clement (1883–1967), British prime minister (1945–51) during the formative period of the Cold War.

Of prosperous middle-class origins, Attlee studied at Oxford and practiced briefly as a lawyer. Then, struck by the poverty he saw in London, he became committed to social reform and socialist ideas, joining the Independent Labour Party in 1908. After being elected to parliament, he served in Britain's first two Labour governments (1924 and 1929–31). As leader of the Labor Party after 1935, having defeated a pacifist politician for the post, Attlee strongly criticized the Conservative government's failure to intervene in the Spanish Civil War. When World War II broke out, he refused to bring Labour into a national government led by Neville Chamberlain. When Winston Churchill became prime minister in 1940, Attlee joined the government as deputy prime minister. He became prime minister during the Potsdam Conference in July 1945 when Labour scored a decisive victory in Britain's first postwar national elections.

Under Attlee's leadership, the Labour government implemented an extensive program of nationalization and social reform, laying the basis for the British welfare state. It nationalized the Bank of England, the gas, electricity, coal, and iron and steel industries, and the railways. Among Attlee's social reforms were the establishment of the National Health Service and educational reforms.

In foreign affairs, it fell to the Attlee government to set Britain's course during the critical early days of the Cold War. Convinced of the dangers of Soviet expansionism, Attlee made British-American cooperation the basis of his foreign policy and allied Britain closely with the United States in its growing confrontation with the Soviet Union. He and his foreign minister Ernest Bevin consistently urged the United States to fortify its commitment to Europe. They welcomed the Truman Doctrine and Marshall Plan and the subsequent formation of NATO. Attlee also supported the Korean War and sent British troops to join the United Nations forces defending South Korea. However, in December 1950, worried that the United States might resort to nuclear weapons in that conflict and that Korea was distracting the United States from its fundamental commitments in Europe, Attlee went to Washington to try to convince Truman to seek a negotiated settlement.

While consistently supporting the United States, Attlee also pursued Britain's independent development of the atomic bomb, convinced that only with atomic weapons could his country remain a first-rate power. At the same time, recognized that Britain's limited resources required reduced foreign commitments. His government therefore ended Britain's role in Greece (the event that precipitated the Truman Doctrine), Palestine, and Egypt and began the dissolution of the British Empire, granting independence to India, Pakistan, Sri Lanka, and Burma.

Berlin, capital of Germany before 1945 and again since 1991, and one of the most important focal points and symbols of the Cold War, when it was divided into **East Berlin** and **West Berlin**. Site of the **Berlin Blockade,** the **Berlin Airlift,** and the **Berlin Wall**.

After being divided into four occupation zones (American, British, French, and Russian) during the Potsdam Conference, attempts to administer Berlin as a single city under the Allied Control Council soon broke down and Berlin became one of the major sources of Cold War tension into the 1960s. Located 110 miles inside the Soviet occupation zone in Germany, West Berlin from the start of the Cold War was a Western outpost deep within the Communist bloc, a hotbed of intelligence operations by both sides, and the best available escape route for East Germans fleeing Communism and Soviet control. Soviet determination to push the Western powers out of Berlin, and thereby discredit the value of American assurances to its allies and the rest of Europe, and the matching Western determination to remain in the city, led to the Soviets imposing the Berlin Blockade on West Berlin in June 1948. The Western powers, foremost among them the United States, undertook to supply West Berlin through air corridors left open to them via the Berlin Airlift. The airlift was successful and the Soviets ended their blockade in May 1949, by which time the United States had reinforced its commitment to Europe's defense through the establishment of NATO. That same year East Berlin was proclaimed the capital of the Democratic Republic of Germany (East Germany), the Soviet-dominated satellite state, and West Berlin designated one of the states of the Federal Republic of Germany (West Germany). In June 1953 workers rioting in East Berlin over poor living conditions were suppressed by Soviet tanks. Subsequent years saw several new Berlin crises. Meanwhile, better living conditions in West Berlin and the West in general led to the massive flight of East Germans to the West via Berlin, where no physical division prevented people from crossing from the eastern part of the city to the western part. This was a great embarrassment to the Communists in both East Germany and the Soviet Union and a serious drain on the East German labor supply, as many of those fleeing westward were young and educated.

To stop the flow, in August 1961 the Communists threw up barriers to isolate West Berlin, marking the beginning of the Berlin Wall. The Wall immediately became the symbol of the Cold War and the division of Europe. In the following decades East German border guards killed dozens of persons attempting to break through or go over the barrier. However, tensions in the city itself eased. December 1963 saw the first of several agreements that permitted West Berliners to visit relatives in the eastern zone. Visits across the Wall and access to West Berlin from West Germany were finally regularized in the Berlin agreement reached among the four powers and the two German states in 1972.

On November 9, 1989, in a desperate attempt to save the tottering East German regime, Egon Krenz, the successor to long-time hard-line party boss Erich Honecker, opened the Berlin Wall. That act led to massive celebrations around and on the Wall, which soon was dismantled along with the East German regime. Shortly after Germany's reunification in 1990, the parliament in June 1991 voted to make Berlin the capital of the country.

Brandt, Willy (1913–92), chancellor of West Germany (1969–74), mayor of West Berlin (1957–66), and the architect as chancellor of the policy of *Ostpolitik* ("Eastern Policy") to normalize West Germany's relations with East Germany and improve them with the Soviet Union and the rest of the Soviet bloc.

Willy Brandt was born Herbert Ernst Karl Frahm, the illegitimate son of a working-class woman in the Baltic port of Lübeck. He first used the name "Willy Brandt" as a pseudonym for his journalistic articles, adopting it as his own after he fled Germany to avoid arrest by the Nazi regime in 1933. A member of the Social Democratic party from his youth, Brandt's staunch opposition to the Nazis forced him to remain in exile until after World War

II. After returning to Germany and resuming his Social Democratic activities, he was elected to parliament and then, in 1957, mayor of West Berlin.

Brandt's election as West Berlin's mayor made him a visible figure in the Cold War. It fell to him to rally the spirits of West Berlin's people to help them weather the 1958 Berlin crisis, when the Soviet Union, having issued an ultimatum that West Berlin's final status had to be settled in six months, pressed to turn Berlin into a demilitarized "free city," which inevitably would have led to its absorption into the Soviet bloc, and especially the erection of the Berlin Wall in August 1961. Brandt's measured but strong public stands against Soviet pressure won him respect abroad and throughout West Germany and made him a potential candidate for the post of chancellor of his country.

Brandt became chancellor after his party's victory in the 1969 national elections. His most important initiative was the policy of *Ostpolitik*. Though he remained committed to Germany's eventual unification, Brandt believed that West Germany could not ignore the reality of a divided Europe. West Germany had to do what it could to reduce Cold War tensions—Brandt called the Cold War a "sterile and dangerous confrontation"—to avoid the outbreak of a war that would leave it devastated. Despite great difficulties, his efforts during the era of détente bore their first fruit in a nonaggression pact with the Soviet Union signed in 1970, in which West Germany accepted both its border with East Germany and Germany's eastern border with Poland, the so-called Oder-Neisse Line. A treaty with Poland followed at the end of the year. In 1971 Brandt was awarded the Nobel Peace Prize. In 1972, the two German states became party to the four-power treaty that provided both security for West Berlin and liberalized travel restrictions between the two parts of the city [see **Berlin**] and then established normal diplomatic relations between themselves.

Brandt also dedicated himself to cleansing the German image of its Nazi past. At a visit to a memorial to Warsaw Ghetto victims who died in the Holocaust, Brandt spontaneously fell to his knees. He visited Israel in 1973.

In 1974, a disastrous spy scandal—one of Brandt's top advisors turned out to be an East German agent—forced Brandt to resign from office. He later chaired an international research group called the Brandt Commission, which in 1980 issued a report calling for the world's industrialized nations to make massive increases in the aid to the poor nations of the Third World.

Brezhnev, Leonid Ilyich (1906–82), leader of the Soviet Union (1964–82), architect of policies to achieve recognition from the United States as an equal superpower, including the massive Soviet nuclear and conventional arms buildup that achieved military parity with the United States, the projection of Soviet power worldwide, the policy of détente, and, ultimately, aggressive measures that caused the collapse of détente in the late 1970s and early 1980s.

Leonid Brezhnev rose from his working-class origins through the ranks of the Communist Party, first as a Stalinist functionary and then as a supporter and protégé of Nikita Khrushchev. He played a central role in the coup of 1964 that overthrew his erratic benefactor and then emerged as the first among equals among his successors. Among the Brezhnev regime's first steps was the reversal of many of Khrushchev's reforms, including his largely unsuccessful economic reforms and his liberalization of cultural policies. Brezhnev's staunch conservatism in domestic affairs and, in particular, his failure to undertake economic reforms ultimately contributed to the decline of the Soviet economy, a growing technological lag vis-à-vis the United States and its allies, extensive corruption, and social problems that created a crisis situation by the early 1980s. It was this legacy that caused Mikhail Gorbachev to refer to the Brezhnev years as the "era of stagnation."

Brezhnev's major concern, like that of his contemporary Richard Nixon, was foreign affairs. He sought to establish a new and more stable relationship between the Soviet Union and the United States. In 1968, when Soviet-bloc troops invaded Czechoslovakia and crushed the reform movement led by Alexander Dubček, the Soviets proclaimed the Brezhnev Doctrine, which asserted that no Communist country could be permitted to revert to capitalism and that the Soviet Union could intervene in the internal affairs of another Soviet bloc nation if Communist rule were threatened.

Meanwhile, Brezhnev pursued the military buildup that by the late 1960s achieved nuclear parity with the United States and gave the Soviet Union unprecedented conventional strength as well, including the country's first deep-water navy. At the same time he pursued détente with the United States and its Western European allies. Détente was responsible for the 1972 SALT treaty that, however flawed, was the first Soviet-American arms control agreement. SALT was followed by the Helsinki Accords in 1975, under which the Soviet Union finally achieved recognition of the post–World War II border changes it imposed in Eastern Europe. Considered a major Soviet achievement at the time, the Helsinki Accords, under which the Soviet Union recognized its obligation to observe human rights, ultimately helped undermine the totalitarianism throughout the Soviet bloc. SALT I was followed by SALT II, signed in 1979, but by then aggressive Soviet activities in the Third World, and especially the invasion of

Afghanistan, had mortally wounded détente. Soviet relations with the United States and Western Europe chilled further with the suppression of the Solidarity union in Poland in 1981. At his death, Brezhnev left behind a Soviet Union with a crisis situation at home and relations with the West chilled to what was being called a "New Cold War."

Bush, George Herbert Walker (1924–), forty-first president of the United States (1989–93) and American leader during the last years of the Cold War.

Bush was the scion of a wealthy and well-connected political family (his father, Prescott Bush, served as a Republican senator from Connecticut). He was a decorated fighter pilot in World War II and a Yale graduate. Bush then won two terms in the House of Representatives before gaining experience in foreign affairs as U.S. ambassador to the United Nations (1971–73), chief of the U.S. liaison office in China (1974–75), and director of the Central Intelligence Agency (1976–77). He served two terms as vice president in the Reagan administration before being elected president in 1989.

Bush became president just as Communism in Eastern Europe was beginning to collapse, an event that unfolded with stunning rapidity during 1989 and culminated in November and December. Just one year later, in late November 1990, at the signing of the Charter of Paris, Bush proclaimed, "The Cold War is over." At the summit of the Conference on Security and Cooperation (CSCE) that same month, NATO and the Warsaw Pact signed the Conventional Forces in Europe (CFE) treaty that provided for drastic cuts in forces stationed in Central Europe. In July 1991 Bush also signed the last arms control agreement between the United States and the Soviet Union, the Strategic Arms Reduction Treaty (START I). The next month saw the unsuccessful coup against Mikhail Gorbachev, which was followed by the dissolution of the Soviet Union the following December.

Outside Europe, the Bush administration engaged in armed intervention in Panama in 1989 to overthrow dictator Manuel Noriega, whose involvement in drug trafficking infuriated Washington. Bush also was at the helm when a longstanding goal inherited from the Reagan administration, the removal of the Marxist Sandinista regime in Nicaragua, was accomplished when the Sandinistas were defeated in a national election, which took place largely due to American economic, political, and military pressure. But it was the invasion of Kuwait by Iraq in August 1990 that provided Bush with his most striking foreign policy achievement. Bush saw Iraq's expulsion by a U.S.-led coalition as a test of American resolve to uphold and enforce what he termed the "new world order." Although the coalition was spectacularly successful in the stated task of expelling Iraq from Kuwait in early 1991, Bush opted not to destroy the Iraqi army. This allowed dictator Saddam Hussein to hold on to power, which over time diminished the luster of the Bush administration's achievement in the crisis.

Byrnes, James Francis (1879–1972), U.S. secretary of state (1945–47) during the opening days of the Cold War.

A former journalist, representative and senator from South Carolina, Supreme Court justice, and advisor to Franklin Roosevelt who accompanied him to Yalta, Byrnes was appointed secretary of state by Harry Truman in July 1945. Relations between the two men always were cool because Byrnes had expected in 1944 to be Roosevelt's running mate and felt that he, rather than Truman, should be president. Known from his years in Congress for his skills as a conciliator and negotiator, Byrnes at first tried to mend postwar differences with the Soviet Union. However, his efforts and skills could not prevent the failure of the London Conference of foreign ministers in September 1945. It was at that conference that Soviet foreign minister Viacheslav Molotov half jokingly asked Byrnes if he had "an atomic bomb in his side pocket" and Byrnes replied, again half jokingly, that if Molotov did not stop his stalling in the current negotiations he would pull an atomic bomb out of his hip pocket "and let you have it." In fact, Byrnes continued to seek diplomatic solutions to Soviet-American differences, efforts which by 1946 put him at odds with those, including President Truman, who believed the United States had to toughen its stand vis-à-vis the Soviet Union. Still, in a dramatic speech in Stuttgart, Germany, in September 1946 Byrnes articulated the toughening American attitude when he declared that the United States would not let Germany become a Soviet satellite and would keep its occupation soldiers in the country as long as necessary. Nonetheless, Byrnes's disagreements with Truman and his personal rivalry with the president led him to resign as secretary of state. His replacement was General George C. Marshall.

Carter, Jimmy (1924–), thirty-ninth president of the United States (1977–81), staunch advocate of human rights in foreign policy.

Jimmy Carter (full name: James Earl Carter Jr.) grew up in a small Georgia town. He graduated from the U.S. Naval Academy and served as a naval officer for seven years, including one tour of duty as a submarine officer and another developing the navy's nuclear submarine program. After leaving the navy and successfully running the family's peanut business, he served a term as governor of Georgia.

Immediately upon assuming office in January 1977 Carter stated he intended to make changes in American foreign policy that stressed support of human rights. He established an office in the State Department for human rights and pardoned thousands of men who left the United States during the Vietnam War era to avoid the draft. However, his appointments reflected the tension between his desire to promote human rights and certain traditional demands of foreign policy in a world dominated by power politics. Carter appointed Cyrus Vance, a career diplomat with liberal sympathies, as secretary of state. At the same time, he appointed Zbigniew Brzezinski, a hard-line anti-Communist émigré from Poland, as his national security advisor, and the two men competed for influence until Vance resigned his office in 1980 after the failed attempt to rescue American hostages in Iran, an enterprise he had opposed.

Carter initially enjoyed some success in foreign affairs. In 1977 his administration completed negotiations, begun under Lyndon Johnson, for returning sovereignty of the Panama Canal Zone to Panama (one treaty guaranteed America's right to defend the "neutrality" of the Canal Zone) and succeeded in winning Congressional ratification in 1978, although only after rancorous debate and by a single vote. In 1978 he brought Prime Minister Menachem Begin of Israel and Anwar Sadat of Egypt to the presidential retreat at Camp David in Maryland for difficult negotiations that finally produced the Camp David Accords, which were the basis of the Egyptian-Israeli peace treaty signed in Washington in March 1979. The year 1979 also saw the establishment of formal diplomatic relations with the People's Republic of China.

As part of its human-rights orientation, the Carter administration joined the successful effort to end white minority rule in Rhodesia (renamed Zimbabwe) and also put pressure on South Africa, this time without success, to reform its system of racial apartheid. He also reduced aid to several Central American dictatorships, including the Somoza regime in Nicaragua, which was subsequently overthrown by the Marxist Sandinista movement that soon established a dictatorship of its own and aligned itself with the Soviet Union.

Carter's human rights campaign backfired in his dealings with the Soviet Union. The Brezhnev regime considered Carter's efforts, especially his support of dissident physicist Andrei Sakharov, to be an unacceptable intrusion into the Soviet Union's internal affairs. Not even the signing of the SALT II arms control treaty prevented the serious deterioration of Soviet-American relations during the Carter years. The treaty, never ratified, was severely criticized by conservatives for being advantageous to the Soviets. The rising tensions were reflected in Carter's decision late in 1979 to increase American military spending and NATO's decision to deploy new American Pershing II ballistic missiles and cruise missiles in Europe to counter Soviet deployment of intermediate-range SS-missiles.

What was left of détente was destroyed in December 1979 when Soviet forces invaded Afghanistan. Carter responded with the Carter Doctrine and a number of measures to punish the Soviet Union. By then, however, his administration was being consumed by the Iran hostage crisis, which began when Iranian students invaded the American embassy in Teheran and took its staff hostage. Carter's weak response, and the disastrous failure of a rescue attempt in April 1980, fatally undermined the rest of his presidency.

Castro, Fidel (1926–), Cuban revolutionary and head of the Communist dictatorship that has ruled Cuba since Castro led it to power in 1959.

The illegitimate son of a prosperous sugarcane farmer, Castro was educated as a lawyer before becoming a full-time revolutionary in the early 1950s. His guerrilla organization, the 26th of July Movement, overthrew the corrupt U.S.-supported dictatorship of Fulgencio Batista on January 1, 1959. At the time the Cuban economy was dominated by American interests, including the United Fruit Company, which controlled much of the sugar industry. Little of substance was known of Castro in Washington—the American press had portrayed him as an populist social reformer—or in Moscow, where as Nikita Khrushchev put it, despite information that there were Communists in Castro's organization, "we had no idea what political course his regime would follow." Of course, Castro, who deeply hated the United States, soon followed a Communist course. During 1959 his regime tried and summarily executed many political opponents, began nationalizing property—including American-owned assets—without compensation, signed a trade agreement with the Soviet Union, and brought in KGB officers to set up a Soviet-style secret police. The Castro regime also instituted sweeping reforms in favor of the poor while disenfranchising the native propertied classes, many of whom fled to the United States where they became a vocal anti-Castro lobby. This trend, and the worsening of relations with the United States, continued in 1960. In January 1961, just before leaving office and with plans moving ahead to invade Cuba and overthrow Castro, the Eisenhower administration broke diplomatic relations with Cuba.

The Bay of Pigs invasion took place in April 1961 and was a complete fiasco that humiliated the United States and its new President, John F. Kennedy. In December 1961, Castro declared himself a Marxist-Leninist and moved even closer to the Soviet bloc. Less than a year later, in October 1962, the world came to the brink of nuclear war when the Soviet plan to place nuclear missiles in Cuba led to the Cuban Missile Crisis. The crisis was defused following tense negotiations and Khrushchev's agreeing to remove the missiles.

For Castro, the Cuban Missile Crisis was a humiliating, though temporary, defeat. He became an influential Third World leader and an icon to many Latin American revolutionaries. He continued to aid revolutionary movements in Latin America. Cuba's socialist economy, boycotted by the United States, was supported by massive aid from the Soviet Union. Cuba meanwhile sent soldiers to support Communist movements in several African countries, an effort bankrolled by the Soviets. However, the recession of the Communist tide after 1989 left Castro high and dry. Soviet aid disappeared and the Cuban economy virtually collapsed. Castro was forced by the desperate need for foreign exchange to open Cuba to tourism, while continuing to clamp down on domestic dissent. In the post–Cold War era, Fidel Castro and his Cuban revolution increasingly appeared to be vestiges of a bygone world.

Chiang Kai-shek (Jian Jieshi) (1887–1975), president of the Nationalist regime in China until its defeat by the Communists in 1949 and the president of the Nationalist regime on the island of Taiwan thereafter.

Although he grew up in poverty, Chiang received a military education in China and then in Japan. He participated in the 1911 revolution that overthrew the Manchu dynasty and joined the Nationalist party (Guomindang) led by Sun Yatsen. He became the movement's leading military specialist and its leader after Sun's death in 1925. He continued the alliance Sun had established with the Communist Party until 1927, when he suddenly turned on the Communists and almost succeeded in wiping them out. Among the Communist leaders who escaped Chiang's murderous campaign was Mao Zedong.

After World War II American attempts to avoid renewed warfare between the Nationalists and Communists failed. In the ensuing civil war (1946–49), the corruption that pervaded Chiang's regime and his military errors contributed to the Communist victory. That victory inflamed the anti-Communist hysteria already growing in the United States. Still, at first it appeared that the United States would do nothing to protect Chiang and the Nationalists on Taiwan from a Communist invasion, but the Korean War changed American policy toward Chiang's refugee regime. The United States sent its navy to protect the Nationalists and, alone among the major Western powers, continued until 1972 to recognize them as the legitimate government of China. The Korean War and America's refusal to recognize the PRC intensified the Cold War in Asia and helped to solidify the Soviet-PRC alliance, which nonetheless began to dissolve in the late 1950s and turned to open hostility in the 1960s. In 1972, three years before Chiang's death, the United States withdrew its recognition of the Nationalists as China's legitimate government and did not object when the United Nations expelled Taiwan and turned over its seats in the General Assembly and Security Council to the PRC. Chiang remained president of the rump regime on Taiwan until his death in 1975.

Churchill, Winston (1874–1965), British prime minister (1940–45, 1951–55), one of Britain's greatest leaders and one of the outstanding political leaders of the twentieth century, and a staunch anti-Communist who first popularized the term "Iron Curtain" in 1946.

The scion of a distinguished British family, Churchill was a soldier and noted author as well as a distinguished politician. Although prior to World War II his political record contained notable failures as well as successes, Churchill rose to greatness upon becoming prime minister in 1940 and rallied Britain from the brink of defeat to heroic resistance and eventual triumph.

As World War II drew to an end, Churchill increasingly feared Soviet expansion into Eastern and Central Europe and unsuccessfully urged both Roosevelt and Truman to take steps to limit that expansion. In 1946, a year after his party's defeat in national elections, ex-prime minister Churchill came to Fulton, Missouri on President Truman's invitation and delivered his famous Iron Curtain speech. While out of power from 1945 to 1951, he supported the Labour government's steps to strengthen the Western allies vis-à-vis the Soviets. During his second term as prime minister Churchill expanded Britain's nuclear program. Those years saw Britain's first atom-bomb test and the start of its hydrogen-bomb program. Notwithstanding the grave dangers these weapons posed, Churchill believed that what he called the "balance of terror" created by nuclear arsenals in the West and the East would serve as a mutual deterrence and thereby preserve peace. At the same time, he slowed Britain's conventional rearmament, despite his desire to built up NATO's conventional forces, in order to meet pressing social needs. After Stalin's death in 1953 Churchill urged a summit meeting with the new Soviet leadership, which he believed might significantly improve East-West relations. However, American reluctance, in large part because of the objections of Secretary of State John Foster Dulles, helped delay the conference until July 1955, by which time Churchill, felled by illness, had retired from public life. He left office with the 1953 Nobel Prize for literature in hand for his magnificent six-volume *The Second World War*.

Cuban Missile Crisis, called the "Gettysburg" of the Cold War, pushed the superpowers and the world as close as they ever came to nuclear war.

After the Bay of Pigs invasion, the Soviet Union increased its support of Fidel Castro's Communist regime in Cuba, and in the summer of 1962 Nikita Khrushchev secretly decided to install medium- and intermediate-range ballistic missiles in Cuba capable of delivering nuclear warheads over much of the eastern United States. The Soviets still had not finished building their missile launching sites when they were discovered by high-flying American U-2 spy planes. After consulting with a specially assembled group of advisors called the "EX Comm," President Kennedy rejected the idea of an immediate air strike against the missile sites and chose instead to follow Secretary of Defense McNamara's suggestion for a naval blockade of Cuba, a step the president publicly called a "quarantine" inasmuch as a blockade in fact would violate international law.

The Cuban Missile Crisis brought the world to the brink of war for almost two weeks. As Khrushchev put it, "the smell of burning hung in the air." Aside from the dangers both sides were aware of, during the crisis miscalculations occurred that could have easily led to war regardless of what Kennedy and Khrushchev were planning. For example, thousands of miles away from Cuba in northeast Asia, a U-2 spy plane strayed over Soviet territory, while in waters near Cuba U.S. warships forced Soviet submarines to surface before presidential orders to that effect were issued. Even worse, unbeknownst to the Americans, Soviet troops in Cuba possessed tactical nuclear weapons that could have been used had the United States invaded the island. Had that happened, in all likelihood the United States would have retaliated with nuclear weapons. "Where would that have ended?" McNamara asked rhetorically many years later. The former secretary of defense answered his own question in three words: "In utter disaster."

The resolution of the Cuban Missile Crisis was widely seen as a serious defeat for Khrushchev, both by Western observers and by Khrushchev's own critics in Moscow, who blamed him for the Soviet Union's military weakness that had forced a humiliating retreat, and it became a major factor in his political demise two years later. However, the Soviet Union did win a public American pledge not to invade Cuba, which in effect allowed Cuba to remain a Soviet base in the Western Hemisphere and rendered the Monroe Doctrine obsolete. Perhaps most important, the crisis induced both sides to seek measures for defusing crises before they reached such menacing proportions — beginning with the telephone hotline between the Kremlin and the White House. It also led to the partial nuclear test ban treaty of 1963, the first, albeit extremely modest, U.S.-Soviet nuclear weapons agreement.

de Gaulle, Charles (1890–1970), French soldier and statesman, founder and first president of his country's Fifth Republic (1959–69), and France's most important leader for three decades beginning in 1940.

De Gaulle, who said, "I feel not a person but an instrument of Destiny," earned his position in history by daring to run against the wind. After compiling a distinguished record as a soldier in World War I, he foresaw and futilely urged his country to prepare for the mechanized warfare by which Germany overwhelmed France in 1940. When the French government agreed to an armistice with the victorious Nazis in June 1940, de Gaulle opposed the surrender and fled to London, where he organized the Free French forces and ultimately emerged as its undisputed leader. However, his wartime experiences with Franklin Roosevelt and Winston Churchill were laced with disagreements, which left him permanently suspicious of both the United States and Britain after the war. He was elected president of the provisional government of France in November 1945, but resigned in January 1946 when it became clear that France's new constitution would not provide for a strong executive leader.

De Gaulle returned to power in 1958 amid political turmoil caused by the military and civilian revolt in Algeria, widely accepted as the only French political figure capable of dealing with the situation. He opposed American domination of NATO, arguing that France should hold an equal position in the organization. As part of his campaign to restore France's stature as a world power, he accelerated its nuclear-weapons program. The first French nuclear test took place in 1960. As part of his policy of increasing French influence in Europe at the expense of both the United States and Britain, he vetoed Britain's membership in the European Common Market in 1963 and fostered ties with both West Germany and the Soviet Union. He also established diplomatic relations with the People's Republic of China. In 1966, he withdrew French forces from NATO and ordered the withdrawal of NATO military installations from France by April 1967.

In effect, de Gaulle played a major role in the evolution of the bipolar early Cold War international scene into a multipolar world. He resigned from office after a series of political defeats in 1970.

Defense, United States Department of, the executive department of the federal government charged with coordinating and supervising all agencies and functions of the government relating directly to national security and

military affairs. Based at the Pentagon, it is divided into three major subsections—the U.S. Army, the U.S. Navy, and the U.S. Air Force. It was created by the National Security Act of 1947 by combining the Departments of
War and Navy and was called the National Military Establishment; it became the Department of Defense when the act was amended in 1949.
James Forrestal pioneered in this reorganization, which ended cabinet status for the secretaries of the Army, Navy, and Air Force, subordinated them
to the secretary of defense, and gave him full cabinet authority over the department. In effect, the Department of Defense became one of the first and
very quickly one of the largest offspring of the Cold War.

Under the act as amended in 1949, the secretary of defense—appointed
by the president with the consent of the Senate —supervises the entire military. Under the secretary is the Joint Chiefs of Staff made up of its chairman, a senior military officer, the heads of the three main services, and the
commandant of the Marine Corps.

The new defense establishment received its first test during the Korean
War. It was generally agreed that the department revealed a capability to
react quickly to crisis, but there was criticism that before the outbreak of the
war too much reliance had been placed on strategic air forces and nuclear
weapons to the neglect of conventional military forces. The Eisenhower administration, concerned about controlling military expenditures, empha-
sized deterring Soviet aggression with massive retaliation with nuclear
weapons, despite critics who advocated additional expenditures on conventional forces. Under Robert McNamara (1961–68), the department
aimed for a more balanced military program and established a new layer of
civilian officials who imported civilian management techniques. In general, the administrations of John F. Kennedy and Lyndon Johnson aimed for
a stronger conventional capability but failed with their counterinsurgency
strategy in the Vietnam War.

During the Cold War, the Department of Defense became a major economic force, mostly through its massive purchases and research invest-
ments in high-technology industries. It played a leading role, for example,
in the growth of the United States aircraft industry. The Pentagon became
the core of the so-called military-industrial complex, a vast interlocking network of the U.S. military, businesses supplying military needs, and universities with departments doing military research. However, the end of the
Cold War and the breakup of the Soviet Union, and the resultant reductions in defense spending, have negatively affected civilian industries that
supply the Department of Defense.

Diem, Ngo Dinh (1901–63), prime minister (1954–55) and president (1955–63) of South Vietnam.

Diem came from an influential Catholic Vietnamese family and established a reputation as a nationalist during World War II. His fervent anti-Communism made him a staunch opponent of Ho Chi Minh's Vietminh, which briefly imprisoned him. After the Geneva Conference and the division of Vietnam, Diem was appointed South Vietnam's prime minister by Emperor Bao Dai in 1954. The next year Diem staged a referendum that ended the monarchy and became South Vietnam's president. Diem's anti-Communism earned him strong American backing, but his regime was based mainly on South Vietnam's Catholic minority and repressed the Buddhist majority. Diem's authoritarianism and the corruption of those around him further alienated his regime from the great majority of his people. His policies provided fertile ground for Communist guerrillas, who were supported and controlled by North Vietnam. His overthrow (but not his murder) in 1963 by a group of military officers took place with the consent of the Kennedy administration.

Doctrines, American and Soviet, major Cold War American and Soviet policies.

The first American policy to be designated a "doctrine" was the Truman Doctrine (1947), which pledged American help to countries threatened by Communist aggression or subversion. It was followed by the Eisenhower Doctrine (1957), which specifically extended the Truman Doctrine to the Middle East. The Johnson Doctrine (1965) proclaimed that the United States would not allow a new Communist government to come to power in the Western Hemisphere. The Nixon Doctrine (1969), announced as the United States was trying to extract itself from Vietnam, said that the United States would supply nations needing help to defend themselves with economic and military assistance but not with American troops. The Carter Doctrine (1980) stated that the United States would use military force if necessary to prevent outside forces, by which Carter meant the Soviet Union, from seizing control of the Persian Gulf and its oil resources. The final American Cold War doctrine was the Reagan Doctrine (1985), which declared that the United States would support anti-Communist "freedom fighters" attempting to overthrow Communist regimes in the Third World.

The only Soviet policy to achieve the status of a "doctrine" was the Brezhnev Doctrine (1968), which proclaimed the Soviet Union's right to intervene to prevent any Soviet bloc country from reverting to capitalism. Two of the most important policy statements of the Cold War, however, did not attain the status of a "doctrine." The first, announced in 1956, was Nikita Khrushchev's principle of "peaceful coexistence," which rejected nuclear war as an instrument of Communist–capitalist competition. Instead, Khrushchev maintained, the competition between the two systems would be peaceful and would result, he insisted, in the victory of Communism because it would provide a better life for its people. The second was Mikhail Gorbachev's concept of "new thinking," which he announced in 1986. New thinking was nothing less than a revolutionary reappraisal of Soviet foreign policy. It rejected completely the idea of competition between capitalism and Communism in favor of normal relations between states and cooperation in solving world problems. Gorbachev's new thinking was the pivotal step in bringing about the end of the Cold War.

Actually, one aspect of new thinking did reach the status of an unofficial doctrine. In 1989, when Gorbachev made it clear that the Soviet Union would not intervene to save the Communist regimes of Eastern Europe, a Soviet commentator dubbed that policy, under which the Eastern Europeans would be allowed to do things "their way," the "Sinatra Doctrine." The reference was to a song, "My Way," made popular by the famous American singer Frank Sinatra. (Perhaps it should have been called the "Anka Doctrine," inasmuch as singer/writer Paul Anka wrote the song.)

Dulles, John Foster (1888–1959), U.S. secretary of state (1953–59).

Dulles was born in Washington, D.C., the grandson of one secretary of state (John Watson Foster, who served under Benjamin Harrison) and the nephew of another (Robert Lansing, who served under Woodrow Wilson). Dulles studied at Princeton University and the Sorbonne in Paris before earning his law degree at George Washington University. Having served as counsel to the United States delegation at the Paris Peace Conference of 1919, Dulles gained prominence as an international lawyer. Dulles supported the League of Nations, was advisor to the U.S. delegation to the founding conference of the United Nations in San Francisco in 1945, and served as a U.S. delegate to the UN General Assembly from 1945 to 1949. He fulfilled several other international assignments prior to becoming Eisenhower's secretary of state including, as ambassador at large, negotiating the United States peace and security treaty with Japan in 1951, which allowed the United States to maintain military bases in Japan and effectively excluded the Soviet Union from any role in Japanese affairs.

Dulles considered Communism to be a moral evil and believed the Soviet Union was determined to overthrow Western democracy. He was a critic of containment, arguing that as practiced by the Democrats it was a "treadmill" policy that would exhaust the United States before it produced results. Dulles therefore advocated taking advantage of U.S. technical superiority and using nuclear weapons, which were far cheaper than large conventional forces, to deter the Soviets and keep them in check, which became the core of Eisenhower's "New Look" foreign policy. Regarding Eastern Europe, Dulles suggested containment be replaced by a policy he called "liberation."

After his appointment as secretary of state, Dulles stressed the collective security of the United States and its allies and the development of nuclear weapons for "massive retaliation" in case of attack, whether nuclear or conventional. However, even with the Eisenhower administration's emphasis on nuclear weapons, in practice the "New Look" remained a policy of containment, as the failure of the United States to act during the Hungarian Revolution convincingly demonstrated. Dulles' hostility toward the neutralism of many Third World leaders often strained U.S. relations with important Third World countries, including Egypt and India. He strongly supported the American commitment to the struggling Diem regime in South Vietnam and to the Nationalist regime on Taiwan and helped develop the Eisenhower doctrine of military and economic help to Middle Eastern countries to thwart Communist expansion in that vital region. Although Dulles certainly was a formidable secretary of state, recent evidence indicates that Eisenhower's role in the formulation and direction of policy was stronger than previously believed.

Eisenhower, Dwight David (1890–1969), American general and supreme Allied commander in Europe during World War II and thirty-fourth president of the United States (1953–61).

After a youth spent in Kansas, Eisenhower won admission to and graduated from the United States Military Academy at West Point. His rise through the ranks of the army was at best routine until a series of rapid promotions during World War II that propelled him to the top of the American military establishment and to the position of commander of all Allied forces in Europe. After the war he served as army chief of staff, president of Columbia University, and commander of NATO forces in Europe. After refusing to get involved in politics, he responded to the urging of the internationalist wing of the Republican Party—the party had a strong isolationist wing led by Senator Robert Taft—and won the Republican presidential nomination in 1952. He then defeated the Democratic nominee Adlai Stevenson in the general election.

Immediately after his election, Eisenhower moved to fulfill his campaign pledge to end the Korean War. His task was simplified somewhat by the death of Joseph Stalin in March 1953. An armistice was finally signed in July, but not until after Eisenhower freed Chiang Kai-shek to bomb mainland China from his bastion on Taiwan and Secretary of State Dulles threatened that the United States might employ atomic weapons to end the war. The Eisenhower-Dulles team, notwithstanding campaign rhetoric, continued the policy of containment, although the "New Look" emphasis on atomic weapons helped reduce the defense budget from its Korean War level of $50 billion to $35 to $40 billion. His administration strongly supported NATO and European unity, which included bringing West Germany into the alliance in 1955. Eisenhower expanded containment efforts in Asia. He supported the French in Indochina until their defeat in 1954 and then backed the South Vietnamese government of Ngo Dinh Diem. In 1954 the United States also played the central role in the creation of the Southeast Asia Treaty Organization (SEATO). The next year, Eisenhower went to Geneva for the first summit between Western and Soviet leaders since World War II.

The Eisenhower administration's reaction to two crises in the fall of 1956 tore the veil from two heretofore at least partially covered truths. The Hungarian Revolution, and America's inaction in the face of Soviet intervention, revealed that the Eisenhower administration's proclamations about the "liberation" of Eastern Europe were a sham. The Suez Crisis, in which the United States forced the British and French to withdraw from Egypt, aside from embittering America's relations with allies, demonstrated that both no longer were first-rate global powers.

During Eisenhower's second term, he announced the Eisenhower Doctrine for the Middle East and in 1958 sent U.S. troops to Lebanon to support that country's pro-Western government. The last years of his administration were frustrating, however. In 1959 Castro came to power in Cuba, and relations with Cuba rapidly deteriorated to the point where Eisenhower broke diplomatic relations with the Castro regime in January 1961. In 1960, a summit meeting with Khrushchev in Paris collapsed when the Soviets downed a U-2 spy plane over their territory and Eisenhower defended the mission rather than offer the Soviets an apology. In his farewell address, Eisenhower warned of the detrimental effects of the developing "military-industrial complex" in the United States as a result of the Cold War.

Espionage, the act of obtaining information secretly. The term applies particularly to the act of seeking military, industrial, and political data about one nation for the benefit of another. Espionage is part of intelligence activity, which is also concerned with analysis of diplomatic reports, newspapers, periodicals, technical publications, commercial statistics, and radio and television broadcasts.

Espionage dates from ancient times. The Egyptians had a well-developed secret service, and spying and subversion are mentioned in the *Bible* and the *Iliad*. The ancient Chinese treatise (c. 500 B.C.) on the art of war by Sun Tzu devotes much attention to deception and intelligence gathering, arguing that most war is based on deception.

Espionage activity increased significantly during the Cold War. The Soviet espionage network, the largest in the world, was the work of two main agencies, the civilian Committee for State Security (KGB) and the military's Chief Directorate of Intelligence (GRU). The KGB, whose activities involved many other activities besides spying, including internal repression, traces its long roots back through Soviet history to the CHEKA, the secret policy organization set up in December 1917, and from there back beyond 1917 to tsarist spy and secret police organizations, the last of which was the Okhrana. The KGB ran the largest spy network in the world, with agents operating under the cover of positions such as diplomats, journalists, and ordinary working people. It succeeded in penetrating both American and British intelligence services, among others, and achieved many espionage coups, including stealing important atomic-bomb secrets in the 1940s and the theft of vital U.S. navy secrets from the 1960s into the 1980s. The KGB's work was supplemented by the GRU, itself a formidable espionage and intelligence-gathering organization.

In the United States, the National Security Act of 1947 created the Central Intelligence Agency (CIA) for intelligence and espionage operations. The CIA became the most important of several U.S. intelligence agencies, among them the Defense Intelligence Agency (DIA), Federal Bureau of Investigation (FBI), and the National Security Agency (NSA). The CIA relied on human operatives as well as on increasingly sophisticated technological and electronic measures. Among its many successful espionage operations was a tunnel built under East Berlin that allowed its operatives, sitting in a comfortable air-conditioned station, to tap into cables carrying top-secret Soviet communications. In the air, the CIA flew the hugely successful U-2 spy planes and their even more remarkable successor, the SR-71, which remained in service well into the age of spy satellites.

Other important Western espionage organizations included Britain's MI5 and MI6. Although these had their notable successes, they also were plagued by infiltration by Soviet double agents, the most notorious of whom was Kim Philby, who ultimately escaped safely to Moscow. Close

French cooperation with American intelligence ended after France terminated its military role in NATO in 1966. At various times during the Cold War the CIA benefited from information and materials provided by Israeli intelligence, including Soviet weapons and electronic gear captured during Israel's wars with Soviet-supplied Arab countries.

During the Cold War, both sides won and lost in the endless struggle to secure defections from the opposition. Probably the most important Soviet intelligence officer who defected to the West was GRU Colonel Oleg Penkovsky, who provided the United States and Britain vital information about Soviet military preparedness and intentions in the early 1960s. Among Western citizens who aided the Soviet Union, none did more damage than physicist Klaus Fuchs, the German-born naturalized British citizen whose theft of nuclear secrets probably speeded up the Soviet atomic bomb program by four years; U.S. Navy officer John Anthony Walker and his collaborators, who for almost two decades provided the KGB with invaluable military information; and career CIA official Aldrich Ames, whose information led to the decimation of the CIA's agent network inside the Soviet Union.

European Community, originally called the European Economic Community (EEC) or Common Market. It grew out of efforts to promote European unity in the aftermath of World War II, when there developed in Europe a revulsion against national rivalries and parochial loyalties. During the postwar recovery stimulated by the Marshall Plan, which required that the European aid recipients work together toward economic recovery, the idea of a united Europe was held up by continental statesmen to be a basis for European strength and security—in terms of being able both to resist Soviet aggression and to compete economically with the United States— and the best way to prevent another European war. Like NATO, the EEC was an effective mechanism for integrating West Germany into a greater European framework. The EEC (it became the EC in the mid-1960s) grew out of the European Coal and Steel Community, a French-German project first proposed in 1950 by French foreign minister Robert Schuman. The Treaty of Rome that established the six-member Common Market (France, West Germany, Italy, and the Benelux countries) was signed in 1957 and the organization itself began functioning in 1958.

Great Britain originally stood aloof from the EC, largely because of its lingering pretensions as a global power. However, in 1963, with the passing from the scene of World War II-era leaders Winston Churchill and Anthony Eden, the British applied for EC membership, only to have their application vetoed by France's Charles de Gaulle. The French president had not forgotten the British-American snubs he had endured during World War II and tended to view Britain as an American puppet. Keeping Britain out of the EC was part of his effort to build a European entity independent of American influence. Nonetheless, in 1973, after de Gaulle's retirement, Britain joined the EC along with Ireland and Denmark. In the 1980s the EC reached twelve members with the admission of Greece (1981), Spain (1986), and Portugal (1986). After the end of the Cold War, efforts at further integration were slowed by economic stagnation and reluctance in several member countries to yield traditional prerogatives of national sovereignty to a supranational European body.

Ford, Gerald Rudolph (1913–), thirty-eighth president of the United States (1974–77) who served during the difficult days of the immediate post-Watergate and post-Vietnam era.

Ford was born Leslie Lynch King Jr. but took his stepfather's name after his mother moved from Nebraska to Michigan and remarried. After excelling as a student and athlete at the University of Michigan—he was an All-American football player—Ford graduated from Yale Law School. He served in the navy during World War II and was elected as a Republican to the House of Representatives. Having risen to the post of House minority leader and earned a reputation for personal integrity, in October 1973 Ford was appointed vice president by Richard Nixon to replace Spiro Agnew, taking office in December. His tenure as vice president was short; when Nixon resigned on August 9, 1974, Ford became president, the first to be appointed under procedures established by the 25th amendment to the Constitution. He pledged to continue Nixon's foreign policy and to work to curb inflation. But his position was weakened by his status as an appointed president and by the pardon he issued to Nixon a month after taking office, despite the fact that many observers agreed with Ford that little could be served by the country further immersing itself in the Watergate scandal and that the time had come to heal the nation's wounds and end what he called "our long national nightmare."

In the wake of Watergate and disillusionment with what had transpired in Vietnam, Ford and his secretary of state Henry Kissinger were unable to convince Congress to provide additional aid to the South Vietnamese and Cambodian regimes in 1975, which hastened their collapse and the end of the American presence in Indochina as Communist forces overran both countries. In May 1975, a month after the hurried American evacuation of Saigon, the new Cambodian Communist regime seized an American merchant vessel, the *Mayaguez*, claiming it was a spy ship. Ford responded by sending American troops to recover the vessel and its crew, which they did despite heavy losses. That same year, Ford and Kissinger again failed to convince Congress to support a non-Marxist faction in the African country of Angola, despite the presence of Soviet-supported Cuban forces backing a Marxist faction, which eventually won that struggle.

Ford continued Nixon's policy of détente. In 1974 he signed an agreement with Leonid Brezhnev in the Soviet city of Vladivostok that established guidelines for continuing SALT II negotiations, but those talks nonetheless bogged down and were not completed when Ford was defeated in 1976 in his reelection bid by Jimmy Carter. The Ford presidency marked what is generally considered the height of détente, the signing of the Helsinki Accords in 1975. Ford's election campaign was weakened by opposition to détente within his own party, notably by Ronald Reagan and his supporters. However, despite his reelection defeat, Ford is credited with helping to bind the nation's wounds during a very difficult period in its history.

Forrestal, James Vincent (1892–1949), U.S. secretary of the navy (1944–47), and first secretary of defense (1947–49).

James Forrestal, a navy aviator during World War I and later an investment banker on Wall Street, was one of the most militant anti-Communists in both the Roosevelt and Truman administrations. In administration discussions over Poland in April 1945 Forrestal urged a tough stance, saying it was better to have a "showdown" with the Russians sooner rather than later. In the months after World War II ended he warned against trying to win the understanding of the Soviet Union, noting, "We tried that once with Hitler." In January 1946, along with former secretary of war Henry Stimson, Forrestal was among those who unsuccessfully advised President Truman to stop the process of American demobilization because of what they said was a growing Soviet threat.

Forrestal welcomed George Kennan's famous Long Telegram of 1946, which stressed the aggressive nature of the Soviet Union, and had hundreds of copies printed for circulation among key people in Washington. He strongly supported the Truman Doctrine and the Marshall Plan. After the passage of the National Security Act of 1947, Forrestal headed the newly created Department of Defense. It was not an easy job. As secretary of defense he had to deal with the rivalries among the army, navy, and air force. His efforts to satisfy their demands were made far more difficult by Truman's budget cuts. The pressures of his job may have contributed to Forrestal's becoming mentally depressed, unbalanced, and paranoid. In 1949, at Truman's request, he resigned his post. He committed suicide shortly after being hospitalized for a nervous breakdown.

Fulbright, J. William (1905–95), long-time senator from Arkansas (1944–74) and chairman of the Senate Foreign Relations Committee (1959–74).

Educated at the University of Arkansas, Oxford (as a Rhodes scholar) and George Washington University law school, Fulbright served as the president of the University of Arkansas and in the House of Representatives before his election to the Senate in 1944. He quickly gained international recognition from the Fulbright Act (1946), which provided for the exchange of students and teachers between the United States and many foreign countries. Although he supported the three basic building blocks of containment—the Truman Doctrine, Marshall Plan, and NATO—his relations with Truman were poor from the time he suggested, after the Republican victory in the Congressional elections of 1946, that Truman resign. Truman's response was to dub the senator from Arkansas "Halfbright."

Although he occasionally took a hard line in foreign affairs, such as urging an invasion of Cuba during the Cuban Missile Crisis, for most of his career Fulbright argued that the United States was overemphasizing anti-Communism in its foreign policy and should be more flexible in its dealings with the Soviet Union and with nationalist movements in the Third World. Before emerging as one of the Senate's leading critics of the Vietnam War, he opposed the Bay of Pigs invasion (1961) and the landing of marines in the Dominican Republic (1965). At the time of the Dominican action, Fulbright complained that the United States was allowing itself to become the tool of Latin American "oligarchs" in their effort to preserve the unfair status quo and to use anti-Communist language to cover up their motives and get American help. After strongly supporting the Gulf of Tonkin resolution in August 1964 that in effect gave Lyndon Johnson a free hand to escalate United States involvement in Vietnam, Fulbright turned against the war. He was convinced that what he called the "arrogance of power" was leading the United States to make excessive commitments abroad that were undermining its democratic institutions at home.

After 1965 Fulbright turned the Senate Foreign Relations Committee into a forum for critics of the Vietnam War. It was during the committee's hearings on war in 1966 that George Kennan testified that containment had been designed for Europe and its system of nation-states and was not applicable to the vastly different situation that existed in Asia. Fulbright continued to oppose the Vietnam War as one of the most articulate "doves" in the Senate. He vigorously supported the Senate's repeal of the Gulf of Tonkin resolution in 1970 and played a major role in the passage of the War Powers Act of 1973, which restricted the President's authority to undertake armed intervention abroad by requiring that failing a declaration of war, any commitment beyond sixty days (ninety days in certain circumstances) have Congressional approval. Fulbright served in the Senate until defeated for reelection in 1974.

Genscher, Hans-Dietrich (1927–), West German foreign minister (1974–90), German foreign minister (1990–92).

Genscher's career as a major player in German and international politics spanned the second half of the Cold War. After serving in various branches of the German military during World War II, Genscher lived in East Germany until fleeing to the West in 1952. He subsequently became a prominent member of the Free Democratic Party, a centrist group standing between the Christian Democratic Union and the Social Democrats. In 1974, the same year he became the chairman of the Free Democrats, Genscher became West Germany's foreign minister and deputy chancellor in the Social Democrat-Free Democrat coalition government. In 1982, after his split with the Social Democrats brought down that government, Genscher took his party into a coalition led by the Christian Democrats, where he continued in his posts as foreign minister and as deputy chancellor. By his retirement in 1992, he was the West's longest-serving foreign minister or secretary.

Genscher was flexible in his approach to dealing with the Cold War division of his country and the continent of Europe. He strongly supported the EEC and European integration. He helped Social Democratic chancellor Willy Brandt and his successor Helmut Schmidt implement the policy of *Ostpolitik*. At the same time, during the Cold War Genscher was a firm believer in the importance to Western European security of a strong American presence in Europe, and therefore supported the deployment of U.S. Pershing II and cruise missiles on the continent. He welcomed Mikhail Gorbachev's peace initiatives after 1985 and worked hard with Chancellor Helmut Kohl to seize the opportunity provided by the collapse of Communism in 1989 to consummate German reunification in 1990. His retirement in 1992 was due to health problems.

Gomulka, Wladyslaw (1905–82), leader of Communist Poland (1956–70).

Gomulka was born into a working-class family and followed his father into socialist activism. As a young man he became a Communist and was arrested several times. He spent much of World War II in German-occupied Poland as a party operative organizing resistance to the Nazis. When the Soviets set up their puppet Polish government Gomulka became deputy premier. However, because his Communism also included elements of Polish nationalism he ran afoul of Stalin. Gomulka was purged from both the government and the party and eventually arrested and imprisoned for several years. He returned to power in 1956 in the wake of the riots that shook the regime and raised the threat of Soviet intervention to restore order. At first Nikita Khrushchev and the Soviet leadership were unwilling to accept Gomulka. But using both threats of Polish resistance and the promise of loyalty to the Soviet Union Gomulka convinced Khrushchev that allowing Poland a small measure of autonomy would strengthen rather than weaken the Soviet bloc. Over the next fourteen years Gomulka used his autonomy to bring about modest social and economic liberalization. However, the modified Stalinism that satisfied the Soviet leaders in Moscow did not in the end satisfy the Polish people, who continued to resent the Communist system and Soviet domination of their country. In 1970, Polish workers reacted to the government's announcement of food price increases with widespread riots. Gomulka was removed from power and replaced by Edward Gierek, who in turn was swept away by another wave of worker protests a decade later.

Gorbachev, Mikhail Sergeyevich (1931–), president of the Soviet Union and general secretary of the Communist Party of the Soviet Union from 1985 until its collapse in 1991 and the man most responsible for ending the Cold War.

Mikhail Gorbachev came to power determined to reform the Soviet system and make it economically competitive with the West. He soon found that the problems he faced were far more serious and required far more radical measures than he had anticipated. Gorbachev also realized that domestic reform required a relaxation of tensions with the United States and its allies—which had deteriorated to the point of what was called the "New Cold War" during the late Brezhnev era—so that the Soviet Union could decrease its enormous defense burden and shift resources to civilian investment and other needs. Over time Gorbachev's program had four main aspects: *perestroika*, or restructuring, a term that referred at once to the entire program and the overhaul and reform of the economy; *glasnost*, or openness, which referred to cultural freedom and reduction of censorship; *democratizatsia*, which meant the democratization of Soviet institutions; and *novomyshlenie*, or new thinking, which implied ending the Soviet

Union's long confrontational relationship with the West and the normal-ization of relations.

It was Gorbachev's new-thinking foreign policy, implemented with the aid of foreign minister Eduard Shevardnadze, that set in motion forces that led to the end of the Cold War. After a 1985 getting-acquainted sum-mit meeting with President Reagan in Geneva and a failed summit in Reykjavik, Iceland, the two leaders had a triumphant meeting in Decem-ber 1987 in Washington where they signed the INF treaty that removed all intermediate nuclear missiles from Europe. More examples of "new thinking" followed in rapid sequence. In February 1988 Gorbachev an-nounced that the Soviet Union would withdraw from Afghanistan in a year; the withdrawal was completed on schedule. In December 1988 Gor-bachev spoke to the UN General Assembly. He rejected the old Soviet as-sumption of security based on military power and maintained that it could be best achieved by recognizing nations' mutual interdependence and their need for cooperation. He then announced the Soviets would unilaterally cut their armed forces by half a million men and ten thou-sand tanks.

In 1989 Gorbachev reached his peak as in international statesman when he refused to intervene to stop the collapse of Communism in East-ern Europe. To have done so would have destroyed in one blow every-thing he had accomplished to improve relations with the West and his re-form efforts at home. The imposition of Soviet control over Eastern Europe under Stalin had instigated the Cold War; the dissolution of that control in effect ended the Cold War. That end was proclaimed in No-vember 1990, after the nations of NATO and the Warsaw Pact signed the Conventional Forces in Europe treaty at the summit meeting of the Con-ference on Security and Cooperation in Europe. Two days later, the Unit-ed States, Canada, the Soviet Union, and every European nation except Albania signed the Charter of Paris for a New Europe, which formally pro-claimed the end of the Cold War.

Gorbachev was awarded the 1990 Nobel Peace Prize for his contribution to world peace, the year after *Time* magazine voted him the "Man of the Decade" for the 1980s. However, his great successes abroad—Gorbachev was far more popular in the West than in the Soviet Union—did not help him at home. Within a year of the signing of the Charter of Paris the Sovi-et Union would collapse and Gorbachev would be pushed from the world stage he had dominated for six years. That did not, in the view of many ob-servers, lessen his remarkable contributions toward ending the Cold War, contributions that made him one of the most remarkable and outstanding statesmen of the twentieth century.

Gromyko, Andrei Andreyevich (1909–89), diplomat, historian, and Soviet foreign minister (1957–89).

Perhaps more than any other single person, Gromyko was at center stage during the entire length of the Cold War. A native of Belarus, Gromyko entered the Soviet diplomatic service in 1939 and advanced rapidly as a protégé of then foreign minister Viacheslav Molotov. He served as Soviet ambassador to the United States from 1943 to 1946 and was present as an advisor to Stalin at both Yalta and Potsdam, the conferences many observers consider the opening bells of the Cold War. After serving as the chief permanent Soviet delegate to the United Nations (1946–48) Gromyko became his country's ambassador to Great Britain (1952–53). Meanwhile, he rose up the Communist Party hierarchy at home, reaching the Central Committee, the party's second ranking political body, in 1956.

For much of his career as foreign minister, Gromyko was a vastly experienced and very important advisor to the Kremlin leadership; however, they, not he, made the policies, which he in turn carried out with great skill. There are few major events in the Cold War in which he did not play a part. He was at the United Nations sitting next to Khrushchev when the Soviet leader unceremoniously pounded his desk with his shoe; he sat face to face with President Kennedy during the Cuban Missile Crisis; he was involved in the numerous crises over Berlin; he helped craft Soviet support for North Vietnam during the Vietnam War; he managed Soviet policy in the Third World; and he was deeply involved in détente and negotiations for arms control.

Gromyko finally reached the Politburo, the highest body of the Communist Party, in 1973. However, he did not control Soviet foreign policy until after Brezhnev's death, when the poor health of his successors created a vacuum that the old experienced diplomat comfortably filled. Although Gromyko was a relative hard-liner vis-à-vis the West, and especially the United States, he unwittingly played a critical role in ending the Cold War by giving Mikhail Gorbachev vital support in the competition to become Soviet leader in 1985. In the aftermath of that selection Gromyko was replaced as foreign minister by Eduard Shevardnadze as the Soviet foreign policy Gromyko had been identified with for his entire career was fundamentally overhauled. He was given the ceremonial post of president of the Soviet Union until Gorbachev took that post for himself in 1988. That marked the removal from office of the last powerful Brezhnev-era holdover and the end of Gromyko's long public career. He was removed from the Central Committee with other old guard leftovers in Gorbachev's "cold purge" of 1989 and died that same year, just as the Communist system he had helped impose on Eastern Europe was suffering its final death throes.

Guerrilla warfare, a term referring to irregular forces' fighting with hit-and-run tactics against enemy occupiers.

Guerrilla warfare did not, of course, begin with the Cold War; it has been used for centuries. The term *guerrilla* was coined to designate Spanish resistance forces fighting French occupiers during the Napoleonic Wars. Guerrilla warfare played a prominent role in resistance to German and Japanese aggression during World War II, especially in Soviet territory occupied by the Germans between 1941 and 1945 and in China, where the Communist Party gained popular support by mounting effective resistance against the Japanese.

Guerrilla warfare played a major role during the Cold War. It was used by nationalist groups fighting to overthrow colonialism, by dissidents to launch civil wars, and, most importantly, by Communist forces fighting Western-supported (and often dictatorial) regimes in the Third World. The most significant Communist guerrilla struggle occurred in Vietnam, where Communist guerrillas first defeated the French and established the independence of North Vietnam in 1954, and then waged a long and bitter struggle against the government of South Vietnam and the United States. In that struggle, North Vietnamese regular troops fought alongside guerrillas from the South, who notwithstanding their claims and those of their supporters abroad were in fact under North Vietnamese control. As the fighting escalated, the North Vietnamese ultimately took over the main burden of the fighting, as did United States troops until American troops left South Vietnam in 1973. Other successful insurgencies that brought Communists to power occurred in Cuba and Nicaragua.

Late in the Cold War the United States borrowed a leaf from the Soviet textbook on the subject and supported anti-Communist guerrilla movements in several countries, including Nicaragua and Afghanistan. American support for Muslim guerrillas in Afghanistan helped turn that country into the Soviet Union's Vietnam and further undermined the ebbing strength of the Soviet regime.

Hammarskjöld, Dag (1905–61), secretary general of the United Nations (1953–61).

Hammarskjöld was an experienced Swedish political figure and diplomat when, having served in the Swedish delegation to the United Nations, he was elected that organization's secretary general in 1953. His tenure coincided with some of the tensest years of the Cold War. He was reelected in 1957 with the support of both the United States and the Soviet Union. The Soviets supported his reelection despite his strong condemnation of their invasion of Hungary in 1956.

Hammarskjöld was an activist secretary general who greatly expanded the influence of the United Nations and the prestige of the post he held. A quiet, tactful, and highly active diplomat, he personally led missions to Beijing (1955), the Middle East (1956, 1958), and elsewhere to lessen tensions or to arrange peace settlements. Under his guidance a UN emergency force was established in 1956 to help maintain peace between Israel and Egypt after the Suez Crisis of that year, and UN observers were sent to Laos and Lebanon. However, beginning in the late 1950s the Soviet Union began to oppose Hammarskjöld. Soviet opposition led to angry attacks on him by Soviet leader Nikita Khrushchev in 1960 over Hammarskjöld's handling of a crisis in the Congo (later known as Zaire). The Soviets wanted the United Nations to give stronger support to Prime Minister Patrice Lumumba, whom they were backing, against secessionist forces backed by Western interests. The Soviets attempted to force Hammarskjöld's resignation and have the post of secretary general replaced by a committee of three, with the West, the Soviet bloc, and the Third World each having one representative. Hammarskjöld survived that challenge, but not his attempt to bring peace to the Congo in 1961. He arrived there in September, a year after Lumumba's ouster and eight months after Lumumba's murder by conservative political forces backed by the West. A plane Hammarskjöld was taking to a peace meeting crashed under mysterious circumstances, killing all aboard; the Soviets were suspected of having caused the crash. He was succeeded by U Thant of Burma. Hammarskjöld was posthumously awarded the 1961 Nobel Peace Prize.

Harriman, William Averell (1891–1986), American diplomat and governor of New York (1955–59), whose service spanned more than three decades from the 1940s to the 1970s.

Harriman was an heir to one of America's great fortunes, built on the ownership of the Union Pacific Railroad. After a successful career in railroads and other businesses, he joined the Roosevelt administration. In 1941 he became the overseas administrator of the lend-lease program.

Harriman was appointed ambassador to the Soviet Union in 1943 and served until 1946. He attended both the Yalta and Potsdam conferences. Although he developed a relatively good relationship with Stalin, Harriman did not trust the Soviet dictator and was among the first, shortly before Roosevelt's death, to warn about Soviet expansionist intentions regarding Eastern Europe. At the time of that warning, Harriman's most important assistant in the U.S. embassy in Moscow was George Kennan, later to become known as the "father" of containment.

In April 1945 Harriman rushed to Washington to present his analysis of the Soviet threat to the newly inaugurated Harry Truman. Harriman's influence was one reason for Truman's bluntly confronting Molotov with "words of one syllable" over Soviet conduct in Poland at the president's first meeting with the Soviet foreign minister two days later. After serving briefly as ambassador to Britain in 1946, Harriman played a major role in winning congressional approval of the Marshall Plan and then in administering that program. He continued to serve Truman as an important foreign policy advisor during the Korean War.

After a term as the governor of New York, Harriman was appointed as ambassador-at-large by John F. Kennedy and negotiated the fourteen-nation treaty that guaranteed the neutrality of Laos. As an undersecretary of state, he negotiated the Nuclear Test Ban treaty of 1963. He again served as ambassador-at-large from 1965 to 1969 under Lyndon Johnson, doing his best to drum up allied support for the U.S. effort in Vietnam. When the Paris peace talks on Vietnam opened in 1968, Harriman initially was the chief U.S. negotiator. By the early 1970s, his early concern about American involvement in Vietnam had turned into an open call for American withdrawal. Harriman's last service in the cause of American foreign policy were several short missions during the Carter administration. Among his published works are *Peace With Russia* (1959) and *America and Russia in a Changing World* (1971).

Ho Chi Minh (1890–1969), Vietnamese nationalist and Communist leader, president of North Vietnam (1954–69).

Born Nguyen That Than in a village in the northern part of Vietnam, then a French colony, Ho left his country in 1911 and spent the next twenty-nine years abroad. When he became involved in politics he took the first of many pseudonyms, Nguyen Ai Quoc, which means "Nguyen the Patriot." In 1941 he took the name Ho Chi Minh, meaning "he who enlightens."

Ho's travels took him to France, the Soviet Union, Britain, the United States, China, and many other countries. After arriving in France in 1917, Ho in 1920 became a founding member of the French Communist Party. During the early 1920s he studied revolutionary tactics in Moscow and in 1925 was sent to China as a agent of the Comintern. While in the Far East he organized Vietnamese revolutionaries and founded the Communist Party of Indochina (later the Vietnamese Communist Party). In the 1930s, Ho lived mainly in the Soviet Union and China. He finally returned to Vietnam after the outbreak of World War II on the heels of France's defeat in 1940 by Nazi Germany. In 1941 he organized the Vietnamese Independence Movement, or Viet Minh, and raised a guerrilla army to fight the Japanese, who had supplanted the French in Vietnam. After Japan's defeat and surrender, Ho in September 1945 proclaimed the independent Republic of Vietnam; his declaration drew heavily from the American Declaration of Independence and the French Declaration of the Rights of Man.

However, France's attempt to reassert control over the country led to the outbreak of war in 1946. The resulting war lasted until 1954. After the Geneva Conference of that year that divided Vietnam at the 17th parallel, Ho became president of an independent North Vietnam. The agreements at Geneva also provided for an election in 1956 to reunify the two Vietnams; however, South Vietnam, backed by the United States, refused to hold the elections. The South Vietnamese charged that fair elections could not be held in the territory controlled by North Vietnam; however, it was widely believed that the elections were scuttled because Ho's popularity would have led to reunification under Communist rule.

Although he cultivated the image of child-loving "Uncle Ho," Ho Chi Minh could also be a ruthless and brutal leader, as he demonstrated in the struggle against the French, in establishing a Communist dictatorship in North Vietnam, and in the struggle against the United States and the South Vietnamese government in the 1950s and 1960s. After 1954 he consolidated his government and the Communist dictatorship in the North. In 1959 Ho and his colleagues decided to begin the armed struggle to take over the South. Ho led that struggle for the next ten years, refusing to bow to American power even as North Vietnam was pounded by American bombers. In 1967, he responded to Lyndon Johnson's offer to stop the bombing in return for the end of North Vietnamese infiltration into the South by accusing the United States of committing war crimes. Ho died in 1969, after peace talks with the United States had begun but almost four years before they reached fruition.

Honecker, Erich (1912–94), Communist Party chief and leader of East Germany (1971–89).

Honecker's Communist activism dated from his youth; his father, a coal miner, was a party member. Arrested by the Nazis in 1935, Honecker remained in prison until the end of World War II. He rose through the ranks of the East German Communist Party and in 1971 replaced Walter Ulbricht as party leader. Honecker was a hard-liner who urged the Soviet Union to invade Poland after the formation of the Solidarity union in 1980. After Mikhail Gorbachev came to power in the Soviet Union in 1985, Honecker rejected any reform in East Germany. He was finally removed from power in October 1989 by a group led by Egon Krenz that turned toward reform in a desperate attempt to save the Communist regime. Honecker fled to Moscow after Germany's reunification to avoid trial for ordering guards at the Berlin Wall to shoot to kill anyone trying to escape to the West. After the collapse of the Soviet Union Honecker returned to Germany and was tried and convicted of manslaughter. However, because of poor health he was allowed to leave Germany for Chile, where he died.

Hoover, John Edgar (1895–1972), director of the Federal Bureau of Investigation (1924–72).

Hoover was born in Washington, D.C., and graduated from George Washington University law school. He joined the Justice Department and served as a special assistant to Attorney General A. Mitchell Palmer, directing the so-called Palmer Raids against allegedly subversive aliens. After becoming head of what was then called the Bureau of Investigation (renamed the FBI in 1935), Hoover turned it into an efficient crime-fighting organization, establishing a centralized fingerprint file, a crime laboratory, and a training school for police. During the 1930s he sought to publicize the work of the agency in fighting organized crime, and participated directly in the arrest of several major gangsters.

Hoover and the FBI were first given the job of combating foreign espionage in the mid-1930s. At that time and during World War II the FBI's main concern was subversion from extreme right-wing groups sympathetic to Nazi Germany. After World War II Hoover focused on the threat of Communist subversion. The FBI played a major investigative role in some of the postwar era's most famous cases of actual or alleged Communist subversion, including the Rosenberg spy case and the charges surrounding Alger Hiss. Hoover himself was a militant anti-Communist who believed that Soviet agents had penetrated many important walks of American life, including the highest levels of the federal government. He made his case in such books as *Masters of Deceit* (1958) and *A Study of Communism* (1962). Hoover became a controversial figure. His critics considered him to be an anti-Communist fanatic. It has been verified that he orchestrated systematic harassment of people he considered dangerous dissenters, whether they were Communists or not, including Martin Luther King Jr. Serving under eight presidents, he accumulated enormous power, in part from his secret files on political leaders and their associates. Although that power began to erode in the 1960s, beginning with the Kennedy administration, Hoover remained entrenched at the FBI until his death.

Hungarian Revolution, the most explosive event to rock the Communist world in the wake of Nikita Khrushchev's supposedly secret destalinization speech of February 1956.

Khrushchev's speech was followed within a few months by the fall of Hungary's dictator and Stalinist stalwart Matyas Rakosi and his replacement in July by Erno Gero, a somewhat less inflexible Stalinist. However, Gero's very minimal reforms did nothing to assuage nationalist and anti-Soviet sentiments in traditionally anti-Russian Hungary. Matters came to a head in October, just as Wladyslaw Gomulka's rise to power in Poland was stabilizing the situation there. Hungarian dissidents were encouraged by the success of the reformers in Poland and, significantly, by propaganda broadcasts by Radio Free Europe and Radio Liberty that led them to believe they would have American support if they expanded their resistance to Soviet rule. Riots late in October brought Gero down and led to Imre Nagy being elevated to the position of premier. Nagy was a reformer who had been in power from 1953 to 1955, during which time he slowed collectivization and otherwise liberalized economic policy and released a number of political prisoners. However, the chain reaction of events in the fall of 1956 soon swept him and Hungary far beyond his earlier reforms.

Nagy proved unable to stem or control the anti-Soviet and anti-Communist sentiments of the young people in the street. Budapest became the scene of street fighting between Hungarian demonstrators and Soviet occupation forces, and anti-Soviet activity spread to towns and villages outside the capital. When Soviet troops withdrew from Budapest in the waning days of October Nagy announced that Hungary would cease to be a one-party dictatorship, would withdraw from the newly established Warsaw Pact, and would become a neutral country like neighboring Austria. Nagy's government also appealed to the United Nations for aid. The Soviet response was a return to Budapest in force. In the bloody fighting that followed between the overmatched Hungarians and Soviet tanks, thousands were killed. An estimated 200,000 Hungarians fled to the West. No help came from the West. The Eisenhower administration's talk of "liberation" in Eastern Europe was exposed as a sham. The United States had no intention of risking war with the Soviet Union by going beyond containment. In 1956, the best it could offer was sympathy for the people Eisenhower called "poor fellows."

Imre Nagy was arrested several weeks after the revolt was suppressed, and he was executed in 1958. His body was buried in an unmarked grave. Meanwhile, the Soviets installed a new Communist regime in Budapest headed by Janos Kadar, who subsequently purged his regime of its most extreme Stalinists and undertook limited reforms that over time slowly won it a modest degree of public support. But Hungary, like the other countries of Eastern Europe, never accepted Communism or Soviet domination. More than four decades later, in 1989, as Hungary was breaking free from them both, one of the first acts of its people was to exhume Nagy's remains and give their fallen leader a hero's funeral.

Iron Curtain, perhaps the single most defining and recognizable term of the Cold War.

February and March 1946 witnessed a rapidly deepening frost in relations between the Western democracies and the Soviet Union. As February began, the Soviet army still occupied parts of northern Iran and Manchuria. On February 9 Stalin made an extremely hard-line speech in which he declared that war between capitalism and Communism was inevitable. A week later, a Soviet nuclear-spy ring was uncovered in Canada. A week after that, George Kennan's Long Telegram arrived in Washington.

These events provided the backdrop to the speech Winston Churchill made on the campus of Westminster College in Fulton, Missouri, on March 5, with Truman sitting behind him on the dais. Using a metaphor he had used several times before without causing any public reaction, Churchill warned that "from Stettin in the Baltic to Trieste in the Adriatic, an iron curtain has descended upon the continent." Nor was that all. Churchill added that the Soviets were trying to avoid war while still gaining the "fruits of war and the indefinite expansion of their power and doctrines."

The speech caused a storm from Moscow to Washington. Stalin denounced it as a "call to war." More than a hundred Labour Party members of Parliament called it a threat to peace, and Prime Minister Attlee expressed his disapproval. Columnists and congressmen in the United States criticized Britain's wartime leader. President Truman, who clearly approved of the speech at first, responded to American criticism by distancing himself from Churchill. He even invited Stalin to visit the United States and come to the University of Missouri to state his point of view, an offer the Soviet dictator declined.

Yet the term *Iron Curtain* survived. More succinctly than any other contemporary expression, it signified the division of Europe and the Soviet domination of Eastern Europe that gave rise to the Cold War. As it was used over and over again, it became a part of the English language and many other languages as well.

Jackson, Henry Martin (1912–83), U.S. senator (1953–83) and leading hard-line figure on defense and foreign policy issues.

Jackson began his career as a traditional liberal Democrat who strongly supported civil rights and organized labor and who denounced Senator Joseph McCarthy. At the same time, throughout his career Jackson took a very hard line regarding the Soviet Union and the defense posture of the United States. During the early days of the Cold War he strongly supported the Marshall Plan and NATO and the development of newer and ever more powerful nuclear arms, as did most of his Democratic colleagues. However, unlike many other liberal Democrats, Jackson always was wary of attempts to negotiate arms agreements with the Soviets, beginning with his opposition to the nuclear test ban treaty of 1963 and culminating with his angry criticism of SALT II and President Jimmy Carter. His suspicions regarding détente led to his sponsorship of the Jackson-Vanik amendment to a Nixon administration trade reform bill. The amendment required the Soviet Union to relax its restrictions on Jews seeking to emigrate in return for being granted most-favored-nation status in its trade relations with the United States. The amendment did not achieve its stated goal, inasmuch as the Soviets denounced it and tightened their restrictions on Jewish emigrants, but it may have served Jackson's agenda of reining in détente. Jackson differed further from many of his Democratic colleagues in his strong and unflagging support for the Vietnam War. Overall, Jackson had a considerable impact on the conservative turn of politics in the 1970s and 1980s, through both his own policy statements and the influence of his supporters and staffers, many of whom later supported Ronald Reagan. Jackson made unsuccessful bids for the Democratic presidential nomination in 1972 and 1976.

John Paul II (1920–), Roman Catholic pope (1978–).

A Pole and the first non-Italian pope since the sixteenth century, John Paul played an active role both in public and behind the scenes in undermining Communism in his native country, as well as supporting Catholic resistance to Communism elsewhere in Eastern Europe. His first visit to Poland as pope in 1979 drew huge crowds, boosted the prestige of the Catholic church, and contributed to the rise of the independent labor movement Solidarity. In January 1981 John Paul had a highly publicized meeting with Solidarity leader Lech Walesa at the Vatican. He also spoke out publicly in support of the union after the Polish government declared martial law and arrested its leaders the following December. Meanwhile, the Vatican secretly cooperated with the Reagan administration to undermine the Soviet grip on Poland and the rest of Eastern Europe.

In 1981 John Paul survived an assassination attempt by a Turkish national linked to the Bulgarian secret police and the Soviet KGB. Two more visits to Poland followed, in 1983, when the pope again met with Walesa, and in 1987, during the Gorbachev era. Nor did John Paul neglect the rest of the world; during his first decade as pope he made thirty-seven trips to more than fifty countries. Meanwhile, as he staunchly supported the West in the Cold War struggle over Eastern Europe, John Paul in 1988 issued an encyclical, *Social Concerns of the Church*, in which he condemned the Cold War as well as the respective flaws of both capitalism and Communism. At the same time, John Paul's concern about Marxist influence in the Third World led him to reject what is known as liberation theology, which mixed Catholic doctrine and advocacy of social justice for the poor, but whose practitioners, according to John Paul, wrongly tended to support violent revolution and Marxist class struggle.

In both his public and extensive secret activities, John Paul was a highly political pope who played a significant role in weakening Communist control of Poland, the original battleground of the Cold War.

Johnson, Lyndon Baines (1908–73), thirty-sixth president of the United States (1963–69).

Having served as a congressman (1937–49), senator (1949–61), and vice president (1961–63), Johnson became president on November 22, 1963, after the assassination of John F. Kennedy. During his Senate years (he became Democratic leader in 1953) Johnson was an advocate of military preparedness. As president, he secured the passage of sweeping civil-rights and social-reform legislation, including the Civil Rights Act of 1964, the Voting Rights Act of 1965, a variety of antipoverty programs, and medical care for the elderly under Social Security (Medicare), all designed to create what he called the Great Society. One of his first major steps in foreign affairs was a largely successful military intervention with twenty thousand troops in the Dominican Republic. This action began in April 1965 and prevented the rise of power of either left-wing forces friendly to Fidel Castro or right-wing forces sympathetic to the fallen Trujillo regime.

Johnson's other major foreign military enterprise—the Vietnam War—was far less successful and undermined his entire presidency. He accepted the so-called domino theory that suggested that the fall of South Vietnam would endanger the rest of Southeast Asia. Taking matters further, he once warned that the if the United States failed to stop the "Reds" in Vietnam it would have to face them in Hawaii "tomorrow" and "next" in San Francisco. After visiting Vietnam in 1961 as vice president, Johnson advocated increased backing for the Vietnamese regime of Ngo Dinh Diem. When he became president in 1963 there were about 16,000 U.S. troops in Vietnam. Johnson increased that force to over 23,000 during 1964, the same year the Tonkin Gulf Resolution gave him broad powers, including the use of armed force, to protect American troops in South Vietnam. Convinced that South Vietnam was about to fall to Communist forces, Johnson began a massive escalation of the American presence that during 1965 increased U.S. forces to over 184,000 and sent American units into combat against the Viet Cong and North Vietnamese. Within three years, there were more than half a million U.S. troops in South Vietnam.

Johnson's escalation, which the North Vietnamese matched, failed to bring victory or bring the North Vietnamese to the negotiating table. Meanwhile, as American battle deaths skyrocketed Johnson's policy aroused widespread popular opposition and generated a large and vocal antiwar movement. Opposition to the war also grew in Congress. As the financial cost of the war mounted, Congress scuttled many of Johnson's domestic programs. Large-scale riots in the black ghettos of major American cities further clouded his presidency, and by the beginning of 1968 he was under sharp attack from all sides. The North Vietnamese/Viet Cong Tet Offensive of January–February 1968 further undermined public support for the war and the Johnson administration's credibility with the American people. After senators Eugene McCarthy and Robert F. Kennedy began campaigns for the Democratic presidential nomination, Johnson announced on March 31 that he would not run for reelection. At the same time, he called a partial halt to the bombing of North Vietnam; two months later peace talks began in Paris.

Despite the Vietnam conflict and the tensions it caused with the Soviet Union, Johnson initiated policies that eventually led to détente and the SALT I arms control negotiations. The SALT I negotiations, originally scheduled to start in 1968, were pushed back to 1969 by the Soviet invasion of Czechoslovakia and suppression of the Prague Spring.

Johnson left behind a nation bitterly divided by the Vietnam War when he left office in 1969. He retired to his ranch in Johnson City, Texas, where he worked on his memoirs. He died of a heart attack on January 22, 1973, five days before U.S. and Vietnamese negotiators signed the cease-fire agreement that led to the withdrawal of the last American troops in Vietnam.

Kennan, George Frost (1904–), U.S. diplomat and the formulator of the Cold War policy of containment.

A graduate of Princeton University, Kennan specialized in Russian language and culture after entering the foreign service. He was posted to Riga, Latvia, prior to Washington's recognition of the Soviet regime and to Moscow after the establishment of diplomatic relations in 1933, serving there until 1937. Kennan developed a deep respect for the Russian people and their culture. In 1944 he again was posted to Moscow as a top advisor to ambassador Averell Harriman. Both men were suspicious of Soviet motives and concerned about Soviet plans for Eastern Europe after the conclusion of World War II.

Kennan's views first became widely known when he responded to a State Department request for an analysis of Soviet intentions in 1946 with his so-called Long Telegram, which warned that Soviet policy was based on an assumption of the permanent hostility toward the Western capitalist powers. The 8,000-word telegram was wide circulated in official Washington and confirmed President Truman's view that new countermeasures were needed to combat Soviet expansionism. In 1947, by which time he was head of the State Department's newly created policy planning staff, Kennan published "The Sources of Soviet Conduct" in the journal *Foreign Affairs*. Kennan repeated much of his Long Telegram analysis and suggested that the United States deal with the Soviets by a policy of "long-term patient but firm and vigilant containment."

Kennan helped to forge the beginning of the containment policy with his work on the Marshall Plan. However, he disagreed with the Truman administration's tendency to focus on the military measures of pursuing containment, in contrast to political and economic policies, and opposed the formation of NATO. This and other disagreements led to his resignation in 1951, although he returned to serve briefly as ambassador to the Soviet Union in 1952. After serving as ambassador to Yugoslavia in the Kennedy administration from 1961 to 1963, Kennan left government service for a position at Princeton. He subsequently opposed the Vietnam War, arguing that American did not have vital interests in the region, and also became a leading critic of the nuclear arms race, urging leaders on both sides to "cease this madness."

Kennedy, John Fitzgerald (1917–63), thirty-fifth president of the United States (1961–63).

Kennedy was the second oldest of nine children of a wealthy and politically prominent Boston Irish family. In 1960 he became both the youngest man and the first Roman Catholic ever elected president of the United States. When he was assassinated in 1963 he became the youngest president to die in office.

Both of Kennedy's grandfathers were prominent politicians in Massachusetts. His father served as American ambassador to Great Britain from 1938 to 1940. Kennedy's senior thesis while at Harvard University, a study of England's unpreparedness for World War II, became a successful book, *Why England Slept* (1940). Kennedy served in the navy during the war and was cited for heroism in saving his crew after the PT boat he commanded was sunk by a Japanese destroyer. He was elected to Congress in 1946 and to the Senate in 1952. Shortly after his election he married Jacqueline Lee Bouvier, the glamorous and beautiful daughter of a Wall Street executive.

Kennedy's early years in Congress marked him as a staunch anti-Communist and Cold Warrior. As a member of the House of Representatives he went so far as to make a speech praising Senator Joseph McCarthy, whose Senate operations subcommittee staff included Robert F. Kennedy, John's younger brother. Although he became more liberal after reaching the Senate, Kennedy continued to take a hard line vis-à-vis the Soviet Union. In 1957 he won the Pulitzer Prize for his book *Profiles in Courage*, studies of eight American political figures who defied public opinion to take public stands according to the dictates of their consciences. Kennedy had tried and failed to win the Democratic vice presidential nomination in 1956, but a concerted campaign, backed by his father's money, won him the party's presidential nomination in 1960. He defeated Richard Nixon in the most closely contested election of the twentieth century.

Kennedy's inaugural address was a ringing restatement of his earlier promises to wage the Cold War with the Soviet Union in a more vigorous manner. Kennedy had criticized Eisenhower for relying too heavily on nuclear weapons to deter and manage the Soviets. The Kennedy doctrine of "flexible response" would make use of strengthened conventional forces, as well as political and economic weapons. They included his "Alliance for Progress" program of economic aid to Latin America and the Peace Corps, under whose auspices thousands of Americans worked in developing countries in programs of economic and social development.

However, Kennedy's first year in office proved to be frustrating. It was marked by the Bay of Pigs invasion fiasco, an unsuccessful meeting with Soviet leader Nikita Khrushchev in Vienna, the fall of a pro-Western regime in Laos and its replacement by a neutral regime, and the building of the Berlin Wall in August, which would leave that city physically divided until the end of the Cold War.

It is likely that these failures contributed to Kennedy's tough stand during the Cuban Missile Crisis of October 1962. That crisis marked the most dangerous moments of the Cold War when the Soviet Union and the United States stood on the brink of a nuclear exchange. Kennedy won praise in many circles for his firm but flexible handling of the crisis, but also has been criticized for unnecessary and reckless brinkmanship. Both Kennedy and Khrushchev, chastened by their brush with nuclear war, then pulled back from the brink; one result was the 1963 partial nuclear test ban treaty which banned all atmospheric nuclear weapons tests. In fact, the two men had taken the first step toward détente and arms control that would develop during the 1970s. At the same time, Kennedy took a major step toward America's greatest Cold War disaster: the war in Vietnam. By 1963 he had significantly increased American support for the corrupt but anti-Communist regime on Diem regime. However, Diem's failure to undertake reform led Kennedy to approve a military plot to remove the South Vietnamese dictator. The president was shocked when the plotters murdered Diem, an event that took place only a few weeks before Kennedy's own assassination.

Kennedy also committed the United States to another Cold War contest: the space race with the Soviet Union. The commitment he made early in his administration led to the United States landing the first man on the moon in 1969.

Khrushchev, Nikita Sergeyevich (1894–1971), Soviet leader, first secretary of the Communist Party of the Soviet Union (1953–64) and premier (1958–64).

Born into a Russian peasant family living near the Ukrainian border, Khrushchev received a limited education before going to work as a metal fitter in the coal mining industry in the Russian Empire's Donbass region. Exempted from military service because of his status as a skilled industrial worker, Khrushchev became a labor activist and ultimately a Bolshevik in 1918. He rose through the party ranks as a Stalin supporter in the 1920s and received major promotions in the 1930s that brought him into the top ranks of the party leadership. He served in the Red Army as a political commissar during World War II and was one of Stalin's top five lieutenants when the Soviet dictator died in 1953. Over the next two years he emerged victorious in the struggle for power. However, neither Khrushchev nor any subsequent Soviet leader exercised anything approaching Stalin's dictatorial power, and in fact Khrushchev barely survived an attempt to remove him from office in 1957.

Khrushchev's tenure as Soviet leader was marked by a series of fitful and frequently unsuccessful reforms in foreign and domestic policy. His own inconsistencies and lack of planning, as well as opposition to his policies within the Communist Party leadership, often forced him to reverse or modify his reforms. In particular, his recklessness and aggressiveness undermined his attempts to improve relations with the United States and its NATO allies. Khrushchev's main doctrinal innovation in foreign policy, the idea of "peaceful coexistence," was announced at the 20th Party Congress, the same meeting where in his Secret Speech he denounced Stalin. In rejecting the inevitability of war between the capitalist and Communist systems, Khrushchev reversed Soviet doctrine that had governed its foreign policy since the days of Lenin. At the same time, peaceful coexistence did not preclude competition for influence on a global scale, which helped embroil Khrushchev and the Soviet Union in crises with the United States on many fronts. Ultimately, it led Khrushchev to blunder into the Cuban Missile Crisis, which brought the Cold War to its most dangerous phase and forced Khrushchev into a humiliating public retreat that gravely weakened his position at home.

Among the major events that defined the conduct of the Cold War that occurred on Khrushchev's watch were the Hungarian Revolution and the Sino-Soviet split. Recent archival discoveries have revealed that in 1956 Khrushchev and the Soviet leadership considered withdrawing from Hungary and seeking a compromise solution to the crisis there, but that they reversed their position in part because of Chinese and Yugoslav pressure. A major cause of the split between Moscow and Beijing was Khrushchev's attempt to improve relations with the United States, which reached its high point in Khrushchev's largely successful visit to the United States in 1959. However, the shooting down of the American U-2 spy plane aborted the scheduled 1960 Paris Soviet-American summit and soured Soviet-American relations for the remainder of the Eisenhower administration. Khrushchev did not help matters much when he behaved outrageously by pounding his shoe on a desk during while attending a meeting of the UN General Assembly in New York in the fall of 1960. The building of the Berlin Wall in August 1961 followed by several years an unsuccessful Khrushchev attempt to pressure the United States, Britain, and France to end the Allied administration of the city, which dated from the end of World War II. Although its construction caused a short-term crisis, the Berlin Wall actually helped stabilize West Berlin's status as a Western enclave inside East German territory, while leaving the city divided for the remainder of the Cold War. Khrushchev's worst foreign-policy mistake was to send nuclear missiles to Cuba in an attempt to redress the Soviet Union's strategic inferiority vis-à-vis the United States and to protect the Castro regime from another American invasion. His retreat from Cuba, notwithstanding concessions he won from Kennedy, gravely weakened his standing in Moscow and infuriated Beijing. He never recovered from that defeat. Two years later his colleagues removed him from office.

Khrushchev lived out his life in a comfortable but severely restricted retirement. His name went unmentioned in the Soviet press until a terse announcement of his death in 1971. In the end, however, the garrulous and irrepressible Khrushchev had the last word with the publication in the West of his memoirs. Unlike other memoirs by Soviet political figures, Khrushchev's were remarkably frank and revealing. The first volume appeared in the West in 1970, while he was still alive. Later volumes appeared after his death.

Kim Il Sung (1912–94), Communist dictator of the Democratic Republic of North Korea (North Korea) from its official establishment in 1948 until his death in 1994.

Kim Il Sung is the only political leader and significant player in the Cold War to be in power for its entire duration. During World War II he built Korea's Communist party into a powerful force that won considerable popular support for its role in resisting Japanese rule. In 1945 he took charge of the Soviet-sponsored People's Committee of North Korea, which became the government of Korea when the Soviets withdrew their troops in 1948. In 1950 Kim convinced Stalin to back his plan to invade and overrun South Korea, which caused the Korean War but which went awry when the United States surprised the Communist dictators by rushing troops to South Korea's defense. After the 1953 armistice North Korea followed a program of Stalinist-style industrialization and became one of the most oppressive societies in the world. Kim's regime survived the collapse of the Soviet Union but began the post–Cold War era with severe economic problems and widespread hardship.

Kissinger, Henry Alfred (1923–), national security advisor (1969–75) and U.S. secretary of state (1973–77).

Kissinger was born in Germany and emigrated with his family to the United States in 1938 to escape Nazi persecution of Jews. He became a citizen in 1943, the same year he entered the U.S. Army, in which he served until 1946. He then entered Harvard University, where he received his B.A. and Ph.D. and later taught. He established his reputation as a leading scholar of foreign policy with his book *Nuclear Weapons and Foreign Policy*, published in 1957. While teaching at Harvard from 1957 to 1969, Kissinger also served as a consultant to government agencies and private foundations. He also became a close advisor to Nelson Rockefeller, a leading figure in the Republican Party and later vice president under Gerald Ford.

Kissinger stepped onto the international stage when Richard Nixon appointed him national security advisor in 1969. Kissinger's most immediate concern was to negotiate an end to the Vietnam War, a frustrating job that ended up taking four years and that resulted in conditions that left South Vietnam vulnerable to a North Vietnamese assault. However, Kissinger's main concern was to reorient American foreign policy to take account of what he believed was an increasingly multipolar—as opposed to a U.S.-Soviet bipolar—world in which Western Europe, Japan, and the People's Republic of China were becoming major players. The Kissinger-Nixon strategy included negotiating the first major arms control agreement with the Soviet Union (SALT I), a broader policy of détente with the Soviet Union, and an opening to the PRC. Kissinger finally succeeded in negotiating the cease-fire that ended U.S. armed involvement in Vietnam in 1973, for which he shared the Nobel Peace Prize with North Vietnamese negotiator Le Duc Tho. His negotiating skill helped arrange a cease-fire in the 1973 Israeli-Arab Yom Kippur War and, employing "shuttle diplomacy" that sent him back and forth between Jerusalem and Cairo, a subsequent separation of forces between Israeli and Egyptian troops.

President Nixon appointed Kissinger as Secretary of State in 1973, but his leverage in dealing with foreign powers was reduced as the Nixon administration was weakened by the Watergate scandal. He continued in office when Gerald Ford succeeded Nixon after the latter's resignation in 1974 and played a central role in the negotiations that laid the basis for SALT II. Since leaving office he has lectured and served as a consultant on international affairs.

Kohl, Helmut (1930–), chancellor of West Germany (1982–90) and of united Germany from 1990 until late 1998.

Kohl rose through the ranks of the Christian Democratic Union and became West Germany's chancellor when its parliament in 1982 turned out the Social Democratic government of Helmut Schmidt in a no-confidence vote. He then led his party to election victories in 1983 and 1987. Kohl was among the more anti-Soviet West German politicians and did not favor proposals to eliminate intermediate-range nuclear weapons in Europe that eventually were realized by virtue of the Soviet-American INF treaty of 1987. Yet he ultimately brilliantly took advantage of the new international conditions that arose out of the Gorbachev era to bring about German re-unification. He moved quickly as the East German state began to collapse in 1989 and overcame not only Soviet concerns but also the reluctance of many of West Germany's allies to secure German reunification in October 1990. Soviet acceptance of reunification and Germany's membership in NATO were secured in part with the promise of billions of dollars of aid to Gorbachev's tottering regime. In December 1990, Kohl won election as united Germany's first chancellor.

Korean War, a conflict that broke out on June 25, 1950, when North Korean troops crossed the 38th parallel and invaded South Korea. The Korean War was the first major military confrontation of the Cold War.

Immediately after the invasion, the United Nations Security Council approved a United States-sponsored resolution condemning North Korea and then a second resolution calling upon its members to aid South Korea. On June 27 President Truman authorized the use of American forces to defend South Korea. A week later the United Nations placed the forces of fifteen other member nations under American command, and Truman appointed World War II hero General Douglas MacArthur as supreme commander.

In the first weeks of the conflict North Korean troops met little resistance and advanced rapidly. By September 10 they had driven the South Korean army and a small American force to a small area around the port of Pusan in southeastern Korea. MacArthur's counteroffensive began five days later with a daring landing of forces behind North Korean lines at Inchon, on South Korea's western coast just south of the 38th parallel. As the North Koreans fell back in panic MacArthur received permission to pursue them into North Korea. By the end of November UN forces were approaching the Yalu River, the North Korean border with China. At that point the Chinese launched a massive counterattack, pitting 300,000 troops against MacArthur's outnumbered forces. The Chinese drove south of the 38th parallel and captured Seoul, the South Korean capital.

By March 1953 the center of fighting returned to near the 38th parallel, where it remained until the end of the war. MacArthur wanted to mount a new assault on North Korea, which would have included attacks on targets in China. The general was convinced that it was in Asia that international Communism had to be stopped. The Truman administration, however, wanted to negotiate an end to the war in Korea and, in any event, was unwilling to risk a full-scale war with China or a direct confrontation with the Soviet Union. It believed that Europe, not Asia, should be the main focus of U.S policy. When MacArthur persisted in public criticism of the president—including making his famous statement, "There is no substitute for victory"—Truman fired him. Although MacArthur had many vocal supporters in the United States who pilloried Truman and accused him of appeasement, ultimately the administration convinced the majority of Americans that containment in Korea was preferable to MacArthur's risky policies, which might have led to a direct confrontation with the Soviet Union.

Despite the opening of truce negotiations in July 1951, the fighting dragged on for two more years. The war became increasingly unpopular as frustrated Americans accustomed to victories in foreign wars watched casualties rise. It played a significant role in the triumph of Republican candidate Dwight Eisenhower in the 1952 presidential elections, which featured a pledge by Eisenhower to go to Korea and end the war. It took nuclear threats against China by Eisenhower to bring about an armistice agreement on July 27, 1953. U.S. losses were more than 54,000 killed and 100,000 wounded. Chinese and Korean casualties were at least ten times as high. A peace treaty to end the war formally was never signed.

Lie, Trygve Halvdan (1896–1968), first secretary general of the United Nations (1946–1953).

A prominent Norwegian politician, Lie headed his country's delegation to the founding conference of the United Nations in 1945. He was elected United Nations secretary general in 1946.

In his efforts to deal with some of the early crises of the Cold War Lie angered the Soviet Union, which accused him of siding with the West. The Soviet Union's extensive use of its veto power in the Security Council weakened both the secretary general and the United Nations itself. Soviet hostility to Lie increased even further after the outbreak of the Korean War, when the United Nations backed the United States in the defense of South Korea. Although American efforts had won him a three-year extension when his initial five-year term expired in 1951, Lie, frustrated by continued Soviet hostility, resigned from office in 1952. Lie continued to serve as secretary general until Dag Hammarskjöld was elected to succeed him in 1953.

MacArthur, Douglas (1880–1964), American general, commander of United Nations forces during the Korean War (1950–51).

MacArthur was a brilliant soldier who served with great distinction in both World War I and World War II. His other military commands included service as superintendent of West Point (1919–22) and as chief of the general staff (1930–35). He retired from the army in 1937 but was recalled to duty in July 1941 to command American forces in the Far East. After the Japanese attack on Pearl Harbor on December 7, 1941, MacArthur commanded the campaign that culminated in the Japanese surrender on September 2, 1945.

MacArthur became a prominent early Cold War figure when he was put in charge of the Allied occupation of Japan. A militant anti-Communist, MacArthur's goal was to turn Japan into a democratic society with a stable economy. His policies, which including writing a new democratic constitution, generally won the support of the Japanese people. In 1948 he was considered for the Republican nomination for president, but his defeat in two primaries deflated his chances. Meanwhile, MacArthur strongly supported Chiang Kai-shek despite Chiang's defeat in the Chinese civil war and flight to Taiwan in 1949.

When the Korean War broke out in 1950 President Truman appointed MacArthur commander of United Nations forces defending South Korea. MacArthur responded with a brilliant landing of troops at Inchon, behind North Korean lines, and quickly drove the North Koreans from South Korea. At that point, having convinced Truman that the Chinese Communists were unlikely to intervene in the war, MacArthur won the president's permission to cross the 38th parallel and unify Korea. As his troops were approaching the Yalu River in late November, with MacArthur promising to get them "home by Christmas," the Chinese attacked with 300,000 troops. UN forces were driven south of the 38th parallel. MacArthur began to urge the United States to bomb Chinese bases in Manchuria that supported the Communist military effort in Korea. Truman refused, being unwilling to risk a general war with China. The general responded by publicly criticizing the president, and Truman dismissed MacArthur from his command in April 1951. MacArthur returned to the United States to a hero's welcome and a rising wave of irresponsible attacks on the Truman administration by his supporters, including Senator Joseph McCarthy. MacArthur was invited to speak to a joint session of Congress, where he was interrupted by applause more than thirty times. He brought down the house by dramatically closing his speech by announcing that like the "old soldier" of a popular army ballad, "I now close my military career and fade away." After an unsuccessful attempt at the Republican presidential nomination in 1952, MacArthur retired from public life, became chairman of the board of a large corporation, and did, indeed, fade away.

McCarthy, Joseph Raymond (1908–57), U.S. senator (1947–57) and fanatical anti-Communist whose irresponsible personal attacks and accusations inflamed anti-Communist hysteria in the United States in the early 1950s.

Before reaching the Senate as a Republican, McCarthy was an obscure Wisconsin politician. His career in the Senate was undistinguished until in 1950 he seized on the issue of alleged Communist subversion and infiltration of the United States State Department. Although a Senate investigation labeled McCarthy's charges without foundation and fraudulent, the senator repeated them. Challenged to produce evidence, he refused and instead made new accusations. Among the most prominent victims of his wild attacks were George Marshall, whom he accused of treason, and Secretary of State Dean Acheson.

McCarthy's rhetoric intensified as the Korean War dragged on without a U.S. victory. During the election of 1952 Republican nominee Dwight Eisenhower declined to defend Marshall, who had sponsored his military career, from McCarthy's attacks. When the Republicans assumed control of the Senate after the elections, McCarthy was given a platform as chairman of a Senate subcommittee. He used his position to exploit the public's fear of Communism and build his own power. Through widely publicized hearings, the use of unidentified informers, and reckless accusation, McCarthy pursued those he identified as Communists or subversives. Careers were ruined on the flimsiest evidence. Public debate was stifled by the fear of being accused of pro-Communist sentiments or disloyalty.

Despite President Eisenhower's refusal to denounce McCarthy, the senator's methods eventually came under increasing attack by the press and his colleagues. In 1954, McCarthy reached too far when he attacked the army for harboring subversives. The army in turn accused McCarthy and his leading aides of seeking preferential treatment for a former staff member who had been drafted. McCarthy's subcommittee then began televised hearings to investigate the charges. The Army-McCarthy hearings lasted more than a month and dominated daytime television, outdrawing the popular soap operas. The hearings, constantly punctuated by McCarthy's refrain—"Mr. Chairman, point of order"—revealed McCarthy's viciousness and the emptiness of his charges and discredited him in front of millions of Americans who viewed the proceedings. Particularly disastrous for McCarthy was his interrogation by army counsel Joseph Welch, who concluded his confrontation with the Wisconsin senator by asking him, "Have you no sense of decency, sir, at long last?" By the end of 1954 the tide had turned and the Senate voted to censure McCarthy. Although his personal influence quickly declined, the damage he did to American political life lasted longer. His conduct gave rise to the term "McCarthyism," which denotes assaults characterized by underhanded tactics and lack of credible evidence.

Macmillan, (Maurice) Harold (1894–1986), British prime minister (1957–63).

Macmillan was a member of the family that founded the publishing house of Macmillan and Company. After World War I, during which he was badly wounded, Macmillan entered politics and was elected to Parliament. During the 1930s he was an outspoken critic of Britain's policy of appeasement. Macmillan worked with General Dwight Eisenhower during World War II, and the two men developed a good personal relationship, which paid dividends when both headed their respective governments in the 1950s.

Macmillan became prime minister in the wake of the Suez Crisis of 1956. The crisis had driven a wedge between the United States and Great Britain and Macmillan's first priority was to restore American-British relations to their former solid status, which he did at a meeting with Eisenhower on Bermuda in early 1957. The two men also agreed to base American nuclear missiles in Britain under joint Anglo-American control. Later agreements led to further cooperation in developing nuclear weapons. In 1958, when the United States sent marines to protect the shaky Lebanese government, Macmillan sent British troops to do the same in Jordan. Macmillan also worked on the partial nuclear test ban treaty and was still in office when it was signed in 1963. He accelerated the process of dismantling Britain's colonial empire, granting independence to Ghana, Nigeria, and Kenya in Africa and to Malaya in Asia. In 1960, in a memorable speech, he criticized the South African parliament for its policy of apartheid, warning that the "wind of change" was blowing through Africa. In 1959, Macmillan became the first British prime minister since World War II to visit the Soviet Union. His efforts to win admission for Britain to the Common Market failed because of opposition from French president Charles de Gaulle. Macmillan resigned as prime minister in 1963 after his government was racked by several scandals.

Malenkov, Georgi M. (1902–88), Soviet leader for a short time after Stalin's death.

One of Stalin's inner circle from the end of World War II until the dictator's death in 1953, Malenkov at first appeared to be the new Soviet leader as the country began the post-Stalin era. During his term as prime minister, Malenkov advocated a more conciliatory approach to the West and presided over the "thaw" of the immediate post-Stalin years that saw, among other things, the end of the Korean War. Malenkov also advocated domestic economic policies designed to raise the miserably low Soviet standard of living. By early 1955 Malenkov had been outmaneuvered by Nikita Khrushchev and was forced to resign as prime minister. He participated in the unsuccessful attempt to remove Khrushchev from power in 1957, after which he was relegated to the obscurity of managing a power plant far from Moscow in Kazakhstan.

Mao Zedong (1893–1976), founder and leader of the People's Republic of China (1949–76).

Mao was born into a prosperous peasant family and received a primary education in the traditional Chinese classics. He later rebelled against his father's authority and left home in order to continue his education and study modern subjects. Mao participated in the 1911 revolution that overthrew the Manchu dynasty, was further radicalized by the May Fourth movement of 1919, and in 1921 attended the founding meeting of the Chinese Communist Party. From the start his Marxism included the belief in the revolutionary potential of China's peasantry, a doctrine that was at variance with traditional Marxist dogma. After the party's disastrous defeats in the late 1920s at the hands of Chiang Kai-shek, Mao retreated to the countryside, where he ultimately built a powerful peasant movement. After taking the lead in resisting the Japanese during World War II, the Chinese Communists under Mao's leadership won control of China in a civil war that lasted from 1946 to 1949.

The Communist victory in China led to an acrimonious debate in the United States about who was responsible for "losing" China and raised American concerns about further Communist expansion in Asia. The 1950 Sino-Soviet alliance treaty further intensified those concerns. But it was the Korean War and the resultant American decision to protect Chiang Kai-shek's Nationalist regime on Taiwan that put Sino-American relations into a deep freeze for more than two decades. During the 1950s Mao became increasingly critical of the Soviet Union, in part because of Khrushchev's attempts to improve relations with the United States. Khrushchev himself was unnerved by Mao's assertions that a nuclear war would lead to the destruction of capitalism and the victory of Communism. These differences led to the Sino-Soviet split, which burst into the open after 1960. Meanwhile, at home Mao dragged China through two disastrous episodes that grew out of his obsession to avoid contamination of his revolution: the Great Leap Forward (1958–59) and the Cultural Revolution

(1966–69). However, in the early 1970s, geopolitics, and in particular Mao's growing fear of the Soviet Union—the two nations had fought several bloody border battles in 1969—dictated a rapprochement with the United States. The main landmark in that development was Richard Nixon's historic visit to China in 1972. The two men—the staunch anti-Communist and the lifelong foe of capitalism—got along extremely well, and Mao invited Nixon to visit China when the latter was forced to resign the presidency in 1974. By then Mao's health was seriously deteriorating, and he lived only two more years while the struggle to succeed him went on behind the scenes.

Marshall, George Catlett (1880–1959), American general, army chief of staff (1939–45), secretary of state (1947–49), and secretary of defense (1950–51).

A career soldier, Marshall was the overall head of American military operations during World War II, the man Winston Churchill called the "true organizer of victory." Between his service as army chief of staff and secretary of state Marshall led a United States mission to China with the task of mediating the conflict between the Nationalists and Communists and avoiding a civil war. The mission failed because both sides were confident of victory. Once hostilities resumed Marshall, convinced that the Nationalists were too corrupt to resist the Communists, counseled against increased American involvement, advice that Truman wisely followed.

Marshall's appointment as secretary of state in January 1947 reflected the hardening American attitude toward the Soviet Union. It was during 1947 that the policy of containment started to take shape. In February Truman announced the Truman Doctrine, while in June, in a speech at Harvard University, Marshall announced what became the European Recovery Program, or Marshall Plan. This plan was a great success and laid the groundwork for the revitalization of Europe and the formation of the North Atlantic Treaty Organization, another project in which Marshall played a major role. Having retired in 1949 because of ill health, Marshall was recalled to Truman's cabinet as secretary of defense after the outbreak of the Korean War in 1950 to rebuild America's shrunken military establishment. He retired permanently in 1951. Two years later he was awarded the Nobel Peace Prize for his role in planning the Marshall Plan and Europe's economic recovery.

Marshall Plan or European Recovery Program, American program to foster economic recovery in Western Europe after World War II. The plan was a response to the continued economic crisis in Europe, which the Truman administration feared would cause despair and instability and lead to the spread of Communism. As such the plan became one of the keystones of America's containment policy.

The Marshall Plan was announced on June 5, 1947, when Secretary of State George Marshall, speaking at Harvard University, urged that European countries decide on their economic needs so that material and financial aid from the United States could be integrated on a broad scale. One development that helped win approval from a reluctant Republican-controlled Congress was the Soviet Union's refusal to participate in the plan, which Foreign Minister Molotov denounced as a "new venture in American imperialism." Another critical element was the increased fear of Soviet expansionism created by the Communist coup in Czechoslovakia in February 1948. Senator Arthur Vandenberg, one of the most influential Republican leaders in Congress, played a vital role in giving the Marshall Plan the bipartisan support it needed to win congressional approval.

President Truman signed the act establishing the Economic Cooperation Administration (ECA) in April 1948. The ECA was created to promote European production, to bolster European currencies, and to facilitate international trade. During 1948 Paul C. Hoffman was named economic cooperation administrator and the participating countries signed an accord establishing the Organization for European Economic Cooperation (later called the European Organization for Economic Recovery and Development). Over $12 billion was dispersed under the program, which lasted until the end of 1951. Although fifteen European nations participated, Britain, France, and West Germany received more than half the American aid. By 1952 European production already was higher than before World War II and within two years it exceeded prewar production by 200 percent. The Marshall Plan not only was a success as an instrument of containment, but it also won admiration as a genuinely humanitarian program that Winston Churchill called "the most unsordid act in history."

McNamara, Robert Strange (1916–), U.S. secretary of defense (1961–68).

McNamara was a brilliantly successful executive with the Ford Motor Company with a reputation as a superb manager when John F. Kennedy brought him to Washington to be secretary of defense. McNamara introduced modern management and efficiency techniques to the Pentagon, took charge of modernizing the nation's nuclear forces, and implemented Kennedy's overall strategy of flexible response, which involved strengthening the country's conventional forces to deal with crises for which nuclear weapons were unsuited. During the Cuban Missile Crisis it was McNamara who first suggested during the meetings of the "Ex Comm" that Cuba be blockaded. After 1964 McNamara, like the rest of the Johnson administration, became caught up in the Vietnam War. He was as closely identified with the war as any member of that administration, although he gradually concluded that it could not be won. He resigned his post in 1968 after Johnson rejected his advice to begin deescalating the American involvement in the war. From 1968 to 1981 he was president of the World Bank. In 1995 McNamara wrote a book, *In Retrospect,* in which he acknowledged critics of American involvement in the Vietnam War had been correct, an admission that garnered him yet more criticism for failing to speak out three decades earlier, when it counted.

Mitterrand, Francois M. (1916–96), president of France (1981–95).

Elected France's president in 1981 after two unsuccessful tries, including a defeat by Charles de Gaulle in 1965, Mitterrand went on to become the longest-serving president in his country's history. Before winning the presidency Mitterrand cobbled together several socialist groups to form a united Socialist Party under his leadership in 1971. Mitterrand was a non-Marxist, moderate socialist. Although he was initially was elected president with Communist support, he quickly marginalized them within his government, and within a few years they left the government altogether.

As president Mitterrand continued the Gaullist program of building an independent French nuclear deterrent against the Soviet Union, as opposed to relying completely on the nuclear umbrella of the United States. At the same time, he was more pro-American and favorably inclined toward NATO than de Gaulle. In the early 1980s Mitterrand supported the basing of new American Pershing II ballistic missiles and cruise missiles in Europe to counter the Soviet Union's SS-20 intermediate-range ballistic missiles. Mitterrand also advocated strengthened ties among the nations of Western Europe and focused on promoting cooperation between France and both West Germany and Great Britain.

Mitterrand's attitude toward the Soviet Union was flexible. He took a hard line on military and certain political matters but promoted economic ties, including large French purchases of Soviet natural gas that were opposed by the Reagan administration. Mitterrand also differed with Reagan on how to deal with radical forces in Latin America and was critical of American attempts to overthrow the Sandinista regime in Nicaragua. Meanwhile, France under Mitterrand continued to maintain a presence in sub-Sahara Africa, sending troops to protect the government of Chad from Libyan interference in 1992. In 1989, Mitterrand proudly presided over elaborate celebrations marking the bicentennial of the French Revolution.

Molotov, Viacheslav M. (1890–1986), Soviet foreign minister (1939–49, 1953–56).

Molotov joined the Bolshevik Party in 1906. His relationship with Stalin, whom he served with total devotion and loyalty throughout his political career, also dates from before the Bolshevik Revolution. Molotov achieved high office by the early 1920s as Stalin's staunch supporter in Bolshevik power struggles. Before becoming foreign minister in 1939 he served Stalin in various capacities, including helping direct the murderous purges of the 1930s. Molotov, who was Soviet premier from 1930 to 1941, when Stalin took the post for himself, was appointed foreign minister in 1939. His first task was to negotiate the notorious Nazi-Soviet nonaggression pact with German foreign minister Joachim von Ribbentrop. That agreement, which shocked the Western democracies, gave Hitler the security on his eastern front that he needed to launch World War II. When the Germans invaded the Soviet Union in June 1941, it was Molotov who substituted for the stunned and temporarily immobilized Stalin and announced the invasion to the Soviet people in a radio broadcast.

During World War II Molotov's task was to strengthen the Soviet Union's alliance with the West. He participated in the founding of the United Nations and took part in every major international conference until 1949. During the early days of the Cold War, his task, as he put it, was "to expand the borders of the fatherland as much as possible." Molotov was a tough and unyielding negotiator, a symbol of both Soviet strength and its hostility toward, and fear of, the West. Winston Churchill, who respected his abilities, referred to Molotov's "smile of Siberian winter." Molotov was on the receiving end of one of the opening verbal salvos of the Cold War when newly inaugurated President Harry Truman spoke angrily to him "in words of one syllable" about Soviet conduct in Poland in April 1945. Undeterred by Truman's criticism, Molotov implemented policies that established postwar Soviet control over Eastern Europe and pushed the world into the Cold War. After walking out of the Paris conference to discuss the proposed Marshall Plan in July 1947, Molotov announced an economic program for Eastern Europe and the Soviet Union that came to be called the Molotov Plan. Molotov did not let his demotion nor the imprisonment of his wife in a labor camp, both of which Stalin ordered in 1949, shake his devotion to the Soviet dictator. He reemerged as foreign minister after Stalin's death in 1953 and served in that office for three years. In 1957 he joined the plot against Nikita Khrushchev; his political career was ended when Khrushchev triumphed over his opponents. Until his death Molotov remained loyal to Stalin and his programs, from the great terror of the 1930s to postwar policies in Eastern Europe.

Nasser, Gamal Abdul (1918–70), president of Egypt (1956–70) and the most important leader in the Arab world from the mid-1950s until his death.

Nasser was the leader of the group of army officers that deposed Egypt's King Farouk in 1952, although he waited two years to become the country's prime minister and did not assume the presidency until he gave Egypt a new constitution in 1956. One reason for Nasser and his associates' over-throwing Farouk was that they blamed him for Egypt's humiliating defeat in the Arab war of 1948–49 to destroy the newly founded state of Israel. Nasser was driven by two obsessions. He envisioned himself as the leader of a pan-Arab nationalist movement, and his efforts toward that end in fact made him one of the world's leading neutralist political figures by the mid-1950s. He also was determined to eliminate Israel, whose very existence he termed an "act of aggression" against the Arab world.

These ambitions were behind Nasser's seizure of the Suez Canal from the British in 1956. Although the resulting Suez Crisis produced yet anoth-er Egyptian military defeat, Nasser's defiance of the British and French and his clash with the Israelis made him a hero in the Arab world. The Suez Crisis provided the opportunity for the Soviet Union to establish its influ-ence in Egypt. The Soviets seized the chance by offering to finance and build one of Nasser's dreams, a giant hydroelectric dam at Aswan in south-ern Egypt. Meanwhile, Nasser's pan-Arab ambitions produced the short-lived United Arab Republic (1958–61), an abortive union between Egypt and Syria, and a disastrous intervention in a civil war in Yemen (1962–67). His hatred of Israel led to another military disaster, the Six-Day War of 1967. Nasser triggered the war by ordering a UN peace force out of the Sinai, in-stituting an illegal blockade of Israel's port of Elat, massing thousands of Arab troops along Israel's borders, and pledging to wipe the Jewish state off the map. The Israelis then struck first, defeated Egypt and its Syrian and Jordanian allies, and occupied Egypt's Sinai Peninsula. Nasser resigned in the wake of this latest humiliation, but returned to office after massive demonstrations of support from Egypt's masses. Nasser meanwhile turned to a program of social and economic development he called Arab Social-ism. Shortly before his death in 1970 the Aswan Dam was completed.

Nasser ruled Egypt as a dictator, and his regime was marred by ineffi-ciency and corruption. Yet he achieved stature in non-Western circles for contributing to the reestablishment of Arab pride, seriously wounded by decades of Western domination. After 1967, his neutralism increasingly took a pro-Soviet tilt as Egypt's dependence on Soviet military and economic aid grew. Nonetheless, as a pan-Arabist and advocate of Third World unity, Nasser was the preeminent Arab leader of his era and one of the most important of the twentieth century.

Nehru, Jawaharal (1889–1964), prime minister of India (1947–64) and one of the leading figures of Third World neutralism in the 1950s and 1960s.

Nehru came from a prominent Indian family and received an exclusive British education. He became involved in the Indian independence movement, which cost him almost nine years in prison, and became a close associate of Mahatma Gandhi.

Nehru became India's first prime minister when the country achieved independence in 1947. His international stature came from both his status as the leader of the most populous country in the Third World and his personal diplomatic skills and charisma. Nehru stressed the importance of the Afro-Asian bloc in international affairs and became one of its leading spokesmen. During the first two decades of the Cold War he was recognized as one of the Third World's leading advocates of neutralism. In 1955 he played a prominent role in the Bandung Conference, a meeting of twenty-nine nonaligned Asian and African nations. Nehru's neutralist stance angered the Eisenhower administration, and especially Secretary of State John Foster Dulles. Nehru vigorously supported decolonialization in the Third World, opposed the formation of military alliances, and urged a moratorium on all nuclear testing. However, his reputation as an opponent of the use of force in international affairs was tainted by India's military clashes with Pakistan over the Kashmir region and its 1961 seizure of Goa, a Portuguese colony on the Indian coast. In 1962, after Indian forces were defeated by the Chinese in a short border war, Nehru turned to the West for military aid. In 1966, two years after Nehru's death, his daughter, Indira Gandhi, became India's prime minister.

Nitze, Paul H. (1907–), U.S. Cold War strategist and public official.

For over forty years and virtually the entire Cold War, Paul Nitze was one of the chief architects of U.S. policy toward the Soviet Union. A graduate of Harvard University and a successful Wall Street banker, Nitze entered government service in 1941. He was vice-chairman of the U.S. Strategic Bombing Survey (1944–46) and joined the policy planning staff of the State Department under George Kennan in 1949. He replaced Kennan in 1950 and served as head of the policy planning staff until 1953. In was in this capacity that Nitze became the main author of NSC 68, which recommended a massive program of American rearmament in order to meet the

Soviet challenge in the Cold War, a document with which he remained identified for the rest of his public life. He also was among those who advised President Truman to authorize development of the hydrogen bomb.

Nitze later served in important defense positions in the Kennedy and Johnson administrations. He was skeptical about fighting a land war in Vietnam from the start, and in 1968 warned newly appointed Secretary of Defense Clark Clifford (who had replaced Robert McNamara) that the war was distorting American foreign policy priorities and damaging its relations with its European allies. From 1969 to 1973 Nitze served on the American negotiating team in the SALT I negotiations. Fearing Soviet rearmament, he subsequently became a critic of détente and opposed ratification of the SALT II treaty (1979). Nitze then became Ronald Reagan's chief negotiator for the Intermediate-Range Nuclear Forces (INF) treaty (1981–84). He later served as a special advisor to the president and secretary of state on arms control.

Nixon, Richard Milhous (1913–94), vice president (1953–61) and thirty-seventh president of the United States (1969–74).

Richard Nixon's career was enmeshed in the waxing and waning of the Cold War for three decades. A native of California, Nixon graduated from Duke University law school and served in the navy during World War II. Nixon built his early career on the issue of anti-Communism. He was elected to Congress in 1946 after a campaign in which he used the anti-Communism issue to defeat his Democratic opponent. As a member of the House Committee on Un-American Activities, Nixon gained national attention by bringing to light evidence that led to the perjury conviction of Alger Hiss, a State Department official during the Roosevelt and Truman administrations who had been accused of spying for the Soviet Union. Nixon won election to the Senate in 1950 in a campaign in which he attacked his Democratic opponent and the Truman administration for failing to meet his anti-Communist standards. In the Senate, Nixon supported Douglas MacArthur and attacked the Truman administration's Asia policy. In 1952 he was elected vice president as Dwight D. Eisenhower's running mate. As vice president Nixon made frequent trips abroad. In 1958 he faced a violent mob in Venezuela that nearly overturned his car; his personal courage in the face of the mob won him applause. Nixon added to his formidable anti-Communist credentials in 1959 when he engaged in an informal "Kitchen Debate" at an American exhibition with Soviet leader Nikita Khrushchev.

John F. Kennedy narrowly defeated Nixon in his 1960 run for the presidency, winning by the closest margin in American history. However, Nixon remained active in the Republican Party and won its presidential nomination and the election against Hubert Humphrey, in another close contest, in 1968. During the campaign Nixon had said he had a "secret plan" to end the Vietnam War. However, his policy of "Vietnamization" proved to be a prolonged withdrawal that lasted until 1973. During that time the Nixon administration expanded the American military effort in into Laos and Cambodia, succeeding mainly in generating more antiwar sentiment in the United States. In fact, for Nixon and his national security advisor and later secretary of state Henry Kissinger, the Vietnam War was a painful distraction and impediment to their overall foreign policy. The Nixon-Kissinger foreign policy program was based on the recognition of a multipolar world that included as major players Western Europe, Japan, and the PRC as well as the United States and Soviet Union. As president, Nixon abandoned his old anti-Communism to seek détente with the Soviet Union and normal relations with the PRC, whose recognition by the United States he had staunchly opposed during the early days of the Cold War. Nixon's "opening" to China became official with a dramatic visit to that country in 1972. Negotiations with the Soviet Union on arms control began in 1969 and yielded the SALT I treaty in 1972. With the withdrawal from South Vietnam finally completed in January 1973, and his overwhelming reelection in hand, Nixon seemed primed for a triumphant second term. However, the Watergate scandal ultimately forced him to resign from office in disgrace in August 1974. During the two decades that followed as a private citizen, his writings and comments on foreign policy issues gradually improved his standing with the public, and he took on the status of an elder statesmen in certain circles both at home and abroad.

The North Atlantic Treaty Organization (NATO) was established on April 4, 1949, during the Berlin Blockade. One of the crucial buildingblocks of the American containment policy, NATO provided for the collective defense of its members; an attack on one was considered an attack against all. In 1949 the United States lacked any effective means of defending Western Europe from Soviet aggression. However, NATO still represented a vital commitment to its European allies at a time of great uncertainty. NATO ultimately became the main military instrument for containing the Soviet Union in Europe as well as an agent for encouraging closer economic, political, and social cooperation among its members. Its signing also marked the first time in its history that the United States entered a military alliance in peacetime. NATO's original members were the United States, Belgium, Canada, Denmark, France, Great Britain, Iceland, Italy, Luxembourg, the Netherlands, Norway, and Portugal. Greece and Turkey were admitted in 1952 and West Germany (the Federal Republic of Germany) in 1955. In 1966 France withdrew from NATO's military command, although it retained its political ties. No other membership changes took place in the alliance for the duration of the Cold War.

As part of its NATO commitment, the United States stationed a large military force in Western Europe, as well as nuclear weapons. The end of the Cold War and the collapse of the Soviet Union created the need for NATO to redefine its purpose and focus in a world lacking the threat that had originally brought the organization into existence.

Nuclear Weapons and Arms Control, a concern of the world's powers since the beginning of the Cold War.

The Cold War gave birth to the nuclear arms race, potentially the most deadly in history. The first atomic bombs dropped on Japan in 1945 demonstrated the overwhelming destructive power of nuclear weapons and the terrible threat posed to humanity by the possibility of nuclear war. At first the United States had a monopoly on nuclear weapons; this ended in the summer of 1949 when the Soviet Union exploded its first atomic bomb. By the mid-1950s, both the United States and the Soviet Union had developed fusion, or hydrogen, bombs whose power was measured in millions of tons of TNT, as against the tens of thousands of tons by which fission, or atomic, bombs were measured. At same time, both superpowers developed weapons to deliver their nuclear weapons, at first strategic bombers with ranges of thousands of miles and later ballistic missiles. The Soviet Union tested the world's first intercontinental ballistic missile in 1957, and that year used one of its huge new missiles to launch the world's first artificial satellite. By the 1960s the United States had more, and more accurate, missiles than the Soviets, including missiles that could be launched from submarines. Both sides also developed tactical nuclear weapons for use on battlefields, and as the Cold War wore on each side built thousands of nuclear weapons of various sorts. Meanwhile, other nations—Great Britain, France, the People's Republic of China, and India—developed nuclear weapons. Pakistan and Israel were also believed to have built such weapons, although this was not officially confirmed.

Early efforts at nuclear arms control were confounded by mutual suspicions among East and West. The first concrete step in nuclear arms control was taken in 1963 when the United States, the Soviet Union, and Great Britain signed the Nuclear Test Ban Treaty, which banned nuclear tests in the atmosphere. However, France and the People's Republic of China refused to sign the treaty and subsequently conducted atmospheric nuclear tests. In 1968 the Soviet Union and the United States submitted a treaty to the United Nations General Assembly designed to prevent the spread of nuclear weapons. Although more than a hundred countries ratified the treaty, a number of countries that intended to develop those weapons refused to sign.

The first treaty that placed any limits at all on nuclear weapons was the SALT I agreement, signed in 1972. It put temporary limits on both land-based intercontinental ballistic missiles (ICBMs) and submarine-launched missiles (SLBMs), and imposed strict limits on defensive antiballistic missile systems. However, it did not stop the modernization of offensive missiles and in particular did not ban development of missiles capable of carrying more than one nuclear warhead, missiles known as MIRVs (multiple independently targetable reentry vehicles). In short, SALT I slowed but did not stop the escalation of the arms race. In 1974, the superpowers signed a second agreement in the Soviet city of Vladivostok that lowered the numbers permitted in SALT I and added bombers to the list of covered weapons. That agreement became the basis of SALT II, which the two superpowers signed in 1979. That agreement, reached as détente was crumbling, was never ratified by either power, but both sides claimed to adhere to it. Arms control agreements that actually reduced the number of nuclear weapons had to await the advent of Mikhail Gorbachev and *perestroika*. The 1987 Intermediate-Range Nuclear Forces Treaty (INF) eliminated an entire class of nuclear weapons from European soil, which accounted for about 4 percent of the superpowers' arsenals. Within a year after the end of the Cold War, and just before the collapse of the Soviet Union, the superpowers signed the START (Strategic Arms Reduction Talks) I treaty, which provided for deep cuts in long-range weapons on both sides. START II, which called for even deeper cuts, was signed by the United States and the Russian Federation in 1993 but remains unratified by the Russians.

Potsdam Conference (July 17–August 2, 1945), the last major conference of World War II.

The Potsdam Conference took place between Germany's surrender and Japan's capitulation. Potsdam, a suburb of Berlin, was the former residence of Prussian and German kings. The three chief representatives were President Harry Truman of the United States, who had succeeded the late President Roosevelt in April; Premier Joseph Stalin of the Soviet Union; and Prime Minister Winston Churchill of Great Britain, who in turn was replaced by Clement Attlee after the Labour Party defeated the Conservatives in British parliamentary elections. The foreign ministers of all three Allied powers were also present.

The conferees managed to reach a number of agreements, but only after hard bargaining. Building on the Yalta agreements, they established an Allied Control Council composed of the military governors of the four occupation zones to oversee the occupation as a whole. Germany was to be treated as a "single economic unit," a formulation that reflected the American and British view that Europe's economic future depended on a healthy German economy. In fact, however, the Soviet Union in practice would reject that formulation. Meanwhile, the conferees found themselves deadlocked over almost every other issue. The Soviet Union's demand for $10 billion in reparations was rejected. The Americans and British reluctantly accepted the Oder-Neisse line as the temporary border between Germany and Poland, which meant large losses of German territory to Poland, inasmuch as Stalin already had turned that territory over to the Poles. The conferees also disagreed about Soviet policies in Poland, Soviet participation in control of the Black Sea straits, and a variety of other matters.

It was during the Potsdam Conference that President Truman received notice of the successful testing of the atomic bomb in the New Mexico desert. After informing Churchill, Truman eventually told Stalin the United States had a new weapon of enormous power. The Soviet leader, who knew about the American-British program to build the bomb through the Soviet spy network, reacted simply by saying he hoped it would be used against the Japanese. According to Churchill, news of the successful test boosted Truman's confidence in negotiations with Stalin; that alleged confidence, however, had little or no effect on the results of the conference. Another product of the conference was the Potsdam Declaration demanding Japan's unconditional surrender, which the Japanese ignored, setting the stage for the dropping of the atomic bomb on Hiroshima four days after the conference ended.

Perhaps the most important outcome of Potsdam was the impression it made on the conferees. President Truman left Potsdam convinced of the Soviets' aggressiveness; overall, disagreement and suspicion characterized the meeting. As a result, the Potsdam Conference marked a major step from wartime cooperation to Cold War confrontation.

Prague Spring, a brief flourishing of democratic reform in Czechoslovakia during 1968 under new Communist Party leader Alexander Dubček. The goal was to reform Soviet-style Marxism-Leninism and create a democratic socialist regime in Czechoslovakia. Dubček's efforts reflected the overwhelming sentiment in Czechoslovakia, which had been the only country in Eastern Europe to have a genuine democracy between World War I and World War II. The Prague Spring was crushed by the Soviet-led Warsaw Pact invasion of Czechoslovakia in August. Dubček and his associates were arrested and taken to Moscow, although they escaped the fate of Hungary's Imre Nagy, who was executed after Hungary's 1956 revolt against Communism, and were eventually allowed return home and live in anonymity. After the suppression of the Prague Spring, Moscow issued a statement saying that it would prevent any "socialist" regime from abandoning socialism for capitalism. This justification of intervention outside Soviet borders came to be called the Brezhnev Doctrine. Despite the shock and anger the crushing of the Prague Spring caused in the West, it only derailed the movement toward détente for a short period. However, in the long run, the Prague Spring intensified the conservative and antireformist attitudes that dominated the Brezhnev regime, which weakened rather than strengthened the Soviet Union and may ultimately have contributed to its collapse.

Reagan, Ronald Wilson (1911–), fortieth president of the United States (1981–89).

Ronald Reagan was a well-known actor before entering politics in the 1960s. By that time he had shed his former liberal views in favor of a staunchly conservative outlook, which included a deep aversion to Communism and the Soviet Union. After switching from the Democratic to the Republican Party, he was elected to two consecutive terms as governor of California (in 1966 and 1970) before being elected president in November 1980.

Before his election Reagan had been a vocal opponent of détente and the SALT II treaty, both of which in his judgment benefited the Soviet Union at the expense of the United States. He also criticized the defense policies of his two immediate predecessors, Ford and Carter, for supposedly compromising the military preparedness of the United States.

Reagan's election occurred in the wake of the fundamentalist Islamic revolution in Iran, the Soviet invasion of Afghanistan, and the crumbling of détente. His policies during his first term increased tensions with the Soviet Union, thereby contributing to what was called the "new Cold War." Reagan responded to the Soviet military buildup of the 1960s and 1970s by instituting the largest peacetime military buildup in history. That buildup included a controversial and expensive space-based defense system against nuclear weapons called the Strategic Defense Initiative (SDI), which was widely known as "Star Wars" after a popular science fiction movie. Reagan backed SDI despite criticism from many scientists that it was technologically unfeasible. In 1983, the same year he proposed SDI, he called the Soviet Union "the Evil Empire." However, Reagan did back new arms control negotiations aimed at reducing, as opposed to simply controlling, nuclear stockpiles. The Strategic Arms Reduction Talks (START) began in 1982. At the same time, the Reagan administration followed the so-called Reagan Doctrine, a policy of employing military force to overthrow Marxist regimes in the Third World. Reagan sent marines to the Caribbean island nation of Grenada in 1983 to remove a regime of radical Marxists that had just seized power from another group of Marxists in a bloody coup. He backed rebel forces (the Contras) battling the Marxist regime in Nicaragua. The United States also supplied weapons to Islamic rebels fighting a Soviet occupation force of 100,000 and the Marxist regime in Afghanistan.

A few months after Reagan began his second term, Mikhail Gorbachev came to power in the Soviet Union and the era of *perestroika* began. At this point Reagan, who had often asserted to his critics that he was willing to negotiate with the Soviets from a position of strength, shifted gears. Anti-Communism gave way to a pragmatic approach to a dramatic change in Soviet attitudes. Reagan met Gorbachev four times between 1985 and 1988. In December 1987 the two leaders signed the Intermediate-Range Nuclear Forces Treaty (INF) that eliminated all intermediate-range missiles from European soil. The INF was the first agreement that actually reduced the nuclear stockpiles of the superpowers. The last years of Reagan's presidency were disrupted by the Iran-Contra scandal. The scandal involved White House complicity in the illegal diversion of profits from arms-for-hostages with Iran to the U.S-supported Contra guerrillas fighting Nicaragua's Sandinista government. However, despite the scandal Reagan concluded his term as a highly popular president who was credited with a major role in winding down the Cold War.

Rhee, Syngman (1875–1965), president of South Korea (1948–60).

Rhee's struggle for Korean independence began before the turn of the century. It cost him several years in prison and forced him into exile in the United States for almost four decades. Rhee became South Korea's first president with American support in 1948. However, his dictatorial methods aroused considerable opposition while his opposition to land reform led to an uprising against his rule. Notwithstanding Soviet support for the North Korean regime, Rhee was determined to reunify Korea as a non-Communist country. Rhee was saved from disaster after the North Korean invasion of South Korea in 1950 by American intervention under United Nations auspices. However, he bitterly opposed talks for a cease fire that would leave Korea divided, just as it had been before the war began. His attempt to sabotage the cease-fire talks failed, but Rhee did win continued American military and economic support for his regime once the fighting ended. His authoritarian methods and his regime's corruption ultimately proved to be Rhee's undoing. His regime fell after fraudulent elections in 1960 caused nationwide student demonstrations. Rhee once again was forced into exile in the United States, where he spent the rest of his life.

Rusk, (David) Dean (1909–94), U.S. secretary of state (1961–69).

Born into a poor Georgia family, Rusk was educated at Davidson College before becoming a Rhodes Scholar at Oxford. His career in the State Department began in 1946 after several years of teaching and service in World War II as an aide to Gen. Joseph Stilwell, the commander of U.S. troops in the China-Burma-India theater. Rusk was a strong supporter of Chiang Kai-shek. After the Nationalist defeat by the Communists in China, Rusk, at the time assistant secretary of state for Far Eastern Affairs, summed up the American position on the PRC by rejecting its legitimacy. He called the Communist regime a "colonial Russian government" and labeled it as "not Chinese." From 1952 until 1961 he served as president of the Rockefeller Foundation.

In 1961 Rusk advised President Kennedy not to undertake the Bay of Pigs invasion because he believed, correctly it turned out, it would fail. In 1962 he was a member of Kennedy's "Ex-Comm" during the Cuban Missile Crisis, during which he apparently came close to a nervous breakdown. However, Rusk's long tenure as secretary of state in the Kennedy and Johnson administrations was dominated by the Vietnam War. A firm believer in the use of military force to prevent Communist aggression, he defended the war till the end. He argued that the battle against Communist forces in Vietnam really was a battle to contain Chinese Communism in Asia. Rusk taught international law at the University of Georgia after his term as secretary of state ended.

Sadat, Anwar al (1918–81), president of Egypt (1970–81).

Sadat became an active Egyptian nationalist during his days at the Abbasia Military Academy in the 1930s, when he first met Gamal Abdul Nasser. Sadat was imprisoned by the British for his activities as a German agent but escaped after two years. He was jailed again (1946–49) for terrorist acts against pro-British Egyptian officials. After taking part in the coup that overthrew King Farouk, Sadat served in a variety of positions before becoming Nasser's vice president in 1969. He became president on Nasser's death in 1970.

Once in office, Sadat surprised many observers with his policies. In 1971, which he called the "year of decision," he made a major diplomatic effort to break the Egyptian-Israeli deadlock over the Sinai Peninsula. No less an authority than Yitzhak Rabin later wrote in his memoirs that Israel may have missed an opportunity to achieve a breakthrough in peace negotiations that year. This was at least in part the result of Sadat's disappointment at the level of Soviet military aid, which was not sufficient to enable Egypt to attack Israel. In 1972 he expelled thousands of Soviet advisors in Egypt, although Egypt subsequently continued to receive Soviet military equipment. Still, Sadat had weakened Soviet influence in the Middle East significantly by denying them a base in Egypt.

Sadat used his Soviet equipment to launch the 1973 Yom Kippur War. Although Egyptian (and Syrian) forces ultimately suffered a decisive military defeat at Israeli hands, Egypt's initial battlefield victories made Sadat a hero in the Arab world. He followed that with his dramatic offer in 1977 to go to Jerusalem to negotiate a peace treaty with Israel. In a stroke Sadat had breached the united Arab front and discarded the policies of his mentor, Gamal Abdul Nasser, by recognizing Israel's right to exist. Long and difficult negotiations, under the auspices of President Jimmy Carter, finally yielded a framework for peace in the 1978 Camp David Accords. Sadat and Israeli prime minister Menachem Begin shared the 1978 Nobel Peace Prize for their achievement. A formal Egyptian-Israeli peace treaty followed in 1979. However, both Egypt and Sadat paid a high price for his willingness to make peace with the Israelis. Egypt was expelled from the Arab League and shunned by the rest of the Arab world. Sadat was called a traitor, and worse; he was assassinated by Muslim extremists opposed to peace with Israel in 1981.

Schmidt, Helmut (1918–), West German chancellor (1973–82).

Schmidt belonged to the Hitler Youth before World War II and served as a officer in the Germany army during the war. After the war he moved to the political left and became a member of the Social Democratic Party. Early in his political career his views placed him at the left wing of the party. Schmidt was critical of the United States and was opposed to placing American nuclear weapons in West Germany. However, his views moderated during the 1960s and he eventually became a firm supporter of a strong American presence in Western Europe and West Germany.

Schmidt became West German chancellor when Willy Brandt was forced to resign when one of his top aides was exposed as an East Germany spy in 1974. He continued Brandt's policy of *Ostpolitik* and promoted better ties with both East Germany and the Soviet Union. In 1975 he met with East German leader Erich Honecker, the first meeting between East and West German leaders. Schmidt also promoted West Germany's ties with France and economic cooperation among Western European nations while maintaining close relations with the United States. After the Soviet Union deployed its modern SS-20 intermediate-range missiles, Schmidt vigorously advocated and supported the deployment of American Pershing II and cruise missiles in Europe. Many members of his Social Democratic party strongly dissented from Schmidt's position on this issue. His government fell in 1982 when its coalition partner, the Free Democrats, switched sides and joined forces with the Christian Democratic Union led by Helmut Kohl.

Shevardnadze, Eduard (1927–), foreign minister of the Soviet Union (1985–90).

Aside from Mikhail Gorbachev, no man played a larger role in bringing the Cold War to a close than Shevardnadze. After rising through the ranks of the Communist Party, Shevardnadze served as the party boss in the Republic of Georgia from 1972 until Gorbachev brought him to Moscow to replace the venerable Cold War warhorse Andrei Gromyko as Soviet foreign minister in 1985. Shevardnadze then played a central role in formulating the "new thinking" on which Gorbachev's foreign policy was based. Gorbachev and Shevardnadze, mindful of the disastrous strain the Cold War was putting on the Soviet Union's economic and social fabric, rejected the idea of a foreign policy based on "class conflict" in favor of establishing a "normal" relationship with the rest of the world, including the United States and its allies. Shevardnadze managed the negotiations that led to the 1987 INF treaty and the Soviet withdrawal from Afghanistan. He was at the foreign-policy helm when the Soviet Union acquiesced in the collapse of Communism in Eastern Europe, the event that laid the Cold War to rest. In August 1990, just three months before the signing of the Charter of Paris marked the formal end of the Cold War, Shevardnadze joined with U.S. Secretary of State James Baker in condemning the Iraqi invasion of Kuwait.

Shevardnadze suddenly resigned his post in December 1990 in protest against Gorbachev's turn toward conservative forces within the Communist Party with the warning that a coup was in the making. After the unsuccessful coup against Gorbachev, Shevardnadze returned as foreign minister briefly as Gorbachev struggled vainly to preserve the crumbling Soviet Union. In 1992 Shevardnadze became president of his native Georgia, which was torn by civil war and secessionist movements. He has struggled since then to restore order to his troubled country.

Shultz, George Pratt (1920–), U.S. secretary of state (1982–89).

Shultz compiled a impressive record as an academic, labor mediator, businessman, and government official (serving in the Nixon administration as secretary of labor from 1969 to 1970 and secretary of the treasury from 1972 to 1974) before becoming secretary of state in 1982 under Ronald Reagan. Shultz's skills as a negotiator were a welcome addition to the Reagan administration, which tended during Reagan's first term to take a confrontational approach to many foreign policy issues. He was among those who urged restraint regarding Reagan's Strategic Defense Initiative, holding that its deployment would violate the 1972 antiballistic missile (ABM) treaty. Shultz was highly respected in many quarters, including the Middle East, where both Arabs and Israelis had confidence in his competence and fair-mindedness. His excellent working relationships with Soviet President Mikhail Gorbachev and Foreign Minister Eduard Shevardnadze helped facilitate the dramatic improvement in Soviet-American relations during Reagan's second term. Although he vigorously supported both the Reagan Doctrine and aid to the Contra rebels fighting the Sandinista regime in Nicaragua, Shultz strongly opposed the hostages-for-arms deal with Iran and was not implicated in the Iran-Contra scandal.

Sino-Soviet Split, division between the world's major Communist powers.

The victory of the Communists in China's civil war and the founding of the People's Republic of China changed the complexion of the Cold War. The shift of the world's most populous country into the Communist camp intensified the anti-Communist mood in the United States and soon was providing grist for McCarthyism. From the Soviet point of view, the Communist victory in China was more evidence that what Moscow called the "correlation of forces" increasingly favored the Communist camp. In February 1950 the two Communist giants signed the Sino-Soviet Treaty of Friendship and Alliance, a step that further increased anxiety in the United States.

However, behind the Marxist façade of supposedly fraternal socialist friendship lay old national rivalries and bitter political disputes about who should be the leader of world Communism. As early as 1956 the Chinese were concerned about Khrushchev's denunciation of Stalin. Other Khrushchev reforms also were viewed in Beijing as "revisionist," or non-Marxist. When Mao Zedong launched his Great Leap Forward toward full-fledged Communism in 1958, he in effect challenged the Soviet Union for leadership of the Communist bloc.

The Chinese, who in the wake of the Korean War were violently anti-American, also opposed Khrushchev's policy of peaceful coexistence. The Soviets meanwhile feared Mao's cavalier attitude toward nuclear war. Khrushchev was deeply unnerved when Mao told him that China could afford to lose millions of people in a nuclear war because such a war would destroy the United States and world capitalism.

These various disputes and disagreements gradually merged and by 1960 the Sino-Soviet split was out in the open. By the mid-1960s the two countries had heavily fortified their four-thousand-mile-long border, itself a serious issue because of Russian annexations of thousands of square miles of Chinese territory in the nineteenth century. In 1969 the Soviet Union and China fought a bloody full-scale battle along the Ussuri River in the Far East.

The Sino-Soviet split changed the complexion of the Cold War no less than the founding of the PRC, although this time in favor of the United States. The Communist world, supposedly a monolith, had been broken in half, even though most Communist regimes sided with the Soviets. Outside the Communist bloc, local Communist parties split into competing groups. Still, it took more than a decade and several changes in the occupant of the White House before the Nixon administration took advantage of the split to improve relations with China. By playing the "China Card," President Nixon and Secretary of State Henry Kissinger were able to put new pressure on the Soviet Union that helped pave the way for détente.

Southeast Asia Treaty Organization (SEATO), defensive alliance organized largely because of American initiatives after the Geneva Conference of 1954 ended the war in Vietnam between the French and the Communist Vietminh and divided the country at the 17th parallel. In addition to the United States, its members were Australia, France, Great Britain, Pakistan, the Philippines, and Thailand. One of several anti-Communist alliances sponsored by the United States, SEATO was envisioned as an Asian equivalent of NATO that would be capable of military action to thwart Communist expansion. However, Britain and France had no interest in such a commitment, and its Asian members were often preoccupied by other matters or local conflicts that had nothing to do with Communism. After lingering in a useless limbo for many years, the alliance finally was dissolved in 1976.

Stalin, Joseph Vissarionovich (1873–53), Communist leader and head of the Soviet Union (1924–53).

Stalin rose from impoverished beginnings in his native Georgia to become unchallenged dictator of one of the world's superpowers. His policies in Eastern Europe during the final months of World War II and in the immediate postwar period were the single greatest cause of the Cold War.

Stalin became converted to Marxism while a seminary student in Georgia and was expelled in 1899. In 1903 he joined the Bolshevik faction of the Russian Social Democratic Party, headed by Vladimir Lenin. He was arrested several times but always managed to secure his freedom one way or another. One of the many rumors about Stalin is that he had dealings with the tsarist secret police. Certainly a number of his revolutionary associates disliked and mistrusted him. However, Lenin was not one of them, and in 1912 he elevated Stalin to the central committee of the Bolshevik Party, which had evolved into an independent party molded by Lenin. Stalin occupied key posts and played a central role in the bitter struggle to retain power that followed the Bolshevik Revolution in November 1917. In 1922, with Lenin's support, he became the party's general secretary, which gave him control of the rapidly growing party bureaucracy and put his hands on key levers of power. Although Lenin soon turned against his former protégé, the old leader's declining health removed him from active political life by the end of 1922, and he died in 1924. By then Stalin already was the most powerful of Lenin's would-be successors; he won the subsequent struggle for power and emerged as the country's dictator by 1929.

In the decade after 1929 Stalin's policies transformed the Soviet Union into an industrial giant at the cost of millions of lives. Collectivization of agriculture and the resulting famine, which Stalin used to break the back of peasant resistance to collectivization, caused an estimated ten million deaths. The Great Purge Stalin launched in 1934 took millions more before he stopped it in 1938. The Soviet Union became the world's second leading industrial power behind the United States, but also a brutalized totalitarian state ruled by a dictator far more powerful than any tsar.

The rise of Nazi Germany increasingly turned Stalin's attention to foreign policy. In August 1939, in the wake of the failure to arrange a common front with the Western democracies against the Germans, the Soviet Union signed the notorious Nazi-Soviet nonaggression pact. The pact divided eastern Europe between the two totalitarian powers, and the Soviets carried out massive deportations in the Baltic and Polish territories that came under their control. For two years the Soviets were Hitler's helpful friends, delivering the raw materials the Nazi war machine needed. Stalin was stunned and temporarily incapacitated when the Germans invaded the Soviet Union, but he recovered and proved to be an able war leader. He demonstrated diplomatic skill at both the Teheran Conference (1943) and Yalta (1945). However, it was the presence of the victorious Soviet Red Army in Poland in Eastern Europe that made it impossible for President Roosevelt or Prime Minister Churchill to win significant concessions from Stalin at Yalta.

Stalin, with Foreign Minister Molotov as his diplomatic point man, used the fluid postwar situation to push Soviet control as far into Eastern and Central Europe as he could. Whether he was acting according to a preconceived plan, reacting to the opportunity created by the westward drive of the Red Army, responding to his indisputably increasing paranoia, or behaving according to some combination of the three is still debated by scholars. Apparently, Stalin believed he could impose Soviet control on the region without provoking a serious response from the United States and the other Western democracies. In this, of course, he was mistaken, and the result was the Cold War.

Another of Stalin's priorities in the immediate postwar era was for the Soviet Union to develop an atomic bomb; this was particularly urgent because with America's possession of the bomb, he said to a group of Russian scientists, "the balance has been broken." Of course, it was not only scientists but also spies that brought Soviet efforts to fruition several years earlier than anyone in the West expected. According to Nikita Khrushchev, Stalin lived in constant fear of the United States. Yet that did not keep him from probing where he suspected weak spots might exist, such as in Iran or Turkey in 1946. Recent research indicates that beginning in 1947, once Stalin became convinced that the Communists in China had a good chance of success and that the United States would not intervene, he sent significant amounts of aid to Mao's forces. It also is now clear that Stalin approved of and helped plan the Korean War, secure in what turned out to be the erroneous assumption that the United States would not intervene.

Given his growing paranoia, the thawing of the early Cold War freeze had to await his death. It came in March 1953 as the man historian Robert Conquest called the "breaker of nations" was planning yet another deadly purge.

Thant, U (1909–74), secretary general of the United Nations (1961–71).

A Burmese diplomat and his country's permanent delegate to the United Nations, Thant was became its secretary general in 1961 after his predecessor Dag Hammarskjöld's death in a plane crash. His selection was a compromise that reflected Cold War tensions. The Soviet Union wanted to replace the position of secretary general with a three-person body (dubbed a "troika" by the media). The Soviets, who had been extremely critical of Hammarskjöld, wanted to weaken the United Nations, which it considered a tool of the United States. The United States wanted to preserve a strong secretary general, which it considered vital to the effective functioning of the United Nations. Thant, from a neutral Asian country, was an alternative both superpowers could accept.

During his tenure, Thant dealt with a number of major crises, ranging from major Cold War issues to Third World conflicts. He is given credit for creating some maneuvering room that helped to defuse the Cuban Missile Crisis. His efforts were important in resolving the civil war in the Congo in 1963, placing a peacekeeping force on Cyprus in 1964, and achieving a cease-fire in the 1965 India-Pakistan war. However, in 1967, his immediate response to President Nasser's demand for removal of the UN peacekeeping force from the Sinai Peninsula in 1967, which probably surprised Nasser and certainly stunned the Israelis, was one of the sparks that ignited the Six-Day War. Thant failed in several attempts to bring about negotiations to end the Vietnam War. During his term in office he also faced a chronic problem of financing United Nations operations. Thant could have had another term as UN secretary general, but chose to retire in 1972.

Thatcher, Margaret (1925–), prime minister of Great Britain (1979–90).

The daughter of a greengrocer, Margaret Thatcher rose to become the leader of Great Britain's Conservative Party, the country's first woman prime minister and its longest serving prime minister in the twentieth century. Before turning to the law and politics, Thatcher studied chemistry and worked as a research chemist. She was elected to Parliament in 1959 and gradually rose to a position of prominence in the Conservative Party, holding a number of government posts in the 1960s and 1970s. During the mid-1970s she was a critic of détente.

Even before she became prime minister Thatcher was known as the "Iron Lady." She demonstrated that she deserved the term when she began dismantling parts of the British welfare state, which she believed was responsible for the country's poor economic performance and stagnating standard of living. Her policy of moving Britain from a welfare state to a free-market economy became known as "Thatcherism" or the "Thatcher Revolution." It included reduced government spending and lower taxes, the privatization of state-owned industries and utilities, and facing down the country's powerful trade unions. Her domestic policies had admirers, who felt they increased Britain's economic competitiveness, and critics, who felt they placed on unfair burden on the working classes and the poor.

Thatcher was no less the Iron Lady in foreign affairs. In 1980 she vigorously supported the basing of American Pershing II ballistic missiles and cruise missiles in Britain. Thatcher strongly supported the United States on most international issues and was a great admirer of President Ronald Reagan, a sentiment he returned in full. In 1986 she allowed the United States to use bases in Britain to bomb Libya in retaliation for Libyan terrorist attacks against American personnel in Europe. On other fronts, in 1980 and 1981 Thatcher stood up to international pressure and refused to make concessions to Catholic militants in Northern Ireland, even as ten hunger strikers in British prisons starved themselves to death. (In 1985 she reached a historic agreement with the Republic of Ireland, giving it a consulting role in governing Northern Ireland.) In 1982 she sent a naval task force to retake the Falkland Islands off South America, which had been seized by Argentina, a action that boosted her popularity and helped her and the Conservatives retain power in the 1983 elections. Another major landmark of the Thatcher years was the 1984 agreement to return Hong Kong to Chinese sovereignty in 1997.

It was Margaret Thatcher who, upon meeting the up-and-coming Soviet politician Mikhail Gorbachev in December 1984, said that she had finally found a "Communist I can do business with." The next year, when he visited Britain as part of his international goodwill trip, the longtime anti-Soviet Thatcher called Gorbachev a "friend." Still, Thatcher continued to urge that the West proceed carefully in its negotiations with the Soviets. By the late 1980s the negative aspects of "Thatcherism," including a growing trade deficit and a variety of economic and political problems, were catching up to the Iron Lady. Her popularity had declined drastically and she faced a strong challenge for leadership of the Conservative party and hence for the post of prime minister. She resigned in November 1990.

Third World, Cold War designation, coined by Chinese Communist leader Mao Zedong, referring to the technologically less advanced parts of Asia, Africa, and Latin America. Third World countries are generally poor and have economies distorted by dependence on the export of agricultural products and raw materials in return for manufactured products from the developed nations. These nations also tend to have high rates of illiteracy and disease, rapid population growth, and unstable governments. During the Cold War the term "Third World" was generally intended to distinguish nonaligned nations formerly dominated by colonial powers from the United States and developed nations aligned with it (the First World) and the Soviet bloc (the Second World). Politically the Third World emerged at the Bandung Conference (1955) and now ranks as the largest group in the United Nations. Since the end of the Cold War the term has retained currency to designate poverty-stricken, underdeveloped countries. A number of nations—such as the newly industrialized nations of East Asia, among them Taiwan and South Korea, and the oil-rich states of the Middle East—have developed in recent decades to the point where they no longer are part of the Third World.

Tito, Josef Broz (1892–1980), Communist dictator of Yugoslavia (1945–80).

Born Josip Broz, Tito was the son of a Croatian blacksmith. His mother was a Slovene. Tito was converted to Communism after being captured during World War I and taken to Russia, where he witnessed the Bolshevik Revolution and fought on the Bolshevik side during that country's civil war. He spent part of the 1930s in the Soviet Union and witnessed Stalin's Great Purge, which almost certainly made him wary of the Soviet dictator. During World War II Tito led a Communist guerrilla group against the German occupiers. His partisan forces were more successful than the non-Communist "Chetniks" and therefore received Allied support. After the war, Tito abolished the Yugoslav monarchy, ruthlessly suppressed all non-Communist opposition, and established a Communist dictatorship.

Tito was a militant Communist and a loyal servant of Stalin and the Soviet Union until 1948. However, unlike the leaders of other Communist rulers in Eastern Europe (with the exception of Albania), Tito was an independent force who had come to power largely on his own and was not Stalin's puppet. Among policies that bothered Stalin was Yugoslavia's support of Communist guerrillas in Greece. However, the real problem was Tito's independence, which set an example the paranoid Soviet dictator could not tolerate. Tension grew until Stalin expelled the Yugoslav Communist Party from the Cominform (Communist Information Bureau, a Soviet-created international organization of Communist parties), and hence from the Soviet bloc.

Tito survived Stalin's attempts to depose him and for the next three decades became a unique international phenomenon. His regime received Western aid, as the United States, in contrast to its attitude vis-à-vis China, decided to exploit the differences between the Soviet Union and an independent Communist state. Tito also became one of the most prominent leaders of the nonaligned nations, along with Nehru of India and Nasser of Egypt. At the same time he continued his support for revolutionary Communist movements in the Third World and, after Stalin's death, patched up some of his quarrels with the Soviet Union. However, the Warsaw Pact invasion of Czechoslovakia once again embittered Yugoslav-Soviet relations. Over time Tito liberalized internal economic policies and relaxed political restrictions so Yugoslavia became by far the world's least repressive Communist regime.

But Tito did little to improve the relations between the quarrelsome ethnic groups that made up Yugoslavia, relying mainly on his dictatorial rule and divide and conquer tactics to keep order. He prevented any other politician from establishing the stature needed to succeed him. Tito therefore bears some responsibility for the disintegration of his country and the disasters that befell many of its people a decade after his death.

Truman, Harry S. (1884–1972), thirty-third president of the United States (1945–53).

Harry Truman succeeded to the presidency on the death of Franklin Roosevelt on April 12, 1945, at a critical time in American history and with almost no preparation for the job. Although he was Roosevelt's vice president, he was not part of Roosevelt's inner circle and therefore was uninformed on most vital policy matters. It fell to Truman to bring World War II to a close, make the decision about using the atomic bomb against Japan, see to the establishment of the United Nations, and formulate a foreign policy in the immediate postwar era as the wartime alliance against Germany dissolved and the Cold War began. Although Truman has his detractors, the growing consensus among historians is that he acquitted himself well, if not with distinction.

Truman grew up in modest circumstances in Missouri, served in World War I as an artillery officer, and briefly went into business before entering politics in the early 1920s. Although he was associated with the corrupt Pendergast political machine, Truman was known as an honest and efficient politician. A avid supporter of the New Deal, he was elected to the Senate in 1934 and again in 1940. During the war he earned a national reputation for heading a Senate committee investigating government war contracts and was selected to be Roosevelt's running mate in 1944. Germany surrendered less than a month after Truman's inauguration as president. A month later Truman attended the Potsdam Conference, where he and Winston Churchill (and after the Labour Party victory in national elections Clement Attlee) attempted unsuccessfully to negotiate a satisfactory postwar settlement with Soviet leader Joseph Stalin. While at Potsdam Truman was notified of the successful testing of the atomic bomb and authorized its use against Japan.

Truman faced a series of foreign policy crises beginning in 1946 that culminated in the containment policy. Containment began in 1947 when the Greek civil war led to the proclamation of the Truman Doctrine. Over the next two years the continuing economic crisis in Western Europe called forth the Marshall Plan, while the Berlin Blockade and the necessity of assuring the European democracies of America's commitment to their defense produced NATO. The Communist victory in China in 1949 and the Soviet Union's successful testing of an atomic bomb led Truman to call for a reevaluation of American defense needs. Before Truman could act, he was faced in 1950 with the Korean War, the event that led directly to a massive increase in U.S. defense spending and rearmament. Truman also authorized the development of the hydrogen bomb.

On the domestic front, Truman had to deal with the rising tide of anti-Communist hysteria and McCarthyism. Despite instituting a loyalty program for checking on government employees, Truman's administration was furiously attacked for its alleged failure to stop Communist expansion abroad and prevent Communist infiltration of the government at home. Truman dismissed charges of internal subversion as a "red herring" and denounced the House Committee on Un-American Activities as the "most un-American thing in America" for violating the constitutional rights of the people it investigated. Truman also did what he could to promote more New Deal policies under his Fair Deal program, but was severely limited when the Republicans won control of Congress in the 1946 elections.

In 1948 Truman won reelection in one of the greatest upsets in American history. However, his popularity declined drastically during his second term and he left office with an extremely low approval rating in the polls. History and historians have been much kinder to him since then. Recently released documents from Soviet archives have tended to support his decisions that implemented containment. Instead of being held responsible for starting the Cold War, Truman is increasingly viewed as having come up with the necessary response to a dangerous situation in which the security of the United States and Western Europe was at risk.

Truman Doctrine, the first major expression of the American policy of containing Communist expansion.

On March 12, 1947, Harry Truman told the United States Congress, "I believe it must be the policy of the United States to support free peoples who are resisting attempted aggression by armed minorities or outside pressure." This policy became known as the Truman Doctrine.

In that speech to Congress, Truman requested $400 million in aid for Greece and Turkey. The government of Greece was threatened by Communist guerrillas and was about to lose the support of Great Britain, whose government had just informed Truman that it could no longer afford to underwrite the tottering Greek regime. Turkey was also under the Soviet shadow, although Soviet pressure there had decreased since 1946. Still, even some of Truman's close advisors said he was exaggerating the situation as it existed at the moment. But the President had been told by Republican Senator Arthur Vandenberg, who supported the aid package, that he would have to "scare the hell out of the American people" in order to get Congress to provide the funds he needed. That is what Truman tried to do, drawing a distinction between two ways of life, one based on freedom and the other on tyranny. Congress approved Truman's request in May, beginning the process that evolved into the overall policy of containment.

Ulbricht, Walter (1893–1973), Communist leader of the German Democratic Republic (East Germany) (1950–71).

The son of a tailor who was an active socialist, Walter Ulbricht joined the German Communist Party after World War I. He fled Nazi Germany in 1933 and went to Moscow, returning to his shattered homeland with victorious Red Army troops in 1945. A hard-line Communist and devout Stalinist, Ulbricht became the party's general secretary and leader of East Germany in 1950, a year after the Soviet satellite regime was set up. He was in charge when East Berlin revolted against harsh living and working conditions. Soviet tanks had to be called in to restore order at the cost of many dead and injured.

Ulbricht's hard-line views led him to oppose normalization of relations with West Germany. His main claim to fame is the building of the Berlin Wall in 1961 to stop the flight of thousands of refugees, many of them skilled young people, to West Berlin. Ulbricht continued to get along well with the Soviet Union and sent East German troops to support the Soviet-led invasion of Czechoslovakia in 1968. However, he became a liability when the Soviet Union, enticed by Willy Brandt's willingness to accept Soviet-drawn postwar borders and other concessions, began pushing the East Germans toward normalization with West Germany. Ulbricht therefore was replaced as East German general secretary by Erich Honecker.

United Nations, international organization founded in April 1945, as World War II was ending and the Cold War was beginning. It replaced the League of Nations, which had proved largely powerless and failed to prevent the outbreak of World War II. The term "United Nations" originally referred to the countries allied in fighting against the Axis powers during World War II. The United Nations' main purpose is to promote international peace and prevent war. It is governed by a General Assembly of all its members. A Security Council—a fifteen-member body in which five major powers (the United States, Russia, China, Britain, and France) have permanent seats and veto power and ten seats are filled by other nations for two-year terms—deals with a variety of major crises and immediate threats to peace. The Secretariat, headed by the secretary general, serves as the organization's executive. The International Court of Justice rules on a variety of disputes between states. A large number of specialized agencies deal with a variety of humanitarian, developmental, education, communications, and other matters of international concern.

During the Cold War United Nations agencies were active in improving conditions in many countries and the organization successfully promoted international cooperation on matters such as the peaceful use of atomic energy and arms limitation on the international seabed. Its peacekeeping forces were able to control violence in a number of localized disputes. The UN's most notable intervention was in the Korean War, when the Soviet absence from the Security Council enabled that body to commit the organization to the defense of South Korea. However, the same Cold War tensions that kept the superpowers apart generally relegated the United Nations to a secondary role in most major world crises. Inside the United Nations, both the General Assembly and the Security Council were often divided by the larger Cold War struggle that dominated so many world arenas.

Vance, Cyrus Roberts (1917–), U.S. secretary of state (1977–80).

A respected international lawyer, Vance served in a number of defense-related and diplomatic posts before becoming secretary of state under Jimmy Carter. Vance disagreed with national security advisor Zbigniew Brzezinski, with Vance favoring flexibility and détente in dealing with the Soviet Union and Brzezinski taking a harder line. The shifting balance between the two men in the struggle to influence the president brought inconsistency to Carter's foreign policy. The Iranian revolution and the coming to power of Islamic fundamentalists in that country in 1979 both disrupted Carter's conduct of foreign policy and led to Vance's leaving his post. In November of 1979 Iranian students stormed the American embassy in Teheran and took its personnel hostage. Vance opposed the military attempt to rescue hostages in April 1980 and resigned when the mission failed.

Vandenberg, Arthur Hedrick (1884–1951), U.S. senator and chairman of the Senate Committee on Foreign Relations (1946–51).

Vandenberg was born in Michigan and was a newspaper reporter and editor before being appointed to the Senate as a Republican in 1928. Before the Japanese bombing of Pearl Harbor he was an isolationist. His view then began to change and he strongly supported President Roosevelt's wartime policies. After 1945 he was a leading proponent of a bipartisan foreign policy and the internationalist stance of President Truman. Vandenberg was a

U.S. delegate to the founding conference of the United Nations and in 1946 a delegate to the UN General Assembly. He played a crucial role in winning support for the Truman Doctrine, the Marshall Plan, and NATO. Although he fell terminally ill with cancer, Vandenberg continued efforts on behalf of an Truman's foreign policy into 1951. When asked about his support for a Democratic administration, Vandenberg explained, "Politics ends at the water's edge."

Vietnam War, conflict in Southeast Asia from the mid-1950s to the mid-1970s between the United States and the government of South Vietnam on one side and North Vietnam and Communist guerrillas in South Vietnam on the other. The war also spread into Laos and Cambodia, the two other countries of Indochina. The Vietnam War was the longest war in United States history, its most unsuccessful and frustrating conflict, and its most serious defeat in the Cold War.

The United States first became involved in Vietnam in 1950 when it began supporting France's effort to defend its colonial presence in Vietnam. After the French defeat by the Communist-dominated Vietminh and the Geneva Conference of 1954, the United States, in an effort to contain Communism in Southeast Asia, supported an anti-Communist regime headed by Ngo Dinh Diem in South Vietnam.

What followed was increasing American involvement in the effort to sustain the corrupt and unpopular Diem regime, which by the early 1960s was tottering in the face of a guerrilla war fought by guerrillas called the Viet Cong but organized and supplied by Ho Chi Minh's regime in North Vietnam. The United States approved Diem's overthrow (but not his execution) by military officers in 1963, but the hoped-for effective South Vietnamese government did not materialize. By then, as a result of increased commitment by the Kennedy administration, more than sixteen thousand American military advisors were in Vietnam. The continued failure of a succession of South Vietnamese governments to cope with the Communist insurgency eventually led to the commitment of U.S. combat troops in 1965. American escalation—190,000 U.S. troops in Vietnam by 1966, 550,000 by 1969—was matched by North Vietnamese escalation. In fact, North Vietnamese regulars were introduced in the South in 1964, a year before U.S. troops.

The war in Vietnam deeply divided the United States at home. The failure to defeat the North Vietnamese and the Viet Cong; the spread of antiestablishment sentiment among young people, especially on college campuses; the graphic coverage of the fighting by the media; and the exposure of deception by successive administrations regarding what was happening in Vietnam all undermined support for the war. Opposition at home and the failure to secure a battlefield victory persisted through the Johnson and Nixon administrations. Neither massive bombing of both South and North Vietnam nor expansion of the war into Cambodia and Laos to interdict North Vietnamese supply routes could bring the war to a successful conclusion. By the time the United States finally withdrew from Vietnam its losses had reached over 58,000 dead and 300,000 wounded. Hundreds of thousands of other U.S. soldiers became addicted to drugs while in Vietnam and had great difficulty in adjusting to civilian life after returning home. Attitudes also changed among the general population, as skepticism about the truthfulness of the government spread and traditional authority was undermined. The war also led to less willingness on the part of later U.S. administrations to undertake foreign commitments, a development that had both supporters and critics. Nor did the enormous American effort in Vietnam prevent a Communist takeover once U.S. soldiers left. The North Vietnamese overran South Vietnam and unified the country in 1975. Communist regimes also came to power in Laos and Cambodia.

Waldheim, Kurt (1918–), secretary general of the United Nations (1972–81), president of Austria (1982–86).

An Austrian, Waldheim served in the German army during World War II and entered diplomatic service after the war. During his tenure at the helm of the United Nations the crises he faced included the 1973 Arab-Israeli war, the Soviet invasion of Afghanistan, and the Iranian hostage crisis. Waldheim's reputation was permanently tarnished in 1986 when documents came to light demonstrating his participation in Nazi atrocities against Jews during World War II. Notwithstanding his denials, the United States labeled Waldheim a suspected war criminal and barred him from entering the country.

Walesa, Lech (1943–), Polish labor leader and president of Poland (1990–96).

Walesa was an electrician and labor activist in the Lenin Shipyard in Gdansk before rising to prominence in 1980 as the leader of Solidarity, the first independent labor union in the history of the Communist bloc. As head of Solidarity he displayed great skill and courage in dealing with Poland's Communist regime during 1980 and 1981. He was jailed when the Polish regime cracked down on and disbanded Solidarity in December 1981 but was released in 1982. In 1983, to the dismay of the Polish government, Walesa was awarded the Nobel Peace Prize. His leadership was crucial in keeping pressure on the Polish government over the next several years. In 1989, faced with widespread passive resistance and with the country's economy in tatters, the Polish government finally yielded; it legalized Solidarity and allowed it to run candidates and campaign in elections to the lower house of parliament. Solidarity's overwhelming victory led to the creation of a coalition government under its leadership, Poland's first non-Communist government of the post–World War II era. The events in Poland in 1989 were part of the earthquake that shattered Communist rule in Eastern Europe that year and led to the end of the Cold War. Walesa, who did not take a post in the government formed in 1989, ran successfully for Poland's presidency in 1990.

Warsaw Pact (Warsaw Treaty Organization), the Soviet-dominated alliance set up in 1955 as a counter to NATO. NATO and Warsaw Pact forces, armed with nuclear weapons, then faced each other in Europe until the end of the Cold War. The Soviet decision to set up the alliance was in part a response to the rearming of West Germany and its admission to NATO. The Warsaw Pact's original members, aside from the Soviet Union, were Albania, Bulgaria, Czechoslovakia, East Germany, Hungary, Poland, and Romania. The initial treaty was binding for twenty years. A unified military command was established in Moscow. By 1962 Albania was no longer an active participant in the alliance; it withdrew officially in 1968, the same year Warsaw Pact forces crushed the Prague Spring in Czechoslovakia. The collapse of Communism in Eastern Europe in 1989 turned the Warsaw Pact into a lifeless hulk. It was officially disbanded in 1991.

Yalta Conference, held on February 4–11, 1945, marked the last meeting of the Big Three leaders—Roosevelt, Churchill, and Stalin—who led the main Allied powers during World War II. President Roosevelt survived the Yalta Conference by only two months, and Churchill fell from power as a result of British elections held five months later. Yalta also was the last conference before the end of the war in Europe and, arguably, the event where the first real chills of the approaching Cold War were felt. The debates surrounding Yalta—especially over whether Roosevelt and Churchill yielded too much to Stalin—probably were unavoidable given the magnitude of the disappointment in the Western democracies with the tense and unsatisfactory peace that followed the great sacrifices of World War II. At the same time, those debates were intensified by the fact that most of the important decisions made at Yalta remained secret until the end of the war for military and political reasons. The complete text of all the agreements was not disclosed until 1947. In particular, the secrecy surrounding the Yalta agreements fed suspicions in militant anti-Communist circles in the United States, where accusations were made that a "betrayal" had taken place that had turned the people of Eastern Europe over to Communist control. Those who believed in the "Yalta Betrayal" were not swayed by certain unavoidable geopolitical realities. They stemmed from the fortunes of war that by 1945 that had left Eastern and Central Europe under the control of the Red Army and the United States convinced it needed Soviet cooperation in the upcoming final struggle with Japan.

The Yalta conferees reached several important agreements. They confirmed the decision made at the Casablanca Conference—the other Big Three wartime meeting—demanding Germany's unconditional surrender. They agreed to a four-power occupation of Germany, to hold war-crimes trials of leading Nazis, and to found the United Nations. Unable to agree on the question of German reparations, the conferees left that matter open for future negotiations. Secret agreements at Yalta included the Soviet pledge to enter the war against Japan three months after Germany's surrender and provisions for Soviet gains in the Far East at the expense of Japan and China. The conferees also agreed on the general outline for Poland's postwar borders, which included losses of territory to the Soviet Union in the east and gains at the expense of Germany in the West.

However, it was Poland, which Churchill called the "most urgent reason for the Yalta Conference," that brought the big chill to Yalta. The paper-thin agreement regarding the composition of the Polish government that the Soviets had unilaterally established in January hardly covered up the deep disagreement about Poland's future. Would Poland be "mistress of her own house and captain of her soul," as Churchill put it, or would what Stalin called the "question of security" for the Soviet Union dominate Poland's house and oppress her soul? The Soviets, whose Red Army occupied Poland, made it clear within months of Yalta that the "question of security" would prevail. This was unacceptable to Great Britain and the United States. Meanwhile, the forward thrust of Soviet control into Poland and the rest of Eastern Europe raised fears over the future of Western Europe. The chill that began at Yalta began to deepen and the postwar peace soon was encrusted in the frosts of the Cold War.

PART III

Concise Chronology

It is impossible to fix an opening date for the Cold War. The most commonly accepted date is February 1945, when the Yalta Conference took place. That is the starting point of this chronology. However, some important events to keep in mind took place prior to that date:

- November 7, 1917: the Bolshevik Revolution begins in Russia
- November 17, 1933: the United States recognizes the Soviet Union
- September 30, 1938: Britain and Germany sign the Munich agreement
- August 23, 1939: the Nazi-Soviet nonaggression pact is signed
- August 10, 1941: the United States and Britain announce the Atlantic Charter
- June 22, 1941: Germany invades the Soviet Union
- June 6, 1944: the Western Allies land in France (D-Day)
- January 17, 1945: Soviet forces take Warsaw

1945

FEBRUARY 4–12: Yalta Conference attended by Roosevelt, Churchill, and Stalin.

APRIL 12: Roosevelt dies. Harry S. Truman becomes president of the United States.

APRIL 23: Truman scolds Soviet foreign minister Molotov for Soviet violations of the Yalta agreements.

APRIL 25: Founding conference of the United Nations begins.

MAY 8: World War II ends in Europe (V-E Day).

JULY 16: The United States successfully tests the world's first atomic bomb.

JULY 17–AUGUST 2: Potsdam Conference attended by Truman, Churchill, and Stalin. Attlee replaces Churchill during the conference.

AUGUST 6: United States drops an atomic bomb on Hiroshima, Japan. It drops a second bomb on Nagasaki on August 9.

AUGUST 14: Japan surrenders unconditionally, ending World War II (V-J Day). The official surrender date is September 2.

1946

FEBRUARY 9: Stalin gives hard-line, anti-Western speech in Moscow, saying the Communist and capitalists worlds are fundamentally incompatible.

FEBRUARY 22: George Kennan sends his Long Telegram to Washington. His analysis will become the basis of the U.S. containment policy.

FEBRUARY: Soviet nuclear spy ring broken in Canada.

MARCH 5: Churchill delivers his "Iron Curtain" speech in Fulton, Missouri.

MARCH 25: In response to Western pressure, the Soviet Union announces it will withdraw its troops from northern Iran.

MAY 26: Czechoslovakia holds free elections, the country's last for forty-four years.

AUGUST: Truman sends an aircraft carrier to the eastern Mediterranean to protect Turkey from Soviet pressure.

SEPTEMBER: Civil war between the British-supported government and Communist guerrillas begins in Greece.

NOVEMBER 25: Truman establishes the Presidential Temporary Commission on Employee Loyalty, better known as the Loyalty Commission.

DECEMBER 19: Communist forces led by Ho Chi Minh begin armed struggle against the French, marking the start of the first Indochina war.

1947

JANUARY 1: United States and Britain combine their occupation zones in Germany to create "Bizonia."

FEBRUARY 21: Britain informs the United States it can no longer provide aid to Greece and Turkey.

MARCH 12: President Truman asks Congress for $400 million for aid to Greece and Turkey. His speech outlines the policy that comes to be called the Truman Doctrine.

JUNE 5: Secretary of State Marshall, speaking at Harvard University, proposes the policy that comes to be called the Marshall Plan.

JULY: The journal *Foreign Policy* publishes "Sources of Soviet Conduct," by "X." The author is George Kennan, who uses the word "containment" to describe his proposed policy for dealing with the Soviet Union.

JULY 26: Truman signs the National Security Act, which is intended to unify the armed forces under the Department of Defense. The act also establishes the Central Intelligence Agency (CIA), National Security Council (NSC), and Joint Chiefs of Staff (JCS).

OCTOBER 18: The House Un-American Activities Committee (HUAC) opens its investigation into Communist infiltration of Hollywood's movie industry.

DECEMBER: Civil war begins in China.

1948

FEBRUARY 25: Communist coup takes place in Czechoslovakia when President Eduard Benes is pressured into appointing a Communist-dominated government under Clement Gottwald. Foreign Minister Jan Masaryk is murdered two weeks later.

MARCH 17: France, Britain, and the Benelux countries sign the Treaty of Brussels, a defense pact clearly aimed at the Soviet Union.

MARCH 31: Congress approves the Marshall Plan. It establishes the Economic Cooperation Administration to operate the plan a few days later.

JUNE 24: The Soviet Union halts land traffic from the West to West Berlin, beginning the Berlin Blockade.

JUNE 28: Yugoslavia is expelled from the Cominform, marking the first split in the Communist bloc.

AUGUST 3: Whittaker Chambers tells HUAC that former State Department official Alger Hiss was a Communist during the 1930s, also accusing Hiss of espionage on behalf of the Soviet Union.

NOVEMBER 2: In a major upset, President Truman wins reelection over Republican candidate Thomas E. Dewey.

1949

JANUARY 22: Chinese Communist forces occupy Beijing.

APRIL 4: Twelve Western nations, including the United States, sign the North Atlantic Treaty establishing NATO, the first time in its history that the United States enters a peacetime alliance.

MAY 12: Soviet Union ends the Berlin Blockade.

MAY 23: Konrad Adenauer proclaims the Federal Republic of Germany (West Germany).

AUGUST 29: The Soviet Union tests its first atomic bomb, developed with American atomic secrets supplied by Soviet spies.

SEPTEMBER 23: President Truman announces the Soviet Union has exploded an atomic bomb. The test was detected by the U.S. Air Force on September 3.

OCTOBER 1: Mao Zedong proclaims the People's Republic of China.

NOVEMBER 1 (APPROXIMATELY): The Soviet Union begins development of a thermonuclear, or hydrogen, bomb.

1950

JANUARY 21: Alger Hiss is convicted of perjury.

JANUARY 31: Responding to the shock of the Soviet atomic test, Truman announces the decision to speed up work on a thermonuclear bomb. He is unaware of Soviet research begun about two months earlier.

FEBRUARY 9: In Wheeling, West Virginia, Senator Joseph R. McCarthy accuses the State Department of harboring Communists. He claims to have a list of 205 Communists in the department.

FEBRUARY 14: Sino-Soviet Treaty of Friendship, Alliance, and Mutual Assistance is signed in Moscow.

APRIL 25: President Truman approves NSC 68, which calls for a massive military buildup in light of the fall of China and Soviet development of the atomic bomb.

JUNE 25: North Korea invades South Korea, beginning the Korean War.

JUNE 27: Truman announces the United States will send air and naval forces to defend South Korea. The UN Security Council passes a U.S.-sponsored resolution calling for the defense of South Korea.

JUNE 30: Truman announces the United States will send ground forces to Korea. He extends the draft for another year.

SEPTEMBER 15: General Douglas MacArthur carries out a successful amphibious landing at Inchon. South Korea quickly is cleared of North Korean forces.

OCTOBER 7: United Nations forces cross the 38th parallel into North Korea. The UN General Assembly passes a resolution calling for a united and democratic Korea.

NOVEMBER 25–26: After probing actions beginning in October, Communists Chinese forces launch massive intervention in Korea.

1951

MARCH 29: Julius and Ethel Rosenberg and Morton Sobol are convicted of passing nuclear secrets to the Soviet Union.

APRIL 11: Truman dismisses General MacArthur as commander of UN forces in Korea, replacing him with General Matthew Ridgeway.

MAY 25: Guy Burgess and Donald Maclean, British Foreign office officials who are also Soviet spies, slip out of Britain. They surface in the Soviet Union several years later.

JULY 10: Armistice talks begin in Korea.

SEPTEMBER 8: The United States and Japan sign a mutual security treaty in San Francisco.

1952

FEBRUARY 23: The NATO countries announce a plan to create an army of fifty divisions.

OCTOBER 3: Britain tests its first atomic bomb.

NOVEMBER 1: The United States tests the world's first thermonuclear device, with a yield of ten megatons.

NOVEMBER 4: Dwight D. Eisenhower is elected president of the United States.

1953

MARCH 5: Joseph Stalin dies. A struggle for power in the Soviet Union begins.

MARCH 6: Georgi Malenkov becomes Soviet premier and first secretary of the Soviet Communist Party.

MARCH 14: Malenkov is forced by his colleagues to give up the post of first secretary. It goes to Nikita Khrushchev.

JUNE 17: German workers in East Berlin strike and riot against increased output requirements and shortages of basic goods. The riots spread across Germany and are put down by Soviet troops.

JUNE 19: Julius and Ethel Rosenberg are executed, despite widespread protests that their sentence is unwarranted.

JULY 27: The United States and North Korea sign an armistice, ending the fighting in Korea.

AUGUST 12: The Soviet Union tests a version of a thermonuclear bomb. However, despite Soviet claims, it is not a full-fledged thermonuclear weapon, or "superbomb."

1954

JANUARY 21: The United States launches the *Nautilus*, the world's first nuclear-powered submarine.

MARCH 1: The United States explodes its first deliverable thermonuclear bomb on Bikini Island in the Pacific. It has a yield of 15 megatons.

APRIL 22: The Army-McCarthy hearings begin in Washington, D.C.

APRIL 26: The Geneva Conference on the war in Indochina opens.

MAY 7: In Vietnam, the French fortress of Dienbienphu falls to Vietminh forces.

JUNE 18: A CIA-sponsored coup overthrows President Jacobo Arbenz of Guatemala.

AUGUST 19: A CIA-sponsored coup in Iran overthrows the government led by nationalist premier Mohammed Mossadegh.

SEPTEMBER 8: The Southeast Asia Treaty Organization (SEATO) is established in Manila.

DECEMBER 2: The U.S. Senate votes to censure Senator McCarthy.

DECEMBER 2: The United States and the Republic of China (Taiwan) sign a mutual defense treaty.

1955

FEBRUARY 8: Georgi Malenkov resigns as premier of the Soviet Union. His replacement is Nikolai Bulganin. However, the real power behind Malenkov's fall is Nikita Khrushchev, who now clearly emerges as the leader in the Kremlin.

APRIL 5: Winston Churchill resigns as British prime minister, ending his political career.

APRIL 5: Britain, Turkey, and Iraq sign the Baghdad Pact, also known as the Middle East Treaty Organization. Iran and Pakistan join later in the year. (Iraq leaves the organization in 1959, and its name is changed to Central Treaty Organization [CENTO].)

MAY 5: West Germany regains full sovereignty. Four days later it joins NATO as a full member.

MAY 14: The Soviet Union and its satellites establish the Warsaw Pact to counter NATO.

JUNE 18: The first summit meeting between Soviet and Western leaders since Potsdam begins in Geneva. However, the "Spirit of Geneva" proves to be ephemeral.

AUGUST 4: The American U-2 spy plane makes its first flight over the Soviet Union.

NOVEMBER 22: The Soviet Union explodes its first true thermonuclear bomb, with a yield of 1.6 megatons.

1956

FEBRUARY 25: Nikita Khrushchev denounces Stalin in his "secret speech" at the 20th Party Congress of the Soviet Communist Party.

JULY 26: Egypt's president Gamal Abdul Nasser nationalizes the Suez Canal.

JUNE 29: Workers riot against poor economic conditions and Communist rule in Poland.

OCTOBER 21: The Soviet leadership accepts Wladlyslaw Gomulka's rise to power in Poland.

OCTOBER 23: The Hungarian Revolution begins. Imre Nagy comes to power on October 30 and in November announces Hungary is leaving the Warsaw Pact. On November 4, Soviet tanks roll into Budapest and begin the bloody job of crushing the rebellion.

OCTOBER 29: The Suez Crisis begins as Israel, backed by Britain and France, attacks Egypt to put a stop to Egyptian-sponsored terrorism against its territory and citizens.

DECEMBER 2: Fidel Castro lands in Cuba with a small band of followers.

1957

JANUARY 5: President Eisenhower announces a Middle East policy that becomes known as the Eisenhower Doctrine.

FEBRUARY 15: Andrei Gromyko becomes Soviet foreign minister. He will serve in that post until replaced by Eduard Shevardnadze in 1985.

MAY 15: Britain tests its first thermonuclear bomb.

JUNE 29: Khrushchev triumphs over opponents who wanted to remove him from power. He now solidifies his position as the leader of the Soviet Union.

OCTOBER 4: The Soviet Union launches the *Sputnik I*, the world's first artificial satellite. It is launched by an SS-6 ICBM, which was first successfully tested in late August. A second and larger satellite, *Sputnik II*, is launched shortly thereafter.

1958

JANUARY 1: The European Common Market, established by the Treaty of Rome in February 1957, comes into existence.

JANUARY 31: After the U.S. Navy's embarrassing failure to launch its Vanguard satellite, the army launches Explorer I, the first American artificial satellite.

MAY: China begins Mao's disastrous Great Leap Forward, which ultimately causes a famine—probably the worst in history—in which an estimated thirty million people die.

JUNE 1: Charles de Gaulle returns to power as premier of France.

JULY–OCTOBER: The United States sends troops to protect Lebanon's pro-Western regime.

JULY 29: The United States establishes the National Aeronautics and Space Administration (NASA).

AUGUST 23: China renews shelling of Quemoy and Matsu in the Taiwan Straits. Previous incidents occurred during 1954 and 1955.

OCTOBER 4: The French Fifth Republic is established.

NOVEMBER 10: Soviet pressure begins the first of several Berlin crises.

DECEMBER 14: The Western Allies reject the Soviet demand that they withdraw their soldiers from West Berlin.

DECEMBER 21: Charles de Gaulle becomes the first president of the French Fifth Republic.

1959

JANUARY 1: Fidel Castro takes power in Cuba.

JULY 24: Vice President Richard Nixon and Soviet leader Nikita Khrushchev have their "Kitchen Debate" at a United States exhibition in Moscow.

SEPTEMBER 15–27: Nikita Khrushchev becomes the first Russian or Soviet leader to visit the United States. He concludes the trip by visiting President Eisenhower at Camp David, but their discussions yield no concrete results.

1960

MARCH 17: Eisenhower approves a CIA plan to overthrow Castro by having Cuban exiles invade Cuba.

MAY 5: Nikita Khrushchev announces that on May 1 the Soviet Union shot down a U-2 spy plane over its territory and captured its pilot, Francis Gary Powers.

MAY 16: The scheduled Paris summit between the Soviet Union and Western leaders collapses when Eisenhower refuses to apologize for the U-2 spy flights. Khrushchev also cancels Eisenhower's invitation to visit the Soviet Union.

JULY: A civil war begins in the Republic of the Congo, which has just received its independence from Belgium. It helps cause the first superpower confrontation in sub-Saharan Africa.

SEPTEMBER 23: Khrushchev arrives in New York to attend the UN General Assembly session. He spends almost a month in the United States, but Eisenhower does not offer to meet with him.

OCTOBER 19: The United States bans most trade with Cuba, excepting only certain goods and medicines.

NOVEMBER 8: John F. Kennedy is elected president of the United States.

1961

JANUARY 3: The United States breaks diplomatic relations with Cuba.

MARCH 1: President Kennedy establishes the Peace Corps.

APRIL 12: Major Yuri Gagarin of the Soviet Union becomes the first man to orbit the earth.

APRIL 17: The disastrous Bay of Pigs invasion by Cuban exiles begins.

MAY: The United States sends its first military advisors to Vietnam.

MAY 5: Alan Shepard becomes the first American in space with a suborbital mission.

MAY 25: President Kennedy commits the United States to putting a man on the moon by the end of the decade.

JUNE 3–4: Kennedy and Khrushchev hold a summit meeting in Vienna.

AUGUST 13: East Germany begins building the Berlin Wall.

SEPTEMBER 18: UN Secretary General Dag Hammarskjöld dies in a plane crash while trying to end the fighting in the Congo.

1962

FEBRUARY 10: The United States trades convicted Soviet spy Rudolf Abel for Francis Gary Powers.

FEBRUARY 20: Lieutenant Colonel John Glenn becomes the first American to orbit the earth.

JULY 23: Fourteen nations sign accords in Geneva guaranteeing the neutrality of Laos.

OCTOBER 14: A U-2 spy plane discovers Soviet missiles in Cuba. The Cuban Missile Crisis begins.

1963

JANUARY 29: France vetoes Britain's entry into the Common Market.

MAY 11: A Soviet court sentences Oleg Penkovsky, the West's most successful spy, to death.

JUNE 20: The United States and the Soviet Union agree to establish a "hot-line" between the White House and the Kremlin.

JULY 25: The United States, Soviet Union, and Great Britain agree on a partial nuclear test ban treaty. The treaty is signed in Moscow on August 5.

NOVEMBER 1: President Ngo Dinh Diem of South Vietnam is overthrown and murdered in a military coup.

NOVEMBER 22: President Kennedy is assassinated in Dallas. Vice President Lyndon Johnson succeeds him as president. Two days later Kennedy's alleged assassin, Lee Harvey Oswald, is murdered while in police custody.

1964

AUGUST 7: The United States Congress passes the Gulf of Tonkin Resolution as American involvement in South Vietnam deepens.

OCTOBER 14: Nikita Khrushchev is removed from office and replaced by Leonid Brezhnev as first secretary of the CPSU. Alexei Kosygin becomes premier.

OCTOBER 16: Communist China tests its first atomic bomb.

NOVEMBER 3: Lyndon Johnson wins election as president.

1965

FEBRUARY 7: Vietcong forces attack the U.S. military base at Pleiku. The United States responds with its first bombing attacks on North Vietnam.

MARCH 2: The United States begins sustained bombing of North Vietnam in Operation Rolling Thunder.

MARCH 8–9: The first United States combat troops arrive in South Vietnam.

APRIL 28: The United States intervenes militarily in the Dominican Republic.

SEPTEMBER 30–OCTOBER 1: The Indonesian army crushes a Communist coup.

The anti-Communist General Suharto follows his victory with a massive massacre of Communists and others. At least 500,000 are killed.

1966

FEBRUARY 6: President Johnson meets with South Vietnamese Premier Nguyen Cao Ky in Honolulu as American involvement in Vietnam deepens.

MARCH 9: France announces that it will withdraw from NATO's military command but remain a part of the alliance.

MAY 1: U.S. bombers attack oil installations in Hanoi and Haiphong, North Vietnam.

OCTOBER 26: President Johnson visits U.S. troops in South Vietnam.

1967

APRIL 21: Right-wing military officers seize power in Greece.

JUNE 5: Six-Day War begins between Israel and two Arab states, Egypt and Syria. Jordan later joins on the Egyptian-Syrian side.

JUNE 17: Communist China tests its first thermonuclear bomb.

JUNE 23: President Johnson and Premier Kosygin hold their first meeting in Glassboro, New Jersey.

OCTOBER 21: Tens of thousands of protesters gather at the Pentagon to protest U.S. involvement in Vietnam.

SEPTEMBER 3: Nguyen Van Thieu is elected president of South Vietnam. Nguyen Cao Ky becomes vice president.

1968

JANUARY 3: Antiwar candidate Senator Eugene McCarthy begins his campaign for the presidency.

JANUARY 5: Reformer Alexander Dubček becomes leader of the Czechoslovak Communist Party. The "Prague Spring" begins in earnest in March.

JANUARY 30: Communist forces begin the Tet Offensive in South Vietnam.

MARCH 16: Robert F. Kennedy announces that he will run for president on an antiwar platform.

MARCH 16: U.S. troops murder civilians in the South Vietnamese hamlet of My Lai.

MARCH 31: Lyndon Johnson announces that he will not be a candidate for president in November. He also orders a pause in the bombing of North Vietnam.

MAY 10–13: The United States and North Vietnam begin peace talks in Paris.

JULY 1: The United States, Soviet Union, and Great Britain sign the Nuclear Non-Proliferation Treaty.

AUGUST 20–21: Warsaw Pact troops invade Czechoslovakia, ending the Prague Spring.

NOVEMBER 5: Richard Nixon defeats Hubert Humphrey to win the presidency in a close election.

1969

MARCH 2: The first military border clash between the Soviet Union and the People's Republic of China occurs along the Ussuri River.

APRIL 28: Charles de Gaulle resigns as French president, ending his political career.

JUNE 8: President Nixon announces the withdrawal of 25,000 U.S. troops from South Vietnam as "Vietnamization" begins.

JULY 20: U.S. astronauts land on the moon.

JULY 25: Nixon declares that Asian nations will have to defend themselves with their own soldiers in future wars. This becomes known as the Nixon Doctrine.

SEPTEMBER 3: Ho Chi Minh dies.

NOVEMBER 17: U.S. and Soviet negotiators begin the Strategic Arms Limitation Talks (SALT) in Helsinki, Finland.

1970

MARCH 18: Backed by the United States, anti-Communist General Lon Nol overthrows Prince Norodom Sihanouk in Cambodia.

APRIL 30: President Nixon announces that U.S. and South Vietnamese troops have invaded Cambodia, setting off a storm of antiwar protest in the United States. A few days later National Guard troops kill four student protesters at Kent State University in Ohio.

AUGUST 12: West Germany and the Soviet Union sign a nonaggression pact, in which West Germany accepts the post–World War II Soviet-imposed border changes between East and West Germany and East Germany and Poland. This agreement is part of Chancellor Willy Brandt's policy of Ostpolitik.

1971

JULY 15: President Nixon announces he will visit the People's Republic of China in 1972 to normalize relations with Beijing. His national security advisor Henry Kissinger had secretly gone to China for negotiations on July 9.

AUGUST 2: China joins the United Nations as the United States ends two decades of blocking Beijing's entry.

1972

JANUARY 22: The European Economic Community (Common Market) agrees to expand admit new members. As a result Britain, Denmark, and Ireland become members in 1973.

FEBRUARY 21: Nixon begins his visit to Communist China.

MARCH 30: North Vietnamese army troops attack South Vietnam across the demilitarized zone at the 17th parallel. The United States responds by intensifying the air war against North Vietnam and, in May, mining and blockading Haiphong harbor.

MAY 26: In Moscow, President Nixon and Soviet Premier Kosygin sign the SALT I and ABM treaties.

JUNE 17: Burglars are arrested at the headquarters of the Democratic National Committee, beginning the Watergate affair.

SEPTEMBER 3: A four-power agreement (United States, Soviet Union, Britain, and France) guarantees Western access to West Berlin.

OCTOBER 8: Détente continues as the Soviet Union and United States sign a three-year trade agreement.

NOVEMBER 7: Nixon is reelected president by a landslide.

DECEMBER 18: After the Paris peace talks break down, having come close to success, the United States launches its "Christmas bombing" raids against North Vietnam.

1973

JANUARY 27: The Vietnam peace agreement is signed in Paris. Direct American involvement in the fighting ends, but the war itself continues.

MAY 17: The Senate opens its Watergate hearings.

JUNE 21: The UN Security Council approves the admission of West and East Germany to the United Nations.

SEPTEMBER 11: A military junta overthrows the Marxist government of Salvador Allende, who dies during the fighting.

SEPTEMBER 21: The Senate confirms Henry Kissinger as secretary of state.

OCTOBER 6: Egypt and Syria attack Israel, beginning the Yom Kippur War.

NOVEMBER 7: Congress overrides President Nixon's veto of the War Powers Act.

1974

JUNE 28: Nixon and Brezhnev begin a summit meeting in Moscow. They agree to reduce the number of ABMs allowed under SALT I.

AUGUST 9: Implicated in illegal actions while in office, Richard Nixon resigns the presidency. He is succeeded by Gerald Ford.

SEPTEMBER 4: The United States begins diplomatic relations with East Germany.

NOVEMBER 23–24: Meeting in Vladivostok, President Ford and Soviet leader Brezhnev agree on a draft for a SALT II treaty.

1975

JANUARY 14: The Soviet-American trade agreement collapses when the Soviets reject the terms of the Jackson-Vannik amendment.

APRIL 17: Cambodia falls to the Khmer Rouge, who soon begin a genocidal campaign against the population that takes between one and two million lives.

APRIL 30: North Vietnamese forces take Saigon, completing their conquest of South Vietnam and ending the Vietnam War.

MAY 12: Cambodia seizes the U.S. merchant ship *Mayaguez*. U.S. marines free its crew in a costly battle with the Cambodians two days later.

JULY 17: Soviet and American spacecraft dock in orbit.

JULY 30–AUGUST 1: Thirty-five countries sign the Helsinki Accords.

OCTOBER 9: Soviet nuclear scientist and dissident Andrei Sakharov is awarded the Nobel Peace Prize.

1976

JULY 2: North and South Vietnam are officially united.

SEPTEMBER 9: Mao Zedong dies.

NOVEMBER 2: Jimmy Carter is elected president of the United States.

1977

MARCH 17: President Carter announces that human rights will be a major concern of U.S. foreign policy.

JUNE 30: Carter rejects production of the controversial B-1 bomber. He prefers launching cruise missiles from B-52 bombers.

SEPTEMBER 1: The World Psychiatric Association condemns the Soviet Union for using psychiatry for political purposes.

NOVEMBER 19: President Anwar Sadat of Egypt begins his visit to Israel, marking the first break in the solid Arab front of rejecting Israel's right to exist.

1978

APRIL 10: Announcement that Arkady Shevchenko, a Soviet diplomat with a high position at the United Nations, has defected to the United States.

APRIL 18: The Senate approves the treaty returning the Panama Canal Zone to Panama, by a margin of one vote.

APRIL 27: Pro-Soviet military officers seize power in Afghanistan.

SEPTEMBER 5–17: President Carter, Anwar Sadat of Egypt, and Menachim Begin of Israel meet at Camp David and agree on the Camp David Accords, the basis of a peace treaty between Israel and Egypt.

OCTOBER 27: Begin and Sadat share the Nobel Peace Prize.

DECEMBER 25: Vietnam invades Cambodia to overthrow the pro-Chinese Khmer Rouge regime.

1979

JANUARY 1: The United States and the People's Republic of China establish normal diplomatic relations. The United States suspends formal diplomatic relations with Taiwan.

JANUARY 16: The Shah of Iran flees as Muslim fundamentalists loyal to the Ayatollah Khomeini take over the country. Khomeini arrives in Iran on February 1.

FEBRUARY 27: Chinese invades Vietnam in retaliation for Vietnam's invasion of Cambodia.

JUNE 8: Presidents Carter and Brezhnev sign the SALT II treaty at their Vienna summit.

MARCH 26: Israel and Egypt sign a peace treaty at the White House.

JUNE 28: The Arab-dominated Organization of Petroleum Exporting Countries (OPEC) engineers a huge jump in oil prices.

JULY 17: Marxist Sandinista guerrillas seize control of Nicaragua, overthrowing the Somoza dictatorship.

NOVEMBER 4: A mob of fundamentalist Iranian students seizes the United States embassy in Teheran. The Iranian hostage crisis begins, lasting 444 days.

DECEMBER 12: NATO's European nations agree to deploy new U.S. Pershing II and cruise missiles on their soil.

DECEMBER 27: Soviet forces seize control of Afghanistan, murdering the incumbent president and installing a new government.

1980

JANUARY 3: In response to the Afghanistan invasion, President Carter withdraws the SALT II treaty from consideration by the Senate. On January 4, he bans high technology sales to the Soviet Union.

JANUARY 24: President Carter announces the United States will use force if its access to Persian Gulf oil is threatened by an outside force (the Soviet Union). This statement becomes known as the Carter Doctrine.

APRIL 7: The United States breaks diplomatic relations with Iran.

APRIL 24: The American attempt to rescue its hostages in Iran is cancelled after a helicopter and transport plane collide in the Iranian desert, killing eight servicemen.

MAY 5: President Tito of Yugoslavia dies. He had been in power since 1945.

JULY 19–AUGUST 3: The United States and forty other nations boycott the Moscow Olympics.

AUGUST 31: After defying Communist authorities and striking for over two weeks, the Solidarity Union, led by Lech Walesa, signs an agreement with the Polish government that legalizes the union.

NOVEMBER 4: Ronald Reagan is elected president of the United States.

1981

APRIL 1: United States suspends aid to the Sandinista regime in Nicaragua.

OCTOBER 6: Muslim fundamentalist military officers assassinate Egyptian president Anwar Sadat. His successor is Hosni Mubarak.

DECEMBER 13: The Polish government declares martial law and arrests Solidarity's leaders.

1982

JANUARY 25: Mikhail Suslov, long-time Soviet kingmaker and chief Communist Party ideologist, dies.

JUNE 6: Israeli forces invade southern Lebanon in an attempt to end terrorism mounted by the Palestine Liberation Organization, which operates from the region with impunity.

NOVEMBER 10: Leonid Brezhnev dies. The old generation of Soviet leaders is passing from the scene. His successor is Yuri Andropov, who is younger than Brezhnev but infirm.

1983

MARCH 23: President Reagan announces his support for the Strategic Defense Initiative.

APRIL 18: Arab terrorists set off a bomb at the U.S. embassy in Beirut, killing sixty-three people.

SEPTEMBER 1: Soviet aircraft shoot down Korean passenger jet KAL 007 after it intrudes into Soviet airspace.

OCTOBER 5: Lech Walesa wins the Nobel Peace Prize.

OCTOBER 23: Arab terrorists in Lebanon drive a truck loaded with explosives into U.S. marine barracks in Beirut, killing 241 soldiers.

OCTOBER 25: U.S. forces invade the Caribbean island of Grenada and overthrow its hard-line Marxist government.

NOVEMBER 23: Deployment of American cruise missiles begins in Europe.

NOVEMBER 25: In response to the deployment of the American missiles, the Soviet Union walks out of Intermediate Nuclear Forces reduction talks in Geneva.

1984

FEBRUARY 9: Yuri Andropov dies. Two days later he is succeeded by Constantin Chernenko, an aged and infirm Brezhnev crony.

MAY 24: Congress bans further aid to the Contras fighting the Sandinista regime in Nicaragua.

JULY 28–AUGUST 12: The Soviet Union and its East European satellites (except Romania) boycott the Los Angeles Olympics.

SEPTEMBER 26: China and Britain sign an agreement calling for the transfer of Hong Kong to Chinese sovereignty in 1997.

NOVEMBER 6: Ronald Reagan is reelected president of the United States.

DECEMBER 15: Mikhail Gorbachev, by now second in command in the Kremlin, begins a state visit to Great Britain.

1985

FEBRUARY 6: President Reagan announces the United States will support anti-Communist rebels fighting Communist regimes in the Third World. This policy comes to be called the Reagan Doctrine.

MARCH 11: Mikhail Gorbachev is chosen as general secretary of the CPSU and thereby becomes the leader of the Soviet Union.

MAY 20: FBI agents arrest naval officer John Anthony Walker Jr., whose delivery of naval intelligence to the Soviet Union makes him one of the most destructive Soviet spies during the Cold War.

JULY 2: Eduard Shevardnadze succeeds Andrei Gromyko as Soviet foreign minister.

JUNE 11: Gorbachev calls for an overhaul of the Soviet economy.

NOVEMBER 19–21: In Geneva, Gorbachev and Reagan hold their first summit meeting.

1986

FEBRUARY 25: Speaking to the 27th Party Congress of the CPSU, on the thirtieth anniversary of Khrushchev's secret speech, Gorbachev forcefully calls for major reforms in the Soviet Union.

APRIL 26: The worst nuclear accident ever occurs at the Chernobyl nuclear power plant near Kiev, in the Soviet Union.

OCTOBER 10–12: Gorbachev and Reagan meet at Reykjavik, Iceland, but fail to reach an arms-control agreement.

NOVEMBER 13: The Iran-Contra scandal breaks.

DECEMBER 16: Gorbachev releases dissident Andrei Sakharov from internal exile in the city of Gorky (today called Nizhni Novgorod).

1987

MAY 5: Congress begins hearings on the Iran-Contra affair.

JUNE 14: Pope John Paul II makes his third papal visit to his native Poland. He is met by enthusiastic crowds and strongly endorses Solidarity.

DECEMBER 8–10: Gorbachev and Reagan meet at another summit, this time in Washington. They sign the INF treaty, which bans all intermediate-range nuclear missiles from Europe.

1988

FEBRUARY 8: Gorbachev announces that the Soviet Union will withdraw its troops from Afghanistan within a year.

MAY 29–JUNE 2: Reagan and Gorbachev hold a summit meeting in Moscow. They exchange ratifications of the INF Treaty.

NOVEMBER 8: George Bush is elected President of the United States.

DECEMBER 7: Gorbachev announces large unilateral reductions in Soviet troop (by 100,000) and tank (by 10,000) strength in Europe during a speech to the UN General Assembly.

1989

JANUARY 11: Hungary introduces political reforms.

JANUARY 15: Czech police crack down on demonstrators. Among those arrested is Vaclav Havel.

JANUARY 19: The Polish government agrees to legalize Solidarity.

FEBRUARY 14: Nicaragua's Sandinista government agrees to hold free elections.

FEBRUARY 15: On schedule, the last Soviet troops leave Afghanistan.

MARCH 26: The Soviet Union holds the first partially free elections in its history. Many dissidents and non-Communists win election to the newly established Congress of People's Deputies.

MAY 2: Hungary begins removing the barbed-wire fence along its border with Austria.

JUNE 3–4: Troops attack and disperse prodemocracy demonstrators in Beijing's Tiananmen Square. Thousands of demonstrators are killed and injured.

JUNE 4, 18: Solidarity scores an overwhelming victory in Poland's first free elections under Communist rule.

JUNE 16: Imre Nagy, executed by the Soviet Union for his role in the 1956 Hungarian Revolution, is reburied as a hero. Hundreds of thousands of people pay tribute to him.

AUGUST 21: Over 200,000 people gather in Prague to protest the Warsaw Pact invasion of Czechoslovakia in 1968.

AUGUST 24: Poland gets its first non-Communist premier and cabinet with a non-Communist majority since World War II.

OCTOBER 9: Demonstrations begin in Leipzig, East Germany. The demonstrations swell over the next two weeks to number more than 100,000 protestors.

OCTOBER 18: Erich Honecker is replaced as head of East Germany's Communist party by Egon Krenz.

OCTOBER 25: Gorbachev publicly rejects the Brezhnev Doctrine.

NOVEMBER 9: East Germany opens the Berlin Wall.

NOVEMBER 20: Over 200,000 people demonstrate in Prague, calling for an end to Communist rule. By November 23, 300,000 are demonstrating.

NOVEMBER 24: Czechoslovakian Communist leader Milos Jakes and his entire politburo resign.

DECEMBER 2–3: Presidents Bush and Gorbachev meet in Malta.

DECEMBER 25: A military tribunal tries and executes Romanian dictator Nicolae Ceausescu and his wife Elena.

DECEMBER 29: Vaclav Havel becomes Czechoslovakia's first non-Communist president since 1948.

1990

MARCH 11: Lithuania declares its independence from the Soviet Union. The process of disintegration in the Soviet Union begins to gain force.

MARCH 13: The Communist Party of the Soviet Union loses its legal monopoly of power when the Congress of People's Deputies repeals Article 6 of the Soviet Constitution. The CPSU's Central Committee agrees to the change two days later.

MAY 30–JUNE 2: Presidents Bush and Gorbachev hold a summit meeting in Washington.

OCTOBER 3: Germany is officially reunited.

OCTOBER 15: Mikhail Gorbachev is awarded the Nobel Peace Prize.

NOVEMBER 18–21: At a full summit meeting of the thirty-four members of the Conference on Security and Cooperation in Europe, NATO and the Warsaw Pact sign the Conventional Forces in Europe Treaty, which limits conventional military forces in both alliances. On November 21 the countries sign the Charter of Paris, which formally ends the Cold War.

1991

JULY 1: The Warsaw Pact officially disbands.

JULY 31: In Moscow, Presidents Bush and Gorbachev sign the Strategic Arms Reduction (START I) Treaty.

AUGUST 19–21: Unsuccessful coup by Communist Party hard-liners against Gorbachev.

DECEMBER 25: Gorbachev resigns as president of the Soviet Union.

DECEMBER 31: The Soviet Union officially ceases to exist. It is replaced by fifteen independent states, the largest of which is Russia.

PART IV

Resources

Looking for Resources

Part IV of this volume is divided into six sections, which in turn are divided into smaller subsections. Section I lists books and articles under thirty-nine key topic headings, ranging from general overviews of the Cold War to highly specialized topics such as "propaganda" and "science and computers." There are headings on every American administration (the Nixon and Ford administrations are combined into a single heading) and every major Soviet leader (the exceptions are Malenkov, Andropov, and Chernenko). Major events, such as the Vietnam War and the Cuban Missile Crisis, also receive separate headings. The final heading in this section is "historiography," which focuses on how historians have looked at and debated the Cold War.

Several of the topic headings are subdivided further in order to help the reader locate materials. "Vietnam" is divided into general overviews, military aspects, policy aspects, and antiwar/domestic aspects. "The Third World" is divided into subsections on overviews, Asia, Latin America, and Africa. "The Cold War at Home" is divided into McCarthyism and domestic politics and effects on American culture and daily life.

More than 90 percent of the resources for research listed here are books. The rest are articles. In both cases, the works listed represent only a tiny fraction of what has been written on the Cold War. The reason for the emphasis on books is that scholars usually elaborate on and refine their articles and then publish them as books. I have also made an effort to include materials written during every period of the Cold War, even if some (but certainly not all) of the older works may be outdated, because this approach provides a flavor of how writing on the Cold War developed.

Most of the works listed are by historians and political scientists. Some are by journalists who demonstrated high professionalism and expertise in their chosen topics. A few articles come from the popular press because they provide a unique bit of information or perspective on some aspect of the Cold War.

Section II is devoted to memoirs and biographies of the participants. The memoirs are list alphabetically by author, whereas the biographies are listed by subject of the volume (e.g., Acheson, Wallace), rather than by author.

Section III is subdivided into bibliographies, reference works, and primary-source collections. The primary-source collections give readers access to speeches, government documents, and other materials that scholars use to do their work. Some of the collections, such as *The Public Papers of the Presidents*, are huge and require painstaking work to find materials relevant to one's particular interest. Others, such as *The American Diplomatic Revolution*, are short collections put together by historians as teaching tools.

Most of the collections focus on the American side of the Cold War, in large part because access to Soviet bloc documents has until very recently been extremely limited. The main exception listed here is the collection on the history of Communism edited by Robert Daniels. Additional documents from the Soviet bloc are becoming available. One of the best sources for them is the Cold War International History Project Bulletin (see Section IV, Journals).

Section IV contains subsections for journals, projects/archives, and presidential libraries. The two archives/projects listed are the Cold War International History Project and the National Security Archive. Neither is an archive in the traditional sense, that is, a place where a government or other institution stores its records. Rather, they are independent institutions whose main agenda is to get documents out of archives in order to make them available to scholars and students.

Section V lists websites, CD-ROMs, and microfiches. The reader should remember that websites are constantly changing when trying to access them.

Section VI covers films and novels. Here there was no attempt to be comprehensive, but only to give the reader a taste of what was produced during the long period of the Cold War. To have tried to do more would have increased the size of this book beyond reasonable limits.

Topics

General Histories

Barnet, Richard J. *The Alliance: America, Europe, Japan: Makers of the Postwar World*. New York: Simon & Schuster, 1983.

The author focuses on key events and on key individuals from Adenauer, Macmillan, and Monnet to Carter, Kissinger, and Reagan. He argues that the United States allowed itself to be manipulated by Germany and Japan, the defeated powers in World War II, who ultimately became cornerstones of the alliance.

Brands, H. W. *The Devil We Knew: Americans and the Cold War*. New York: Oxford University Press, 1993.

The Cold War was a conflict of national interests during which great powers did "what great powers had done as long as there had been great powers." Although he is less critical of the United States than other revisionist historians, Brand maintains that Washington deserves part of the blame for the Cold War because the United States was by far the more powerful of the two antagonists.

Brzezinski, Zbigniew. "How the Cold War Was Played." *Foreign Affairs* 51:1 (October 1972): 181–209.

Brzezinski identifies six main phases of the Cold War. He sees it as the result more of long-term and "ineluctable" historical forces than human error or evil intent.

Carlton, David, and Herbert M. Levine, eds. *The Cold War Debated*. New York: Mc-Graw-Hill, 1988.

A textbook that examines the Cold War from several perspectives: historical issues, the international system, goals, instruments of power, and formal constraints on power. Nineteen issues are debated in a yes/no format (for example, "Has Franklin Roosevelt Been Unfairly Criticized for Yalta?").

Crockatt, Richard. *The Fifty-Year War: The United States and the Soviet Union in World Politics, 1941–1991*. New York: Routledge, 1995.

This highly readable volume examines how the United States and the Soviet Union adapted, or failed to adapt, to global change. The author makes use of newly available material concerning a number of issues, including the origins of the Cold War and the Cuban Missile Crisis. The system of states concept is used to make sense of the global context of the American-Soviet rivalry.

Feste, Karen A. *Expanding the Frontiers: Superpower Intervention in the Cold War.* New York: Praeger, 1992.

A highly theoretical overview of the importance, rationales, and trends regarding interventions by the superpowers in the Cold War. Chapters cover events in Greece ("Cold War Origins"), the Middle East ("Cold War Extension"), and Afghanistan ("Cold War Renewal").

Gaddis, John Lewis. *The Long Peace: Inquiries Into the History of the Cold War.* New York: Oxford University Press, 1987.

Gaddis's thesis is that the Cold War era was one of general peace and stability, notwithstanding the many conflicts that occurred, because both superpowers, deterred by nuclear weapons, made efforts to control their rivalry. He discusses how the United States came to see the Soviet Union as the main threat to its security, developed security commitments around the world, and tried to split the Soviet bloc.

——. *Now We Know: Rethinking Cold War History.* New York: Oxford University Press, 1997.

On the basis of the most recently available documents and research by scholars, Gaddis concludes that "as long as Stalin was running the Soviet Union a Cold War was unavoidable." He points out the limits of military power, noting it was a lack of ideological, cultural, and moral power that cost the Soviet Union its superpower status.

Gillon, Steven M., and Dianne B. Kunz, eds. *America During the Cold War.* Orlando: Harcourt Brace Jovanovich, 1993.

An overview of America during the Cold War, with selections by various authors treating both foreign and domestic developments. Topics covered include the origins of the Cold War, the Cold War at home, the struggle for civil rights, the women's movement, Vietnam, the Great Society, and the end of the Cold War. Contributors include Stanley Karnow, Betty Friedan, Allen Matusow, Gaddis Smith, Lou Cannon, and Paul Nitze.

Halle, Louis J. *The Cold War as History.* New York: Harper & Row, 1967.

A former member of the U.S. State Department Policy Planning Staff, Halle covers the period from 1945 to 1962. While viewing the Cold War as a traditional struggle between great powers, Halle sees the Soviet Union, which suddenly expanded into Eastern Europe, as the aggressor. The Cold War, he maintains, was fought to restore the balance of power in Europe after the defeat of Germany.

Hyland, William G. *The Cold War: Fifty Years of Conflict.* New York: Random House, 1990.

Hyland argues the Cold War was "Stalin's war," which began as a straightforward power struggle in Europe. The Cold War was inherent in Stalin's "paranoia and megalomania," as well as in the system he built in the Soviet Union and tried to "transplant" in Eastern Europe. Khrushchev expanded the Cold War into a global contest when he tried to enlist former European colonies in the Third World as allies. A concise, readable volume, excellent for undergraduates.

LaFeber, Walter. *America, Russia, and the Cold War, 1945–1992,* 7th ed. New York: McGraw-Hill, 1993.

A New Left revisionist analysis that attributes the Cold War to American aggressiveness in its pursuit of capitalist economic interest, which required an "open world marketplace" after World War II. Stalin's priority after the war was Soviet security and his own personal power. The first edition of this book was published in 1967.

Levering, Ralph B. *The Cold War, 1945–1991: A Post–Cold War History.* Arlington Heights, Ill.: Harlan Davidson, 1994.

A short survey that views the origins of the Cold War in terms of the United States' reacting to Soviet actions within the context of an unstable international situation. The author also emphasizes domestic factors as essential for understanding American foreign policy. The stakes in the Cold War were "immense": whether Communism ("inevitably totalitarian") or capitalism ("often democratic") would become the world's dominant social system in the late twentieth century. Excellent for the general reader and undergraduates.

Lukacs, John. *A History of the Cold War.* New York: Doubleday, 1961.

A traditionalist survey whose two heroes are Ernest Bevin and Harry Truman. The author maintains that Stalin caused the Cold War and that Truman stopped the spread of Communism with the Truman Doctrine and the Marshall Plan. A third edition of this book appeared in 1966 as *A New History of the Cold War.*

McCormick, Thomas. *America's Half Century: United States Foreign Policy in the Cold War,* 2d ed. Baltimore: Johns Hopkins University Press, 1989.

A revisionist overview. The author takes an economic deterministic approach in explaining American postwar policy, focusing on United States postwar efforts to reorder the world according to free-market principles. This American expansionism, as opposed to Soviet resistance to it, is seen as the primary cause of the Cold War.

Nogee, Joseph, and John Spanier. *Peace Impossible, War Unlikely: The Cold War Between the United States and the Soviet Union.* Glenview, Ill.: Scott Foresman, 1988.

An overview of the Cold War from both a historical and theoretical point of view. The

Soviet state and its leaders bear the primary responsibility for the Cold War. The Cold War will "endure" until there is a fundamental change in the Soviet regime.

Pessen, Edward. *Losing Our Souls: The American Experience in the Cold War*. Chicago: Ivan R. Dee, 1993.

A revisionist analysis that is harshly critical of U.S. foreign policy. The author argues that the United States misrepresented Soviet interests, causing serious damage to domestic freedoms in the process. Despite the Soviet Union's "deplorable actions," the United States should not have regarded it as an enemy, inasmuch as the two countries were not at war.

Powaski, Ronald E. *The Cold War: The United States and the Soviet Union, 1917–1991*. New York: Oxford University Press, 1997.

The author argues that the roots of the Cold War are centuries old, stretching back to tsarist Russia and the infancy of the American nation. He adds that both countries were expansionist and that each believed it had a unique mission in history. The distortions that the long struggle wrought on American institutions raises the question whether anyone won the Cold War.

Smith, Joseph. *The Cold War: Second Edition, 1945–1991*. Oxford and Malden, Mass.: Blackwell, 1998.

A concise overview by a British historian. Good for undergraduates.

Walker, Martin. *The Cold War: A History*. New York: Holt, 1994.

A highly readable and comprehensive account by a British journalist who was the *Manchester Guardian* Moscow correspondent for several years during the 1980s. The Cold War was a conflict of national interests that the United States won because it could harness the power of the late twentieth-century international economy and bankrupt the Soviet Union. Nonetheless, the cost of the Cold War turned both powers into "superlosers."

Weisburger, Bernard A. *Cold War, Cold Peace: The United States and Russia Since 1945*. Introduction by Harrison Salisbury. New York: American Heritage, 1984.

A readable narrative covering almost four decades of the Cold War, although the emphasis is on the period through the Nixon administration. The two superpowers regarded each other with suspicion before the collapse of the wartime alliance. The author discusses how living with the nuclear threat has affected the American people and the concentration of power in the executive branch at the expense of Congress.

White, Donald W. *The American Century: The Rise and Decline of the United States as a World Power*. New Haven: Yale University Press, 1997.

A cultural and intellectual overview of the United States after World War II. The author surveys foreign-policy writing, literature, movies, poetry, and other topics to analyze America's loss of confidence since the early 1960s.

Wohlforth, William C. *The Elusive Balance: Power and Perceptions During the Cold War*. Ithaca: Cornell University Press, 1993.

An overview of Soviet and American perceptions of the balance of power. The author discusses how the Soviet elite saw their country's capabilities and sources of power and compares their outlook to American views. A highly abstract analysis.

Origins

Allen, Thomas B., and Norman Polmar. *Code Name Downfall: The Secret Plan to Invade Japan—and Why Truman Dropped the Bomb*. New York: Simon & Schuster, 1995.

In this popularly written volume, two military historians maintain that Japan was not ready to surrender until after the dropping of the second atomic bomb on Nagasaki and the Soviet entry into the war. Truman was justified in his decision to use atomic bombs to end World War II.

Alperovitz, Gar. *Atomic Diplomacy: Hiroshima and Potsdam: The Use of the Atomic Bomb and the American Confrontation with Soviet Power*. New York: Simon & Schuster, 1965.

The author's controversial "atomic diplomacy" thesis is that the main reason the United States used atomic weapons against Japan in August 1945 was to intimidate the Soviet Union in postwar negotiations. Revised editions of this book appeared in 1985 and 1995.

Buhite, Russell D. *Decision at Yalta: An Appraisal of Summit Diplomacy*. Wilmington, Del.: Scholarly Resources, 1986.

The author sees Yalta as the first Soviet-American attempt at détente. However, a severe "asymmetry of views" prevented an agreement. Yalta is an example of how summit diplomacy often promises more than it can deliver.

Butow, Robert Joseph. *Japan's Decision to Surrender*. Foreword by Edwin O. Reischauer. Stanford: Stanford University Press, 1954.

A carefully documented study of the effect of the "unconditional surrender" policy of the allies on Japanese leaders.

Churchill, Winston. *Triumph and Tragedy*. Boston: Houghton Mifflin, 1953.

The final volume of Churchill's *History of the Second World War* covers the period from D-Day (June 6, 1944) to Potsdam. He emphasizes that the "Soviet menace . . . has replaced the Nazi foe." Many postwar problems arose because of the "deadly hiatus" that lasted from Roosevelt's final illness and death to Truman's taking a strong grip on the American ship of state.

Clemens, Dianne Shaver. *Yalta*. New York: Oxford University Press, 1970.

A revisionist analysis that covers the major issues raised at Yalta. The author often makes conjectures regarding the motives of the principles and tends to see the Soviet Union as conciliatory and accept Stalin's rationales.

Davis, Lynn Etheridge. *The Cold War Begins: Soviet-American Conflict in Eastern Europe*. Princeton: Princeton University Press, 1974.

The author focuses on American policy in Eastern Europe between 1941 and 1945. The United States did not start the Cold War, she maintains, and the revisionists who say it did are guilty of shoddy research and analysis. The Soviet Union was aggressive in Eastern Europe and the State Department often overruled U.S. officials on the scene who wanted a stronger American policy.

Donnelly, Desmond. *The Struggle for the World: The Cold War, 1917–1965*. New York: St. Martin's Press, 1965.

An orthodox account that sees the root cause of the Cold War in traditional Russian expansionism but that also speaks of the "Communist drive for world domination." The book contains many details about British diplomacy and is dedicated to Ernest Bevin and Dean Acheson.

Drea, Edward J. *MacArthur's ULTRA: Codebreaking and the War Against Japan, 1942–1945*. Lawrence: University Press of Kansas, 1992.

Drea is a military historian fluent in Japanese. He argues that the intelligence provided by ULTRA, which revealed a massive Japanese buildup to resist an invasion, played a central role in the American decision to use the atomic bomb.

Feis, Herbert. *Churchill, Roosevelt, Stalin: The War They Waged and the Peace They Sought*. Princeton: Princeton University Press, 1957.

The author has a background as both a historian and public official (as special consultant to three secretaries of war). This volume covers wartime relations through the Yalta Conference. Feis defends Roosevelt against charges that he "sold out" to the Soviets at Yalta. He blames the Cold War on Stalin's ambitions in Eastern Europe.

———. *Between War and Peace: The Potsdam Conference*. Princeton: Princeton University Press, 1960.

A continuation of *Churchill, Roosevelt, Stalin: The War They Waged and the Peace They Sought*. Feis traces the breakdown of the Grand Alliance, which set the stage for the Cold War. He rejects criticism that the West exhibited a lack of firmness or insight in dealing with the Soviets.

———. *Japan Subdued: The Atomic Bomb and the End of World War II*. Princeton: Princeton University Press, 1961.

Feis provides an overview of planning and activities of the allies and Japan during 1945 and concludes that the use of the bomb was justified because American policymakers believed it was necessary to end the war and save lives. A revised version of this book, *The Atomic Bomb and the End of World War II*, appeared in 1966.

———. *From Trust to Terror: The Onset of the Cold War, 1945–1950*. New York: W. W. Norton, 1970.

While not uncritical of American policy, Feis offers an orthodox interpretation that views the Soviet Union as expansionist and is sympathetic to the American effort to stop Communist expansion. He rejects the idea that the United States engaged in "atomic diplomacy."

Fleming, D. F. *The Cold War and Its Origins*. 2 vols. New York: Doubleday, 1961.

Along with W. A. Williams's *The Tragedy of American Diplomacy*, this is one of the two classic early revisionist analyses of the Cold War's origins. Fleming argues the Cold War began because the United States could not accept one of the main consequences of World War II: Soviet control over Eastern Europe. He criticizes Truman for reversing Roosevelt's policy of accommodation.

Gaddis, John Lewis. *The United States and the Origins of the Cold War, 1941–1947*. New York: Columbia University Press, 1972.

Gaddis, an early postrevisionist, argues that many factors — economic considerations, domestic politics, bureaucratic inertia, personality characteristics, and perceptions of Soviet intentions — affected American policymakers. The Soviet Union was more to blame for the Cold War than the United States. The author criticizes revisionist historians for being overly interested in assigning blame and overlooking the complexity of human behavior.

Gallicchio, Marc S. *The Cold War Begins in Asia: American East Asian Policy and the Fall of the Japanese Empire*. New York: Columbia University Press, 1988.

The author focuses on the last nine months of 1945. He maintains that Truman deemphasized Roosevelt's decolonialization policy and introduced a policy that stressed unilateral control of Japan, the Open Door in Asia, and the promotion of "free and friendly" regimes in Korea and China.

Gardner, Lloyd, Arthur Schlesinger, and Hans Morgenthau. *The Origins of the Cold War*. J. J. Huthmacher and W. I. Sussman, eds. Waltham, Mass.: Ginn-Blaisdell, 1970.

The authors present their differing views and their rejoinders to each other. Gardner (revisionist) and Morgenthau (realist) wrote original articles. Schlesinger (orthodox) is represented by a reprint of his 1967 *Foreign Affairs* article.

Gormly, James L. *The Collapse of the Grand Alliance, 1945–1948*. Baton Rouge: Louisiana State University Press, 1987.

The collapse of the Grand Alliance was a return to prewar antipathies. The author tends to see the interests of both sides as equally valid and downplays the role of Stalinism. He makes extensive use of British archival materials.

———. *From Potsdam to the Cold War: Big Three Diplomacy, 1945–1947*. Wilmington, Del.: SR Books, 1990.

The author argues that the United States made little effort at Potsdam to assure Moscow that cooperation was possible or that the United States did not seek the Soviet Union's destruction. The Truman administration is faulted for its unwillingness to downplay differences with the Soviets.

Hammond, Thomas T., ed. *Witnesses to the Origins of the Cold War*. Seattle: University of Washington Press, 1982.

A collection of twelve essays by U.S. officials serving in eastern or southern Europe during the early days of the Cold War, including George Kennan (Soviet Union), C. E. Black (Bulgaria), and William H. McNeill (Greece). In his commentary Hammond blames Stalin for the Cold War and rejects the Alperovitz theory of "atomic diplomacy."

Harbutt, Fraser. *The Iron Curtain: Churchill, America, and the Origins of the Cold War*. New York: Oxford University Press, 1986.

The Cold War resulted from longstanding Anglo-Soviet differences. The United States was a reluctant Cold Warrior and took up the challenge only after Churchill's efforts and provocative Soviet actions in the Near East.

Herring, George C. *Aid to Russia, 1941–1946: Strategy, Diplomacy, and the Origins of the Cold War*. New York: Columbia University Press, 1973.

The author maintains that ending Lend-Lease was not an attempt to pressure the Soviet Union, although it did arouse Soviet suspicions and anger. American aid would not have moved the Soviets to compromise in Eastern Europe. A postrevisionist interpretation of the origins of the Cold War.

Horowitz, David. *The Free World Colossus: A Critique of American Foreign Policy in the Cold War*. New York: Hill and Wang, 1965.

One of the first New Left analyses of the origins of the Cold War. Horowitz blames the Cold War on the United States, citing the Truman Doctrine as a turning point. He carries the story into the early 1960s. By the end of the Cold War, Horowitz had repudiated his New Left beliefs and his criticism of the United States.

Kaiser, Robert G. *Cold Winter, Cold War*. New York: Stein and Day, 1974.

Tracing events from D-Day to the Truman Doctrine, the former Moscow correspondent for the *Washington Post* challenges the "tenets of Cold War revisionism." American policy was not to promote world capitalist domination but was a sensible effort to contain Soviet power.

Kennan, George F. "Sources of Soviet Conduct." *Foreign Affairs* 26 (July 1947): 566–82.

Kennan, writing as "X," proffers his classic statement of the reasons for Soviet expansionism and his recommended policy of "patient but firm and vigilant containment" to deal with that expansionism.

Kolko, Gabriel. *The Politics of War: The United States and Foreign Policy, 1943–1945.* New York: Random House, 1968.

A Marxist economic-determinist analysis. Kolko argues that U.S. foreign policy was an effort to create an "Open Door" world dominated by American capitalism. He depicts Washington policymakers as blind to human suffering.

Kolko, Joyce, and Gabriel Kolko. *The Limits of Power: The World and United States Foreign Policy, 1945–1954.* New York: Harper & Row, 1972.

This volume continues the Marxist "Open Door" argument made in Gabriel Kolko's *Politics of War.* The class structure of the United States, which is dominated by big business, determines American foreign policy. The alleged threat posed by the Soviet Union was really a tool used to manipulate the public into supporting Truman's policies.

Kuniholm, Bruce R. *The Origins of the Cold War in the Near East: Great Power Conflict and Diplomacy in Iran, Turkey, and Greece.* Princeton: Princeton University Press, 1980.

A postrevisionist analysis that views the Soviet Union as expansionist, but for geopolitical rather than ideological reasons. The author argues that although economic considerations played a role in U.S. policy, they were not the dominant factors that determined that policy.

Larsen, Deborah Welch. *Origins of Containment: A Psychological Explanation.* Princeton: Princeton University Press, 1985.

The author asks why Truman and his top advisors abandoned all hope for a "constructive civilized relationship" with the Soviet Union and embarked on an "altruistic if sometimes futile effort" to prevent Soviet gains throughout the world. The author relies on a social psychological approach to explain the shifts in U.S. policymakers' attitudes toward the Soviet Union after 1947.

Leffler, Melvyn P. "Inside Communist Archives: The Cold War Reopened." *Foreign Affairs* 75 (July/August 1996): 120–35.

The author argues for "more nuanced conclusions" than those of historians who maintain that recently opened Eastern bloc and Soviet archives affirm the traditional, prerevisionist interpretations of the origins of the Cold War.

———. *Preponderance of Power: National Security, the Truman Administration, and the Cold War.* Stanford: Stanford University Press, 1992.

The focus of this volume is on the United States because the author believes that Soviet aims and motives "remain unknowable." The analysis is generally revisionist: had the United States taken Soviet security concerns into account the Cold War could have been avoided. The author analyzes American policy worldwide, focusing on the relationship among military, political, and economic goals.

———. *The Specter of Communism: The United States and the Origins of the Cold War, 1917–1953.* New York: Hill and Wang, 1994.

In this concise, readable volume, Leffler traces the origins of the Cold War to the American reaction to the Bolshevik Revolution of 1917. He argues that America's ideological hostility to the Soviet Union did not turn into a sense of "mortal danger" until the Soviets occupied much of Eastern Europe in the wake of World War II. Then the Cold War developed "when a sense of ideological rivalry merged with a fear of Soviet power."

Lippman, Walter. *The Cold War.* New York: Harper & Row, 1947.

Lippman's columns in the *New York Herald Tribune*, collected in this volume, critique George Kennan's containment theory and opened the debate on the origins of the Cold War. Lippman urges diplomatic rather than military pressure on the Soviet Union and protests the broad scope of the Truman Doctrine. Lippman calls containment a "strategic monstrosity" that did not distinguish between vital and tangential interests. A second edition of this book, published in 1972, includes Kennan's "X" article.

Macdonald, Douglas J. "Communist Bloc Expansion in the Early Cold War: Challenging Realism, Refuting Revisionism." *International Security* 20:3 (Winter 1995): 153–88.

The author maintains that newly available archival evidence supports the traditional interpretations for the origins of the Cold War and "pose a challenge to the other schools of thought."

Maddox, Robert James. *Weapons for Victory: The Hiroshima Decision Fifty Years Later.* Columbia: University of Missouri Press, 1995.

Maddox strenuously challenges what he considers revisionist distortions of the historical record. He makes use of recently released archival material to argue that the Japanese were not prepared to surrender prior to the atomic bombing of Hiroshima. Truman and his advisors were convinced that tenacious Japanese resistance lay ahead if the bomb were not used. The documentary evidence refutes Alperovitz's "atomic diplomacy" thesis.

Mastny, Vojtech. *Russia's Road to Cold War: Diplomacy, Warfare, and the Politics of Communism, 1941–1945.* New York: Columbia University Press, 1979.

The first close examination of Soviet wartime diplomacy, making use of newly available Soviet sources. Mastny covers from the 1941 German invasion of the Soviet Union to the Potsdam Conference. He sees the Cold War as being inevitable primarily because of Stalin's policy of imperialist expansion into Eastern Europe that already was being implemented during World War II. Revisionist arguments are rejected.

———. *The Cold War and Soviet Insecurity: The Stalin Years*. New York: Oxford University Press, 1996.

This volume is based on newly opened archives in Russia and its former satellites. The author sees Stalin's inordinate insecurity as the primary cause of the Cold War and marshals evidence to demonstrate that both Stalin and Molotov were Marxist-Leninist ideologues. Mastny provides new insights into the Stalin-Mao relationship, the Korean War, and other crises between 1945 and 1953. He argues that the Cold War lasted for more than four decades because U.S. and Soviet values were diametrically opposed.

McNeill, William H. *America, Britain, and Russia: Their Cooperation and Conflict, 1941–1946*. New York: Oxford University Press, 1953.

A "realist" approach that sees conflicting national interests as the underlying cause of the collapse of the Grand Alliance.

Minor, Steven Merrit. "Revelations, Secrets, Gossip and Lies: Sifting Warily Through the Soviet Archives." *The New York Times Book Review*, May 14, 1995, 18–21.

A survey of new evidence emerging from the Soviet archives and what they tell about various aspects of Soviet history, including foreign affairs.

Morgenthau, Hans. *In Defense of National Interest: A Critical Examination of American Foreign Policy*. New York: Knopf, 1951.

One of the earliest "realist" analyses of the origins of the Cold War, and one of the standard works of that school. Soviet policies are rooted in traditional Russian interests, not Communist ideology. In order to avoid intensifying the Cold War, U.S. national interests must be analyzed unemotionally. The United States must avoid previous errors in its diplomacy that have ranged from utopianism to neoisolationism.

Osgood, Robert C. *Containment, Soviet Behavior, and Grand Strategy*. Berkeley: University of California Press, 1981.

The Soviet Union is an expansionist power and American postwar policy was a proper response to a "Soviet threat to American security interests." This volume includes additional commentary by nine scholars.

Parrish, Thomas. *Berlin in the Balance, 1945–1949: The Blockade, the Airlift, the First Major Battle of the Cold War*. Reading, Mass.: Addison-Wesley, 1998.

A volume popularly written for the general reader, but also thoroughly researched. Parrish strongly endorses Truman's priorities and says his response to the situation in Berlin was a key step in halting Soviet expansion in Europe.

Paterson, Thomas G. *On Every Front: The Making of the Cold War*. New York: Norton, 1979.

This revisionist volume views the Cold War as arising from three "closely intertwined" sources: the conflict-ridden international system, the contending needs and ideas of the United States and the Soviet Union, and the diplomatic tactics of Soviet and American leaders. A new edition of this book, subtitled "The Making and Unmaking of the Cold War," appeared in 1992. Good for general readers and undergraduates.

Paterson, Thomas G., and Robert J. McMahon, eds. *The Origins of the Cold War*, 3d ed. Lexington, Mass.: D.C. Heath, 1991.

Contributors include Arthur Schlesinger, Melvyn Leffler, Vojtech Mastny, John Lewis Gaddis, Thomas J. McCormick, Geir Lundestad, and Paterson and McMahon, who also provide an introduction. The book is divided into three sections: Explanations, Origins, and Toward a Global Cold War.

Perkins, Dexter. *The Diplomacy of a New Age*. Bloomington: Indiana University Press, 1967.

Perkins traces the America's movement away from isolationism and its development of massive military and economic power. He rejects revisionist arguments that American power has been misused or misdirected.

Pollard, Robert A. *Economic Security and the Origins of the Cold War, 1945–1950*. New York: Columbia University Press, 1986.

The policymakers who moved the United States from a policy of isolationism to multilateralism believed that economic interdependence increased prosperity and security. The international economic institutions created after World War II have been very successful. The author challenges revisionist criticism of U.S. postwar economic policy.

Raack, R.C. *Stalin's Drive Toward the East, 1938–1945: The Origins of the Cold War*. Stanford: Stanford University Press, 1995.

Based on research in recently opened East European archives (the German Central Party Archive), Raack affirms that Stalin planned the seizure of Eastern and Central Europe for ideological, not defensive reasons. He rejects revisionist views on the Cold War's origins.

Rees, David. *The Age of Containment: The Cold War*. New York: St. Martin's Press, 1967.

An orthodox analysis that says that the Soviet Union violated the Yalta accords and ultimately compelled the United States to "respond." The antagonists in the Cold War are totalitarianism and democracy.

Reynolds, David, ed. *The Origins of the Cold War in Europe: International Perspectives.* New Haven: Yale University Press, 1994.

Experts from the United States, Russia, and Western European nations contributed to this volume, giving it an unusually broad perspective. Along with chapters on the United States and the Soviet Union ("The Big Two") are chapters on Britain and France ("The Other Two"), Germany and Italy ("The Vanquished"), and on the Benelux countries and Scandinavia. Reynolds contributes an comprehensive introduction to an invaluable volume that reflects the most recent research. Excellent for undergraduates and graduate students.

Schlesinger, Arthur Jr. "Origins of the Cold War." *Foreign Affairs* 46 (October 1967): 23–52.

Schlesinger offers a traditional analysis of the origins of the Cold War while criticizing the revisionist for treating Stalin as "just another Realpolitik statesman" and failing to recognize the Soviet Union as a totalitarian state driven by a messianic Leninist ideology.

Senarclens, Pierre. *From Yalta to the Iron Curtain: The Great Powers and the Origins of the Cold War.* Trans. Amanda Pingrel. New York: Berg Publishers, 1995.

Senarclens, a professor at the University of Lausanne, wrote this book to fill a gap in the French historical literature. He provides a Western European perspective based on French and British archival records. He argues that in the early Cold War Stalin sought hegemony over Central Europe, the Balkans, and Asia, struggling to subdue conquered territory as a base for later expansion. He adds that France, the United States, and Britain wanted to regain imperial control in areas freed from colonialism by World War II. The author is strongly critical of American revisionist historians for focusing on economic arguments while neglecting the intense European reaction to Communist brutality and Stalin's early intransigence.

Sherwin, Martin. *A World Destroyed: The Atomic Bomb and the Grand Alliance.* New York: Knopf, 1975.

Sherwin, a revisionist, asks whether different American and British policies could have brought atomic weapons under international control. Roosevelt, influenced by Churchill, kept exclusive control of those weapons and initiated atomic diplomacy, which Truman then followed. Based largely on American and British sources, the book says little about Stalin's character.

Woods, Randall B., and Howard Jones. *Dawning of the Cold War: The United States' Quest for Order.* Athens: University of Georgia Press, 1991.

A postrevisionist analysis, the first post-*glasnost* monograph on Cold War origins, and a synthesis of recent scholarship on British and American policy between 1945 and 1949.

The authors maintain that the Soviet Union was intent on territorial and ideological expansion and that containment, in the form of the Truman Doctrine, Marshall Plan, and NATO, was necessary. Excellent for the general reader, undergraduates, and graduate students.

Yergin, Daniel. *Shattered Peace: The Origins of the Cold War and the National Security State*. Boston: Houghton Mifflin, 1977.

Yergin maintains that the "Yalta Axioms," which said diplomacy with the Soviet Union was possible and were accepted by Roosevelt, were replaced as the basis of American policy under Truman by the "Riga Axioms," which said that diplomacy was useless because the Soviet Union was intent on world conquest. The Truman administration misread Soviet intentions by seeing them as unyielding and hostile. A revisionist analysis.

Zubok, Vladislav, and Constantine Pleshekov. *Inside the Kremlin's Cold War: From Stalin to Khrushchev*. Cambridge: Harvard University Press, 1996.

The first scholarly look at the Cold War's origins by Russian historians using recently opened Soviet archives. Stalin hoped to avoid confrontation with the West because he believed an inevitable postwar economic crisis would give him the space he needed for geopolitical maneuvering. But Russian imperialism and Marxist globalism "predestined" Soviet expansion. Khrushchev was a romantic revolutionary who could not resist adventures in the Third World.

Soviet-American Relations

Fungigiello, Philip J. *American-Soviet Trade in the Cold War*. Chapel Hill: University of North Carolina Press, 1988.

The author explains why and how the United States after World War II applied economic sanctions toward the Soviet Union to achieve certain foreign policy goals. He maintains that these sanctions failed to contain or modify Soviet international behavior. He offers little analysis from the Soviet side of the equation.

Gaddis, John Lewis. *Russia, the Soviet Union, and the United States: An Interpretive History*, 2d ed. New York: McGraw-Hill, 1990.

The two powers had good relations when "particularist" (national interest) approaches predominated over "universalist" (ideological) concerns in both countries. The second half of the book covers the Cold War in four stages: origins (to 1953), "confrontation to confrontation" (1953–62), "confrontation to negotiation" (1962–76), and the "Rise and Fall of the Second Cold War" (1976–88).

Garthoff, Raymond L. *Détente and Confrontation: Soviet-American Relations From Nixon to Reagan*. Washington, D.C.: Brookings Institution, 1985.

A massively detailed work by a scholar and diplomat. Détente failed because of conflicting understandings of the concept, exacerbated by a lack of sympathy on both sides. Garthoff puts more blame on the United States than on the Soviet Union for the failure of détente. He marshals considerable evidence when criticizing the United States, but in assessing Soviet policy he tends to focus on the Kremlin's statements rather than its actions.

Halliday, Fred. *From Kabul to Managua: Soviet-American Relations in the 1980s.* New York: Pantheon, 1989.

Halliday focuses on key turning points in Soviet-American relations with the Third World during the 1980s. A more aggressive U.S. posture and the Soviet Union's inability to finance Third World revolutions tilted the balance in that arena. The author sees Third World upheavals occurring for reasons unrelated to the superpower rivalry.

Hyland, William. *Mortal Rivals: Superpower Relations from Nixon to Reagan.* New York: Random House, 1987.

An editor of *Foreign Affairs* maintains that every administration since Nixon has settled on something like the détente policies developed by Nixon and Kissinger. However, Kissinger's successors were not as skillful as he was in managing the new balance of power. Hyland, a participant in four summit meetings as a senior assistant to Kissinger, provides an insider's description of events.

Kennan, George F. *The Nuclear Delusion: Soviet-American Relations in the Atomic Age.* New York: Pantheon, 1982.

The nuclear arms race has never been based on a fully realistic American assessment of the USSR. Nuclear calculations and concern over the strategic balance has needlessly hurt relations between Moscow and Washington.

Killen, Linda R. *The Soviet Union and the United States: A New Look at the Cold War.* Boston: Twayne Publishers, 1988.

This volume covers the main events of the Cold War and includes a chronology and glossary. It is sketchy on the period from Nixon to Reagan.

Knight, Jonathan. "The Great Power Peace: The United States and the Soviet Union Since 1945." *Diplomatic History* 6:2 (Spring 1982): 169–84.

Knight analyzes how peace between the United States and the Soviet Union has been preserved since 1945. Although each considered the other an opponent, what they both most feared the destructiveness that would result from another war.

McDougall, Walter. *The Heavens and the Earth: The Politics of the Space Age.* New York: Basic Books, 1985.

The most comprehensive history of the relationship between the space age and international politics available. The author analyzes the political decisions that began and perpetuated the space race and how the United States and Soviet Union went about the business of technological development.

Shulman, Marshall D. "The Superpowers: Dance of the Dinosaurs." *Foreign Affairs* 66:3 (1988): 494–515.

Shulman argues that both superpowers are overmilitarized. He chronicles Gorbachev's changes in Soviet foreign policy and the improved bilateral relations that have come about as a result. He concludes that the competition between the two powers will turn on which nation can adapt to the new requirements of international life.

Sivachev, Nikolai V., and Nikolai N. Yakovlev. *Russia and the United States*. Chicago: University of Chicago Press, 1979.

The authors, both Soviet scholars, cover U.S.-Russian relations from 1776. They blame the United States for the Cold War, citing memoirs and speeches to demonstrate American hostility. They also cite with approval American revisionist historians.

Stevenson, Richard W. *The Rise and Fall of Détente: Relaxation of Tensions in U.S.-Soviet Relations*. Champaign: University of Illinois Press, 1985.

The author examines the major efforts at cooperation during the Cold War, not just the détente of the mid-1970s but "mini-détentes" such as the 1955 Spirit of Geneva, the 1959 Spirit of Camp David, and the post–Cuban Missile Crisis relaxation of tensions. The goal is to understand factors that promoted and blocked U.S.-Soviet cooperation in the four decades after World War II.

Stoessinger, John G. *Nations in Darkness: China, Russia, and America*. New York: Random House, 1971.

Stoessinger examines ten cases (five dealing with Sino-American and five with Soviet-American relations) in which "misconceptions had concrete and specific effects on policy decisions." He shows how self-image and the image of the antagonist has governed the powers' relationships with each other, often to their detriment. A sixth edition of this book—*Nations in Darkness, Nations at Dawn*—was published in 1994.

Ulam, Adam. *The Rivals: America and Russia Since World War II*. New York: Viking, 1971.

A study of the two powers' policies toward each other. Russia skillfully plays a generally cautious power politics game seeking concrete advantages. The American responses are conditioned by a failure to understand what Moscow is up to and by moralistic prejudices. The way to deal with the Russians is by tough and tenacious diplomacy over the long haul.

Wells, Samuel F., and Robert Litwak, eds. *Strategic Defense and Soviet-American Relations*. Cambridge: Ballinger Publishing Company, 1987.

A collection of essays by strategic experts examining strategic defense from Soviet and American perspectives.

U.S. Foreign Policy: Overviews

Ambrose, Stephen E., and Brinkley, Douglas G. *Rise to Globalism: American Foreign Policy Since 1938*, 8th ed. New York: Penguin, 1997.

The first edition of this revisionist overview of American foreign policy appeared in 1971. Ambrose, who wrote the first seven editions of this work, is highly critical of Truman, Kennedy, and Johnson. He is more favorable toward Eisenhower for showing restraint at certain junctures.

Barnet, Richard. *The Roots of War*. New York: Atheneum, 1972.

Barnet sees the key determinants of twentieth-century American foreign policy as domestic factors such as the economy and domestic politics, not foreign threats. He is extremely critical of what he calls the "national security managers." He argues that this elite, drawn largely from law and banking, determines American foreign policy and is immoral, ruthless, hypocritical, and "fascinated by lethal technology."

Betts, Richard K. *Soldiers, Statesmen, and Cold War Crises*. Cambridge: Harvard University Press, 1977.

A comparison of military versus civilian attitudes toward the use of force as an agent of foreign policy. Betts finds that military leaders are less eager to begin hostilities but more prepared to escalate force usage once the decision has been made.

Blechman, Barry. *The Politics of National Security: Congress and U.S. Defense Policy*. New York: Oxford University Press, 1990.

Since Vietnam, Congress has taken a more active role in the creation of foreign policy, despite presidential efforts. This is the result of the increased impact of foreign and security issues on American voters in the last quarter century.

Boll, Michael M. *National Security Planning: Roosevelt Through Reagan*. Lexington: University of Kentucky Press, 1988

A broad analysis of most aspects of national security planning since 1945. Boll analyzes the Reagan administration's change from a "defensive" strategy to a series of offensive plans that included emphasis on rolling back Communism by supporting rebels in Afghanistan and Nicaragua.

Chace, James, and Caleb Carr. *America Invulnerable: The Quest for Security from 1812 to Star Wars*. New York: Summit Books, 1988.

An overview of American foreign and military policy that portrays the United States as expansionistic and interventionist and obsessed with achieving perfect security.

Chang, Gordon. *Friends and Enemies: The United States, China, and the Soviet Union, 1948–1972*. Stanford: Stanford University Press, 1990.

Chang argues that the United States never assumed Communism to be a monolithic movement. The United States tried to promote a Sino-Soviet split; this, Chang says, was Kennedy's primary motive in negotiating the 1963 nuclear test-ban treaty.

Cohen, Warren I. *The Cambridge History of American Foreign Relations*, vol. 4, *America in the Age of Soviet Power, 1945–1991*. New York and London: Cambridge University Press, 1993.

Cohen sees the Soviet-American Cold War conflict as systemic. He focuses on the nature of the Soviet Union under Stalin to explain the course of that confrontation. At the same time, he finds that American leaders exaggerated the threat abroad to enhance their powers at home. Overall, he maintains the world "was a better place" than it would have been without American resistance to "Joseph Stalin's vision."

Combs, Jerald A., with Arthur G. Combs. *A History of American Foreign Policy*, vol. 2, *Since 1900*, 2d ed. New York: McGraw-Hill, 1997.

A postrevisionist/realist overview. Combs includes extensive discussion of conflicting interpretations of events described in each chapter. About two thirds of the book is devoted to the post–1945 era.

Dester, I. M., Leslie Gelb, and Anthony Lake. *Our Own Worst Enemy: The Unmaking of American Foreign Policy*. New York: Simon & Schuster, 1984.

The authors argue that the twenty years after World War II were the golden years of American foreign policy, but that since then the country's government and society have broken down. They urge that the United States substitute pragmatism for ideological warfare in its foreign policy.

Forsythe, David P. *Human Rights and U.S. Foreign Policy: Congress Reconsidered*. Gainesville: University of Florida Press, 1988.

The author traces the role of Congress in framing American human-rights policy between 1973 and 1984. Congress played a largely positive role in shaping the issues and implementation of general and country-specific legislation.

Gaddis, John Lewis. *Strategies of Containment: A Critical Appraisal of Postwar American National Security Policy*. New York: Oxford University Press, 1982.

The author explains national-security policy from Kennan's appointment as director of the State Department Policy Planning Staff to Henry Kissinger's retirement as secretary of state. He sees a pattern of oscillation between Nitze's view mandating a strong response to every challenge and Kennan's view stressing making distinctions between peripheral and vital interests. The result was the failure to develop "a coherent approach" to containment.

Gates, Robert M. *From the Shadows: The Ultimate Insider's Story of Five Presidents and How They Won the Cold War.* New York: Simon & Schuster, 1996.

Gates, former head of the CIA, argues that American policy toward the Soviet Union demonstrated continuity from the Nixon through the Bush administrations. American nuclear policy, notwithstanding criticism made at the time, helped bring the Cold War to a peaceful conclusion, with the United States victorious after a fifty-year struggle.

George, Alexander. *Deterrence in American Foreign Policy: Theory and Practice.* New York: Columbia University Press, 1975.

The author discusses the nature of crisis deterrence and how it has both worked and failed. He uses crises drawn from the Cold War, from the Berlin Blockade to the Cuban Missile Crisis, to make his case.

Jones, Howard. *Quest for Security: A History of U.S. Foreign Relations,* vol. 2, *From 1897.* New York: McGraw Hill, 1996.

Jones generally follows a postrevisionist analysis, supportive of containment. About 70 percent of the book is devoted to the Cold War era.

McCalla, Robert B. *Uncertain Perceptions: U.S. Cold War Crisis Decision-Making.* Ann Arbor: University of Michigan Press, 1992.

On the basis of a study of several Cold War crises, the author finds several shortcomings in crisis decision-making. Among them are that statesmen often are led astray by a lack of information or the power of their beliefs. For advanced undergraduates and graduate students.

Melanson, Richard A. *Reconstructing Consensus: American Foreign Policy Since the Vietnam War.* New York: St. Martin's Press, 1990.

The author surveys foreign policy from Nixon to Bush. His main interest is the relative success each president had in forging a national consensus for their programs. Reagan was the most successful. A second edition of this book, under the title *American Foreign Policy Since the Vietnam War: The Search for Consensus from Nixon to Clinton* (M. E. Sharpe), was published in 1996.

Nathan, James A., and James K. Oliver. *United States Foreign Policy and World Order,* 4th ed. Glenview, Ill.: Scott, Foresman, 1989.

Covering the Cold War era, the authors consider the impact of domestic politics, military power, and strategic issues on American foreign policy.

Paterson, Thomas G., J. Gary Clifford, and Kenneth Hogan. *American Foreign Rela-tions: A History Since 1895*, 4th ed. Lexington, Mass.: D. C. Heath, 1995.

A revisionist history of American foreign policy. About 60 percent of the volume is de-voted to the Cold War era. A revised and abridged edition of this book—by Paterson and Clifford—was published in 1997 with the title *America Ascendant: U.S. Foreign Re-lations Since 1939* (D. C. Heath).

Radosh, Ronald. *Prophets on the Right: Profiles of Conservative Critics of American Globalism*. New York: Simon & Schuster, 1975.

All of the author's subjects, including historian Charles A. Beard and Senator Robert A. Taft, were isolationists before World War II. Yet their concerns—about the growth of presidential power, the erosion of congressional warmaking power, neglect of domestic needs, the militarization of U.S. foreign policy—have relevance to the Cold War era.

Rostow, Walt Whitman. *The United States in the World Arena: An Essay on Recent His-tory*. New York: Harper & Row, 1960.

The author traces the interplay between domestic and external affairs for 150 years prior to World War II before considering the evolution of American society during World War II and the first two postwar administrations. The problem for the United States, he writes, is how to protect national interests in a world where power is rapid-ly becoming diffused.

Schlesinger, Arthur M. Jr. *The Imperial Presidency*. Boston: Houghton Mifflin, 1993.

Schlesinger surveys the "200 years of conflict" resulting from the constitutional division of power. He sees the executive branch unchecked in foreign policy and employment of the armed forces and urges a restoration of the constitutional balance between pres-idential and Congressional powers.

Shafer, Michael D. *Deadly Paradigms: The Failure of U.S. Counterinsurgency Policy*. Princeton: Princeton University Press, 1988.

American policymakers have misunderstood the political context of revolutionary war. American counterinsurgency as a result has been based on false premises and has there-fore failed. The author discusses the Greek civil war, the Huk uprising in the Philip-pines, and Vietnam.

Smith, Tony. *America's Mission: The United States and the Worldwide Struggle for Democracy in the Twentieth Century*. Princeton: Princeton University Press, 1994.

The author considers the impact of foreign policy on democracy abroad, beginning in the late nineteenth century. He traces "liberal democratic internationalism" through the postwar and Cold War years. Suitable for upper-division undergraduates and grad-uate students.

Spanier, John, and Steven W. Hook. *American Foreign Policy Since World War II*, 13th ed. Washington, D.C.: Congressional Quarterly Press, 1995.

An orthodox analysis that places the Cold War in the context of the state balance of power system. Soviet expansionism caused the Cold War and American policy was a necessary response to that threat. The first edition of this book (by Spanier alone) was published in 1960.

Williams, William Appleman. *The Tragedy of American Diplomacy*. New York: World Publishing Company, 1959.

Williams blames the Cold War on American economic expansionism, which is driven by a need for markets abroad. He traces America's "open door" economic policy to the nineteenth century. Domestic economic concerns, not the Soviet threat, drove American policy after World War II. Williams's work in general, and this book in particular, was the fountainhead for the New Left school of historiography regarding the Cold War. Critics of his work have pointed to his failure to provide documentary evidence to back his thesis. Revised editions of this book appeared in 1962 and 1972. It was translated into Russian and published in Moscow in 1960.

Soviet Foreign Policy: Overviews

Bialer, Seweryn. *The Soviet Paradox: External Expansion, Internal Decline*. New York: Knopf, 1980.

Bialer examines the impact of domestic factors on Soviet international ambitions under Brezhnev. The main Soviet dilemma is the discrepancy between military strength and economic weakness. Soviet foreign policy is basically opportunistic rather than ideological.

Clemens, Walter C. *The USSR and Global Interdependence: Alternative Futures*. Washington, D.C.: American Enterprise Institute for Public Policy Research, 1978.

Examines the debate in the Soviet Union between advocates of foreign trade and advocates of autarchy.

Day, Richard B. *Cold War Capitalism: The View From Moscow, 1945–1975*. Armonk, N.Y.: M. E. Sharpe, 1995.

Day considers the extent to which Soviet officials shared the Western illusion of the Soviet Union as a military-industrial colossus and the United States as a nation in decline. The book provides insights into the origins of the Cold War and the tenacity with which it was fought.

Garthoff, Raymond L. *Deterrence and the Revolution in Soviet Military Doctrine*. Washington, D.C.: Brookings Institution, 1990.

Garthoff argues that the Soviet Union always viewed deterrence as a defensive policy, in contrast to the United States, which he says treated deterrence as a means of backing an offensive-minded containment policy. Under Gorbachev, the Soviets have moved further from an emphasis on aggressive nuclear warfighting capabilities to a defensive doctrine of minimally sufficient deterrence.

Gorodetsky, Gabriel, ed. *Soviet Foreign Policy, 1917–1991: A Retrospective*. London: Frank Cass, 1994.

A collection of articles by specialists on various aspects of Soviet foreign policy. Contributors include Jonathan Haslam ("Litvinov, Stalin, and the Road Not Taken"), Mikhail Narinsky ("Soviet Foreign Policy and the Origins of the Marshall Plan"), and Gorodetsky himself ("The Formulation of Soviet Foreign Policy: Ideology and Realpolitik").

Gromyko, Andrei A., and Boris Ponomarev, eds. *Soviet Foreign Policy, 1917–1980*, 4th ed. 2 vols. Moscow: Progress Publishers, 1981.

The Soviet view of what it considers to be its struggle against imperialism, written by a committee of scholars. Gromyko is the long-time Soviet foreign minister. Volume 1 covers the period to 1945 and volume 2 the period since 1945.

Hoffman, Erik P., and Robin F. Laird. *"The Scientific-Technical Revolution" and Soviet Foreign Policy*. New York: Pergamon, 1982.

A study of the Soviet leadership's debate on how to respond to scientific and technological advances. At issue was self-sufficiency versus seeking increased ties with the advanced Western industrial powers.

Lebedev, Nikolai. *The USSR in World Politics*. Moscow: Progress Publishers, 1980.

A professor of history at Moscow University gives the Soviet perspective on the Cold War. He maintains that the United States started the Cold War with its policy of containment. A second edition of this book was published in 1982.

Lenczowski, John. *Soviet Perceptions of U.S. Foreign Policy: A Study of Ideology, Power, and Consensus*. Ithaca: Cornell University Press, 1984.

The Soviet elite is divided between "traditionalists," who have a "primarily orthodox Marxist analysis of capitalism," and "realists," whose more sophisticated view accounts for political forces and trends that reflect the strategic parity existing between the Soviet Union and the United States. Traditionalists emphasize American weaknesses, whereas realists acknowledge American strengths.

MacKenzie, David. *From Messianism to Collapse: Soviet Foreign Policy, 1917–1991*. Fort Worth: Harcourt Brace College Publishers, 1994.

An up-to-date overview that includes a description of the Gorbachev era.

Nichols, Thomas M. *The Sacred Cause: Civil-Military Conflict and Soviet National Security, 1917–1992.* Ithaca: Cornell University Press, 1993.

The "sacred cause" is the primacy of the Marxist historical mission to which the Soviet
officer corps remains loyal. Soviet military-civilian relations have a long history of conflict, and that relationship has become more unstable because of Gorbachev's reforms.

Rubinstein, Alvin. *Soviet Foreign Policy Since World War II: Imperial and Global,* 4th
ed. New York: HarperCollins, 1992.

An account of the evolution, objectives, and impact of Soviet foreign policy since 1945.
A traditionalist approach: Moscow is seen as aggressive, governed by a set of values different from those in the West.

Schmid, Alex P. *Soviet Military Interventions Since 1945.* New Brunswick: Transaction
Press, 1985.

A broad overview, covering the Soviet Union's "intrabloc" use of military force in the
occupation and maintenance of control in Eastern Europe and along the Chinese border, its use or non-use in "interbloc conflicts" (Iran in 1945–46, the Greek civil war, the
Korean War, and the Soviet withdrawal from Austria), and in "extrabloc" conflicts in
the Third World. Ellen Berends provides case studies.

Stalin, Joseph V. *Economic Problems of Socialism in the USSR.* New York: International Publishers, 1952.

Stalin's last theoretical work, which posits conflict between the capitalist states as the
main cause of war. The Soviet Union therefore must be ready for war and focus on
building heavy industry at home.

Tatu, Michael. *Power in the Kremlin: From Khrushchev to Kosygin.* New York: Viking,
1969.

Le Monde's correspondent in Moscow from 1957 to 1964 traces Khrushchev's conflicts
with his Kremlin colleagues, covering a variety of foreign policy episodes in the process.
He says that Khrushchev's main objective in the Cuban Missile Crisis was to take Berlin.

Taubman, William. *Stalin's America Policy: From Entente to Cold War.* New York: Norton, 1982.

Stalin was cautious and conservative and viewed the West as hostile and dangerous. His
détente was designed to undermine Western interests. The author sees détente as a recurring tactic in Soviet diplomacy, even under Stalin.

Ulam, Adam. *Expansion and Coexistence: A History of Soviet Foreign Policy, 1917–1967.*
New York: Praeger, 1968.

A standard text. The author analyzes the perceptions, ideology, and political factors that shaped Soviet foreign policy. He sees Stalin as driven by ideology and equating security with expansion, and therefore largely responsible for the Cold War. Ulam tends toward a realist interpretation of Soviet policy, and his views have been cited by various schools of thought in the Cold War debate to support their views. A second edition appeared in 1974.

Zisk, Kimberly Martin. *Engaging the Enemy: Organization Theory and Soviet Military Innovation, 1955–1991*. Princeton: Princeton University Press, 1993.

A highly theoretical volume for specialists and the sophisticated reader that examines the development of Soviet military doctrine in the post-Stalin era. It examines Soviet reaction to changes in military doctrine adopted by the United States and NATO.

Truman and Containment

Bernstein, Barton, ed. *Politics and Policies of the Truman Administration*. Chicago: Quadrangle Books, 1970.

Five revisionist historians—Bernstein, Thomas Paterson, Lloyd Gardner, David Green, and Athan Theoharis—critique the Truman administration, including aspects of Truman's foreign policy.

Blum, Robert. *Drawing the Line: The Origins of American Containment Policy in East Asia*. New York: Norton, 1982.

The author covers the debate of a new China policy between the White House, Congress, the State Department, the military, and the China Lobby after the fall of the Guomindang. He also discusses how containment led the United States into Vietnam.

Cohen, Michael J. *Truman and Israel*. Berkeley: University of California Press, 1992.

The author says that "Truman never really knew his own mind" and he received conflicting advice. Ultimately, Truman decided pragmatically to support the creation of the Jewish state because it seemed politically rewarding and consistent with the national interest.

Davison, W. Philips. *The Berlin Blockade: A Study in Cold War Politics*. Princeton: Princeton University Press, 1958.

A staff member of the Rand Corporation, Davison consulted U.S. occupation officials, Air Force officers, Berlin politicians, and journalists. He examines the determined resistance of the Berliners, the brilliant improvisation of the airlift, and the unity and clear-headedness of Allied governments.

Gimbel, John. *The American Occupation of Germany: Politics and the Military, 1945–1949*. Stanford: Stanford University Press, 1968.

The occupation policies had continuity and unity. The goals included safeguarding

American security, promoting economic recovery in Germany and Europe, and containing the Soviet Union.

———. *The Origins of the Marshall Plan.* Stanford: Stanford University Press, 1976.

The Marshall Plan was not a unified plan devised at the State Department on Marshall's orders but a series of ad hoc measures growing out of bureaucratic infighting between the State Department and the Army. The compromise solution that emerged favored the Army.

Graebner, Norman. *The New Isolationism: A Study in Politics and Foreign Policy Since 1950.* New York: Ronald, 1956.

The author defends the Truman-Acheson approach to foreign policy against Republican criticism, which he sees as neo-isolationism. The book was published in the midst of the 1956 presidential campaign.

Grose, Peter, ed. "The Marshall Plan and Its Legacy: Special Commemorative Section." *Foreign Affairs* 76 (May/June 1997): 157–221.

Includes George Marshall's original Harvard speech, contributions by historians Dianne Kunz ("The Marshall Plan Reconsidered") and David Reynolds ("The European Response"); profiles of Marshall and Acheson by James Chace, and one of Will Clayton (considered the "idea man" behind the Marshall Plan) by Gregory Fossedal and Bill Mikhail; a memoir by Charles P. Kindleberger; and "reflections" by Roy Jenkins, Walt W. Rostow, and Helmut Schmidt.

Haynes, Richard F. *The Awesome Power: Harry S. Truman as Commander in Chief.* Baton Rouge: Louisiana State University Press, 1973.

The Cold War required an increase in presidential powers as commander in chief, which Truman willingly exercised. Generally favorable to Truman, although critical of his failing to order a test demonstration of the atomic bomb for the Japanese in 1945.

Hixon, Walter. *George F. Kennan: Cold War Iconoclast.* New York: Columbia University Press, 1989.

Hixon, a revisionist, argues that Kennan, who became a critic of the military and global nature of the U.S. policy of containment during 1946 and 1947, was himself responsible for those tendencies. Hixon argues that there is evidence that Kennan worried about the effect of Communist victories in Greece, Italy, and South Korea during the early Cold War.

Hogan, Michael. *The Marshall Plan: America, Britain, and the Reconstruction of Western Europe.* New York: Cambridge University Press, 1987.

The Marshall Plan, described as "the New Deal Synthesis," brought together the "technocorporative formulations of the 1920s" with the "ideological adaptations of the 1930s" in a policy that combined "the freetraders' and planners' approaches." It was a nonviolent way of protecting America's interests by creating an alliance with an integrated and reconstructed Europe that would discourage Communist aggression.

Jones, Howard. *"A New Kind of War": America's Global Strategy and the Truman Doctrine in Greece*. New York: Oxford University Press, 1989.

A study of American policy toward Greece as the focal point in the development of a global containment strategy. The "new kind of war" in Greece was based on infiltration, subversion, propaganda, and guerrilla tactics. The American response under the Truman Doctrine was restrained, flexible, effective, and justified.

Kaplan, Lawrence S. *The United States and NATO: The Formative Years*. Lexington: University of Kentucky Press, 1984.

NATO brought about fundamental changes in world politics. It assimilated West Germany into Western Europe and contributed to the United States shedding "the substance as well as the language of isolationism."

Kennan, George F., and John Lukacs. *George F. Kennan and the Origins of Containment: The Kennan-Lukacs Correspondence*. Columbia: University of Missouri Press, 1997.

Between 1944 and 1946, while serving at the American embassy in Moscow, Kennan exchanged a series of letters with Lukacs. They show the evolution of Kennan's ideas about how to deal with the Soviet Union after World War II.

Kuklick, Bruce. *American Policy and the Division of Germany: The Clash With Russia Over Reparations*. Ithaca: Cornell University Press, 1972.

A revisionist analysis that finds the United States primarily responsible for the division of Germany and the conflict with the Soviet Union. The American goal was to integrate Germany into a U.S.-controlled world economy, which denied the Russians the reparations they had a right to expect.

Kuniholm, Bruce. *The Origins of the Cold War in the Near East: Great Power Conflict and Diplomacy in Iran, Turkey, and Greece*. Princeton: Princeton University Press, 1980.

A postrevisionist analysis in which the Soviet Union is seen as expansionist with a geopolitical framework. The American policy of containment evolved within the context of Soviet activities in Turkey and Iran, the collapse of the Balkans, and Britain's inability to fulfill its traditional role in Greece. The Truman Doctrine stimulated a crusading spirit that damaged national interests.

Lundestad, Geir. *America, Scandinavia, and the Cold War, 1945–1949*. New York: Columbia University Press, 1980.

America's postwar goal was to get the Scandinavian states to adhere to the Western alliance. A generally postrevisionist analysis that sees American policy toward the Soviet Union as flexible rather than completely dominated by anti-Communism.

May, Ernest R., ed. *NSC Sixty-Eight: Blueprint for American Strategy in the Cold War.* New York: St. Martin's Press, 1993.

This volume assesses the impact of NSC 68. Most of the contributors to this volume, with the exception of Paul Nitze, the principal author of NSC 68, criticize the document and do not see it as a sound basis for policy planning.

Mayers, David A. *George F. Kennan and the Dilemmas of U.S. Foreign Policy.* New York: Oxford University Press, 1988.

An analysis of what Kennan was proposing as containment and how it was changed against his wishes into a ring of military alliances encircling the Soviet Union.

McClellan, David S. *Dean Acheson: The State Department Years.* New York: Dodd, Mead and Company, 1976.

The author defends Acheson against his right-wing and left-wing critics. Acheson's policies in Europe were the best that could be implemented at the time. His major errors were in Asia.

McCullough, David G. *Truman.* New York: Simon & Schuster, 1992.

The author's focus is Truman, "an ordinary man who became an extraordinary figure." A sweeping narrative, popularly written and filled with interesting detail.

McGlothen, Ronald. *Controlling the Waves: Dean Acheson and U.S. Foreign Policy in Asia.* New York: Norton, 1993.

The focus is on Acheson's foreign-policy initiatives as undersecretary of state (1946–47) and secretary of state (1949–53). The author covers the reconstruction of Japan, the commitment to the security of Korea and Taiwan, and Acheson's role in America's early involvement in Vietnam.

Miscamble, Wilson D. *George F. Kennan and the Making of American Foreign Policy, 1947–1950.* Princeton: Princeton University Press, 1992.

Containment was not worked out as a clearly delineated strategy but rather formed in a piecemeal and pragmatic manner. A traditionalist approach that sees the United States as having reacted to foreign crises and developments. Kennan was less an "architect" with plans than "one of the on-site builders" of containment.

———. "The Foreign Policy of the Truman Administration: A Post-Cold War Appraisal." *Presidential Studies Quarterly* 24:3 (Summer 1994): 479–94.

Truman's policies were a necessary response to the realities of the postwar world and the Soviet threat to Western Europe and the Mediterranean. Truman did not have an overall plan. Rather, containment received its form and meaning as the Truman administration adopted specific policies between 1947 and 1950.

Ninkovich, Frank A. *The Diplomacy of Ideas: U.S. Foreign Policy and Cultural Relations, 1938–1950.* New York: Cambridge University Press, 1981.

The author argues there was a conflict between advocates of using cultural programs to further international understanding and those who wanted them to serve as an arm of U.S. foreign policy. The latter triumphed in the postwar era as a result of America's overall anti-Communist foreign policy.

Osgood, Robert E. *NATO: The Entangling Alliance.* Chicago: University of Chicago Press, 1962.

A study supportive of Truman that examines the military and strategic problems of NATO in light of the political and technological changes of that era.

Paterson, Thomas G., ed. *Cold War Critics: Alternatives to American Foreign Policy in the Truman Years.* Chicago: Quadrangle Books, 1971.

Contributors discuss critics of Truman's foreign policy, including senators Robert Taft and Claude Pepper, journalists Walter Lippman and I. F. Stone, presidential candidate Henry Wallace, and black dissenters W. E. B. DuBois and Paul Robeson.

Reid, Escott. *Time of Fear and Hope: The Making of the North Atlantic Treaty, 1947–1949.* Philadelphia: Lippincott, 1977.

Written from the Canadian point of view, this volume covers the divergent goals and bargaining strategies of the various countries involved and crucial questions regarding NATO's identity: for example, should NATO be an economic and military alliance and should non-Europeans be allowed to join?

Snetsinger, John. *Truman, the Jewish Vote, and the Creation of Israel.* Stanford: Hoover Institution Press, 1974.

The author maintains that Truman vacillated regarding Israel. At times he heeded the state and defense departments, which did not want to antagonize oil-rich and strategic Arab states, and at other times he listened to Democratic Party staffers who wanted to cultivate the Jewish vote. With the approach of the 1948 election Truman finally assumed a pro-Israel position.

Stephanson, Anders. *Kennan and the Art of Foreign Policy.* Cambridge: Harvard University Press, 1989.

Stephansen argues the United States blundered in 1948 when instead of negotiating with the Soviet Union over Germany it combined with Britain and France to divide the country. Kennan and other U.S. experts on the USSR did not understand Soviet ideology and attributed to the Soviets ambitions they did not have. A settlement was possible.

Wittner, Lawrence. *American Intervention in Greece, 1943–1949*. New York: Columbia
   University Press, 1982.

A revisionist, Wittner attacks Truman's ideological rigidity and support for the Greek
government. He portrays the Greek Communists in a favorable light.

Eisenhower, Dulles, and the "New Look"

Anderson, David L. *Trapped by Success: The Eisenhower Administration and Vietnam,
   1953–1961*. New York: Columbia University Press, 1991.

Eisenhower's handling of Vietnam after the decision not to intervene in Dienbienphu
was a disaster. His administration mistook Diem's façade of stability for success, and this
misconception trapped his administration and those of his successors in Vietnam.

Arnold, James R. *The First Domino: Eisenhower, the Military, and Intervention in Vietnam*. New York: Morrow, 1991.

The author argues that political considerations held Eisenhower back from intervention in Vietnam in 1954, but that in 1955 he made crucial decisions that led to increased
American involvement in that country.

Beschloss, Michael R. *Mayday: Eisenhower, Khrushchev, and the U-2 Affair*. New York:
   Harper & Row, 1986.

The author discusses the CIA spy program that was exposed when Francis Gary Powers
was shot down over the Soviet Union in 1960. He covers the technological background
of the U-2 and provides capsule biographies of Khrushchev and Dulles, as well as of
Trevor Gardner and Kelly Johnson, the two men who developed the spy plane. This
popularly written book for the general reader also focuses on Khrushchev's dangerous
antics and Eisenhower's mistakes in handling the crisis.

Brands, H. W. *Cold Warriors: Eisenhower's Generation and American Foreign Policy*.
   New York: Columbia University Press, 1988.

A collective biography of Eisenhower's foreign-policy team, including John and Allen
Dulles, Milton Eisenhower, and Walter Bedell Smith. Brands criticizes them for apa-
thy toward disarmament and making commitments that exceeded capabilities, but he
credits them for generally keeping the Cold War cold.

Burr, William. "Avoiding the Slippery Slope: The Eisenhower Administration and the
   Berlin Crisis, November 1958–January 1959." *Diplomatic History* 18:2 (Spring 1994):
   177–206.

The author maintains that in response to Khrushchev's speech that triggered the Berlin
Crisis Eisenhower exercised restraint and recognized the necessity of building a consensus with America's allies.

Divine, Robert A. *Eisenhower and the Cold War*. New York: Oxford University Press, 1981.

A positive assessment of Eisenhower that rejects the idea, still accepted at the time, that he deferred to Dulles. Eisenhower's conduct of foreign policy was adroit and underrated. The author praises him for defusing crises and avoiding war.

Finer, Herman. *Dulles Over Suez*. Chicago: Quadrangle Books, 1964.

A critical account of the 1956 crisis on a highly detailed, day-by-day basis. The crisis resulted in a defeat for the United States, for which Dulles was to blame. The author consulted over thirty people who worked with Dulles or the president.

Freiberger, Steven Z. *Dawn Over Suez: The Rise of American Power in the Middle East, 1953–1957*. Chicago: I. R. Dee, 1992.

The Suez Crisis was only the culmination of a poorly conceived American policy directed against Britain in the Middle East. The author maintains that American strategy alienated the Arabs and permitted Soviet expansion in the Middle East. The Eisenhower Doctrine was a device to replace Britain and block Soviet expansion in the region.

Hoopes, Townsend. *The Devil and John Foster Dulles*. Boston: Little Brown, 1973.

Highly critical of Dulles, who is portrayed as a rigid anti-Communist. Dulles' piety and patriotism and his "innate moral and spiritual strength" proved to be a weakness in the pragmatic give-and-take of world politics.

Immerman, Richard, ed. *John Foster Dulles and the Diplomacy of the Cold War*. Princeton: Princeton University Press, 1990.

A collection of papers from the John Foster Dulles Centennial Conference and Princeton University's Woodrow Wilson School of Public and International Affairs. Contributors include Immerman, John Gaddis, George Herring, and Stephen Rabe; topics covered include relations with Western Europe, Latin America, the Middle East, and China and Taiwan.

Kaufman, Burton T. *Trade and Aid: Eisenhower's Foreign Economic Policy, 1953–1961*. Baltimore: Johns Hopkins University Press, 1982.

The author traces the transition from a "trade not aid" to a "trade and aid" policy regarding the Third World. Eisenhower was a "strong activist" president and a political leader of talent and keen intellect, although he did not always provide successful economic policies.

Kunz, Dianne. *The Economic Diplomacy of the Suez Crisis*. Chapel Hill: University of North Carolina Press, 1991.

A study of how U.S. economic policy precipitated the crisis, defined its course, and affected Egypt, Great Britain, France, and Israel. Most of the author's attention is on Great Britain.

Lewis, Roger, and Roger Owen, eds. *Suez 1956*. New York: Oxford University Press, 1989.

A reassessment of the significance of the Suez War of 1956 in light of new evidence, mostly from British archives. The volume contains twenty-two contributions from specialists and an overview by the editors.

Marks, Frederick W. *Power and Peace: The Diplomacy of John Foster Dulles*. Westport, Conn.: Praeger, 1993.

Marks rejects the picture of Dulles as an inflexible ideologue. Instead, he was a professional diplomat whose behind-the-scenes pragmatism and readiness to compromise belied his Cold War rhetoric. He was cautious and pragmatic in dealing with Moscow.

Melanson, Richard A., and David Mayers, eds. *Reevaluating Eisenhower: American Foreign Policy in the 1950s*. Champaign: University of Illinois Press, 1987.

An overview of reevaluations of Eisenhower made since the late 1960s. Among the contributors are Melanson and Mayers, Kenneth Thompson, Norman Graebner, and Richard Immerman. Topics covered include United States relations with the Soviet Union and China, the 1954 decision against military intervention in Indochina, and economic policy toward Latin America.

Parmet, Herbert S. *Eisenhower and the American Crusades*. New York: Macmillan, 1972.

A positive assessment that sees Eisenhower as a pragmatic president who followed a conservative middle-of-the-road path. He could be duplicitous without seeming to be so and was his own man. Parmet traces Eisenhower's career from his decision to resign as NATO commander in June 1952 through his presidency.

Rabe, Stephen G. *Eisenhower and Latin America: The Foreign Policy of Anti-Communism*. Chapel Hill: University of North Carolina Press, 1988.

A critical assessment of Eisenhower's "policy of anti-Communism" in the Western Hemisphere.

Roman, Peter J. *Eisenhower and the Missile Gap*. Ithaca: Cornell University Press, 1996.

In the wake of the Soviet launching of the world's first artificial satellite, the uncertainty about Soviet intentions and capabilities required changes in U.S. strategic nuclear policy. Roman argues that Eisenhower was actively involved in all nuclear policymaking.

Taylor, Maxwell D. *The Uncertain Trumpet*. New York: Harper & Row, 1959.

A critique of Eisenhower's defense policies. Taylor, who served as Army Chief of Staff from 1955 to 1959, calls for a "complete reappraisal" of U.S. strategy. The book's appendix includes an article the author wrote for *Foreign Affairs* in 1956 that was denied clearance by military censors. Taylor later played a major role in the Kennedy administration.

Trachtenberg, Marc. *History and Strategy*. Princeton: Princeton University Press, 1991.

The author focuses on the military strategy of the post–World War II era. He discusses the shift in nuclear strategy between 1949 and 1954, the nuclearization of NATO, the Berlin Crisis of 1958–62, and the Cuban Missile Crisis.

Kennedy and Flexible Response

Ball, Desmond. *Policy and Force Levels: The Strategic Missile Program of the Kennedy Administration*. Berkeley: University of California Press, 1980.

Ball is critical of Kennedy, who, despite his efforts for a nuclear test ban treaty, created a missile force that Robert McNamara called "both greater than we had originally planned and in fact more than we require." The author cites bureaucratic momentum, technical ambitions, and deep feelings regarding "weakness" and "strength" as factors promoting the size of the buildup, which the author says bore little relationship to America's security needs.

Beschloss, Michael R. *The Crisis Years: Kennedy and Khrushchev, 1960–1963*. New York: Ballantine, 1991.

An account of Cold War episodes including the Bay of Pigs, the 1961 Vienna Summit, the Berlin Wall, and the Cuban Missile Crisis. Beschloss provides vivid portraits of important actors from heads of state to KGB agents. It is a detailed and scholarly volume, but is written to appeal to the general reader. It shows how the United States and the Soviet Union nearly blundered into World War III.

Castigliola, Frank. "The Failed Design: Kennedy, de Gaulle, and the Struggle for Europe." *Diplomatic History* 8:3 (Summer 1984): 227–52.

Kennedy's grand design was to shape European development while addressing the relative decline in American power. De Gaulle resisted and ultimately thwarted that design, which he saw as a plan for a Europe dominated by the United States, while asserting French independence in both economic and military matters.

Catudal, Honore M. *Kennedy and the Berlin Wall Crisis: A Case Study in Decision Making*. Berlin: International Publication Service, 1980.

Kennedy's response to the crisis was measured and a compromise between the hawks and doves among his advisors. It was not, as some revisionist historians maintain, "a capitulation to the hard line."

Halberstam, David. *The Best and the Brightest*. New York: Random House, 1972.

A perceptive study of the decision-making process that "got us into Vietnam and kept us there." The book focuses on presidents Kennedy and Johnson and the Kennedy-

Johnson intellectuals, including Robert Kennedy, Robert McNamara, McGeorge Bundy, and General Maxwell Taylor, brilliant men who crafted what the author maintains was a disastrous policy. Written for the general reader.

Hilsman, Roger. *To Move a Nation: The Politics of Foreign Policy in the Administration of John F. Kennedy*. New York: Doubleday, 1967.

Hilsman served both the Kennedy and Johnson administrations. He describes seven foreign-policy crises from the Bay of Pigs to South Vietnam. Despite some criticism, the author praises Kennedy and lists his policies and actions on Laos, the Congo, the Cuban Missile Crisis, China, and Vietnam as successes.

Kaufman, William. *The McNamara Strategy*. New York: Harper & Row, 1964.

A positive evaluation of McNamara's influence. The author covers changes McNamara made in Pentagon operations, his search for a deterrent balanced between nuclear and non-nuclear arms, and his efforts to get the capacity for "flexible response" to various types of threats. The author served as a consultant to the Defense Department, at the Rand Corporation, and as a professor of political science at MIT.

Miroff, Bruce. *Pragmatic Illusions: The Presidential Politics of John F. Kennedy*. New York: McKay, 1976.

A critical overview of Kennedy from a New Left perspective that sees him as counter-revolutionary abroad and conservative at home. Miroff discusses the Cuban Missile Crisis, Vietnam, and the Alliance for Progress, among other issues.

Paterson, Thomas G., ed. *Kennedy's Quest for Victory: American Foreign Policy, 1961–1963*. New York: Oxford University Press, 1989.

Eleven essays on various aspects of Kennedy's foreign policy from a revisionist point of view, uniformly critical of Kennedy. Topics covered include Cuba, Vietnam, Africa, Western Europe, and the Peace Corps.

Reeves, Richard. *President Kennedy: Profile of Power*. New York: Simon & Schuster, 1993.

An account of Kennedy's three years as president, with emphasis on his leadership techniques. Anti-Communism was Kennedy's main visible ideology. The author says that the Berlin Wall, the Cuban Missile Crisis, and Vietnam and the diplomacy of arms reduction all show Kennedy restrained by a Cold War fear of monolithic Communism.

Rice, Gerald T. *The Bold Experiment: JFK's Peace Corps*. South Bend, Ind.: University of Notre Dame Press, 1985.

An account of the development of the Peace Corps, from its genesis as a campaign notion in 1960 to its integration into American foreign policy. The study traces the Peace Corps' early accomplishments and concludes with Kennedy's death.

Schlesinger, Arthur M. Jr. *A Thousand Days: John F. Kennedy in the White House*. Boston: Houghton-Mifflin, 1965.

A "personal memoir" by an historian who also was a special assistant to Kennedy. He strongly endorses his policies and performance as president. Schlesinger supports Kennedy's program of flexible response and praises his handling of various crises, including the Cuban Missile Crisis. He labels the Bay of Pigs a mistake.

Seaborg, Glenn T. *Kennedy, Khrushchev and the Test Ban*. Berkeley: University of California Press, 1982.

Seaborg was the head of the Atomic Energy Commission for ten years, serving in the Kennedy, Johnson, and Nixon administrations. His account covers the five years of negotiations that led to the Limited Test Ban Treaty in August 1963. Seaborg maintains the critical factor in the eventual success of the negotiations was the personal relationship between Kennedy and Khrushchev.

Walton, Richard J. *Cold War and Counter-Revolution: The Foreign Policy of John F. Kennedy*. Baltimore: Penguin, 1973.

A revisionist account that portrays Kennedy as a conventional Cold Warrior. He "accelerated" the anti-Communist policies of Truman and Eisenhower.

Wyden, Peter, *Bay of Pigs: The Untold Story*. New York: Simon & Schuster, 1979.

Considered the standard account of the Bay of Pigs invasion. The author says that factors contributing to the fiasco included ambitions of the CIA's independent ways under Allen Dulles and Kennedy's predisposition to action.

The Johnson Administration (Excluding Vietnam)

Brands, H. W. *The Wages of Globalism: Lyndon Johnson and the Limits of American Power*. New York: Oxford University Press, 1995.

Covers the diplomacy of the Johnson administration, putting Vietnam in the context of other crises and the commitment to global containment. The author discusses Johnson's relations with his foreign-policy advisors and major issues of the mid-1960s, including the Dominican Republic, India/Pakistan, Indonesia, the roles of France and Germany in NATO, Cyprus, the Six-Day War, and Vietnam.

Cohen, Warren I., and Nancy Bernkoph Tucker, eds. *Lyndon Johnson Confronts the World: American Foreign Policy, 1963–1968*. New York: Cambridge University Press, 1995.

An overview of the Johnson administration's foreign policy, including the preoccupation with Vietnam that shaped foreign policy elsewhere in the world. Contributors include

Waldo Heinrichs, Richard Immerman, Robert J. McMahon, and Walter LaFeber, as well as the editors.

Geyelin, Philip. *Lyndon Johnson and the World*. New York: Praeger, 1966.

This volume is in part a character study of Johnson as a molder of U.S. foreign policy. It deals with the NATO issues of that era, the intervention in the Dominican Republic, and Vietnam. The author says Johnson overestimated the utility of his political talents for dealing with problems outside the United States.

Goldman, Eric. *The Tragedy of Lyndon Johnson*. New York: Knopf, 1968.

Goldman was a Princeton University professor who served as special consultant to Johnson until September 1966. The bulk of the book is on Johnson's first year in office.

Seaborg, Glenn T., with Benjamin S. Loeb. *Stemming the Tide: Arms Control in the Johnson Years*. Lexington, Mass.: Lexington Books, 1987.

Seaborg, a Nobel Prize-winning chemist, chaired the Atomic Energy Commission for a decade. He says that Johnson supported legislation to limit the spread of nuclear weapons as an angry reaction to the efforts in that area of Robert Kennedy. Johnson's policies charted the way for others to follow.

The Nixon and Ford Administrations

Ambrose, Stephen E. *Nixon: The Triumph of a Politician, 1962–1972*. New York: Simon & Schuster, 1989.

Ambrose, a revisionist, provides extensive coverage of the opening to China, détente, and the Vietnam War.

Bell, Coral. *The Diplomacy of Détente: The Kissinger Era*. New York: St. Martin's Press, 1977.

Bell's focus is on Kissinger as a theorist and executor of American foreign policy from 1969 to 1977. The author praises Kissinger and strongly endorses his policy of détente and its contribution to arms control, as well as in relation to Vietnam and other international problems.

Bowker, Mike, and Phil Williams. *Superpower Détente: A Reappraisal*. London: Sage for Royal Institute of International Affairs, 1988.

Superpower relations have always been a mixture of cooperation and competition, and the détente of the 1970s was a relative shift toward cooperation. It was not a consequence of American weakness, but of the Nixon-Kissinger team's realistic strategy to cope with changing conditions by managing the rise of Soviet power. The Soviet Union undermined détente by using it as an opportunity to neutralize the United States in the Third World.

Brown, Seyom. *The Crisis of Power: Foreign Power in the Kissinger Years*. New York: Columbia University Press, 1979.

The author generally praises Kissinger's "Grand Design," which was crafted with reference to the power capabilities of the United States, as applied to the opening to China, diplomacy in the Middle East, and efforts to improve relations with the Third World. He is critical of Kissinger's negotiations with North Vietnam.

Kalb, Bernard, and Marvin Kalb. *Kissinger*. Boston: Little, Brown, 1974.

Two CBS correspondents generally admire Kissinger for his diplomatic achievements. He moved American foreign policy away from "utopian illusions" and was a pragmatic diplomat. Kissinger "set aside idealism and does not seek perfection; a product of the Weimar Republic, he seeks only stability." The Kalbs fault Kissinger on several issues, including the India-Pakistan crisis and his handling of Japan during the opening to China.

Korbel, Josef. *Détente in Europe: Real or Imaginary?* Princeton: Princeton University Press, 1972.

The author is skeptical of détente, seeing it as limited in nature and scope and of uncertain durability.

Litwak, Robert S. *Détente and the Nixon Doctrine*. New York: Cambridge University Press, 1984.

The Nixon Doctrine was a strategic devolution to maintain United States commitments at decreased costs. The doctrine is analyzed as it applied to Vietnam and other areas of interest.

Morris, Roger. *Uncertain Greatness: Henry Kissinger and American Foreign Policy*. New York: Harper & Row, 1977.

Kissinger's successes are his opening to China, détente with the Soviet Union, and his Middle East diplomacy. His failures are in Bangladesh, Chile, and Biafra. The author, who served in the White House, State Department, and Senate as a staffer, depicts Kissinger as brilliant but cold-blooded.

Nelson, Keith L. *The Making of Détente: Soviet-American Relations in the Shadow of Vietnam*. Baltimore: Johns Hopkins University Press, 1995.

Both countries moved toward détente because they faced a "scarcity or potential scarcity" of resources necessary to maintain their societies, economies, and governments. The leaders of both countries sought arrangements that lessened the demands on them while allowing them to maintain current foreign and domestic policies.

Pipes, Richard. *U.S.-Soviet Relations in the Era of Détente: A Tragedy of Errors*. Boulder: Westview, 1981.

A conservative critique of Kissinger. The author maintains the Soviet Union believes it can fight and win a nuclear war and will not compromise with the United States. Pipes, a specialist on the Soviet Union, served on Ronald Reagan's National Security Council.

Schulzinger, Robert D. *Henry Kissinger: Doctor of Diplomacy*. New York: Columbia University Press, 1989.

The author covers what he sees as Kissinger's grand failures and stunning successes. A readable and well-documented volume.

Sheehan, Edward F. *The Arabs, Israelis, and Kissinger*. New York: Readers Digest Press, 1976.

Kissinger's efforts led to tactical successes but strategic failures. The author maintains that Kissinger should have put more pressure on Israel to secure a comprehensive peace that included a Palestinian state and Palestine Liberation Organization (PLO) participation in the government.

Stoessinger, John G. *Henry Kissinger: The Anguish of Power*. New York: Norton, 1976.

A sympathetic biography by a former Kissinger classmate. The author explains Kissinger's general philosophy of foreign policy and the connection between Kissinger the scholar and statesman. Kissinger's search for stability is based on the encouragement and preservation of legitimate states and the elimination of revolutionary forces.

Sulzberger, C. L. *The World and Richard Nixon*. New York: Prentice-Hall, 1987.

The author sees Nixon as an adept and far-sighted statesman who will be remembered for his contributions to American foreign policy. His achievements included the rapprochement with China, ending the Vietnam War, negotiations that led to the SALT I treaty, and the Middle East armistice that led to Camp David. Nixon's foreign policy should not be denigrated because it was flawed by the Vietnam situation he inherited or overshadowed by Watergate.

The Carter Administration

Christopher, Warren, et al. *American Hostages in Iran: The Conduct of a Crisis*. New Haven: Yale University Press, 1985.

This volume contains highly detailed accounts by Carter administration officials involved in the negotiations. Among the contributors are Christopher and Harold H.

Saunders, the former assistant secretary of state for the Near East and the head of the Iran Working Group.

Hogan, Michael J. *The Panama Canal in American Politics: Domestic Advocacy and the Evolution of Policy*. Carbondale: Southern Illinois University Press, 1986.

The author examines the debate over the two 1977 treaties to clarify the "perceived realities" reflected in the arguments for and against the treaties.

Jordan, Hamilton. *Crisis: The Last Year of the Carter Administration*. New York: Putnam, 1982.

Jordan, a Carter insider, writes this book in a diary format. He reveals the tensions and inner workings of the White House from the seizure of the hostages until Carter's meeting them after their release.

Lake, Anthony. *Somoza Falling, The Nicaraguan Dilemma: A Portrait of Washington at Work*. Boston: Houghton-Mifflin, 1989.

The author was director of policy planning at the State Department during the Carter administration. Focusing on policymaking, he reveals the tug-of-war between officials appointed by the president and career officials.

Ledeen, Michael, and William Lewis. *Debacle: The American Failure in Iran*. New York: Knopf, 1980.

An account of American-Iranian relations during the crisis of 1978–79. The authors maintain that Carter did not appreciate the realities of the Iranian revolution and was unwilling to impose a clear line on advisors at the State Department and National Security Council. Carter's human-rights policy is attacked for confusing the Iranians. Force properly applied could have saved the Shah.

Moffett, George D. *Limits of Victory: The Ratification of the Panama Canal Treaty*. Ithaca: Cornell University Press, 1985.

The author shows why, after thirteen years of negotiations, forty days of congressional hearings, and the longest floor debate in the Senate in fifty years, a coalition barely produced the necessary votes for passage of the Panama Canal Treaty. He concludes that treaties were Pyrrhic victories for Carter. Moffett was on the White House staff at the time.

Mower, A. Glenn. *Human Rights and American Foreign Policy: The Carter and Reagan Experiences*. Westport, Conn.: Greenwood Press, 1987.

The author compares the Carter and Reagan administrations regarding how they used human rights as a foreign-policy tool. He covers both administrations in general and their policies toward South Korea and South Africa in particular, concluding that Carter had a stronger commitment to human rights than his successor.

Muravchik, Joshua. *The Uncertain Crusade: Jimmy Carter and the Dilemmas of Human Rights*. London: Hamilton Press, 1986.

The author describes Carter's human rights policies and then focuses on four dilemmas associated with those policies: determining the proper relationship between human rights policies and East/West conflict; defining human rights; developing a consistent application of these policies; and devising appropriate punitive measures. Muravchik emphasizes the difficulties of translating human rights principles into concrete policies and maintains that Carter pulled his punches when it came to strategically placed allies or key energy suppliers.

Quandt, William B. *Camp David: Peacemaking and Politics*. Washington, D.C.: Brookings Institution, 1986.

Quandt was the senior Middle East staff member on the National Security Council from 1977 to 1979. This account of the negotiations before and during the 1978 Camp David meeting focuses on the American role, especially that of President Carter.

Rosati, Jerel A. *The Carter Administration's Quest for Global Community: Beliefs and Their Impact on Behavior*. Columbia: University of South Carolina Press, 1987.

The author argues that the Carter administration made a sharp break with postwar American policy by attempting to promote a global community based on an idealistic image rather than focus on preventing the spread of Communism via containment.

Sick, Gary. *All Fall Down: America's Tragic Encounter With Iran*. New York: Random House, 1985.

Sick was the principal White House aide for Iran on the National Security Council in the Carter administration. He is critical of those who believed the Iranian revolution would be moderate. President Carter is pictured as decent and serious, slow to appreciate the Shah's weaknesses, and reluctant to use military power. Sick is generally supportive of Cyrus Vance and critical of Zbigniew Brzezinski.

Smith, Gaddis. *Morality, Reason, and Power: American Diplomacy During the Carter Years*. New York: Hill and Wang, 1986.

The author maintains that Carter's foreign policy was informed by reason and morality to a degree not seen since Woodrow Wilson's presidency. Political considerations at the end of Carter's term caused an increased emphasis on power politics.

Sullivan, William H. *Mission to Iran: The Last U.S. Ambassador*. New York: Norton, 1981.

Sullivan served as ambassador from June 1977 to April 1979. He covers the period immediately preceding the crisis, criticizing the State Department and the lack of clear instructions from the White House.

Reagan: From the New Cold War to Negotiation

Arnson, Cynthia J. *Crossroads: Congress, the Reagan Administration, and Central America*. New York: Pantheon, 1990.

A chronological account of the making of American policy toward El Salvador and Nicaragua during the Reagan era. The author focuses on the tug-of-war between the president and Congress and how efforts to circumvent Congress led to the Iran-Contra scandal.

Bell, Coral. *The Reagan Paradox: American Foreign Policy in the 1980s*. New Brunswick: Rutgers University Press, 1990.

The paradox of Bell's title is the disparity between declarations and operational policies. Bell, a researcher at the Australian National University, argues that in the face of international political realities the Reagan administration had to abandon ideological principles.

Burns, E. Bradford. *At War in Nicaragua: The Reagan Doctrine and the Policy of Nostalgia*. New York: Perennial Library, 1987.

The author criticizes the Reagan administration for its desire to return to the old days of Pax Americana in Latin America, thereby becoming obsessed with the Sandinistas in Nicaragua. He argues that the main issue is whether the developing world will be allowed to seek its own path of political and economic development.

Emerson, Steve. *Secret Warriors: Inside the Covert Military Operations of the Reagan Era*. New York: Putnam, 1988.

The author chronicles how the Pentagon, disgusted with the CIA failure in Iran, conducted its own covert military operations abroad, often without Congressional knowledge.

Fisher, Beth A. *The Reagan Reversal: Foreign Policy and the End of the Cold War*. Columbia: University of Missouri Press, 1997.

The author rejects the idea that the Reagan administration simply played a reactive role vis-à-vis Gorbachev's "new thinking" in the diplomatic process that ended the Cold War. Fisher instead argues that Reagan began seeking a rapprochement with Moscow fifteen months before Gorbachev took office.

Garthoff, Raymond L. *The Great Transition: American-Soviet Relations and the End of the Cold War*. Washington, D.C.: Brookings Institution, 1994.

A account of the Soviet-American relationship under Reagan and Bush from the end of the Brezhnev era to the transformation of the Soviet Union under Gorbachev. Garthoff argues that the Cold War was not won by the Reagan military buildup but ended when a new generation of Soviet leaders realized how badly their policies at home and abroad had failed. Very critical of Reagan, who is pictured as having done nothing right; Gorbachev and Moscow get the credit for bringing the Cold War to a close.

Gutman, Roy. *Banana Diplomacy: The Making of American Policy in Nicaragua, 1981–1989.* New York: Simon & Schuster, 1988.

The author interviewed most of the leading players, from the Contra leaders to Secretary of State George Shultz. He chronicles the struggle between hard-liners and advocates of negotiation in Washington. A good journalistic account by the national security correspondent for *Newsday*.

Kyvig, David E., ed. *Reagan and the World.* Westport, Conn.: Greenwood Press, 1990.

A collection of papers presented at a 1989 symposium on Reagan's foreign policy at the University of Akron. John Lewis Gaddis covers policy toward the Soviet Union, Akire Iriye comments on U.S. relations with East Asia, Geir Lundestad discusses policy toward Western Europe, Philip S. Khoury focuses on the Middle East, Randall Rotberg discusses Africa, and Susanne Jones looks at Central America. Kyvig provides an introduction.

Lagon, Mark P. *The Reagan Doctrine: Sources of American Conduct in the Cold War's Last Chapter.* Westport, Conn.: Praeger, 1994.

The author examines the roots of the Reagan doctrine by looking at aid to several different insurgencies. Theoretical and dense; for advanced undergraduates and up.

Oberdorfer, Don. *The Turn: From the Cold War to a New Era. The United States and the Soviet Union, 1983–1990.* New York: Poseidon Press, 1991.

An account of improvements in Soviet-American relations after the shooting down of the Korean Airlines jet in 1983 to the 1990 summit meeting in the United States. The author, a foreign-affairs correspondent for the *Washington Post*, had access to Reagan, Bush, and George Shultz, and received a Soviet insider's perspective from General Sergei Akhromeyev, the former head of the Soviet General Staff.

Talbott, Strobe. *Deadly Gambits: The Reagan Administration and the Stalemate in Nuclear Arms.* New York: Knopf, 1984.

Talbott examines the START and INF nuclear arms negotiations. He says that Reagan differed from previous presidents in believing that arms-control efforts had weakened the United States and that the Soviets were untrustworthy. Reagan's negotiations therefore were a "gambit" to stalemate arms control. The author, a diplomatic correspondent for *Time* who later served in the Clinton administration, also criticized Reagan in *The Russians and Reagan* (1984).

Tucker, Robert W. "Reagan's Foreign Policy." *Foreign Affairs* 68:1 (1989): 1–27.

Tucker sees Reagan as a "combination of the ideologue and the realist" and credits him with improving America's security position. However, he faults Reagan for failing to confront the American people with the reality that his policies required sacrifices. Instead, he ran up the federal debt.

Bush and the End of the Cold War

Beschloss, Michael, and Strobe Talbott. *At the Highest Levels: The Inside Story of the End of the Cold War.* Boston: Little Brown, 1993.

Bush was slow to react to Gorbachev's offers and late in shifting to Yeltsin as Gorbachev's authority eroded. Between 1989 and 1991 Bush and Gorbachev often operated on the basis of understandings reached in secret "at the highest levels." This enabled them to maintain cooperation despite domestic opposition both faced, but caused them to lose touch with their domestic constituencies. The authors tend to rely excessively on unattributed sources.

Jentleson, Bruce W. *With Friends Like These: Reagan, Bush, and Saddam, 1982–1990.* New York: Norton, 1994.

A highly critical survey of the Reagan-Bush policy toward Iraq, including why the United States tilted toward Iraq during the Iran-Iraq war during the 1980s.

Stalin

Beloff, Max. *Soviet Policy in the Far East, 1944–1951.* New York: Oxford University Press, 1953.

This volume covers China, the Chinese borderlands, Japan, Korea, and (in a chapter by Joseph Frankel) Southeast Asia. The author says that Stalin did not foresee events or act with Machiavellian cleverness.

Djilas, Milovan. *Conversations With Stalin.* New York: Harcourt, Brace, and World, 1962.

Djilas was Tito's liaison with Stalin and met with all the top Soviet leaders between 1944 and 1948. He sees Stalin as expansionist and ruthless, a "monster who . . . could recognize only success—violence, physical and spiritual extermination." Djilas, who had been imprisoned by Tito between 1957 and 1961, was returned to prison after this book—which is part memoir and part history—was published.

Fisher, Louis. *The Road to Yalta: Soviet Foreign Policy, 1941–1955.* New York: Harper & Row, 1972.

A journalistic overview that excels at describing the personalities and motivations of Stalin, Roosevelt, and Churchill. The author criticizes Roosevelt's generosity toward Stalin and his belief that the two superpowers "would guard the globe." He argues that the Soviet Union was expansionistic.

Raack, R.C. "Stalin Plans His Post-War Germany." *Journal of Contemporary History* 28:1 (1993): 53–73.

Basing his conclusions on recently opened East German archives, the author stresses Stalin's "intentionally direct role" in bringing about the postwar division of Germany as part of his ultimate plan to achieve "a Soviet future for all Germans."

Rieber, Alfred J. *Stalin and the French Communist Party, 1941–1947*. New York: Columbia University Press, 1962.

The author describes how the policies of the French Communist Party were determined in Moscow and how the party was hurt by following the Moscow line.

Shulman, Marshall D. *Stalin's Foreign Policy Reappraised*. New York: Atheneum, 1965.

Shuman argues that Stalin's policy was changing during his last years, approximately from the end of the Berlin Blockade in 1949 to the 19th Congress of the CPSU in November 1952. The Soviets were returning to formulations that marked the moderate foreign policy after 1921 and the popular-front strategy between 1933 and 1936.

Stavrakis, Peter J. *Moscow and Greek Communism, 1944–1949*. Ithaca: Cornell University Press, 1989.

Stalin tried to establish Soviet influence in Greece, but pulled back to preserve other wartime gains that appeared threatened by political instability in the Balkans. He was prepared to sacrifice the Greek Communist insurgency to achieve broader Soviet foreign policy goals. The author traces the role the perceived threat to Greece had in bringing about the Truman Doctrine and the Cold War.

Zubok, Vladislav M. " 'To Hell With Yalta!'—Stalin Opts for a New Status Quo." *Cold War International History Project Bulletin* 6–7 (Winter 1995/1996): 24–27.

During his meetings with Mao in late 1949 and early 1950, Stalin was cautious before abandoning the status quo strategy of Yalta and opening a new Cold War front against the United States. He changed policies only after the United States indicated that it was focusing on the defense of its core strategic interests in Japan and Southeast Asia.

Khrushchev and Peaceful Coexistence

Bloomfield, Lincoln, et al. *Khrushchev and the Arms Race*. Cambridge: MIT Press, 1966.

The authors analyze the factors that appeared to influence Soviet arms control policy and describe Soviet negotiating techniques. Among their conclusions is that contrary to the situation before 1953, Soviet proposals under Khrushchev were calculated to achieve an agreement. The book is divided into three periods: Khrushchev's rise to power (1954–56), from Sputnik to the Cuban Missile Crisis (1957–62), and the period of "Détente and Limited Arms Control Agreements" (1962–64).

Dallin, David. *Soviet Foreign Policy After Stalin*. Philadelphia: Lippincott, 1961.

Dallin, a former Menshevik, begins with a discussion of the situation at the end of the Stalin era. He then covers the Malenkov/Molotov era and the evolution of policy under Khrushchev. The focus is on the years 1953 to 1957.

Horelick, Arnold, and Myron Rush. *Strategic Power and Soviet Foreign Policy*. Chicago: University of Chicago Press, 1966.

An examination of the forces and events that shaped the Soviet leadership's attitudes to the political use of nuclear power, focusing on the period from Sputnik to the Cuban Missile Crisis. The authors discuss the "missile gap" myth Khrushchev helped to foster and its use in Soviet policies, especially in the Soviet offensive against West Berlin from 1958 to 1962.

Slusser, Robert M. *The Berlin Crisis of 1961: Soviet-American Relations and the Struggle in the Kremlin, June–November 1961*. Baltimore: Johns Hopkins University Press, 1973.

In examining Soviet foreign policy during 1961, Slusser sees a bitter struggle for power in the Kremlin that climaxed at the 22nd Congress of the CPSU and influenced Soviet foreign policy, especially regarding the United States. He rejects the thesis that Khrushchev alone made policy decisions.

The Brezhnev Era (Including Andropov and Chernenko)

Bialer, Seweryn. *Stalin's Successors: Leadership, Stability, and Change in the Soviet Union*. Boulder: Westview Press, 1980.

Focuses on the impact of succession at the top on the Soviet perception of foreign affairs. The author urges the United States to overcome its obsession with the "specter" of a "largely illusory" potential Soviet strategic superiority.

Dallin, Alexander. *Black Box: KAL 007 and the Superpowers*. Berkeley: University of California Press, 1985.

The author examines possibilities why the KAL airliner strayed over Soviet airspace—rejecting the idea that it was simply mechanical or human error—and the political fallout of the incident. He says the Soviet air defense forces did not know they were dealing with a civilian airliner.

Edmunds, Robin. *Soviet Foreign Policy, 1962–1973: The Paradox of Superpower*. New York: Oxford University Press, 1975.

A British diplomat provides a detailed account of Soviet diplomacy up to détente.

Gaiduk, Ilya V. *The Soviet Union and the Vietnam War*. Chicago: Ivan R. Dee, 1996.

The author, a research scholar at the Institute of Universal History of the Russian Academy of Sciences, had access to Communist Party archives that were closed until the collapse of the Soviet Union. He argues that Moscow provided aid to North Vietnam in order to maintain the Soviet Union's revolutionary status and as part of its competition with Communist China. However, the Soviets simultaneously pursued détente with the United States and attempted to negotiate whenever possible to avoid being drawn deeper into the conflict.

Hyland, William G. "Brezhnev and Beyond." *Foreign Affairs* 58 (Fall 1979): 51–66.

Hyland argues that Brezhnev's strengthening of the Soviet Union's strategic security position has been bought at a high cost to the domestic economy. An American policy of accommodation that will ease the military burden may be very attractive to Brezhnev's successors.

Mitchell, R. Judson. *Ideology of a Superpower: Contemporary Soviet Doctrine on International Relations*. Stanford: Hoover Institution Press, 1982.

The author discusses doctrinal changes of the Brezhnev era, which he says are linked to the need for ideological legitimization.

Solzhenitsyn, Aleksandr. *Détente: Prospects for Democracy and Dictatorship*. New Brunswick: Transaction Books, 1976.

This volume consists of two addresses Solzhenitsyn gave to the AFL-CIO in 1975, in which he maintains that the Soviet Union is still predatory and is using détente as a device to lull the West into a false sense of security.

Steele, Jonathan. *Soviet Power: The Kremlin's Foreign Policy—Brezhnev to Andropov*. New York: Simon & Schuster, 1983.

The author, a Moscow correspondent of the *Guardian* (London), concludes that although Soviet military power has increased since Khrushchev, its influence has declined. The Soviet Union is not expansionist but seeks security and détente in the face of United States hostility.

Tamarov, Vladislav. *Afghanistan: Soviet Vietnam*. San Francisco: Mercury House, 1992.

Tamarov provides both text and pictures to chronicle his tour of duty as a Soviet conscript in Afghanistan. His chief purpose is to describe the disorientation and malaise that gripped the *Afghansi*, as Soviet veterans of that war are known. A graphic account of a fruitless war.

Ulam, Adam. *Dangerous Relations: The Soviet Union in World Politics, 1790–1982*. New York: Oxford University Press, 1983.

The author maintains that Moscow's adherence to dogmas is responsible for entanglements that bring it no gains but damages the situation at home. Moscow's perception of Western strength and unity is a central factor in shaping Soviet foreign policy.

Gorbachev and the End of the Cold War

Blacker, Coit. *Hostage to Revolution: Gorbachev and Soviet Security Policy*. New York: Council on Foreign Relations Press, 1993.

The author provides an overview of the shift in Soviet security policy under Gorbachev from intransigence to cooperation, the relationship of security policy to domestic policy, and the Western, and especially American, response to that shift. He argues that the need to revitalize the Soviet economy led Gorbachev to reappraisal of Soviet security policy.

Brown, Archie. *The Gorbachev Factor*. New York: Oxford University Press, 1996.

The focus is on Gorbachev's attempt to reform the Soviet system and his role in ending the Cold War. The author argues that Gorbachev's failures regarding the economy and minority nationalities are far outweighed by his successes in the realms of democratization and foreign policy.

Gorbachev, Mikhail. *Perestroika: New Thinking for Our Country and the World*. New York: Harper & Row, 1987.

In discussing foreign policy, Gorbachev stresses the need for cooperation and recognition of mutual interdependence.

Levgold, Robert. "The Revolution in Soviet Foreign Policy." *Foreign Affairs* 68:1 (1989): 82–99.

Levgold surveys the fundamental changes Gorbachev made in Soviet foreign policy, arguing that Gorbachev changed the Soviet concept of national security and rejected the Leninist idea of the struggle between capitalism and Communism.

Miller, Robert. *Soviet Foreign Policy Today: Gorbachev and New Political Thinking*. New York: Unwin Hyman, 1991.

Covers the evolution of Soviet policy and its changes under Gorbachev. The author argues that Gorbachev's approach "really differs" from the traditional Soviet practice of seeking a temporary "breathing space" to gather strength before returning to the offensive.

USSR Ministry of Foreign Affairs. "The Foreign Policy and Diplomatic Activity of the USSR (April 1985–October 1989)." *International Affairs* (Moscow), January 1990: 5–111.

An detailed overview, from the Soviet perspective, of Soviet foreign policy under Gorbachev and Shevardnadze.

The Korean War

Blair, Clay. *The Forgotten War: America in Korea, 1950–1953*. New York: Times Books, 1988.

This detailed overview of the military operations of the war is based on U.S. Army records and interviews with participants. It provides an excellent portrait of the American officer corps at war. It also details the struggles between MacArthur and Truman and MacArthur and the Joint Chiefs of Staff.

Cumings, Bruce. *The Origins of the Korean War*, vol. 1, *Liberation and the Emergence of Separate Regimes, 1945–1947*. Princeton: Princeton University Press, 1981; vol. 2, *The Roaring of the Cataract, 1947–1950*. Princeton: Princeton University Press, 1990.

A New Left Marxist analysis extremely critical of U.S. policy in Korea. Cumings maintains that the origins of the war can be traced to 1945 and were "civil and revolutionary in character." The military battles that began in 1950 "only continued this war by other means." He argues that the after 1945 the United States treated South Korea much like an enemy country, suppressing leftist forces and favoring conservatives because of a perceived Communist threat. The author, whose sympathies lie with South Korean leftists and North Korea, makes extensive use of Korean and English-language sources.

Dingman, Roger. "Atomic Diplomacy During the Korean War." *International Security* 13:3 (Winter 1988/89): 50–91.

Dingman argues that atomic diplomacy was part of American statecraft under Truman throughout the Korean War, not just in its waning months under Eisenhower. The main lesson learned was that atomic weapons proved "cumbersome" and imposed more responsibility for restraint than usable power.

Dobbs, Charles M. *The Unwanted Symbol: American Foreign Policy, the Cold War, and Korea, 1945–1950*. Kent, Ohio: Kent State University Press, 1981.

The United States initially sought to disengage from Korea without loss of prestige once hopes of cooperation with the Soviet Union faded. The United States tried to build up South Korea in order to withdraw, but in doing so made South Korea into an inviting target. The fall of China made the United States determined to defend Korea.

Foot, Rosemary. *The Wrong War: American Policy and the Dimensions of the Korean Conflict, 1950–1953*. Ithaca: Cornell University Press, 1985.

Foot sees the Korean War, coming as it did in the early days of the Cold War, as "pivotal" in undermining America's relationship with the Soviet Union and China. It gave definite shape to American policy toward those countries that persisted for decades.

Goncharev, Sergei, John W. Lewis, and Xue Litai. *Uncertain Partners: Stalin, Mao, and the Korean War*. Stanford: Stanford University Press, 1993.

The authors make use of newly available archival material, including the testimony of Ivan Kovalev, Stalin's personal representative to Beijing in 1949; cables sent by Mao Zedong; and other documents. They conclude by saying that Kim Il Sung proposed the war and received extensive help from Stalin in planning and launching the invasion. Mao backed the war reluctantly.

Hastings, Max. *The Korean War*. New York: Simon & Schuster, 1986.

The editor of the *British Daily Telegraph* interviewed Chinese and North Korean veterans, who were off limits to most Western historians. The result is an excellent battlefield history of the war.

MacDonald, Callum A. *Korea: The War Before Vietnam*. New York: Free Press, 1987.

The author covers the political background, especially within the United States. He stresses the fundamental importance of the global strategy the Truman administration adopted in 1950 based on NSC 68 and discusses how the Korean War led to the growth of the American nuclear arsenal.

Matray, James I. *The Reluctant Crusade: American Foreign Policy in Korea*. Honolulu: University of Hawaii Press, 1985.

An overview of American policy in Korea from the attack on Pearl Harbor to Truman's decision to send combat troops in 1950. The shift from indifference to limited commitment to direct military intervention took place within the context of, and in turn influenced, the transition from isolationism to internationalism.

Rees, David. *Korea: The Limited War*. New York: St. Martin's Press, 1964.

An orthodox analysis that maintains that the decision to fight in Korea grew out of the policy of containment. The author provides an outline of the fighting and an analysis of the Truman-MacArthur controversy. The war is seen as a phase in the broader struggle against Communism.

Spanier, John W. *The Truman-MacArthur Controversy*. Cambridge: Harvard University Press, 1959.

The author examines the nature of the controversy but also analyzes the problems of civilian-military relations in a limited war. Although he argues that MacArthur had to be fired, Spanier also focuses on the problems the general faced trying to do his best militarily while operating under restraints imposed from above.

Stein, Arthur A. *The Nation at War*. Baltimore: Johns Hopkins University Press, 1980.

Limited war, as opposed to total war, creates decreased cohesion at home. The author uses quantitative methods, economic models, and statistics to support his thesis.

Stueck, William. *The Necessary War: An International History of the Korean War*. Princeton: Princeton University Press, 1995.

Stueck focuses on the international context of the war. Several Communist states coordinated their efforts just before North Korea launched its invasion of the South. Without Soviet involvement there would have been no war in Korea. The American response to the attack, followed by Western rearmament, deterred an "opportunistic" Stalin from pushing too far elsewhere and possibly igniting World War III.

Toland, John. *In Mortal Combat: Korea, 1950–1953*. New York: Morrow, 1991.

A historian who writes for the general reader, Toland makes good use of hundreds of interviews and secondary literature to create a panoramic and gripping account of the Korean War.

Tomedi, Rudy. *No Bugles, No Drums: An Oral History of the Korean War*. New York: John Wiley, 1993.

The author's goal is to "personalize the Korean conflict in a way that most standard narratives fail to do." Each of thirty-three chapters is told from the perspective of an individual soldier. It covers battles from the Pusan perimeter to the air war. The author fought in Vietnam and was a journalist in Korea.

Whiting, Allen S. *China Crosses the Yalu: The Decision to Enter the Korean War*. New York: Macmillan, 1960.

Whiting focuses on diplomatic maneuvering at the United Nations. China did not participate in the original planning for the war and did not intervene due to Soviet pressure. The author assumes a degree of Chinese-Soviet partnership and emphasizes Chinese aspirations to Asian leadership.

Withersby, Kathryn. "To Attack or Not to Attack: Stalin, Kim Il Sung, and the Prelude to War." *Cold War International History Project Bulletin* 5 (Spring 1995): 1–4.

Withersby analyzes recently released Soviet documents that "vividly" reveal Kim's dependence on the Soviet Union. Stalin decided to permit Kim to invade South Korea only after becoming convinced the United States would not intervene. Seven of the 216 documents turned over to South Korea by Boris Yeltsin in 1994 follow the article.

Vietnam

General Overviews

Bartiz, Loren. *Backfire: A History of How American Culture Led Us Into Vietnam and Made Us Fight the Way We Did*. New York: Morrow, 1985.

The author of this polemical volume examines American cultural values, bureaucratic processes, and what he sees as the worship of political power to analyze American's entry and conduct in Vietnam.

Braestrum, Peter, ed. *Vietnam as History: Ten Years After the Peace Accord*. Washington, D.C.: University Press of America, 1984.

The proceedings of a conference held at the Smithsonian Institution in 1983, attended by fifty leading historians, and analysis. Most of the participants agree that American intervention was a mistake, but also that in a military sense the war could have been "won." They also tended to answer "no" to the questions: Did Hanoi wage and win a "people's war" in South Vietnam? Was the U.S. commitment "immoral"? Was Johnson eager to put U.S. troops into Vietnam? Did U.S. hopes for a negotiated settlement rest on solid ground? Participants included Richard Betts, Harry G. Summers Jr., Larry Berman, and George C. Herring.

Butler, David. *The Fall of Saigon: Scenes From the Sudden End of a Long War*. New York: Simon & Schuster, 1985.

Butler was NBC news bureau chief in Saigon in 1975. His memoirs, drawn from his experiences and interviews with many eyewitnesses, are dramatic and gripping.

Colby, William. *Lost Victory: A Firsthand Account of America's Sixteen-Year Involvement in Vietnam*. Chicago: Contemporary Books, 1989.

Colby started in Vietnam as CIA assistant chief of station in Saigon and participated in CORDS, the intensive 1967–68 pacification program. He says that the war could have been won had more attention been paid to political and social issues, pacification, and fighting an unconventional war. Another error, he says, was the failure to support the South Vietnamese government in 1975.

Duiker, William J. *U.S. Containment Policy and the Conflict in Indochina*. Stanford: Stanford University Press, 1994.

Duiker argues that South Vietnam could not have been kept independent at acceptable cost. Although the North Vietnamese leaders were Marxist, the driving power behind their struggle for unification was nationalism. The bulk of the book focuses on the period up to 1965, when U.S. combat forces arrived in Vietnam.

——. *The Communist Road to Victory in Vietnam*, 2d ed. Boulder: Westview Press, 1996.

An updated version of a 1982 volume by the same name that makes use of new information about the Communist side. The author, who served as a foreign service officer in the U.S. embassy in Saigon, explains why Communist forces were victorious. Suitable for high school students and undergraduates.

Engleman, Larry. *Tears Before the Rain: An Oral History of the Fall of South Vietnam*. New York: Oxford University Press, 1990.

The author conducted more than seventy interviews with Americans and Vietnamese about their experiences during the last days of the Saigon regime. Among those interviewed were some from the Communist side, boat people, and individuals on the last flight out of Saigon.

Fall, Bernard. *Vietnam Witness, 1953–1966*. New York: Praeger, 1966.

A collection of articles that Fall chose based on their long-range accuracy and overall relevance. They cover topics ranging from the French occupation of Vietnam to U.S. involvement and the evolution of the war.

———. *Anatomy of a Crisis: The Laotian Crisis of 1960–1961*. New York: Doubleday, 1969.

Fall, a journalist highly respected for his reporting from Indochina, was killed in Vietnam as he was completing this book, a comprehensive and critical narrative of the origins, major battles, and political developments of the crisis. Fall sees American policies in Laos as aggravating the civil war and as having been doomed to failure.

FitzGerald, Frances. *Fire in the Lake: The Vietnamese and Americans in Vietnam*. Boston: Little, Brown, 1972.

A journalist, FitzGerald spent sixteen months in Vietnam reporting on the war. She argues that the United States misunderstood the nature of the conflict and that its policies exacerbated rather than solved South Vietnam's problems.

Gardner, Lloyd C. *Approaching Vietnam: From World War II through Dienbienphu, 1941–1954*. New York: Norton, 1988.

The author deals primarily with the Eisenhower administration, focusing on 1954. He traces the factors that paved the way for the United States to assume the whole burden for preserving South Vietnam.

———. *Paying the Price: Lyndon Johnson and the Wars for Vietnam*. Ivan R. Dee: Chicago, 1996.

Gardner argues that Vietnam was not just Johnson's war, but is a conflict traceable to New Deal liberalism and Cold War diplomacy. He shows the confusion and despair Johnson and his advisors faced as they confronted the deepening crisis in Vietnam.

Gurtov, Melvin. *The First Vietnam Crisis: Chinese Communist Strategy and U.S. Involvement, 1953–1954*. New York: Columbia University Press, 1967.

This volume focuses on the crisis of 1953–54, primarily on perceptions and policy in Washington and Beijing. The author examines the strengths and weaknesses of American diplomacy and policy decisions.

Halberstam, David. *Ho*. New York: Knopf, 1971.

Halberstam argues that the United States never understood Ho Chi Minh, who symbolized the Vietnamese desire to rid itself of Western domination. The bulk of the book covers Ho up to 1954. The portrait of Ho seems somewhat idealized.

Hallin, Daniel C. *The "Uncensored War": The Media and Vietnam.* New York: Oxford University Press, 1986.

An analysis of *New York Times* and network coverage of the war from 1961 to 1973. The media supported and legitimized Washington's policies before turning against U.S. strategy in 1968.

Hellman, John. *American Myth and the Legacy of Vietnam.* New York: Columbia University Press, 1986.

A study of American memoirs, novels, and films dealing with Vietnam and how they related to this country's national myths.

Herr, Michael. *Dispatches.* New York: Knopf, 1977.

Herr covered the war for *Esquire* magazine during 1967 and 1968. His reporting emphasizes how the war was fought: the details of the violence, the language of the troops, the way the land looked. He is critical of what he considers American delusions and deceptions.

Herring, George. *America's Longest War: The United States and Vietnam, 1950–1975.* New York: John Wiley, 1979.

Vietnam is seen as part of the failure of global containment. The American leadership was unwilling to recognize Vietnam's marginal importance to its United States interests. The United States never developed an appropriate military strategy, relying on massive and ultimately counterproductive firepower. This is considered to be one of the most balanced overviews of the Vietnam War. A third edition was published in 1995.

Isaacs, Arnold R. *Vietnam Shadows: The War, Its Ghosts, and Its Legacy.* Baltimore: Johns Hopkins University Press, 1997.

Isaacs, who covered the war as a correspondent for the *Baltimore Sun*, has written eight essays on the legacy of the war. He rejects as "a sentimental fable" the idea that an idealistic new generation by opposing the war forced a corrupt political establishment to change course. At the same time he refutes the assertions that inept civilians and a hostile press prevented the military from winning the war. Isaacs also argues that the United States treated its Vietnam veterans poorly. He is equally critical of conservative notions of Vietnam as a "noble cause" and leftist academics who have used the Vietnam war as tool for indoctrinating students in their classrooms.

Karnow, Stanley. *Vietnam: A History.* New York: Viking, 1983.

A comprehensive history with extensive coverage of the French occupation of Vietnam, considered one of the standard works on the subject. It became the basis of a television documentary series. The author calls the Vietnam War "The War Nobody Won," ending his account with a chapter called "The Peace That Never Was." A revised edition of this book appeared in 1991.

Kolko, Gabriel. *Anatomy of a War: Vietnam, the United States, and the Modern Historical Experience*. New York: Pantheon, 1985.

Kolko strongly supports what he refers to as "the Revolution" in Vietnam. He severely criticizes the United States for opposing the "irresistibility" of Communism's triumph. The author covers the impact of the war on South Vietnamese society but neglects the atrocities committed by Communist forces.

Lewy, Guenther. *America in Vietnam*. New York: Oxford University Press, 1978.

One of the standard defenses of the American effort in Vietnam. Lewy says that the United States was not guilty of illegal or grossly immoral conduct in Vietnam. Using newly available material, he documents North Vietnamese control of the war in the south from its early stages. The United States exaggerated the geopolitical importance of Vietnam, but the "sad fate" of the local population since 1975 lends authority to the argument that American intervention "was not without moral justification."

Lomperis, Timothy J. *The War Everyone Lost—and Won: America's Intervention in Vietnam*. Baton Rouge: Louisiana State University Press, 1984.

A defense of the American war effort. The author argues that the Communists never won legitimacy in the eyes of the South Vietnamese people. "Thus, although they won, they also lost." The United States could have won the war had the South Vietnamese government not been so weak it required U.S. troops, whose presence undermined the regime's already limited legitimacy.

Nixon, Richard M. *No More Vietnams*. New York: Arbor House, 1985.

Nixon, who was president from 1969 to 1974, claims that "we had won the second Vietnam war" and tries to explain "how we lost the peace." He blames congressional "irresponsibility" for refusing the South Vietnamese air support and supplies and the "outcry of Watergate," which prevented him from countering North Vietnamese violations of the Paris Peace Accords.

The Pentagon Papers. 1971–72.

There are three versions of the *Pentagon Papers*. The first is *The Pentagon Papers: As Published by* The New York Times, by Neal Sheehan and others (Chicago: Quadrangle Press, 1971/New York: Bantam Books, 1971). It contains the complete *New York Times* reporting by Sheehan and others and is edited by Hedrick Smith, E. W. Kenworthy, and Fox Butterfield. This volume contains 134 documents. The second version is *The Pentagon Papers: The Definitive Defense Department History of United States Decisionmaking on Vietnam—The Senator Gravel Edition* (Boston: Beacon Press, 1972). This version was read into the Congressional Record by Senator Mike Gravel of Alaska. It contains two thousand pages of narrative, seven hundred pages of documents, and two hundred pages of statements by government officials. It consists of five volumes.

The third version came from the Department of Defense and was published by the Congressional Printing Office in limited quantities. Published in twelve volumes, it contains almost twice as much material as the so-called Gravel Edition. Its formal title is *United States-Vietnam Relations, 1945–1967: A Study Prepared by the Department of Defense*. None of these editions is complete, all offer pitfalls to the historian, and many documents from different periods are incomplete, neglected, or missing.

Podhoretz, Norman. *Why We Were in Vietnam*. New York: Simon & Schuster, 1982.

Podhoretz sees America's Vietnam effort as a noble cause. But three presidents failed there for different reasons: Kennedy sought a military victory "on the cheap," Johnson erred by simultaneously trying to win and keep his Great Society domestic programs going, and Nixon erred by thinking Vietnamization would work.

Randle, Robert R. *Geneva 1954: The Settlement of the Indochinese War*. Princeton: Princeton University Press, 1969.

The author traces the background of the conference with an emphasis on America's diplomacy of nonintervention. What resulted from the conference was not a peace but a military agreement calling for a cease-fire and regrouping of forces.

Schulzinger, Robert D. *A Time for War: The United States and Vietnam, 1941–1975*. New York: Oxford University Press, 1997.

An overview of the war as a whole, including the debate within the U.S. political establishment concerning war policy.

Shawcross, William. *Sideshow: Kissinger, Nixon, and the Destruction of Cambodia*. New York: Simon & Schuster, 1979.

A correspondent for the *London Sunday Times*, Shawcross argues that the American bombing of Cambodia helped bring about the Khmer Rouge victory in that country.

Sheehan, Neil. *A Bright Shining Lie: John Paul Vann and America in Vietnam*. New York: Random House, 1988.

A biography of the legendary American military advisor who later became a civilian official in Vietnam and was killed there in a plane crash in 1972. The book combines Vann's biography with a history of the Vietnam War and Sheehan's case against American involvement. Sheehan is the *New York Times* reporter who obtained *The Pentagon Papers* from Daniel Ellsberg.

Smith, R. B. *An International History of the Vietnam War*, vol. 1, *Revolution versus Containment*. New York: St. Martin's Press, 1983; vol. 2, *The Kennedy Strategy*. New York: St. Martin's Press, 1985; vol. 3, *The Making of a Limited War*. New York: St. Martin's Press, 1991.

Smith stresses roles of Soviet and Chinese global strategies in the breakdown of the

Geneva Accords of 1954 and the subsequent war in Vietnam (vol. 1). He says the coup against Diem was the most important cause for the deterioration of the situation in South Vietnam in 1963, and faults the United States for its role in that coup (vol. 2). Smith also supports the decisions of Lyndon Johnson that Americanized the war, maintaining that it was justified by the international situation at the time (vol. 3).

Todd, Oliver. *Cruel April: The Fall of Saigon.* New York: Norton, 1990.

Oliver covers the last four months of the Saigon regime. He is sympathetic to the South Vietnamese.

Military Aspects

Caputo, Philip. *A Rumor of War.* New York: Holt, Rinehart, and Winston, 1978.

The gripping memoirs of a young marine combat officer who later became a journalist. Written from the point of view of a soldier, the book conveys the stifling jungle heat, the raw nerves of the weary soldiers, and the general misery of the war. Caputo captures the war as it was.

Clodfelter, Mark. *The Limits of Power: The American Bombing of North Vietnam.* New York: Free Press, 1989.

A history professor at the Air Force Academy, Clodfelter argues that American air commanders and political leaders were formed by their experiences in World War II and Korea and believed, incorrectly, that they were fighting a similar war in Vietnam.

Davidson, Phillip. *Vietnam and War: A History, 1946–1975.* Novato, Cal.: Presidio Press, 1988.

A comprehensive military history. The author uses materials about Communist forces from captured documents, intensive interviews of Vietcong soldiers, and recent North Vietnamese writings. He discusses three wars: the French (1946–54), the American (1964–73), and the Vietnamese (1973–75). He argues that Tet was a victory stolen from the United States by the press, which portrayed it as a defeat.

Fall, Bernard. *Hell in a Very Small Place: The Siege of Dien Bien Phu.* Philadelphia: Lippincott, 1966.

An highly detailed account of the fifty-five-day siege in 1954. Fall says that U.S. air power, which was promised but not provided, could have saved the French fortress.

Gibson, James William. *The Perfect War: Technowar in Vietnam.* New York: Atlantic Monthly Press, 1986.

The author argues that the United States relied too much on technology, while American officers saw themselves as managers rather than combat leaders. Gibson says little about the brutalities inflicted by the North Vietnamese and Vietcong.

Goldman, Peter, et al. "What the Vietnam War Did to Us: Survivors of Charlie Company Relive the War and the Decade Since." *Newsweek*, December 14, 1981, 46–97.

A gripping collective memoir based on interviews with many of the men of Charlie Company and relatives of those who died.

Krepinevich, Andrew F. Jr. *The Army in Vietnam*. Baltimore: Johns Hopkins University Press, 1986.

A member of the Strategic Planning and Policy Division of the army analyzes U.S. military policy in Vietnam from 1954 to 1973. The U.S. mission was "foredoomed from the start" because the military used conventional tactics applicable to Europe. It should have used counterinsurgency tactics.

Moore, Harold G., and Joseph L. Galloway. *We Were Soldiers Once—and Young: Ia Drang, the Battle That Changed the War in Vietnam*. New York: Random House, 1992.

A gripping account of the fierce battle fought between U.S. troops and North Vietnam regulars in November 1965. It is an hour-by-hour and blow-by-blow account of the fighting, which lasted for four days and four nights. Moore, who was a lieutenant colonel and battalion commander during the battle, and Galloway, who was a reporter for United Press International, spent ten years researching and conducted hundreds of interviews to write this book.

Palmer, Bruce Jr. *The 25-Year War: America's Military Role in Vietnam*. Lexington: University of Kentucky Press, 1984.

Palmer was a field commander in Vietnam who graduated in the same class (1936) as William Westmoreland; his book is part history, part memoir, and part critique. He blames America's top political and military leaders and the faulty strategy they followed for the defeat.

Pisor, Robert L. *The End of the Line: The Siege of Khe Sanh*. New York: Norton, 1982.

Pisor was in Vietnam during 1967–68 as a war correspondent for the *Detroit News*. He describes the history, politics, and strategies of the battle for Khe Sanh. Pisor argues that General Westmoreland's figures of 205 American dead and 10,000–15,000 Vietnamese dead were, respectively, a deception and a fiction.

Specter, Ronald H. *Advice and Support: The Early Years of the United States Army in Vietnam, 1941–1960*. New York: Free Press, 1985.

This volume is the first of a series planned by the Center for Military History and is supportive of the U.S. effort in Vietnam. Still, the author criticizes the U.S. leadership for underestimating the strength of Vietnamese nationalism and that of the U.S. Army for believing that military power alone could achieve American goals in Vietnam.

———. *After Tet: The Bloodiest Year in Vietnam.* New York: Free Press, 1993.

The year after Tet (1968) was the bloodiest of the war for American forces. The author is critical of the high price the United States paid for empty victories and the failure of American leaders to see that what for them was a limited war was for the Vietnamese an unlimited war for survival. The author, a professor of international affairs, served in Vietnam as a marine during that year.

Summers, Harry G. Jr. *On Strategy: A Critical Analysis of the Vietnam War.* Novato, Cal.: Presidio Press, 1982.

Summers served on the staff of the Strategic Studies Institute of the Army War College. He argues that the war was winnable. But a lack of understanding of military theory and the relationship between military strategy and national policy undermined the U.S. effort in Vietnam.

Westmoreland, William C. *A Soldier Reports.* New York: Doubleday, 1976.

The commander of American forces in Vietnam devotes most of his book to his service in Vietnam between 1964 and 1968. He argues that Tet was a serious defeat for the Communists and that the war, though winnable, was lost because the civilian leadership in Washington failed to supply sufficient resources to do the job.

Wirtz, James J. *The Tet Offensive: Intelligence Failures in War.* Ithaca: Cornell University Press, 1991.

The author analyzes the Communist strategy of deception that preceded the Tet offensive and the American failure to see what was happening. A technical volume suitable to upper-division undergraduates and graduate students.

Policy Aspects

Berman, Larry. *Planning a Tragedy: The Americanization of the War in Vietnam.* New York: Norton, 1982.

An overview of how Johnson and his advisors decided to commit massive numbers of American troops to support South Vietnam in July 1965. American officials were oblivious to the nature of Vietnamese Communism. However, national security advisor McGeorge Bundy was skeptical and hesitant.

———. *Lyndon Johnson's War: The Road to Stalemate in Vietnam.* New York: Norton, 1989.

A sequel to *Planning a Tragedy.* The author examines the flawed decision-making that led to stalemate. He puts the blame on President Lyndon Johnson, but also shows how generals protecting their careers and close advisors unwilling to dissent played important roles.

Berman, William C. *William Fulbright and the Vietnam War: The Dissent of a Political Realist*. Kent, Ohio: Kent State University Press, 1988.

An in-depth overview of Fulbright's views and his change of heart from being the floor manager for the Gulf of Tonkin Resolution to becoming one of the leading congressional opponents of the war.

Buttinger, Joseph. *Vietnam: The Unforgettable Tragedy*. New York: Horizon Press, 1977.

Buttinger was involved in the effort to install, maintain, and depose Diem. He sees U.S. involvement as "ill advised." Among the reasons it failed were ignorance, unexamined ends, and the lack of political courage to admit error.

Buzzanco, Robert. "Prologue to Tragedy: U.S. Military Opposition to Intervention in Vietnam, 1950–1954." *Diplomatic History* 17:2 (Spring 1993): 201–22.

The American military opposed intervention in Vietnam on several grounds. Senior officers doubted that the United States had resources available in light of its worldwide commitments, especially in Europe. They also argued that conditions in Vietnam were not favorable in light of the deep indigenous roots of the independence struggle. Government leaders ignored "clear and detailed" warnings and "knowledgeable counsel" as they increased the U.S. commitment in Vietnam.

Dileo, David L. *George Ball, Vietnam, and the Rethinking of Containment*. Chapel Hill: University of North Carolina Press, 1991.

Ball was deputy secretary of state from 1961–1966. The author profiles Ball's opposition to the American role in Vietnam and his efforts to stop escalation.

Gelb, Leslie H., and Richard K. Betts. *The Irony of Vietnam: The System Worked*. Washington, D.C.: Brookings Institution, 1979.

The bureaucratic system provided Johnson and his advisors with good information as it was supposed to. However, Johnson escalated because he feared the political fallout that would result from defeat.

Gibbons, William Conrad. *The United States Government and the Vietnam War: Executive and Legislative Policy and Relations*. Part I, 1945–1960. Part II, 1961–1964. Princeton: Princeton University Press, 1986.

This study was prepared for the Senate Committee on Foreign Relations by the Congressional Research Service. It originally was published by the U.S. Government Printing Office.

Holsti, Ole, and James R. Rosenau. *American Leadership in World Affairs: Vietnam and the Breakdown of Consensus*. Boston: Allen and Unwin, 1984.

American foreign policy, as viewed by people in positions of leadership in the 1976 and 1980 elections, was in disarray. The war in Vietnam was the cause of that disarray.

Hoopes, Townsend. *The Limits of Intervention: An Inside Account of How the Johnson Policy of Escalation Was Reversed*. New York: McKay, 1969.

Hoopes, who served as undersecretary of the Air Force from 1967 to 1969, was a participant in the decision to stop the bombing of North Vietnam. He provides a critical view of the policy struggles and people involved that led to the decision to deescalate in March 1968. The author criticizes Johnson's inflexibility and his hawkish advisors.

Hunt, Michael H. *Lyndon Johnson's War: America's Cold War Crusade in Vietnam, 1945–1968*. New York: Hill and Wang, 1996.

The author criticizes American policymakers for viewing Vietnamese problems strictly within the context of the Cold War. He is critical of Eisenhower for ignoring Vietnamese nationalism and of Kennedy for his strict Cold War outlook, but is most critical of Johnson for viewing Vietnam in terms of 1930s Europe. The author provides a good bibliographical essay for students.

Isaacs, Arnold. *Without Honor: Defeat in Vietnam and Cambodia*. Baltimore: Johns Hopkins University Press, 1983.

The author covered Vietnam for the *Baltimore Sun* from 1972 to 1978. America viewed Indochina through a Cold War prism. Its failure was not one of will but resulted from ignorance of local conditions.

Kahin, George McT. *Intervention: How America Became Involved In Vietnam*. New York: Knopf, 1986.

Kahin chronicles the development of American involvement from 1945 to 1966, indicating opportunities the United States had to get out. Johnson was reluctant to bomb North Vietnam and send American combat troops to the south, but ultimately listened to "expert military advice" and did both.

Newman, John M. *JFK and Vietnam: Deception, Intrigue, and the Struggle for Power*. New York: Warner Books, 1992.

The author is a retired army officer and military historian with broad experience in Southeast Asia. Based on an extensive study of the available documents, he argues that Kennedy never would have sent combat troops to Vietnam. He planned to withdraw military advisors in 1965. Newman also maintains that in 1963 Kennedy told senators Mike Mansfield and Wayne Morse, both opponents of the war, that he planned to withdraw.

Rotter, Andrew J. *The Path to Vietnam: Origins of American Containment in Southeast Asia*. Ithaca: Cornell University Press, 1987.

An analysis of the Truman administration's decision to provide economic and military aid to the nations of Southeast Asia. The goal was to revive Southeast Asia economically and strengthen it against Communist expansion.

Rust, William J. *Kennedy in Vietnam*. New York: Scribner's, 1985.

This volume focuses on 1963 and the military coup that overthrew Diem. Rust argues that Kennedy would have withdrawn from Vietnam after 1964. Suitable for upper-division undergraduates.

Snepp, Frank. *Decent Interval: An Insider's Account of Saigon's Indecent End*. New York: Random House, 1978.

Snepp was a CIA analyst posted to the Saigon embassy. He says American officials failed to heed the portents of disaster and persisted in the illusion of a negotiated settlement. He details the infighting within the various American agencies operating in Vietnam.

Thies, Wallace J. *When Governments Collide: Coercion and Diplomacy in the Vietnam Conflict, 1964–1968*. Berkeley: University of California Press, 1980.

An examination of President Johnson's efforts between 1964 and 1968 to coerce the government of North Vietnam to cease its activities in South Vietnam, beginning with covert operations and culminating in the Rolling Thunder bombing campaign. The author also discusses North Vietnamese decision-making.

Antiwar Movement/Domestic Aspects

DeBenedetti, Charles. *An American Ordeal: The Antiwar Movement of the Vietnam Era*. Syracuse, N.Y.: Syracuse University Press, 1990.

The author explains the emergence of opposition to the Vietnam War in the United States, the relationship of the movement to changing popular moods, and the interaction between the antiwar dissenters and the U.S. government. He argues that the movement was both cultural and political, and that its central paradox was that its cultural power compromised its political effectiveness.

Garfinkle, Adam M. *Tell-Tale Hearts: The Origins and Impact of the Vietnam Antiwar Movement*. New York: St. Martin's Press, 1995.

Garfinkle explores the impact of the Vietnam experience on American society from the perspective of the antiwar movement. He concludes that the movement was counterproductive at crucial junctures of the war, that it was the product of broader changes in American society, and that it has had a continuing role in American society. Garfinkle is critical of the antiwar movement and the contemporary left, arguing that the war was winnable and that the antiwar movement actually prolonged the war.

Heineman, Kenneth J. *Campus Wars: The Peace Movement at American State Universities in the Vietnam Era*. New York: New York University Press, 1993.

An overview of the rise of the political left and peace activities from the beginning of the Vietnam War to 1972 at four major state universities: Michigan State, Pennsylvania State, Kent State, and the State University of New York at Buffalo. The author concludes that just as state universities reflected the heartland of America, their student protests illustrated the depth of the anguish over U.S. involvement in Vietnam.

Levy, David. *The Debate Over Vietnam*. Baltimore: Johns Hopkins University Press, 1991.

Levy surveys the cultural issues, foreign-policy concerns, social movements, and political anxieties that shaped the debate over Vietnam. The main division between opponents and supporters of the war was the issue of whether the war was just or not; in that sense the Vietnam War was not unique in American history, but lies within the tradition that includes the Civil War, the Mexican War, and the Spanish-American War.

Rudensteine, David. *The Day the Presses Stopped: A History of the Pentagon Papers Case*. Berkeley: University of California Press, 1997.

A chronicle of the Nixon administration's unsuccessful attempt to stop the *New York Times* and *Washington Post* from publishing these materials. The case is considered a landmark in protecting the press from censorship. Yet the author, an associate dean at Cardozo Law School, supports the government case that the Pentagon Papers contained information that damaged national interest.

Zaroulis, Nancy, and Gerald Sullivan. *Who Spoke Up? American Protests Against the War in Vietnam, 1963–1975*. New York: Doubleday, 1984.

An overview of the sources, operation, and changing nature of American opposition to the war. The author focuses on the movement's leftist leadership and sees the protests as a true expression of American conscience and patriotism.

Cuba and the Cuban Missile Crisis

Abel, Elie. *The Missile Crisis*. New York: Bantam, 1966.

An NBC correspondent sketches the background and then provides an hour-by-hour account of the thirteen days of the crisis. The book includes the Defense Department photos that proved Soviet missiles were in Cuba. An excellent short account for the general reader.

Allison, Graham. *Essence of Decision: Explaining the Cuban Missile Crisis*. Boston: Little, Brown, 1971.

The author examines policymaking during the crisis. An attempt to combine political science theory and an analytical narrative.

Anderson, Jon Lee. *Che Guevara: A Revolutionary Life*. New York: Grove Press, 1997.

Anderson, a journalist, has written the first major biography of Guevara. The author argues that Guevara's resignation from his posts in Castro's government did not signify a break between the two men. While publicly following the Soviet line, Castro agreed with Guevara that the only way for Cuba to break out of its isolation was to foment revolution elsewhere in Latin America.

Blight, James G., and David A. Welch, eds. *On the Brink: Americans and Soviets Reexamine the Cuban Missile Crisis*. New York: Hill and Wang, 1989.

This volume contains the edited transcript of the 1987 Hawk's Cay Conference that brought together major participants from the Kremlin and the White House, the edited transcript of the Cambridge conference that included American and Soviet participants, and additional interviews with Dean Rusk, Robert McNamara, Douglas Dillon, and Paul Nitze. The editors add analysis and commentary and biographical sketches of thirty-one participants.

Dinerstein, Herbert. *The Making of the Missile Crisis: October 1962*. Baltimore: Johns Hopkins University Press, 1976.

The author shows how American anti-Communist policies, Soviet strategic goals, the ambitions of the Latin American left, and Castro's revolution combined to lead to the crisis.

Divine, Robert A., ed. *The Cuban Missile Crisis*. New York: A. Wiener Publishers, 1988.

A collection divided into several sections: international reactions to the crisis, the problem of Soviet motivation, the continuing debate, and scholarly assessments. Among the contributors are Theodore Sorenson, Barton Bernstein, Thomas Paterson, and James A. Nathan.

Duncan, W. Raymond. *The Soviet Union and Cuba: Interests and Influence*. New York: Praeger, 1985.

An overall assessment of the Cuban-Soviet relationship. The author examines the stresses in the relationship and the extent to which Cuba serves as a Soviet client.

Furchenko, Aleksandr, and Timothy Naftali. *"One Hell of a Gamble": Khrushchev, Castro, and Kennedy, 1958–1964*. New York: Norton, 1997.

The authors, a member of the Russian Academy of Sciences and an American-educated historian, had unprecedented access to Soviet archives. They stress the close ties between Fidel Castro, Che Guevara, and Moscow and discuss President Kennedy's effort to foster détente in the two years prior to the crisis. The Soviet leadership decided to put missiles in Cuba to remind Washington of Soviet power and to demonstrate to Castro the Soviet commitment to defend his revolution. Khrushchev was prepared to use nuclear missiles against an American invasion force in this story of "unintended consequences" that has "neither heroes nor villains."

Garthoff, Raymond. *Reflections on the Cuban Missile Crisis*. Washington, D.C.: Brookings Institution, 1987.

Garthoff was a participant in the crisis deliberations as a State Department official. He discusses the origins, unfolding, and consequences of the crisis and analyzes the Soviet understanding of the crisis and the lessons they may have drawn from the event.

Higgins, Trumbull. *The Perfect Failure: Kennedy, Eisenhower, and the CIA at the Bay of Pigs.* New York: Norton, 1987.

The author focuses on Kennedy before and after the invasion and argues that Kennedy warily implemented the project that was flawed from the start. Faulty intelligence from the CIA contributed to the defeat.

Kennedy, Robert F. *The Thirteen Days: A Memoir of the Cuban Missile Crisis.* New York: Norton, 1969.

Kennedy describes the president's advisors in their working sessions, providing insight into decision-making at the highest level. The memoir also shows the effects of extreme stress in a crisis situation.

Morley, Morris H. *The Imperial State and Revolution: The United States and Cuba, 1952–1986.* New York: Cambridge University Press, 1987.

A New Left, highly economic-deterministic analysis that sees American policy toward Cuba governed by "the interests and demands of capitalists."

Nathan, James A., ed. *The Cuban Missile Crisis Revisited.* New York: St. Martin's Press, 1992.

Contributors include Barton Bernstein, Ned Lebow, and Lawrence Chang and are generally critical of Kennedy's handling of the crisis. This volume tends to view Khrushchev, rather than Kennedy, as the winner in the crisis.

Smith, Wayne. *The Closest of Enemies: A Personal and Diplomatic Account of U.S.-Cuban Relations Since 1957.* New York: Norton, 1987.

A former foreign service officer who resigned in 1982, Smith is critical of American reliance on covert action and isolation rather than diplomacy vis-à-vis Cuba.

Welch, Richard E. Jr. *Response to Revolution: The United States and the Cuban Revolution, 1959–1961.* Chapel Hill: University of North Carolina Press, 1985.

An examination of Washington's response to Castro's revolution as well as the public's reaction, and how that reaction affected policymaking. The author is critical of both Eisenhower and Kennedy. He also focuses on the Cuban revolution as it moved from a reformist to a radical Marxist path.

Nuclear Weapons, Arms Control, and Military Policy

Ball, Howard. *Justice Downwind: America's Atom Testing Program in the 1950s.* New York: Oxford University Press, 1986.

The author chronicles the impact of nuclear tests at the Yucca Flats test site in Nevada between 1951 and 1963 on 100,000 people in Nevada, Arizona, and southern Utah. He argues that the Atomic Energy Commission behaved irresponsibly.

Blacker, Coit D. *Reluctant Warriors: The United States, the Soviet Union, and Arms Control*. New York: W. H. Freeman, 1987.

The author covers Soviet-American relations since the advent of nuclear weapons and the radical change those weapons have had on the concepts of offense, defense, and deterrence. The book is clearly written in understandable language and features a chronology and glossary of terms. Blacker is at the Center for International Security and Arms Control at Stanford University.

Borowski, Harry R. *A Hollow Threat: Strategic Air Power and Containment Before Korea*. Westport, Conn.: Greenwood Press, 1982.

America's Strategic Air Command was not a capable nuclear deterrent before the Korean War. They key bottleneck was the lack of assembly teams—there were only three—to put the atomic bombs together, not the number of bombs.

Brians, Paul. *Nuclear Holocausts: Atomic War in Fiction, 1895–1897*. Kent, Ohio: Kent State University Press, 1987.

A survey of fiction, including plays, published in English, depicting nuclear war and its aftermath. The bibliography contains more than eight hundred entries.

Brown, Harold. *Thinking About National Security*. Boulder: Westview, 1983.

President Carter's secretary of defense examines the security relationship between the Soviet Union and the United States. Topics covered include nuclear weapons strategy, regional security threats, arms limitations, and the problem of managing the "massive U.S. defense establishment."

Bundy, McGeorge. *Danger and Survival: Choices About the Bomb in the First Fifty Years*. New York: Random House, 1988.

A political history of the nuclear age by a former national security advisor to presidents Kennedy and Johnson. More detailed on the earlier period (Roosevelt through Eisenhower), including forty pages on the bombing of Hiroshima. Bundy argues that nuclear superiority does not help the United States and never has; parity with the Soviet Union is sufficient.

Bundy, McGeorge, George F. Kennan, Robert S. McNamara, and Gerard Smith. "Nuclear Weapons and the Atlantic Alliance." *Foreign Policy* 60 (Spring 1982): 753–68.

The famous statement advocating a NATO policy of no-first-use regarding nuclear weapons. The authors argue that even the use of nuclear weapons on the smallest scale is likely to lead to disastrous escalation.

Cox, Arthur. *Russian Roulette: The Superpower Game.* Soviet commentary by Georgy Arbatov. New York: Times Books, 1982.

A critique of Reagan administration nuclear strategy by an advocate of détente. Arbatov was the top Soviet expert on the United States.

Dinerstein, Herbert S. *War and the Soviet Union: Nuclear Weapons and the Revolution in Soviet Military and Political Thinking.* New York: Praeger, 1959.

An analysis of Soviet nuclear strategy in the years after Stalin's death, which the author suggests has switched to an offensive and "pre-emptive" mode. The study was done for the Rand Corporation.

Evangelista, Mathew. *Innovation and the Arms Race: How the United States and the Soviet Union Develop New Military Technologies.* Ithaca: Cornell University Press, 1988.

The author argues that in the United States decisions are made "from the bottom," that is, at the initiative of corporation or government researches. In the Soviet Union they are made "from the top," that is, in response to foreign developments. This argument seemed superficial to some critics.

Freedman, Lawrence. *The Evolution of Nuclear Strategy.* New York: St. Martin's Press, 1981.

Covers strategic thinking and the debates surrounding it from World War II to Carter. Among the topics covered are massive retaliation, limited nuclear war, counterforce targeting, and MAD (mutual assured destruction). The author has served as head of policy studies at the Royal Institute of International Affairs, London.

Glynn, Patrick. *Closing Pandora's Box: Arms Races, Arms Control, and the History of the Cold War.* New York: Basic Books, 1993.

The author argues that the arms race was not destabilizing. Instead, military strength serves as a deterrent to aggression. Idealists and revisionists are to blame for the Cold War. The Reagan administration's strategy—first building up America's strength and then offering reciprocal détente—planted the seeds for the collapse of Communist power.

Halperin, Morton. *Nuclear Fallacy: Dispelling the Myth of Nuclear Strategy.* New York: Ballinger, 1987.

Eisenhower institutionalized the assumption that nuclear weapons can be used to fight and win wars. Halperin argues that this is fallacious: nuclear weapons on the battlefield will destroy what they are supposed to defend. Written for the general reader.

Herken, Greg. *The Winning Weapon: The Atomic Bomb and the Cold War.* New York: Knopf, 1981.

An overview of how American policymakers viewed the atomic bomb during the period of this country's nuclear monopoly (1945–49) and the growing role the bomb played in diplomatic and military policy. There was widespread wishful thinking in the government bureaucracy, despite evidence to the contrary, that the nuclear monopoly would last a long time.

Holloway, David. *The Soviet Union and the Arms Race.* New Haven: Yale University Press, 1983.

The author examines the doctrinal, economic, political, and technical factors that influence Soviet arms policies. He argues that they are a product of specific decisions made in a distinct institutional setting under the influence of particular circumstances. They cannot be explained by theoretical models. The Soviets value nuclear weapons both for their potential military utility and political effect. They have made the Soviet Union a superpower, but at great economic cost. A balanced and highly regarded analysis.

Huntington, Samuel P. *The Common Defense: Strategic Programs in National Politics.* New York: Columbia University Press, 1961.

A highly regarded analysis of military policy under Truman and Eisenhower. The author analyzes the politics of decision-making that shaped changes in American military policy between 1945 and 1961.

Kissinger, Henry. *Nuclear Weapons and Foreign Policy.* New York: Harper & Row, 1957.

A pioneering work regarding the development of nuclear weapons and their effects on foreign policy that defined the concept of deterrence.

Mandelbaum, Michael. *The Nuclear Question: The United States and Nuclear Weapons, 1946–1976.* New York: Cambridge University Press, 1979.

Mandelbaum traces the development of U.S. nuclear-weapons policies. His thesis is that only deterrence should determine strategy and choice of weapons. Deterrence has worked for more than thirty years and will continue to work. The nuclear age is a "continence, with some modifications, of the history of politics among nations."

Newhouse, John. *Cold Dawn: The Story of SALT.* New York: Holt, Rinehart, and Winston, 1973.

The author discusses the political and technical problems of the SALT talks. Although it is written primarily from an American perspective, the book contains valuable information on Soviet negotiating behavior. Among the topics covered are differences in Soviet and American strategic concepts and the working of U.S. bureaucracies.

Pach, Chester J. Jr. *Arming the Free World: Origins of United States Military Assistance Programs, 1945–1950.* Chapel Hill: University of North Carolina Press, 1991.

A definitive work that covers the roots of postwar military assistance programs in the Lend-

Lease program of World War II, the early orientation toward Latin America, and the shift toward Europe and the Near East with the intensification of the Cold War after 1947.

Powaski, Ronald. *March to Armageddon: The United States and the Nuclear Arms Race, 1939 to the Present*. New York: Oxford University Press, 1987.

A history of the arms race from the Manhattan Project to the Iceland Summit of 1980. The theme is that despite the rhetoric of commitment to arms control, every president has increased the size of America's nuclear arsenal. The author holds a revisionist view of the Cold War.

Quester, George H. *Nuclear Diplomacy: The First Twenty-Five Years*. New York: Dunellen Publishing Company, 1970.

The author covers the emergence of nuclear deterrence, arms proliferation, and domestic as well as international factors affecting the Soviet Union and the United States.

Rhodes, Richard. *The Making of the Atomic Bomb*. New York: Simon & Schuster, 1987.

Rhodes begins with the birth of modern physics in the late nineteenth century and chronicles the story to the first hydrogen bomb tests by the United States (1954) and Soviet Union (1955). He includes interesting portraits of key individuals from Albert Einstein to Robert Oppenheimer and a lengthy bibliography. Suitable for the general reader.

——. *Dark Sun: The Making of the Hydrogen Bomb*. New York: Simon & Schuster, 1995.

A panoramic overview of the making of the hydrogen bomb and other aspects of United States and Soviet nuclear programs. The author often is critical of U.S. military strategy. He draws on recently released American and Soviet files for interesting anecdotes and details. Very well written by a novelist and writer of nonfiction and suitable for the general reader.

Roberts, Chalmers. *The Nuclear Years: The Arms Race and Arms Control, 1945–1970*. New York: Praeger, 1970.

The author, a journalist, discusses the inability of nations to cooperate in the nuclear age. The emphasis is on the changes in U.S. policy from the Baruch Plan to the Nixon administration. Topics covered include the Limited Nuclear Test Ban Treaty of 1963 and the Non-Proliferation Treaty of 1968.

Sherry, Michael S. *The Rise of American Air Power: The Creation of Armageddon*. New Haven: Yale University Press, 1987.

The author, using a cultural analysis, discusses American thinking regarding aerial bombing from the early twentieth century through the bombings of Germany and Japan and the early Cold War years.

Smoke, Richard. *National Security and the Nuclear Dilemma: An Introduction to the American Experience*. New York: McGraw-Hill, 1984.

A study of the impact of nuclear weapons on American strategic thinking since World War II. The author considers what the United States has done in the face of the increased threats to its security and what efforts have been made to achieve effective agreements to limit nuclear arms. A third edition of this book appeared in 1993.

Solokovsky, V. D. *Soviet Military Strategy*. New York: Crane Russak, 1975.

Solokovsky, a Soviet marshal, was one of his country's leading Soviet nuclear strategists. The editor compares his current writings with earlier ones.

Stares, Paul B. *The Militarization of Space: U.S. Policy, 1945–1984*. Ithaca: Cornell University Press, 1985.

A study of American space policy from Truman to Reagan. The author argues that plans for the militarization of space are not new; the SDI concept was around a long time before it won presidential support.

———. *Space and National Security*. Washington, D.C.: Brookings Institution, 1987.

The author makes a case against the deployment of antisatellite (ASAT) space weapons.

Talbott, Strobe. *Endgame: The Inside Story of SALT II*. New York: Harper & Row, 1979.

Talbott discusses the weapons, personalities, and technical issues of SALT II. His main focus is on United States policymaking and policymakers.

———. *The Masters of the Game: Paul Nitze and the Nuclear Peace*. New York: Knopf, 1988.

A sequel to *Endgame* and *Deadly Gambits*. Talbott reviews the history of the nuclear age from the Manhattan Project to SDI. He points out the sharp differences Nitze had with leading players in the American security debates.

Wolfe, Thomas W. *The SALT Experience*. Cambridge: Ballinger Publishing Company, 1979.

Wolfe covers the history of the SALT I and SALT II negotiations. He stresses the centrality of the Mutually Assured Destruction doctrine (MAD) to U.S. strategic thinking and views SALT as neither a clear success nor a failure in halting the arms race.

Zuckerman, Solly. *Nuclear Illusions and Reality*. New York: Viking, 1982.

Zuckerman has served as a science advisor to British governments since the 1950s. He discusses the enormous cost of the arms race and criticizes the philosophy that "if it works it is obsolete." The "nuclear illusion" is that nuclear weapons might be usable.

They can only serve as a deterrent. The author stresses the importance of NATO's conventional forces.

Western Europe

Alexander, G. M. *The Prelude to the Truman Doctrine: British Policy in Greece, 1943–1949*. Oxford: Oxford University Press, 1982.

Disagreeing with revisionist historians, the author says Britain supported a moderate constitutional monarchy in Greece. Alexander traces how Britain, unable to achieve its objectives, turned to the United States. He relies on recently released British documents.

Anderson, Terry H. *The United States, Great Britain, and the Cold War, 1944–1947*. Columbia: University of Missouri Press, 1981.

The author argues that British resistance to Soviet expansion determined the American stance at Yalta, during the Iran crisis of 1946, and following Churchill's "Iron Curtain" speech. It also was a key factor leading to the policy of containment.

Best, Richard A. Jr. *"Cooperation With Like-Minded Peoples": British Influence on American Security Policy, 1945–1949*. Westport, Conn.: Greenwood Press, 1986.

The author focuses on the diplomacy that led to the formation of NATO in 1949. He discusses Britain's concern with America's desire to disengage from Europe after World War II and sees a large British role in fostering American globalism.

Blechman, Barry, and Cathleen S. Fisher. *The Silent Partner: West Germany and Arms Control*. New York: Ballinger, 1988.

This volume examines the issue of national security in West Germany. It covers the evolution of positions and internal debates within the major political parties.

Costigliola, Frank. *France and the United States: The Cold Alliance Since World War II*. Boston: Twayne Publishers, 1992.

The author argues that the United States had the power to impose its will on France after World War II but that the power relationship became more balanced after Charles de Gaulle came to power in 1958. America's preoccupation with events outside Europe allowed the French to play an increased role in that arena.

Deighton, Anne. *The Impossible Peace: Britain, the Division of Germany, and the Origins of the Cold War*. New York: Oxford University Press, 1990.

The British and French worked to keep Germany divided in early 1946. The goal was to link western Germany with Western Europe and confine Communism to the Soviet zone.

De Porte, A. W. *Europe Between the Superpowers: The Enduring Balance*. New Haven: Yale University Press, 1979.

The defeat and division of Germany brought about "the death of the classical European state system." It was replaced by a bipolar system no longer centered on Europe that has been consolidated to the point where it "stands quite independent of its Cold War origins."

Fileppeli, Ronald L. *American Labor and Postwar Italy, 1943–1953: A Study of Cold War Politics*. Stanford: Stanford University Press, 1989.

Fearful that the fall of Mussolini would benefit Italy's Communists, the United States tried to divide the movement and supported the Christian Democrats. It enlisted the AFL-CIO in this effort. The author argues that this created a situation in which conservative democracy survived, but at the expense of the working class's winning decent wages and a voice in industrial affairs. That in turn helped to create a powerful Communist workers' movement.

Fulbrook, Mary. *The Divided Nation: A History of Germany, 1918–1990*. New York: Oxford University Press, 1992

Two thirds of the book is devoted to Germany since 1945. The author focuses on international developments, the roles of different elites, the economy, and the role of dissident groups. She also discusses the historical debates surrounding German history.

Gori, Francesca, and Silvio Pons, eds. *The Soviet Union and Europe in the Cold War, 1943–1953*. New York: St. Martin's Press, 1996.

A collection of essays, based on recently available Russian archival materials, focusing on the Soviet Union and the postwar order, the Cominform and the Soviet bloc, and relations between the Soviet Union and Western Europe. The contributors are Russian, European, and American specialists.

Hanrieder, Wolfram F. *Germany, America, and Europe: Forty Years of German Foreign Policy*. New Haven: Yale University Press, 1989.

The author outlines the problems and opportunities West German leaders from Konrad Adenauer to Helmut Kohl have faced internationally. He focuses on strategic security, national division, international economic integration, and domestic politics.

Harrison, Michael M. *The Reluctant Ally: France and Atlantic Security*. Baltimore: Johns Hopkins University Press, 1981.

An analysis of French alliance policies since World War II. The author argues that de Gaulle's policy of independence was pragmatic and flexible and not harmful to NATO.

Hathaway, Robert M. *Ambiguous Partnership: Britain and America, 1944–1947*. New York: Columbia University Press, 1981.

The author stresses the tensions and clashes in the Anglo-American relationship. Among the topics he discusses are British colonialism, economics and trade, the treatment of the defeated powers, and relations with the Soviet Union.

Hooper, John L. *America and the Reconstruction of Italy, 1945–1948*. New York: Columbia University Press, 1986.

This volume focuses on American aid and economic policies. The author also traces how different groups in the U.S. government worked to build ties with their Italian counterparts in order to revamp the Italian economy.

Kent, John. *British Imperial Strategy and the Origins of the Cold War*. Leicester: Leicester University Press, 1994.

British policy after World War II was not a response to Soviet activities but an "imperial strategy" designed to preserve its status as a major power. A revisionist view of British policy that sees the conflict with the Soviet Union as a "clash between rival imperialisms."

Large, David Clay. *Germans to the Front: West German Rearmament in the Adenauer Era*. Chapel Hill: University of North Carolina Press, 1996.

An overview of West Germany's rearmament in the context of the Western alliance. Large argues this process was promoted by Cold War tensions, a desire for a united Europe, and shrewd political strategy by German leaders. The integration of German forces into the NATO command structure helped democratize the German military establishment.

Lundestad, Geir. "Empire by Invitation? The United States and Western Europe, 1949–1952." *Journal of Peace Research* 23:3 (September 1986): 263–78.

American expansion after World War II had a greater impact than did Soviet expansion, as it was felt all over the world. However, in contrast to the Soviet empire, the American "empire" in Europe was largely an "empire by invitation," inasmuch as the countries of Western Europe urged the United States to play an active economic and military role on the continent.

Miller, James Edward. *The United States and Italy, 1940–1950: The Politics and Diplomacy of Stabilization*. Chapel Hill: University of North Carolina Press, 1986.

An analysis of the successful effort to integrate Italy into the Western alliance after World War II. As the Cold War intensified, the United States operated more freely in Italy and intervened often to stimulate the economy and undermine the Italian Communist Party. The author is critical of a policy he says helped to prevent necessary social and economic reforms.

Milwood, Alan S. *The Reconstruction of Western Europe, 1945–1951*. Berkeley: University of California Press, 1984.

An overview of how Western Europe's economic recovery began and continued and how integration succeeded and prolonged the economic boom.

Morgan, Kenneth. *Labour in Power, 1945–1951*. New York: Oxford University Press, 1984.

The author examines the achievements of the Attlee government in domestic and foreign policy, including the departure from India and the formation of NATO.

Ninkovich, Frank A. *Germany and the United States: The Transformation of the German Question Since 1945*. Boston: Twayne Publishers, 1988.

An analysis of the Soviet-American postwar conflict over Germany and an evolution of a new German identity in the age of the superpowers.

Ovendale, Ritchie. *The English-Speaking Alliance: Britain, the United States, the Dominions, and the Cold War, 1945–1951*. Boston: Allen and Unwin, 1985.

Ovendale covers Ernest Bevin's efforts to create a Western alliance that included the United States and Britain's "white" dominions: Canada, Australia, New Zealand, and South Africa.

Tusa, Ann. *The Last Division: A History of Berlin, 1945–1989*. Reading, Mass.: Addison-Wesley, 1997.

A history of Berlin during the Cold War, from its administrative division in 1945 to its physical division in 1961 and the fall of the Berlin Wall in 1989. The author discusses both the city's role in world affairs and the lives of its ordinary citizens.

Weiler, Peter. *British Labour and the Cold War*. Stanford: Stanford University Press, 1988.

An overview of the political role of the British labor movement in the early days of the Cold War. The author argues that the trade-union establishment cooperated with the Labor government to build a Cold War consensus and delegitimate radical working-class movements in Britain and abroad.

Woods, Randall B. *The Changing of the Guard: Anglo-American Relations, 1940–1946*. Chapel Hill: University of North Carolina Press, 1990.

Using recently available American and British archival material, the author chronicles the final state of a fifty-year process during which the United States displaced Britain as the world's leading capitalist power. He argues that the United States was not prepared to become the arbiter of European affairs.

Young, John W. *Britain, France, and the Unity of Europe, 1945–1951*. Leicester: Leicester University Press, 1984.

Young traces the postwar Labour government's policies toward France, asking why the two countries cooperated as members of the Western alliance but stayed fundamentally divided in their approach to European unity. The author sympathizes with Britain's gradualist approach toward European integration and sees the French goal of moving quickly toward European integration as premature and unrealistic.

―――. *France, the Cold War, and the Western Alliance: French Foreign Policy and Post-War Europe.* New York: St. Martin's Press, 1990.

A chronicle of how France, which entered into an alliance with the Soviet Union in 1944, came to join the NATO alliance directed against Moscow in 1949.

―――. *Cold War Europe.* New York: Arnold, 1991.

The author discusses the rise and fall of political tensions, the movement toward Western European unity, the triumph of liberal democracy in southern Europe, and the failure of Communism in Eastern Europe.

―――. *Winston Churchill's Last Campaign: Britain and the Cold War, 1951–1955.* New York: Oxford University Press, 1996.

The author's focus is on Churchill's attempt to bring about an East-West summit in the early 1950s. Despite the failure of Churchill's efforts, Young sees him as the "forefather of détente."

Eastern Europe/Soviet Bloc

Ascherson, Neal. *The Polish August.* Harmondsworth: Penguin, 1981.

A dramatic account of the Polish upheaval of 1980–81 by a skilled journalist who witnessed the events.

Ash, Timothy Garton. *The Magic Lantern: The Revolution of 1989.* New York: Random House, 1990.

Ash, a leading European journalist, witnessed events in Warsaw, Budapest, Berlin, and Prague. He chronicles the events in the four cities and adds an introduction and closing essay on the meaning of Eastern Europe's rejection of Communism. The title comes from the Magic Lantern theater in Prague, where the author watched Vaclav Havel in action as the Czech revolution surged forward.

Bruce, Valerie. "The Empire Strikes Back: The Transformation of the Eastern Bloc From a Soviet Asset to a Soviet Liability." *International Organization* 39:1 (Winter 1985): 1–46.

During the postwar era Eastern Europe's contribution to Soviet national security, economic growth, and stability declined. The reasons were the tensions between the Eastern European regimes and society, the Soviet role as a political and economic monopoly, and the unexpected costs resulting from Eastern Europe's economic opening to the West.

Brzezinski, Zbigniew K. *The Soviet Bloc: Unity and Conflict,* revised ed. Cambridge: Harvard University Press, 1971.

The author discusses the relationship between power and ideology as he traces the transformation of the Soviet bloc into what he sees as a polycentric system.

Dawisha, Karen. *Eastern Europe, Gorbachev, and Reform: The Great Challenge.* New York: Cambridge University Press, 1988.

The author traces the factors leading to reforms and the difficulties in putting them into practice.

Dedijer, Vladimir. *The Battle Stalin Lost: Memoirs of Yugoslavia 1945–1953.* New York: Viking, 1971.

Dedijer, the director of information in the Yugoslav government, chronicles Stalin's attempt to control Yugoslavia between 1948 and 1953. Although he wrote this history/memoir in the wake of the 1968 Soviet invasion of Czechoslovakia, the author remained what he calls a "utopian communist."

Gati, Charles. *The Bloc That Failed: Soviet-East European Relations in Transition.* Bloomington: Indiana University Press, 1990.

Gati traces the evolution of Soviet policy from Stalin to Chernenko, the early Gorbachev reforms and their impact on Eastern Europe, and the revolutionary upsurge of 1988–89.

Kovrig, Bennett. *The Myth of Liberation: East-Central Europe in U.S. Diplomacy and Politics Since 1941.* Baltimore: Johns Hopkins University Press, 1973.

The author argues that President Roosevelt's naiveté allowed the Soviet Union to take control of Eastern Europe. Since then the United States has tried to undermine that control, first by containment, then by the rhetoric of liberation, and finally by détente.

Lundestad, Geir. *The American Non-Policy Toward Eastern Europe, 1943–1947: Universalism in an Area Not of Essential Interest to the United States.* New York: Columbia University Press, 1978.

The author rejects both revisionist and orthodox interpretations regarding events in postwar Eastern Europe. He sees no consistent U.S. policy and says the United States did little to stop Soviet economic domination of the region. He also argues that except for Poland and Bessarabia the Soviet Union lacked predetermined plans for expansion.

Maier, Charles S. *Dissolution: The Crisis of Communism and the End of East Germany.* Princeton: Princeton University Press, 1997.

Maier argues that events validated Western patience in dealing with East Germany. East Germany's collapse ultimately stemmed from economic decline, the weakening of ideological commitment in the population, and the general upheavals in Eastern Europe that occurred in the wake of Gorbachev's reforms in the Soviet Union.

Stokes, Gale. *The Walls Came Tumbling Down: The Collapse of Communism in Eastern Europe*. New York: Oxford University Press, 1993.

The author traces the decline and fall of Eastern European Communism over two decades. Topics covered include the growing economic crises in the Soviet bloc, the attempts at managed economic reform, and the changes in Soviet policy toward the region.

Ulam, Adam B. *Titoism and the Cominform*. Cambridge: Harvard University Press, 1952.

The author covers how Tito prepared the groundwork for the Communist seizure of power in Yugoslavia and his later break with Stalin.

Valenta, Jeri. *Soviet Intervention in Czechoslovakia, 1968*. Baltimore: Johns Hopkins University Press, 1979.

The author argues that there was a divergence of opinion in the Soviet bloc about whether to invade Czechoslovakia. Among those who were reluctant to act was Mikhail Suslov, the Kremlin's chief ideologist. A good overview of decision-making in the Kremlin and of the invasion itself.

Vali, Ferenc. *Rift and Revolt in Hungary*. Cambridge: Harvard University Press, 1961.

Vali, a Hungarian scholar who spent five years in prison, explains the revolt in terms of nationalism versus Communism. He chronicles the split in the Hungarian Communist Party that contributed to the events of 1956.

Westad, Odel Arne, Sven Holtsmark, and Ivor B. Neumann, eds. *The Soviet Union in Eastern Europe, 1945–1989*. New York: St. Martin's Press, 1994.

Contributors included Leonid Gibiansky on the Soviet-Yugoslav conflict, Krystyna Kersten on 1956 as a crucial turning point, and Karel Kratky on Czechoslovakia and the Marshall Plan.

The Middle East

Cotton, Richard. *Iran and the United States: A Cold War Case Study*. Pittsburgh: University of Pittsburgh Press, 1988.

American policy toward Iran was crafted within a Cold War context dominated by real or imagined Soviet threats, which was not the basis for a sound relationship. The American-sponsored coup of 1953 and uncritical support for the Shah ultimately produced undesirable results.

Dawisha, Karen, ed. *The Soviet Union in the Middle East: Policies and Perspectives*. New York: Holmes and Meier, 1982.

This volume covers Soviet policies regarding the Arab world, the "northern tier," and the Horn of Africa. It also discusses the Soviet Union's use of proxies, trade matters, the Soviet-American rivalry in the Middle East, and Soviet theories on the region.

Eveland, Wilbur Crane. *Rope of Sand: America's Failure in the Middle East*. New York: Norton, 1980.

A harsh critique of American policy in the region. The author argues that U.S. failures in the region since 1950 were related to the use of covert action in place of diplomacy. As a result, Washington was not prepared for a series of wars and crises in the region.

Gasiorowski, Mark J. *U.S. Foreign Policy and the Shah: Building a Client State in Iran*. Ithaca: Cornell University Press, 1991.

The author argues that by bolstering the Shah's repressive regime in the 1950s and 1960s the United States indirectly contributed to the Iranian Revolution of 1979.

Ginat, Rami. *The Soviet Union and Egypt, 1945–1955*. London: Frank Cass, 1993.

An examination of the roots of Egyptian policy and the Soviet policy of supporting nationalist anticolonial regimes in the decade before the Bandung Conference. Ginat argues that a relationship between the two countries was developing even before the 1952 Egyptian military coup and Stalin's death in 1953.

Glassman, Jon D. *Arms for the Arabs: The Soviet Union and War in the Middle East*. Baltimore: Johns Hopkins University Press, 1975.

A survey of Soviet involvement in the region over two decades, focusing on the wars of 1956, 1967, and 1973 and the Soviet use of arms as a diplomatic weapon.

Hahn, Peter L. "Containment and Egyptian Nationalism: The Unsuccessful Effort to Establish the Middle East Command, 1950–1953." *Diplomatic History* 11:1 (Winter 1987): 23–40.

The first U.S. attempt to play an active peacetime role in guaranteeing stability and security in the Middle East failed because the United States sided with Great Britain and never considered Egypt as an equal partner.

——. *The United States, Great Britain, and Egypt, 1945–1956*. Chapel Hill: University of North Carolina Press, 1991.

A survey of the U.S. search for a independent diplomatic and strategic role in the Middle East and its involvement in the struggle between Britain and Egypt during the early Cold War.

Kaufman, Burton. *The Arab Middle East and the United States*. Boston: Twayne Publishers, 1995.

An analysis of United States-Middle Eastern relations in the context of two problems: America's involvement in the Arab-Israeli conflict and its interest in Middle Eastern oil.

Laqueur, Walter A. *The Struggle for the Middle East: The Soviet Union and the Mediterranean, 1958–1968.* Baltimore: Penguin, 1970.

Laqueur focuses on various aspects of Soviet policy in the region, including concerns over oil, its military presence, and Middle East Communist parties. He demonstrates how the Soviets established close relations with most Arab countries and adapted their ideology to allow cooperation with non-Communist nationalist regimes, at the expense of local Communist parties.

Lenczowski, George. *The Middle East in World Affairs,* 4th ed. Ithaca: Cornell University Press, 1980.

The author provides background material on the Ottoman and Persian empires before World War I. He covers the settlement after World War II that shaped the modern Middle East and other postwar developments.

Lytle, Mark Hamilton. *The Origins of the Iranian-American Alliance, 1941–1953.* New York: Holmes and Meier, 1987.

The author argues that both the United States and the Soviet Union tried to incorporate Iran into their regional security systems, setting the stage for conflict. Therefore the United States must share the blame for the confrontations over Iran during and after World War II. American concerns included a desire for Middle Eastern oil and containment of the Soviet Union. A revisionist analysis.

Quandt, William B. *Decade of Decisions: American Policy Toward the Arab-Israeli Conflict, 1967–1976.* Berkeley: University of California Press, 1977.

Quandt covers the 1967 war, abortive U.S. peace efforts in 1969 and 1970, the 1970 Jordanian civil war, the 1970–73 period of neglect, and the October 1973 war and its aftermath. He stresses the persistent American effort to limit Soviet influence and the key presidential role in policymaking.

Reich, Bernard. *Quest for Peace: United States-Israel Relations and the Arab-Israeli Conflict.* New Brunswick: Transaction Books, 1977.

Reich focuses on the period after 1967. He covers the 1973 war and subsequent disengagement agreements. He places the U.S.-Israeli relationship within the context of broader American Middle East interests and policies.

Rubin, Barry. *The Great Powers in the Middle East, 1941–1947.* London: Frank Cass, 1980.

A survey of the relations between the Great Powers from the Soviet Union's entry into World War II to the Truman Doctrine. The author traces the Anglo-American rivalry in the region and the view in Washington during the war that the British were a greater threat to American interests than the Soviets. However, 1945–46 was America's "year of learning" when it became convinced of Soviet aggressive intentions.

———. *Paved With Good Intentions: The American Experience in Iran*. New York: Oxford University Press, 1980.

Rubin traces American-Iranian relations from 1824 onward, with the main focus on the late 1970s. He argues that postwar cooperation between the two nations was based on misconceptions: Iran's overestimation of America's influence on the Shah and American overestimation of the Shah's ability to implement vital reforms.

Safran, Nadav. *Israel: Embattled Ally*. Cambridge: Harvard University Press, 1978.

A survey of the relationship between the United States and Israel, including an analysis of the policies of Henry Kissinger. The author concludes that American protection of Israel is compatible with friendly relations with the Arab states.

Samii, Kuross A. *Involvement by Invitation: American Strategies of Containment in Iran*. University Park: Pennsylvania State University Press, 1987.

The author focuses on U.S. policy from 1950 to 1953, with an epilogue on the 1970s. Until the 1950s Iran preferred democratic America to its experiences with British and Russian power. This perception changed as U.S. concern with the Cold War increased.

Schoenbaum, David. *The United States and the State of Israel*. New York: Oxford University Press, 1993.

The author examines the strategic, cultural, economic, and domestic political factors that have shaped U.S.-Israel relations since the 1940s. The United States gradually came to see Israel as an unofficial ally, but the process was neither smooth nor inevitable.

Spiegel, Stephen L. *The Other Arab-Israeli Conflict: Making American Middle East Policy, From Truman to Reagan*. Chicago: University of Chicago Press, 1985.

A survey of how several American presidents dealt with the Arab-Israeli conflict. American friends of Israel did not determine U.S. policy; the philosophic orientation of the president was the key ingredient. American leaders have made the faulty assumption that solving the conflict would solve other problems in the region, such as Soviet expansionism, Arab radicalism, or the instability of energy supplies.

Stooky, Robert. *America and the Arab States: An Uneasy Encounter*. New York: John Wiley, 1975.

Two thirds of the book covers the postwar era. The author emphasizes the Arab-Israeli conflict and the importance of the rise of Arab radicalism. He sees the need for accommodation rather than confrontation vis-à-vis Soviet interests in the region. Stooky served in the region as a foreign service officer and reflects the generally Arabist view of the State Department.

Tillman, Seth P. *The United States and the Middle East: Interests and Obstacles.* Bloomington: Indiana University Press, 1982.

A study of American policy toward the Arab-Israeli conflict by a former staff member of the Senate Foreign Relations Committee. He sees the need for the United States to synthesize for interests: the need for oil, Israeli security, détente with the Soviet Union, and peaceful solutions of disputes and struggles for self-determination. Tillman favors a Palestinian state.

Vassukuev, Akexei. *Russian Policy in the Middle East: From Messianism to Pragmatism.* Reading: Ithaca Press, 1993.

A survey from 1917 to the present. The author, a well-respected Russian journalist, discusses the various Arab states and the fates of local Communist parties. He also focuses on Iran and Afghanistan, Israeli-Arab relations, and the significance of the changes that took place in the Soviet-American relationship. The book includes a chart showing how Soviet foreign policy was made.

Zonis, Marvin. *Majestic Failure: The Fall of the Shah.* Chicago: University of Chicago Press, 1991.

The author blames the Shah for his own downfall and examines his psychological character.

The People's Republic of China

Borisov, O. B., and B. T. Koloskov. *Soviet-Chinese Relations, 1945–1970.* Bloomington: Indiana University Press, 1975.

In this translated volume, two Soviet scholars discuss Soviet-Chinese relations and anti-Soviet tendencies in China before 1960.

Grasso, June M. *Harry Truman's Two-China Policy, 1949–1950.* Armonk, N.Y.: M. E. Sharpe, 1987.

This study considers various aspects of the Truman administration's policy toward China, including security considerations, the question of Taiwan, control of China's UN seat, and the impact of the Korean War. Truman's goal was not to maintain Chiang Kai-shek or Nationalist rule on Taiwan, but to hold on to it for strategic purposes.

He Di. "The Most Respected Enemy: Mao Zedong's Perception of the United States." *China Quarterly* 137 (March 1994): 144–59.

The author traces Mao's view of the United States from his youthful admiration to his assumptions in the 1950s, based on his own ideological viewpoint and American containment policy, that American imperialism was the main threat to China. His assumptions in the 1950s prevented him from gaining experiences that might have given him a more balanced assessment.

Hunt, Michael H. *The Genesis of Chinese Communist Foreign Policy.* New York: Columbia University Press, 1996.

The goals of Mao and his generation were to restore China's glory and state power. The problems was how to get Western knowledge essential to rebuilding China's strength without absorbing Western values. Mao was flexible and opportunistic. The author revives the "lost chance" theory: that Mao was prepared to deal with the United States in the 1940s, but put off by American rigidity.

Lewis, John W., and Litai Xue. *China Builds the Bomb.* Stanford: Stanford University Press, 1988.

The authors review China's decision to build nuclear weapons, the influence of China's relationship with the Soviet Union and United States on that decision, and the organization put together to build the weapons. They detail the actual work from the mining of uranium to the test of a weapon, as well as the assistance received from the Soviet Union.

Mayers, David. *Cracking the Monolith: U.S. Policy Against the Sino-Soviet Alliance, 1949–1955.* Baton Rouge: Louisiana State University Press, 1986.

Mayers claims both Truman and Eisenhower did their best to encourage a Sino-Soviet split. They were aware of the strains in the alliance and expected normal American-Sino relations. Normal relations were delayed until the 1970s because of American domestic politics and Chinese suspicions of American intentions.

Westad, Add Arne. *Cold War and Revolution: Soviet-American Rivalry and the Origins of the Chinese Civil War.* New York: Columbia University Press, 1993.

A study of the interaction of superpower competition and Third World revolution from mid-1944 to May 1946. The author shows how the Chinese Communist Party and the Guomindang tried to manipulate the superpowers.

Zhai, Qiang. *The Dragon, the Lion, and the Eagle: Chinese-British-American Relations, 1949–1958.* Kent, Ohio: Kent State University Press, 1994.

Zhai examines the diplomatic processes by which China, Britain, and the United States dealt with each other during this period. Events discussed include the Chinese conquest of Tibet, the Korean War, Indochina and the Geneva Accords of 1954, and the Taiwan Strait offshore islands crises of 1954–55 and 1958. The United States and Britain failed to formulate a unified policy for the Far East.

Zhang, Shu Guang. *Deterrence and Strategic Culture: Chinese-American Confrontations, 1949–1958*. Ithaca: Cornell University Press, 1993.

The author applies deterrence theory to Sino-American relations. Using newly available sources, he examines seven cases of conflict. He concludes that neither power had aggressive designs on the other but both failed to understand that because of cultural differences regarding national security and ignorance of those differences.

——. *Mao's Military Romanticism: China and the Korean War*. Lawrence: University of Kansas Press, 1995.

An overview of China's behavior in the Korean War. Mao's belief in human will and its ability to overcome technology created a romantic attitude toward the use of force. As a result, in Korea he chose to behave aggressively instead of calculating the risks involved in going to war. Suitable for upper-division undergraduates and graduate students.

Japan

Borden, William. *The Pacific Alliance: United States Far East Policy and Japanese Trade Recovery, 1947–1955*. Madison: University of Wisconsin Press, 1984.

The author argues that the desire to restructure Japan as a market for U.S. goods was more important than Cold War ideology in the decision to rebuild Japan after 1947.

Prestowitz, Clyde V. Jr. *Trading Places: How We Are Giving Our Future to Japan and How to Reclaim It*. New York: Basic Books, 1988.

An insider view of U.S.-Japan trade negotiations by a veteran American trade negotiator. He argues that Japanese trade policy is based on rules totally different from the American approach.

Scalapino, Robert A., ed. *The Foreign Policy of Modern Japan*. Berkeley: University of California Press, 1978.

The common theme of the contributors is Japan's dependence on economics as the basis of foreign policy. Japan tries to balance its strong economic status and its vulnerability to political and economic shifts.

Schaller, Michael. *The American Occupation of Japan*. New York: Oxford University Press, 1985.

An account of the occupation and how it fit into American postwar policy. Schaller argues that MacArthur's occupation policies were subordinated to Cold War objectives.

——. "MacArthur's Japan: The View From Washington." *Diplomatic History* 10:1 (Winter 1986): 1–24.

The author provides an overview of the tension between MacArthur and the Truman administration during his tenure as Supreme Commander for Allied Powers (SCAP) in Japan. Schaller argues that although MacArthur tested Washington's patience, he accepted its policies after 1948. The Korean War rescued him from "near oblivion."

Schonberger, Howard B. *Aftermath of War: Americans and the Remaking of Japan, 1945–1952*. Kent, Ohio: Kent State University Press, 1989.

The author focuses on eight men, including MacArthur and John Foster Dulles, who contributed to American occupation policy. The book's main focus is the "reverse course" away from reform to favoring Japan's business elements.

The Third World

OVERVIEWS

Bills, Scott. *Empire and Cold War: The Roots of United States-Third World Antagonism*. New York: St. Martin's Press, 1990.

This study focuses on U.S. responses to independence movements in various parts of the Third World during 1945–47. The author argues that the United States had "no interest" in global revolution and sided with the European colonialists. This outlook intensified with the Cold War, as the United States increasingly viewed colonial revolutions in the Third World as a Communist tool.

Brands, H. W. *The Specter of Neutrality: The United States and the Emergence of the Third World, 1947–1960*. New York: Columbia University Press, 1990.

An overview of American relations under Truman and Eisenhower with various nonaligned nations. The author contrasts the ideological rhetoric of U.S. officials with non-ideological actions that were highly successful.

Colburn, Forrest D. *The Vogue of Revolution in Poor Countries*. Princeton: Princeton University Press, 1994.

A comparative study of revolutions in poor countries between 1945 and 1990. The author stresses the importance of ideas to revolutionaries, who held surprisingly similar viewpoints in the twenty-two countries surveyed. A key common influence was the exposure to European socialist traditions.

Donaldson, Robert H., ed. *The Soviet Union and the Third World: Successes and Failures*. Boulder: Westview, 1980.

Twenty-one specialists from academia, government, and the military assess the Soviet record of successes and failures in the Third World. The general consensus is that Soviet influence remains limited.

Hosmer, Stephen T., and Thomas W. Wolfe. *Soviet Policy and Practice Toward the Third World*. Lexington, Mass.: Lexington Books, 1983.

A historical overview that includes recommendations for limiting Soviet influence.

MacDonald, Douglas J. *Adventures in Chaos: American Intervention for Reform in the Third World*. Cambridge: Harvard University Press, 1992.

The author sees two American approaches in granting aid to Third World Countries: unrestricted assistance and assistance tied to the implementation of reform. He provides three case studies: China (1946–48), the Philippines (1950–53), and Vietnam (1954–63).

Menon, Rajnan. *Soviet Power in the Third World*. New Haven: Yale University Press, 1986.

A study focusing on the uses of Soviet military power in the Third World. Topics covered include arms transfers, doctrine, and Soviet capabilities to intervene directly. The author concludes that the Soviet Union is averse to risky military interventions.

Rodman, Peter W. *More Precious Than Peace: The Cold War and the Struggle for the Third World*. New York: Scribner's, 1994.

A survey of American and Soviet diplomatic competition and its effect on Third World nations. American victories during the Reagan administration in Angola, Afghanistan, and Central America helped defeat Communism. The author, a foreign policy official in several Republican administrations, argues that the United States finds it difficult to reconcile moral convictions with strategic responsibilities.

Saivets, Carol R., and Sylvia Goodby. *Soviet-Third World Relations*. Boulder: Westview Press, 1985.

Looking at both Soviet doctrine and the historical record from the end of World War II to the mid-1980s, the authors see Moscow becoming increasingly pragmatic in its policies.

ASIA

Bradsher, Henry S. *Afghanistan and the Soviet Union*. Durham: Duke University Press, 1983.

A survey of the decade before 1983, with emphasis on events after 1978, by a journalist and scholar very familiar with Afghanistan.

Brands, H. W. *India and the United States: The Cold Peace*. Boston: Twayne Publishers, 1990.

This survey covers events from Indian independence in 1947. The best coverage is on the Nehru years (1947–84). The author relies mainly on American materials.

Buhite, Russell D. *Soviet-American Relations in Asia, 1945–1954*. Norman: University of Oklahoma Press, 1982.

This survey focuses on areas that became part of the Soviet-American competition: China, Taiwan, Korea, and Indochina. Buhite sees the Soviet Union as expansionist with goals that included hegemony in Mongolia, Sinkiang (Xinjiang), Manchuria, Korea, and Japan. The United States refused to accept all of these ambitions and used force in Korea and Indochina to contain the Soviets. The United States was neither paranoid nor imperialistic but read Soviet intentions fairly accurately.

Donaldson, Robert H. *Soviet Policy Toward India: Ideology and Strategy*. Cambridge: Harvard University Press, 1974.

Donaldson focuses on the Soviet attempt to modify Marxist-Leninist doctrine to comply with Moscow's policy toward India.

Hammond, Thomas T. *Red Flag Over Afghanistan: The Communist Coup, the Soviet Invasion, and the Consequences*. Boulder: Westview Press, 1984.

The author provides an overview of Soviet-Afghan relations and the events surrounding the coup and the subsequent Soviet invitation. He argues that by taking over a buffer state the Soviets upset the strategic balance in the region.

Hess, Gary R. *The United States' Emergence as a Southeast Asian Power, 1940–1950*. New York: Columbia University Press, 1987.

Although the author is interested in the American role in Vietnam, he puts that subject in the larger context of Southeast Asia as a region of major interest to the United States. American policies in the region reflected its perceived needs in Europe and Japan rather than local conditions, which eroded U.S. prestige in the region after 1945.

Iriye, Akira. *The Cold War in Asia: A Historical Introduction*. Englewood Cliffs, N.J.: Prentice-Hall, 1974.

The author surveys U.S.-Asian relations, American political alternatives, and the structure of the international order in postwar Asia. He covers from the 1940s to the 1970s, but the heart of the book focuses on 1941–46.

Jukes, Geoffrey. *The Soviet Union in Asia*. Berkeley: University of California Press, 1973.

The book focuses on the period after Stalin's death. Jukes finds the Soviet Union pragmatic and opportunistic. He stresses the frequent division between ideology and practice, especially regarding support for existing governments instead of local Communist parties.

Kahin, Audrey R. *Subversion as Foreign Policy: The Secret Eisenhower and Dulles Debacle in Indonesia*. New York: New Press, 1995.

The Eisenhower administration mounted a major covert effort to overthrow Sukarno. The operation not only failed, says Kahin, but was counterproductive as it led to an authoritarian regime that remains in power.

Kasnacheev, Alexsandr. *Inside a Soviet Embassy: Experiences of a Russian Diplomat in Burma*. Philadelphia: Lippincott, 1962.

The author, a Russian who defected to the West, describes his education and disillusionment as well as the inner workings of a Soviet diplomatic mission in the Third World. He also covers Soviet intelligence operations and the rivalry with China.

McMahon, Robert J. *Colonialism and Cold War: The United States and the Indonesian Struggle for Independence, 1945–1949*. Ithaca: Cornell University Press, 1981.

The author explains the U.S. response to the Indonesian revolution within the context of America's overall foreign policy. Washington, convinced that it needed raw materials and foreign markets, favored a gradualist approach to colonial independence. U.S. support for Indonesia was based on Cold War pressures that made Indonesia an important country to cultivate.

——. *The Cold War on the Periphery: The United States, India, and Pakistan*. New York: Columbia University Press, 1994.

The book surveys American policy in the region from the late 1940s to the mid-1960s. The author argues that the U.S. alliance with Pakistan increased local tensions, drove India closer to the Soviet Union, and contributed to the India-Pakistan war of 1965.

Rostow, Walt Whitman. *The United States and the Regional Organization of Asia and the Pacific, 1965–1985*. Austin: University of Texas Press, 1985.

Rostow covers the origins of the Asian development program in the Johnson administration. He sees Johnson, whom he served as special assistant for national security affairs, as a farsighted and capable diplomat.

Wolpert, Stanley. *Roots of Conflict in South Asia: Afghanistan, Pakistan, India and the Superpowers*. New York: Oxford University Press, 1982.

An evaluation and critique of American policy in the region over a thirty-year period. The author argues that the United States must do more to solve the region's problems.

LATIN AMERICA

Alexander, Robert J. *The Tragedy of Chile*. Westport, Conn.: Greenwood Press, 1978.

The book covers Christian Democratic government before the election of Salvador Allende, the Allende years, and military rule after Allende's overthrow, which the author calls the tragedy of Chile. He finds the causes for the tragedy largely within Chile itself and maintains that Allende did not have a mandate to take Chile to socialism.

Ashby, Timothy. *The Bear in the Back Yard: Moscow's Caribbean Policy*. Lexington, Mass.: Lexington Books, 1987.

Ashby argues that the Soviet Union is pursuing a global plan to undermine the United States in the Caribbean basin, using Cuba as an example. His discusses covert and open Soviet aid to various Marxist-Leninist movements and urges U.S. countermeasures, such as aid to the Contras in Nicaragua.

Bailey, Samuel. *The U.S. and the Development of Latin America, 1945–1974*. New York: New Viewpoints, 1976.

The author maintains that America's concern with maintaining a non-Communist Latin America has resulted in dictatorships and economies that benefit the wealthy few.

Blasier, Cole. *The Hovering Giant: U.S. Responses to Revolutionary Change in Latin America*. Pittsburgh: University of Pittsburgh Press, 1976.

The author discusses Mexico (1910–17), Bolivia (1952), Guatemala (1954), and Cuba (after 1959). He says that the United States accepted revolutionary change in the first two cases. He is generally critical of U.S. policy.

Chace, James. *Endless War: How We Got Involved in Central America and What Can Be Done*. New York: Vintage, 1984.

A critical view of U.S. policy. The author, a former editor of *Foreign Affairs*, advocates policies to demilitarize the region. America's most important security concern in the region is Mexico, whose problems demand economic solutions.

Clark, Paul C. Jr. *The United States and Somoza, 1933–1956*. Westport, Conn.: Praeger, 1992.

Clark, who served as a foreign area specialist in Latin America for a decade, challenges the view that the Somoza dictatorship existed because of U.S. support. He argues that Washington never wanted Somoza but could not prevent his rise to power in the non-interventionist 1930s. He adds that Washington opposed Somoza after World War II, pointing to a temporary withdrawal of recognition in 1947. But Somoza "survived despite firm opposition from Washington."

Connell-Smith, Gordon. *The United States and Latin America*. New York: John Wiley, 1974.

A British scholar provides an overview of United States-Latin American relations. Two out of eight chapters cover the postwar period. The author sees the United States as being caught between idealism and self-interest.

Immerman, Richard H. *The CIA in Guatemala: The Foreign Policy of Intervention*. Austin: University of Texas Press, 1982.

The main reason for the success of the coup in 1954 was propaganda and the fear it caused. The author argues that the success of the coup led to miscalculations at the Bay of Pigs and in subsequent relations with other Latin American countries.

Jordan, William J. *Panama Odyssey*. Austin: University of Texas Press, 1984.

A study of the treaty process during 1964–78 whereby the United States returned sovereignty of the Panama Canal Zone to Panama. The author served on the National Security Agency staff under Johnson and Nixon and as U.S. ambassador to Panama (1974–78). His report is candid and discusses both the negotiations and the personalities involved.

Kagan, Robert. *The Twilight Struggle: American Power and Nicaragua*. New York: The Free Press, 1996.

Kagan covers American policy during the Carter, Reagan, and Bush administrations. Carter was of different minds about how to handle the Sandinista regime. Reagan, conversely, set the United States squarely against the Sandinistas and used political and paramilitary power against them. Moscow meanwhile hoped to turn Nicaragua into a second Cuba. Kagan credits Reagan, in whose administration he served as a Latin American specialist, for holding the course despite opposition at home, even in the wake of the Iran-Contra affair. He makes use of recently declassified documents.

LaFeber, Walter. *Inevitable Revolutions: The United States and Central America*. New York: Norton, 1983.

LaFeber traces 150 years of U.S.-Central American relations. He argues that the existing revolutionary climate is in large part an outcome of U.S. policy.

Langley, Lester. *America and the Americas: The United States in the Western Hemisphere*. Athens: University of Georgia Press, 1989.

The first comprehensive overview of U.S.-Latin American relations since Samuel Flagg Bemis's *The Latin American Policy of the United States*, published in 1943. The author argues that the United States should have greater respect for Latin American culture.

Pastor, Robert A. *Condemned to Repetition: The United States and Nicaragua*. Princeton: Princeton University Press, 1987.

The author discusses why those involved in recent U.S.-Nicaraguan affairs "repeated the history of United States-Cuban relations when both sides wanted a different outcome." Pastor served as director of Latin American affairs on the National Security Council in the Carter administration.

——. *Whirlpool: U.S. Foreign Policy Toward Latin America and the Caribbean*. Princeton: Princeton University Press, 1993.

The author reviews the policies of the Carter, Reagan, and Bush administrations. Especially strong on economic policy vis-à-vis Mexico.

Schlesinger, Stephen, and Stephen Kinzer. *Bitter Fruit: The Untold Story of the American Coup in Guatemala*. New York: Doubleday, 1982.

The authors argue that although the coup succeeded, it did long-term damage to U.S. relations with Latin America. They see the Arbenz era in Guatemala as one of significant social reform.

Schoultz, Lars. *Human Rights and United States Policy Toward Latin America*. Princeton: Princeton University Press, 1981.

A survey of policy from 1960 to 1980. The author defends President Carter's much criticized human-rights policies, arguing that previous administrations used the alleged threat posed by Communism to justify intervention to stop social and economic change.

———. *National Security and U.S. Policy Toward Latin America*. Princeton: Princeton University Press, 1987.

The author surveys instability in the region and the U.S. need for raw materials, military bases, and sea lines of communication. He concludes that events in the region are not a threat to U.S. security.

Sigmund, Paul E. *The Overthrow of Allende and the Politics of Chile, 1965–1976*. Pittsburgh: University of Pittsburgh Press, 1977.

The author surveys the causes and consequences of the 1973 coup against Salvador Allende. He argues that internal factors were primarily responsible for the coup and that Allende's economic policies were self-defeating.

Trask, Roger R. "The Impact of the Cold War on United States-Latin American Relations, 1945–1949." *Diplomatic History* 1:3 (Summer 1977): 271–84.

The Cold War increasingly influenced U.S. policy toward Latin America after 1945. The Organization of American States and the Rio Pact were both early examples of containment and prototypes for later Cold War collective defensive treaties and regional organizations, argues the author.

AFRICA

Coker, Christopher. *NATO, the Warsaw Pact, and Africa*. New York: St. Martin's Press, 1985.

A survey of the activities of both alliances in Africa and the Soviet challenge to the West on that continent.

———. *The United States and South Africa, 1968–1985: Constructive Engagement and Its Critics*. Durham: Duke University Press, 1986.

The author sees "seriousness of purpose" in Nixon-Reagan efforts in South Africa, but concludes that by 1985 the Reagan administration "had very little to show for its efforts." He contrasts Carter's approach to those of Nixon and Reagan.

Kalb, Madeline. *The Congo Cables: The Cold War in Africa—From Eisenhower to Kennedy*. New York: Macmillan, 1982.

The author focuses on the years 1960–63, putting U.S. Congo policy within a broader context that includes the Bay of Pigs and the Cuban Missile Crisis.

Korn, David A. *Ethiopia, the United States, and the Soviet Union*. Carbondale: Southern Illinois University Press, 1986.

The author see the government of Col. Mariam Haile Mengisto as consistently anti-American and pro-Soviet and argues that American attempts at rapprochement are futile. Mengisto courted the Soviet Union, not vice versa.

Noer, Thomas J. *Cold War and Black Liberation: The United States and White Rule in Africa, 1948–1968*. Columbia: University of Missouri Press, 1985.

Noer argues that conflicting strategic priorities and the intransigence of Africa's white rulers doomed American efforts to direct change along a peaceful path.

Oil and Other Economic Issues

Anderson, Irving H. *Aramco: The United States and Saudi Arabia: A Study in the Dynamics of Foreign Oil*. Princeton: Princeton University Press, 1981.

A examination of American efforts during World War II to assure permanent access to Saudi oil and the postwar development of the joint Saudi-American oil concern Aramco and its role in the evolution of America's "special relationship" with Saudi Arabia.

Chester, Edward A. *United States Oil Policy and Diplomacy: A Twentieth-Century Overview*. Westport, Conn.: Greenwood Press, 1983.

An overview from 1857 to 1981. The authors show the twists and turns of diplomacy affecting the oil market. The book suggests reasons for concern regarding the influence of oil companies over diplomacy.

Cohen, Benjamin I. *In Whose Interest? International Banking and American Foreign Policy*. New Haven: Yale University Press, 1986.

The author presents four case studies to illustrate the relationship between "high finance and high politics." He criticizes U.S. banks for overextending loans to foreign governments in the expectation that they will be profitable.

Jentleson, Bruce W. *Pipeline Politics: The Complex Political Economy of East-West Energy Trade*. Ithaca: Cornell University Press, 1986.

Jentleson traces the declining cohesiveness of NATO as a trade front vis-à-vis the Soviet bloc with the rise of Soviet oil and natural-gas sales to the West.

Kelly, J. B. *Arabia, the Gulf, and the West: A Critical View of the Arabs and Their Oil Policy*. New York: Basic Books, 1980.

The author traces the withdrawal of British power from Aden and the Persian Gulf and what he sees as the disastrous results of that withdrawal for Britain, Western Europe, and North America. He blames the oil-price explosion of 1973 on Western weakness, wishful thinking, and ignorance.

Miller, Aaron David. *Search for Security: Saudi Arabian Oil and American Foreign Policy*. Chapel Hill: University of North Carolina Press, 1981.

An examination of Saudi-American relations during World War II and immediately thereafter. The author describes how the Saudis and their oil shaped American attitudes toward the Middle East and how this was connected to the official opposition of the State and Defense Departments to Israeli statehood.

Stoff, Michael. *Oil, War, and American Security*. New Haven: Yale University Press, 1980.

Stoff maintains that the United States failed to develop a coherent Persian Gulf oil policy after World War II because of opposition from the oil companies and because the American government wanted to placate the British.

Yergin, Daniel. *The Prize: The Epic Quest for Oil, Money, and Power*. New York: Simon & Schuster, 1991.

A history of the oil industry from the discovery of oil in 1859 in Titusville, Pennsylvania, to the Iraqi invasion of Kuwait. Yergin traces the relationship among oil, politics, and national power.

Espionage and Covert Operations

Ambrose, Stephen, and Richard H. Immerman. *Ike's Spies: Eisenhower and the Espionage Establishment*. New York: Doubleday, 1981.

The authors trace the establishment and growth of the U.S. intelligence network through Eisenhower's military and civilian career. They criticize the performance of CIA chief Allen Dulles.

Andrew, Christopher, and Oleg Gordievsky. *The KGB: The Inside Story of Its Foreign Operations from Lenin to Gorbachev*. New York: HarperCollins, 1990.

A British historian and a KGB agent who defected in 1985 chronicle the history of the KGB, tracing its roots back to the sixteenth century and Ivan the Terrible's political police. The authors argue that Soviet politicians' preconceptions often overrode the facts presented to them.

Barron, John. *KGB: The Secret Work of Soviet Secret Agents*. Pleasantville, N.Y.: Readers Digest Press, 1973.

A lively overview by a journalist with a naval intelligence and Russian-language background.

Cline, Ray S. *Secrets, Spies, and Scholars*. Washington, D.C.: Acropolis Books, 1976.

The former deputy head of the CIA combines personal history with a history of the organization. He argues that secret intelligence is enormously beneficial, but only if political leaders protect an open society and do not make improper use of their secret intelligence agencies.

Jeffreys-Jones, Rhodri. *The CIA and American Diplomacy*. New Haven: Yale University Press, 1989.

A history of the CIA from its founding in 1947. The author, an British espionage expert, sees the CIA as the free world's most effective intelligence agency. Its success has depended on its ability to convince policymakers in Washington of the quality of its analysis.

Klehr, Harvey, and Harvey Radosh. *The Amerasia Spy Case: Prelude to McCarthyism*. Chapel Hill: University of North Carolina Press, 1996.

An account of the 1945 case involving classified material published by the journal *Amerasia*. The authors argue that Philip Jaffe, the journal's editor and publisher, was in contact with Soviet agents and had probably passed on information to them, demonstrating that not all the victims of the McCarthy era were innocent. The authors make use of recently released FBI files.

Kotek, Joel. *Students and the Cold War*. New York: St. Martin's Press, 1996.

Kotek describes how Soviet intelligence attempted to manipulate youth organizations in the West and how Western intelligence agencies, particularly the CIA, reacted.

Murphy, David, Sergei Kondrashev, and George Bailey. *Battle Ground Berlin: CIA versus KGB in the Cold War*. New Haven: Yale University Press, 1997.

This is an insider's account of espionage at the Cold War's heart. Murphy served as chief of the CIA's Berlin base, directing operations against the Soviet Union, East Germany, and the Soviet bloc; Kondrashev is a retired KGB lieutenant colonel and former head of its German department; and Bailey is a former director of Radio Liberty. The book covers the period from 1945 to the building of the Berlin Wall in 1961.

Penkovsky, Oleg. *The Penkovsky Papers*. New York: Doubleday, 1965.

The story of the spy who between April 1961 and August 1962 provided Britain and the United States invaluable top secret information. Penkovsky was attached to the Soviet general staff but grew to hate the Soviet system. He was executed in 1963. His notes about his amazing double life were smuggled out of the Soviet Union just before his death.

Persico, Joseph E. *Casey: From the OSS to the CIA*. New York: Viking, 1990.

Two-thirds of the text covers Casey's six-year service as head of the CIA. The author had access to 300,000 pages of Casey's private papers but provides no source notes.

Powers, Thomas. *The Man Who Kept the Secrets: Richard Helms and the CIA*. New York: Knopf, 1979.

A history of the CIA centered on the career of Helms, who headed the organization from 1966 to 1973. The author discusses the role of a secret service in a democracy as well as the bureaucratic and personal rivalries within the American intelligence network.

Ranelagh, John. *The Agency: The Rise and Fall of the CIA*. New York: Simon & Schuster, 1986.

The author surveys the history of the CIA, concluding with the status of the agency under Reagan and its shift from human intelligence to a highly technical operation. Includes many character profiles.

Schecter, Jerrold L., and Peter S. Deriabin. *The Spy Who Saved the World: How a Soviet Colonel Changed the Course of the Cold War*. New York: Scribner's, 1992.

An account of the life and career of Oleg Penkovsky, with a title that exaggerates matters somewhat. The authors say that information provided by Penkovsky told the United States that Khrushchev was bluffing about Soviet strength during the Cuban Missile Crisis. Deriabin, himself a Soviet defector, translated *The Penkovsky Papers*.

Stanglin, Douglas, et. al. "Secrets of the Cold War." *U.S. News and World Report*, March 15, 1993, 30–36.

More than ten thousand recently declassified documents reveal the extent of American losses of planes and crew members during overflights of the Soviet bloc between 1950 and 1970.

Sudoplatov, Pavel, and Anatolii Sudoplatov. *Special Tasks: The Memoirs of an Unwanted Witness—A Soviet Spymaster*. Boston: Little, Brown, 1994.

A controversial memoir. Many of Pavel Sudoplatov's claims about Soviet espionage and his role in it have been challenged. Most commentators agree that the information in the book must be checked and rechecked to find out which of Sudoplatov's revelations are reliable.

Weinstein, Allen. *Perjury: The Hiss-Chambers Case*. New York: Knopf, 1978.

The author, a professor of history at Smith College, began his research believing in Hiss's innocence, then changed his mind as he uncovered new evidence. Hiss was both a perjurer and a spy, although power-hungry politicians like Richard Nixon exploited the entire affair. A revised edition of this book was published in 1997.

Wolf, Markus, and Anne McElvoy. *The Man Without a Face: The Autobiography of Communism's Greatest Spymaster.* New York: Times Books, 1997.

As the head of East Germany intelligence, Wolf was responsible for some of the most spectacular intelligence coups of the Cold War. It took twenty years before the West even knew what he looked like. Wolf's planting of Günther Guillaume in the West German government brought about the fall of Willy Brandt.

Woodward, Bob. *Veil: The Secret Wars of the CIA, 1981–1987.* New York: Simon & Schuster, 1987.

A journalistic survey of the agency under William Casey during the Reagan administration. Short on documentation.

The Cold War at Home

McCarthyism and Domestic Politics

Belknap, Michael R. *Cold War Political Justice: The Smith Act, the Communist Party, and American Civil Liberties.* Westport, Conn.: Greenwood Press, 1977.

Belknap recounts the 1948 trial and conviction of eleven Communist leaders accused of conspiracy to overthrow the government. He begins his account in the late 1930s and continues the story until the last government attacks against the Communist Party in the late 1950s.

Caute, David. *The Great Fear: The Anti-Communist Purge Under Truman and Eisenhower.* New York: Simon & Schuster, 1987.

A survey by a British journalist. The author covers congressional investigations, the FBI informer system, the Loyalty Program of 1947, the attempts to identify Communists in areas such as education and show business, and other aspects of the anti-Communist fever in the United States.

Ceplair, Larry, and Stephen Englund. *The Inquisition of Hollywood: Politics in the Film Community.* New York: Anchor Press/Doubleday, 1980.

The authors see the Hollywood Ten as necessary victims of an hysterical anti-Communist era. They characterize the Communist outlook of the Hollywood Ten as the idealism of reformers who meant well. They argue the attack from some quarters was intended to eliminate all liberal film content.

Fried, Richard M. *Nightmare in Red: The McCarthy Era in Perspective*. New York: Oxford University Press, 1990.

There was far more to the McCarthy era than Joseph McCarthy. The author argues that Americans developed an obsession with domestic Communism that exceeded the actual threat and hurt civil liberties. He traces three decades of American anti-Communism from the Depression to John F. Kennedy's New Frontier.

Klehr, Harvey, John Earl Haynes, and Fridrikh Igorevich Firsov. *The Secret World of American Communism*. New Haven: Yale University Press, 1995.

A narrative with documents, including translations of Russian materials. The authors conclude that the evidence shows that the Communist Party of the United States of America (CPUSA) "assisted Soviet intelligence and placed loyalty to the Soviet Union ahead of loyalty to the United States." The Party "certainly" was a radical movement of dissent, but also "a conspiracy financed by a hostile power" that developed an extensive apparatus. The authors acknowledge that excesses were committed against the CPUSA, but maintain that "the secret world of the CPUSA made such excesses possible."

Kutler, Stanley J. *The American Inquisition: Justice and Injustice in the Cold War*. New York: Hill and Wang, 1982.

A constitutional historian examines the U.S. government's prosecution and harassment of Communists and suspected subversives during the Cold War. He sees a perversion of justice and the prosecutions for political or propaganda purposes illegal under the constitution.

Matusow, Allen J. *Joseph R. McCarthy*. Englewood Cliffs, N.J.: Prentice-Hall, 1970.

This volume includes selections from McCarthy's speeches, appraisals pro and con, and evaluations of the impact of McCarthyism. An excellent short introduction for students.

Mitgang, Herbert. *Dangerous Dossiers: Exposing the Secret War Against America's Greatest Authors*. New York: Free Press, 1988.

A chronicle of the FBI's files on thirty-five American writers who were subject to investigations and had their ideas distorted through misinformation. Mitgang begins in the 1920s.

Navasky, Victor S. *Naming Names*. New York: Viking, 1980.

Navasky, long-time editor of *The Nation*, chronicles the HUAC investigation of Hollywood in the 1950s and how the film community caved in to the pressure. He interviewed both informers and people they informed on, allowing both sides to be heard. Although he is hard on the informers, he also is critical of the Communists for their "overresponsiveness to Soviet policy" and believes that they caused some of their own problems.

Oshinsky, David M. *A Conspiracy So Immense: The World of Joe McCarthy*. New York: Free Press, 1983.

An excellent scholarly biography that covers both the man and the fearful atmosphere in which he thrived.

Powers, Richard Gid. *Not Without Honor: The History of American Anti-Communism*. Free Press: New York, 1995.

The first comprehensive account of American anti-Communism. Powers argues that American anti-Communism was a pluralistic movement whose reputation has been badly tarnished by a small group of fanatics in its ranks. The bulk of the movement was valid and valuable and has been robbed of the respect it merits. The excesses of McCarthy, the Vietnam War, and the softening of the Cold War alienated many liberals from anti-Communism and delegitimated it. But it persisted until Communism itself collapsed.

Radosh, Ronald, and Joyce Milton. *The Rosenberg File: A Search for the Truth*. New York: Holt, Rinehart, and Winston, 1983.

The authors make a strong case that Julius Rosenberg was guilty but that his wife Ethel was hardly involved — and that the U.S. government knew it. They argue that the death sentences imposed on the Rosenbergs were too harsh and were carried out because of the temper of the times. A revised edition, with a new introduction containing recent information from the National Security Agency and Soviet sources, was published in 1997. The new information supports the authors' original thesis.

Rovere, Richard H. *Senator Joe McCarthy*. New York: Harcourt Brace, 1959.

McCarthy was a demagogue without convictions who was responsible for his own demise. This biography was written only two years after McCarthy's death.

Schrecker, Ellen W. *No Ivory Tower: McCarthyism and the Universities*. New York: Oxford University Press, 1986.

Schrecker chronicles the dilemma of hundreds of professors called before HUAC. The author maintains that there was no Communist threat. The investigators were self-promoting, their victims well-intentioned people acting out of the highest motives. The universities caved in and did not defend the accused.

——. *The Age of McCarthyism: A Brief History with Documents*. Boston: Bedford Books, 1994.

The author surveys the international and domestic roots of American anti-Communism, the espionage cases of the 1940s and 1950s, investigations at the local and state levels, the destruction of Communist Party fronts and leftist trade unions, blacklisting, and other topics. McCarthy himself is viewed within the broader context of the time. The book includes nearly fifty documents.

Small, Melvin. *Johnson, Nixon, and the Doves*. New Brunswick, N.J.: Rutgers University Press, 1988.

An attempt to evaluate the antiwar movement's effect on American public opinion and the conduct of foreign policy in the Johnson and Nixon administrations. He concludes that policymakers tried to fashion a policy to neutralize the dissenters. The continuing protests produced a garrison mentality among Johnson and his advisors.

Steinberg, Peter L. *The Great "Red Menace": United States Prosecution of American Communists, 1947–1952*. Westport, Conn.: Greenwood Press, 1984.

Steinberg traces the political dishonesty in the FBI, HUAC, the courts, and the White House. But he also says the CPUSA contributed to its own problems by adopting an underground structure and mindlessly defending Soviet diplomacy.

Wittner, Lawrence S. *Rebels Against War: The American Peace Movement, 1941–1960*. New York: Columbia University Press, 1969.

An analysis of the shifting support for the peace movement over two decades. Wittner is sympathetic to the movement and attempts to refute criticism that it was naive.

Effects of the Cold War on American Culture and Daily Life

Boyer, Paul. *By the Bomb's Early Light: American Thought and Culture at the Dawn of the Atomic Age*. New York: Pantheon, 1986.

Boyer covers the impact of the atomic bomb on American culture and public opinion from 1945 to 1950. He discusses the small but energetic pacifist movement. Boyer argues that public opinion never transcended an ambivalent but anxious complacency.

Bremmer, Robert H., and Gary W. Richard, eds. *Reshaping American Society and Institutions, 1945–1960*. Columbus: Ohio State University Press, 1982.

The contributors discuss the social and cultural forces that helped shape the United States during the early Cold War years.

Clowse, Barbara B. *Brainpower for the Cold War: The Sputnik Crisis and the National Defense Education Act of 1958*. Westport, Conn.: Greenwood Press, 1982.

The launching of Sputnik led to the NDEA of 1958 to improve American education. America's leaders concluded that education was failing its national security role.

Doherty, Thomas. "Hollywood Agit-Prop: The Anti-Communist Cycle, 1948–1954." *Journal of Film and Video* 40:4 (Fall 1988): 1–14.

The author discusses forty anti-Communist films produced in Hollywood between 1948 and 1954. He provides a detailed analysis of Leo McCarey's *My Son John* and Edward Ludwig's *Big Jim McLain*.

Elsom, John. *Cold War Theater*. New York: Routledge, 1992.

A readable account of the theatrical history of the Cold War era in the context of the existing political climate. The author covers politics and theater in many countries and provides character sketches of many theatrical figures.

Gitlin, Todd. *The Sixties: Years of Hope, Days of Rage*. New York: Bantam Books, 1987.

Gitlin focuses on the New Left and radical student politics. He describes the culture and sensibilities that spawned the New Left and traces its violent decline.

Hinds, Lynn Boyd, and Theodore Otto Windt Jr. *The Cold War as Rhetoric*. Westport, Conn.: Praeger, 1991.

An examination of public discourse during the early Cold War. A good overview of speeches and comments by figures such as Alger Hiss, George Kennan, Henry Wallace, Harry Truman, Winston Churchill, and others.

Inglis, Fred. *The Cruel Peace: Everyday Life and the Cold War*. New York: Basic Books, 1991.

This overview by a British scholar includes coverage of significant events, chapter-length profiles of important actors and interpreters of the Cold War era, and discussions of fiction and films.

Leslie, Stuart W. *Cold War and American Science: The Military-Industrial Complex at MIT and Stanford*. New York: Columbia University Press, 1994.

The author focuses on the changing organizations and the changes in the scientists' values as a result of defense-research imperatives in materials science, physics, aeronautical engineering, and electronics. He sees damage to the United States as science was mortgaged to the Pentagon. The book includes engaging descriptions of important individuals.

MacDonald, J. Fred. *Television and the Red Menace: The Video Road to Vietnam*. New York: Praeger, 1985.

MacDonald sees the television networks functioning as conduits for official lies of the Cold War. Television reflected Cold War orthodoxies for twenty years, and blacklists kept many progressives and Stalinists off the air. Entertainment programs paid homage to the military and newscasts and documentaries uncritically supported established policies.

Miller, James. *"Democracy in the Streets": From Port Huron to the Siege of Chicago*. New York: Simon & Schuster, 1987.

The author traces the birth of the Students for a Democratic Society, focusing on key individuals, including Tom Hayden. Miller is sympathetic but not uncritical.

Oakes, Guy. *The Imaginary War: Civil Defense in American Cold War Culture*. New York: Oxford University Press, 1994.

Oakes writes that the civil-defense program was designed to lessen the American people's fears of nuclear war by suggesting that survival was possible. However, by the early 1950s authorities had no confidence in the program, a fact that was kept from the public.

Sayre, Nora. *Running Time: Films of the Cold War*. New York: Dial Books, 1982.

The author analyzes the political and financial pressures that changed the shape of Hollywood films after 1947. She examines social themes, such as the portrayal of sexuality, anti-Semitism, and racism.

Whitfield, Stephen J. *The Culture of the Cold War*. Baltimore: Johns Hopkins University Press, 1990.

An excellent examination of postwar American culture "as it responded to the threat and fear of Communism." The author covers politics, religion, cultural institutions, and films and novels that dealt with issues related to Communism. He focuses on the mass media and the celebrities it created. Whitfield concludes that "Communism was a threat *to* the United States . . . but it was not a threat *in* the United States, where the danger was often wildly overestimated."

Terrorism

Laqueur, Walter. *The Age of Terrorism*. Boston: Little, Brown, 1987.

A survey of the different types of modern terrorist groups. The author discusses the terrorist vision of the cleansing power of violence and absolutist values of right and wrong.

Martin, David C., and John Walcott. *Best Laid Plans: The Inside Storm of America's Fight Against Terrorism*. New York: Harper & Row, 1988.

Covers the period from Carter's Iran-hostage rescue disaster through the Reagan years. The authors—Martin is a Pentagon correspondent for CBS News and Walcott the national security correspondent for *The Wall Street Journal*—interviewed involved individuals from witnesses to policymakers.

The Fall of the Soviet Union

Brzezinski, Zbigniew. *The Grand Failure: The Birth and Death of Communism in the 20th Century*. New York: Scribner's, 1989.

This volume appeared just as the collapse of Communism in Eastern Europe was beginning. Brzezinski called the Gorbachev reforms the start of the disintegration of the Soviet system.

Gwertzman, Bernard, and Michael Kaufman, eds. *The Collapse of Communism*. New York: Times Books, 1990.

A collection of articles from *The New York Times* from the winter of 1988–89 to the winter of 1989–90. Gwertzman wrote an introduction and Kaufman an epilogue.

Loory, Stuart, and Anne Imse. *Seven Days That Shook the World: The Collapse of Soviet Communism*. Atlanta: Turner Publications, 1991.

A collection of remarkable photographs accompanied by an explanatory text giving a blow-by-blow account of the unsuccessful August 1991 coup against Gorbachev. This volume includes a historical overview, a time line covering the years 1848–1991, and biographies of the main individuals on both sides of the barricades. Eight CNN reporters contributed to this volume.

Matlock, John F. Jr. *Autopsy of an Empire: The American Ambassador's Account of the Collapse of the Soviet Union*. New York: Random House, 1995.

Matlock was at the heart of events from 1987 to 1991. Fluent in Russian and very knowledgeable about Russian culture, he has written a dramatic account for the general reader. He tries to answer several big questions, including: How and why did it all happen? Was a democratic Soviet Union possible? What lessons can be drawn from what happened? Matlock's book includes a useful chronology.

Pryce-Jones, David. *The Strange Death of the Soviet Empire*. New York: Metropolitan Books, 1995.

The author is a British journalist and historian. He provides a vivid picture of how the Soviet Union collapse was experienced by the men at the top of the Soviet empire from Eastern Europe to eastern Siberia.

Remnick, David. *Lenin's Tomb: The Last Days of the Soviet Empire*. New York: Random House, 1993.

Remnick, a *New Yorker* staff writer, offers a vivid glimpse of both ordinary Soviet citizens and their leaders from 1986 to 1991. He argues that the restoration of the truth about the Soviet Union's brutal past and bleak present was the most important force in sweeping away the Soviet system.

Legacies

Brzezinski, Zbigniew. "The Cold War and Its Aftermath." *Foreign Affairs* 71 (Fall 1992): 31–49.

Brzezinski see three major phases in the Cold War: from 1945 to Stalin's death, when both sides were motivated "more by fear than by aggressive designs": from the late 1950s to the late 1970s, when the Soviet Union was on the offensive; and from 1979 to 1991, when the West recaptured the ideological initiative, the Soviet Union entered a crisis, and the United States made the "final and decisive push" in the arms race.

Duedney, Daniel, and G. John Ikenbury. "Who Won the Cold War?" *Foreign Policy* 87 (Summer 1992): 123–39.

The authors reject the arguments of what they call the "Reagan victory school" that the hard-line military policies and tough ideological stance of the Reagan administration won the Cold War. They see Reagan's willingness to engage the Soviets, mutual weakness, and Western cultural influences that undermined Soviet ideology as important factors in the Cold War's end.

Gaddis, John Lewis. *The United States and the End of the Cold War: Implications, Reconsiderations, Provocations*. New York: Oxford University Press, 1992.

Gaddis discusses topics such as the objectives of American foreign policy, the objectives of containment, and the role of morality in the conduct of foreign policy. He concludes that although the Cold War was one of the most peaceful eras in European history, "we would do well to welcome the obsolescence of great-power authority."

Hogan, Michael J., ed. *The End of the Cold War: Its Meaning and Implications*. New York: Cambridge University Press, 1992.

A collection of essays examining various issues such as the origins of the Cold War, why it ended, its costs, and its winners and losers. Contributors include twenty-one experts from the United States, Europe, and the former Soviet Union.

Kennan, George. *At Century's Ending*. New York: Norton, 1996.

Kennan covers a variety of topics, including the consequences of the collapse of Communism and costs of the Cold War. He sees many perils ahead, including an endangered environment and the corrosive effects of the militarization of civilian life.

Kennedy, Paul. *The Rise and Fall of the Great Powers: Economic Change and Military Conflict from 1500 to 2000*. New York: Random House, 1988.

Kennedy warns that the United States overextended itself militarily and in terms of its worldwide commitments during the Cold War. As a result it is undergoing the same process of decline that plagued other overextended great powers in the past.

LeBow, Richard Ned, and Janice Gross Stein. *We All Lost the Cold War*. Princeton: Princeton University Press, 1994.

The authors argue that deterrence prolonged rather than shortened the Cold War. The military policies of the Reagan administration did not speed up but impeded Gorbachev's decision to reach an accommodation with the West.

Nau, Henry R. *The Myth of America's Decline: Leading the World Economy Into the 1990s.* New York: Oxford University Press, 1990.

A comprehensive assessment of the U.S. role in the world economy since 1945. Nau helped formulate President Reagan's economic policies in the 1980s. He argues that America's real global power is based not so much on material strength as on political leadership.

Nye, Joseph S. *Bound to Lead: The Changing Nature of American Power.* New York: Basic Books, 1990.

Nye argues that the United States remains the dominant power in the world. Only the United States has all the traditional bases of power: territory and population, military strength, economic vitality, and technological skill. Nye warns that the past teaches that if the world's strongest power does not lead, then instability will increase.

Propaganda

Hixon, Walter L. *Parting the Curtain: Propaganda, Culture, and the Cold War, 1945–1991.* New York: St. Martin's Press, 1997.

The author maintains that the Truman and Eisenhower administrations tried to use "psychological warfare" and cultural infiltration to undermine the Eastern European and Soviet regimes. Programs that showcased the good life in the West played a key role in that campaign. By the late 1950s, Pepsi-Cola, Cadillac convertibles, and fashion models had become American weapons in the Cold War.

Rawnsley, Gary D. *Radio, Diplomacy, and Propaganda: The BBC and VOA, 1956–1964.* New York: St. Martin's Press, 1996.

Rawnsley focuses on the impact of radio, which could "reach" into areas where television was limited. He argues that both the BBC and VOA might have done more by stressing national interests rather than suspicion and war.

Science and Computers

Edwards, Paul N. *The Closed World: Computers and the Politics of Discourse in the Cold War.* Cambridge: MIT Press, 1996.

A highly technical survey of how computers were used during the Cold War. The author provides case studies of how they affected the military, as well as other areas of American life.

Jones, Greta. *Science, Politics, and the Cold War*. New York: Routledge, 1988.

Focusing mainly on Great Britain, Jones argues that science was central to several crucial political battles of the postwar world. Moreover, scientists were often involved in nonscientific as well as scientific organizations.

Historiography

Combs, Jerald A. *American Diplomatic History: Two Centuries of Changing Interpretations*. Berkeley: University of California Press, 1983.

Several chapters of this survey are devoted to the Cold War. One full section of the book (out of six) deals with Vietnam.

Divine, Robert A. "Vietnam Reconsidered." *Diplomatic History* 12:1 (Winter 1988): 79–94.

At first, historians of the war were highly critical of U.S. involvement, a reversal of the usual pattern in American wars. Beginning in the late 1970s some historians offered a "belated justification" of the U.S. effort. The recent synthesis seems closer to the original critique, viewing the war as "more and more as a national tragedy."

Ferris, John. "Coming in From the Cold War: The Historiography of American Intelligence, 1945–1990." *Diplomatic History* 19:1 (Winter 1995): 87–116.

A comprehensive overview of books and articles on American intelligence during the Cold War.

Gaddis, John Lewis. "The Emerging Post-Revisionist Synthesis on the Origins of the Cold War." *Diplomatic History* 7:3 (Summer 1983): 171–90.

Gaddis argues that as new evidence comes to light, a synthesis is emerging out of the debate between orthodox and revisionist historians on the origins of the Cold War. Although he says that postrevisionism is more than "orthodoxy plus archives," he is more supportive of the orthodox than the revisionist analysis.

——. "On Moral Equivalency and Cold War History." *Ethics and International Affairs* 10 (1996): 131–48.

Gaddis argues against viewing the United States and Soviet Union in terms of "moral equivalency" and seeing the Cold War as little more than a power struggle devoid of moral context, as many American historians have done. Rather, the domestic systems of the Western democracies and Marxist-Leninist states were radically different, and those in the West, in terms of their morality, were decidedly preferable. In the end, the Cold War was "about individual freedom and the ability to pass it along to our kids." Western historians, while avoiding "self-congratulation," should also avoid "self-flagellation" when evaluating the two sides that fought the Cold War.

Haines, Gerald K., and J. Samuel Walker, eds. *American Foreign Relations: A Historiographic Overview.* Westport, Conn.: Greenwood Press, 1981.

A broad-ranging overview of American foreign relations with contributions from a wide range of scholars. The volume includes an essay on the origins of the Cold War and essays on U.S. relations in the twentieth century with Asia, sub-Saharan Africa, the Middle East, and Latin America.

Hammond, Thomas Taylor, ed. *Soviet Foreign Relations and World Communism: A Selected, Annotated Bibliography of 7000 Books in 30 Languages.* Princeton: Princeton University Press, 1965.

A comprehensive bibliography of books through the early 1960s.

Hogan, Michael G., ed. *America and the World: The Historiography of American Foreign Relations Since 1941.* New York: Cambridge University Press, 1995.

The most up-to-date collection of essays and historiographical surveys of the Cold War. Some of the chapters were previously published in scholarly journals. Many of the most prolific and respected scholars of American foreign policy contributed to this volume. The historiographical surveys cover material that has been published since 1981, when *American Foreign Relations: A Historiographical Overview* (Gerald K. Haines and J. Samuel Walker, eds.) was published.

Jones, Howard, and Randall B. Woods. "Origins of the Cold War in Europe and the Near East: Recent Historiography and the National Security Imperative." *Diplomatic History* 17:2 (Spring 1993): 251–76.

The authors examine works on the subject published during the previous decade. They see common factors suggesting an approach based on "the national security imperative." A detailed and comprehensive overview.

Lundestad, Geir. "Moralism, Presentism, Exceptionalism, Provincialism, and Other Extravagances in American Writings on the Early Years of the Cold War." *Diplomatic History* 13:4 (Fall 1989): 527–45.

A critique of American historical writing. Lundestad suggests that "the study of American foreign policy should focus less on America" and more on the broader context in which that policy was formulated. It should also make "relevant" comparisons between American policies and those of other countries.

Maddox, Robert. *The New Left and the Origins of the Cold War.* Princeton: Princeton University Press, 1973.

Maddox criticizes seven leading revisionist historians—including William Appleman Williams, D. F. Fleming, and Gar Alperovitz—of deliberately distorting the evidence. This book became the focus of angry debate among professional historians.

Siracusa, Joseph M. *New Left Diplomatic Histories and Historians: The American Revisionists*. Port Washington, N.Y.: Kennikat Press, 1973.

A survey of New Left historical works dealing with American foreign relations between 1898 and 1950. The author argues that revisionists have an essentially economic interpretation of American foreign policy, an approach that he finds inadequate.

Thompson, Kenneth W. *Cold War Theories*, vol. 1, *World Polarization, 1943–1953*. Baton Rouge: Louisiana State University Press, 1981.

Thompson outlines and defines three schools of thought regarding the Cold War: orthodox, revisionist, and what he says are a "small group of writers" who have been called "interpreters-critics." He says that the revisionists have provided a "healthy corrective" but that "the orthodox historians and the revisionists alike are guilty of similar errors however much they inveigh against one another." Thompson identifies with the "interpreters-critics," who he says include George Kennan, Walter Lippman, and Hans Morgenthau.

Tucker, Robert W. *The Radical Left and American Foreign Policy*. Baltimore: Johns Hopkins University Press, 1971.

Tucker analyzes the radical left's argument that the United States is an aggressive power and a threat to world peace whose foreign policy is dominated by the needs of capitalism. He rejects this argument, maintaining that the view of American foreign policy driven by capitalist needs for markets and Third World raw materials is "archaic."

Memoirs and Biographies

Memoirs

AMERICAN

Acheson, Dean. *Present at the Creation: My Years at the State Department.* New York: Norton, 1969.

Covers Acheson's years as assistant secretary of state (1941–45), undersecretary of state (1945–47), and secretary of state (1949–53).

Adams, Sherman. *First Hand Report: The Story of the Eisenhower Administration.* New York: Harper & Row, 1961.

Among the topics discussed are Dulles, McCarthy, the Suez Crisis, the arms race, and the U-2 incident. Adams admired Eisenhower but criticized Dulles as being too rigid.

Baker, James. *The Politics of Diplomacy: Revolution, War, Peace, 1989–1992.* New York: Putnam, 1995.

Baker provides extensive details on how horse trading works between nations at the highest level. Although he is circumspect on many issues (he says he has not written a "kiss and tell account"), Baker does sketch a vivid portrait of Soviet Foreign Minister Eduard Shevardnadze.

Ball, George. *The Past Has Another Pattern: Memoirs.* New York: Norton, 1982.

Ball served as undersecretary of state to presidents Kennedy and Johnson. He was involved in many important Cold War events, including the Cuban Missile Crisis, but is best known for his dissenting views on Vietnam and warning Johnson that the war could not be won.

Bissell, Richard M. *Reflections of a Cold Warrior: From Yalta to the Bay of Pigs.* New Haven: Yale University Press, 1996.

Bissell helped write the Marshall Plan. His many other activities included involvement in the 1954 Guatemala coup, which he later regretted. During his service as a highly placed CIA officer he was in charge of the U-2 and development of reconnaissance satellites.

Bohlen, Charles E. *Witness to History, 1929–1969.* New York: Norton, 1973.

A friend of John F. Kennedy and expert on the Soviet Union, Bohlen was involved in important dealings with the Soviet Union for four decades, helping to open the American embassy in Moscow in the 1930s. He provides views of Byrnes, McCarthy, Churchill, de Gaulle, Stalin, Khrushchev, and others.

Brzezinski, Zbigniew. *Power and Principle: Memoirs of the National Security Advisor, 1977–1981.* New York: Farrar, Straus & Giroux, 1983.

Brzezinski says that President Carter's accomplishments included Camp David, the Panama Canal treaty, and the Carter Doctrine issued after the Soviet invasion of Afghanistan. He also defends Carter's human-rights policy and the SALT II negotiations.

Byrnes, James F. *Speaking Frankly.* New York: Harper & Row, 1947.

Byrnes covers the period from Yalta to October 1946. He speaks of the frustrations of negotiating with the Soviets in an attempt to conclude a fair postwar settlement. A second volume of memoirs, *All in One Lifetime,* was published in 1958.

Carter, Jimmy. *Keeping Faith: Memoirs of a President.* New York: Bantam Books, 1982.

One quarter of this book is devoted to the Iran hostage crisis, the event that so damaged Carter's presidency.

Chambers, Whittaker. *Witness.* New York: Random House, 1952.

In this volume of more than eight hundred pages Chambers recounts his life as a Communist, his rejection of Communism, and the Hiss-Chambers trial.

Clifford, Clark. *Counsel to the President: A Memoir.* New York: Random House, 1991.

Clifford served as a government official for only six years but was an important advisor to presidents for decades. He was Johnson's secretary of defense when the decision was made to begin deescalation of the Vietnam War.

Eisenhower, Dwight D. *The White House Years: Mandate for Change, 1953–1956.* New York: Doubleday, 1963.

Eisenhower focuses primarily on foreign policy. A second volume of memoirs, *The White House Years: Waging Peace, 1956–1961,* appeared in 1965.

Haig, Alexander. *Caveat: Realism, Reagan, and Foreign Policy.* New York: Macmillan, 1984.

Haig recounts foreign-policy problems and the clashes within the White House during his eighteen months as secretary of state. He defends himself against charges that he tried to usurp presidential foreign-policy functions.

Harriman, W. Averell. *Special Envoy to Churchill and Stalin, 1941–1946.* New York: Random House, 1975.

Harriman recounts his wartime and early Cold War diplomacy. His account is detailed and easily accessible to the general reader.

Johnson, Lyndon. *The Vantage Point: Perspectives of the President, 1963–1969.* New York: Holt, Rinehart, and Winston, 1971.

Johnson pictures himself as a Hamlet, a brooding man who was often misunderstood. The writing was done by a changing group but clearly carries Johnson's personal stamp.

Kennan, George. *Memoirs.* 2 vols. Boston: Little, Brown, 1967 and 1972.

Covers Kennan's entire career, beginning with his student years. He criticizes Roosevelt and his top advisors for their credulity regarding the Soviet Union and its postwar intentions.

Killian, James P. *Sputnik, Scientists, and Eisenhower: A Memoir of the First Special Assistant to the President for Science and Technology.* Cambridge: MIT Press, 1978.

Killian served as president of MIT before being asked by Eisenhower to serve as White House science advisor. Among the topics he discusses are beginning of the U.S. space program and NASA, the development of ICBMs, and arms-control discussions with the Soviet Union.

Kissinger, Henry. *The White House Years.* Boston: Little, Brown, 1979.

The first volume of Kissinger's memoirs covers from 1969 to the Vietnam peace agreement of January 1973. The second volume, *Years of Upheaval* (Boston: Little, Brown, 1982), covers the period from February 1973 to Nixon's resignation in August 1974.

Kistiakowsky, George. *A Scientist in the White House: A Private Diary of President Eisenhower's Special Assistant for Science and Technology.* Cambridge: Harvard University Press, 1976.

Kistiakowsky served as Eisenhower's chief science advisor for eighteen months. His memoir is a window into government decision-making on matters of science at the highest levels.

McNamara, Robert S. *In Retrospect: The Tragedy and Lessons of Vietnam.* New York: Times Books, 1995.

In a controversial memoir that was greeted with both anger and respect, McNamara argues that the United States should have withdrawn from Vietnam either in late 1963, after Diem's overthrow, or in late 1964 or early 1965. He writes, "We were wrong, terribly wrong. We owe it to future generations to explain why."

Nixon, Richard M. *RN: The Memoirs of Richard Nixon*. 2 vols. New York: Grosset & Dunlop, 1978.

Nixon's accounts of his foreign-affairs efforts are detailed and compelling.

———. *Leaders*. New York: Warner Books, 1982.

Nixon's main subjects are Churchill, de Gaulle, Macmillan, Shigeru Yashida, Adenauer, Khrushchev, and Zhou Enlai. He also discusses Ben-Gurion, Sadat, Golda Meir, and the Shah of Iran. The book includes comments on the problems of leadership in the second half of the twentieth century.

Rusk, Dean. *As I Saw It*. New York: Norton, 1990.

Rusk had to be persuaded by his son to record these memoirs. The son was not afraid to ask the hard questions, although he did not always get satisfactory answers.

Shultz, George Pratt. *Turmoil and Triumph: My Years as Secretary of State*. New York: Scribner's, 1993.

Shultz has written an insider's view of "life . . . in the cockpit of the free world" and of how the Cold War ended. He is critical of Caspar Weinberger and William Casey.

Truman, Harry. *Memoirs*. Vol. 1, *Years of Decisions, 1945*. New York: Doubleday, 1955. Vol. 2, *Years of Trial and Hope*. New York: Doubleday, 1956.

Volume 1 covers Truman's years in the Senate and his first year as president, 1945. Volume 2 covers the years 1946–52, including the decision to build the hydrogen bomb. Truman includes many speeches and documents, but also provides a vivid self-portrait.

Vance, Cyrus. *Hard Choices: Critical Years in American Foreign Policy*. New York: Simon & Schuster, 1983.

This volume covers Vance's thirty-nine months as secretary of state. He resigned in April 1980 over the decision to attempt a military rescue of the American hostages in Iran, an action that he believed to be both illegal and morally wrong.

Weinberger, Caspar A. *Fight for Peace: Seven Critical Years in the Pentagon*. New York: Warner Books, 1990.

Weinberger oversaw the Reagan military buildup as secretary of defense. He says that both Reagan's success and his unfavorable reputation in some circles have the same source: Reagan's refusal to accept what Weinberger says was the misguided "conventional wisdom" of the defense and foreign-policy establishments in Washington.

SOVIET

Burlatsky, Fedor. *Khrushchev and the First Russian Spring: The Era of Khrushchev Through the Eyes of His Advisor*. New York: Scribner's, 1988.

A chronicle covering both domestic and foreign struggles, including the Cuban Missile Crisis.

Dobrynin, Anatoly. *In Confidence: Moscow's Ambassador to America's Six Cold War Presidents (1962–1986)*. New York: Times Books, 1995.

Dobrynin took part in every Soviet-American summit from 1955 to 1990. A strong defender of détente, he blames most Cold War crises on the Soviet leadership. He says their isolation and ideological blinders hindered his efforts in Washington, which he in turn strongly criticizes for its own anti-Soviet outlook. Dobrynin maintains that Reagan's SDI program forced Moscow to move toward arms control.

Gromyko, Andrei Andreevich. *Memoirs*. New York: Doubleday, 1989.

Gromyko knows more than he is willing to tell. His tenure at the top extended from the World War II Allied conferences through the 1980s. What he does say demonstrates the rigid and adversarial conduct of Stalinist diplomacy and appears to contradict the revisionist case that the United States could have avoided the Cold War.

Khrushchev, Nikita. *Khrushchev Remembers*. Boston: Little, Brown, 1970. *Khrushchev Remembers: The Last Testament*. Boston: Little, Brown, 1974. *Khrushchev Remembers: The Glasnost Tapes*. Boston: Little, Brown, 1990.

Khrushchev dictated his reminiscences secretly during the last years of his life. Although he is hardly objective, he is always remarkably frank and very interesting to read.

Molotov, Viacheslav. *Molotov Remembers: Inside Kremlin Politics: Conversations with Felix Chuev*. Chicago: Ivan R. Dee, 1993.

Chuev, an Molotov admirer, recorded 140 interviews with the aging former Soviet foreign minister, who speaks at length about his tenure in that post. Molotov's comments on Soviet intentions in Europe after World War II—he says his task was to expand Soviet borders "as much as possible"—support the traditional view about the origins of the Cold War and undermine the revisionist view.

Biographies

Acheson, Dean

Brinkley, Douglas. *Dean Acheson: The Cold War Years, 1953–1971*. New Haven: Yale University Press, 1992.

After his tenure as secretary of state, Acheson was an advisor to presidents Kennedy, Johnson, and Nixon. Brinkley discusses his role in matters such as debates over NATO, crises in Berlin and Cuba, the Vietnam War, and relations with France and de Gaulle, whom he judges to be a rigid Cold Warrior.

Smith, Gaddis. *Dean Acheson*. New York: Cooper Square, 1972.

A part of the publisher's series on American secretaries of state. Smith defends Acheson against his critics, especially Richard Nixon.

Ball, George

Bill, James A. *George Ball: Behind the Scenes in U.S. Foreign Policy*. New Haven: Yale University Press, 1997.

Ball played a role in the making and implementation of American foreign policy for four decades. He was a notable dissenter regarding American involvement in Vietnam. This book reveals the workings of the second tier of foreign policymakers, just below the Cabinet.

Bevin, Ernest

Bullock, Alan. *Ernest Bevin: Foreign Secretary, 1945–1951*. London: Heineman, 1983.

Bullock, a distinguished biographer, portrays a lonely man who played a major role during the early days of the Cold War. He details Bevin's role in many developments, including the Marshall Plan, NATO, and the division of Germany. Bullock postponed this volume until he could get access to Bevin's papers.

Bohlen, Charles

Ruddy, Michael T. *The Cautious Diplomat: Charles Bohlen and the Soviet Union, 1929–1969*. Kent, Ohio: Kent State University Press, 1986.

Bohlen was a member of the first U.S. delegation to Moscow after diplomatic relations were established in 1933. Ruddy rejects the view of Bohlen as a rigid Cold Warrior and instead pictures him as a sophisticated diplomat who believed that the Soviets mistrusted the West but were not bent on world domination.

Castro, Fidel

Geyer, Georgie Ann. *Guerrilla Prince: The Untold Story of Fidel Castro*. Boston: Little, Brown, 1991.

Geyer is a syndicated journalist familiar with Latin America. She sees Castro as a charismatic leader with an insatiable will to power.

Quirk, Robert E. *Fidel Castro*. New York: Norton, 1993.

A scholarly and exhaustively researched study that includes good portraits of Raul

Castro, Che Guevara, and other associates. Quirk is highly critical of Castro and his revolution.

Szulc, Tad. *Fidel: A Critical Portrait*. New York: Morrow, 1986.

Szulc, a journalist, was able to interview Castro. His focus is on the period between 1945 and 1961. Szulc consults newly available evidence regarding Castro's turn to Soviet-style Communism in the early 1960s.

de Gaulle, Charles

Cook, Don. *Charles de Gaulle*. New York: Putnam, 1984.

A major biography. Cook praises de Gaulle for getting France out of Algeria but is critical of his policies after 1962, particularly his decision to take France out of NATO.

Ledwidse, Bernard. *De Gaulle*. New York: St. Martin's Press, 1982.

A sympathetic biography, especially supportive of de Gaulle's effort to achieve a Europe outside Anglo-American control, which was achieved by entente with West Germany and the Soviet Union.

Dulles, John Foster

Gerson, Louis. *John Foster Dulles*. New York: Cooper Square, 1967.

Part of the publisher's series on American secretaries of state. Gerson is supportive of Dulles's policies. He maintains that Eisenhower had a good grasp of foreign affairs.

Guhin, Michael. *John Foster Dulles: A Statesman and His Times*. New York: Columbia University Press, 1972.

The author argues that Dulles's anti-Communist rhetoric was a tactic used to win support for his policies. In fact, he was flexible and realistic.

Hoopes, Townsend. *The Devil and John Foster Dulles*. Boston, 1973.

A highly critical study that pictures Dulles as a narrow-minded moralizer, a rigid ideologue, and a cowardly accomplice of McCarthy.

Pruessen, Ronald M. *Dulles: The Road to Power*. New York: Free Press, 1982.

Covers Dulles's career through his role as the chief negotiator of the Japanese peace treaty (1950–52). Pruessen rejects the image of Dulles as merely a Cold Warrior. Instead, Dulles was an economic pragmatist, who used moral and ethical comments as justifications for his economic preoccupations.

Eden, Anthony

Carlton, David. *Anthony Eden: A Biography*. Bloomington: Indiana University Press, 1981.

Eden served as Britain's foreign secretary before, during, and after World War II before becoming prime minister in 1955. Carlton argues that although Eden erred in the Suez Crisis of 1956, he was poorly served by some colleagues and by the United States.

Eisenhower, Dwight David

Ambrose, Stephen. *Eisenhower: The President*. New York: Simon & Schuster, 1984.

Although he views Eisenhower as a Cold Warrior, Ambrose praises his restraint. He faults Eisenhower for not doing more to improve relations with the Soviet Union and not understanding Third World nationalism.

Forrestal, James

Hoopes, Townsend, and Douglas Brinkley. *Driven Patriot: The Life and Times of James Forrestal*. New York: Knopf, 1992.

Chronicles Forrestal's role in World War II, his postwar role in defense matters, and his tragic suicide in 1949. Hoopes is a former Forrestal aide.

Fulbright, William

Woods, Randall Bennett. *Fulbright: A Biography*. New York: Cambridge University Press, 1995.

A lengthy (700-page) biography that covers Fulbright's role in the major events of the Cold War era. Woods explains how Fulbright changed from an advocate of presidential power in foreign affairs to a defender of the role of Congress.

Khrushchev, Nikita

Khrushchev, Sergei. *Khrushchev on Khrushchev: An Inside Account of the Man and His Era*. Boston: Little, Brown, 1990.

A look at Khrushchev's career by his son, who has since taken up residence in the United States.

Kissinger, Henry

Isaacson, Walter. *Kissinger: A Biography*. New York: Simon & Schuster, 1992.

A critical overview by the managing editor of *Time* magazine. The author does credit Kissinger for the clarity of his vision and skillful diplomacy.

Marshall, George C.

Ferrell, Robert H. *George C. Marshall*. New York: Cooper Square, 1966.

Part of a series on American secretaries of state. Ferrell stresses Marshall's ability to evoke the confidence of those around him, including President Truman.

Pogue, Forrest C. *George C. Marshall: Statesman*. New York: Viking, 1987.

The concluding volume of Pogue's four-volume work, which ranks as the standard biography of Marshall. Pogue, Marshall's official biographer, labored at his task for three decades. Thoroughly researched and balanced in its approach, this volume covers Marshall's activities as special ambassador to China, secretary of state, and secretary of defense. The author credits Marshall's vision and understanding of U.S. responsibilities for helping to save Europe from economic collapse and political turmoil.

Stoler, Mark. *George C. Marshall: Soldier-Statesman of the American Century*. Boston: Twayne, 1989.

A balanced biography. One of the author's concerns is Marshall's understanding of the use of power.

McNamara, Robert

Shapley, Deborah. *Promise and Power: The Life of Robert McNamara*. Boston: Little, Brown, 1993.

The author depicts McNamara as a paradox of contradictory traits, but mainly as an arrogant Cold Warrior whose explanations of the Vietnam War are self-serving. She discusses his concerns by 1965 that the war could not be won.

Nitze, Paul

Callahan, David. *Dangerous Capabilities: Paul Nitze and the Cold War*. New York: HarperCollins, 1990.

Callahan sees Nitze's career as a fifty-year effort to prevent the underestimation of the Soviet threat. He also chronicles Nitze's struggles with Kennan, Dulles, Kissinger, Weinberger, and others. Callahan admires Nitze's dedication but sees him as having been blinded by Cold War obsessions.

Nixon, Richard

Ambrose, Stephen. *Nixon*. 3 vols. New York: Simon & Schuster, 1987–1991.

The three volumes are *Nixon: The Education of a Politician, 1913–1962* (1987), *Nixon: The Triumph of a Politician (1962–1972)*(1989), and *Nixon: Ruin and Recovery, 1973–1990* (1991). The first volume deals with Nixon as a young Cold Warrior, including his involvement in the Alger Hiss case. The second covers détente, the opening to China, and other aspects of Nixon's foreign policy. The third covers his downfall and reemergence, in many though certainly not all quarters, as an elder statesman.

Stalin, Joseph

Ulam, Adam. *Stalin: The Man and His Era*. Boston: Beacon Press, 1973.

Probably the standard biography on Stalin by an expert on Soviet foreign policy.

Truman, Harry S.

Ferrell, Robert H. *Harry S. Truman: A Life*. Columbia: University of Missouri Press, 1994.

Ferrell is considered America's foremost Truman scholar. Although he is somewhat more critical than David McCullough (see the next entry), Ferrell supports both Truman's decision to use the atomic bomb against Japan to end World War II and his policy of containment.

McCullough, David G. *Truman*. New York: Simon & Schuster, 1992.

A sweeping narrative filled with interesting details supportive of Truman, an "ordinary man who became an extraordinary historical figure." Aimed at the general reader.

Wallace, Henry A.

Walker, J. Samuel. *Henry A. Wallace and American Foreign Policy*. Westport, Conn.: Greenwood Press, 1976.

The author shows how Wallace developed his foreign-policy ideas and gives them a sympathetic description.

Bibliographies, Reference Works, and Primary-Source Collections

Bibliographies

Black, J. L. *Origins, Evolution, and Nature of the Cold War: An Annotated Bibliographical Guide*. Santa Barbara, Cal.: ABC-CLIO, 1986.

The most comprehensive available bibliographical guide on the Cold War. Includes entries on books, articles, theses, and documentary collections.

Burns, Richard Dean. *Guide to American Foreign Relations Since 1700*. Santa Barbara, Cal.: ABC-CLIO, 1983.

The most comprehensive available guide to materials on American diplomatic history as a whole. There are two chapters dealing with the Cold War.

Burns, Richard Dean, and Milton Leitenberg. *The Wars in Vietnam, Cambodia, and Laos, 1945–1982*. Santa Barbara, Cal.: ABC-CLIO, 1984.

A bibliography containing more than 6,200 entries.

Reference Works

Arms, Thomas A. *Encyclopedia of the Cold War*. New York: Facts on File, 1994.

Consists of nearly seven hundred alphabetically arranged entries, each entry followed by a short list of readings for further information.

Brogan, Patrick. *The Fighting Never Stopped: A Comparative Guide to World Conflict Since 1945*. New York: Vintage, 1990.

Covers more than eighty wars fought after 1945, which collectively caused the deaths of 15 to 30 million people and created more than 30 million refugees.

Brune, Lester H. *Chronological History of United States Foreign Relations, 1776–January 20, 1981*, vol. 2. New York: Garland, 1985.

A day-by-day account of American foreign relations. Part D of this volume covers the Cold War in three sections: "Origins" (1945–52), "Struggles" (1953–68), and "Détente or Cold War?" (1969–81).

de Conde, Alexander, ed. *Encyclopedia of American Foreign Policy: Studies of Principal Movements and Ideas.* 3 vols. New York: Scribner's, 1978.

A collection of essays on a vast array of topics about American foreign relations. Many are concerned with the Cold War. Volume three also contains short biographies on important individuals in the history of American diplomacy.

Findling, John E. *Dictionary of American Diplomacy.* 2d ed. Westport, Conn.: Greenwood Press, 1989.

Entries on six hundred persons associated with American foreign policy through 1988, along with another six hundred nonbiographical entries on items connected with foreign policy "from crises to catch words." Each entry concludes with a short bibliography.

Frankel, Benjamin, ed. *The Cold War, 1945–1991.* Detroit: Gale Resources, 1992.

A three-volume set. The first volume contains the biographies of 149 important figures from the United States and Western Europe. The second contains 134 biographies of leading figures from the Soviet Union, Eastern Europe, China, and the Third World. The third includes a chronology, historical overview, and other information, including a bibliography.

Hoover Institution. *Yearbook on International Communist Affairs.* Stanford: Hoover Institution Press, 1966– .

The Hoover Institution has published this volume annually since its founding. It contains mainly country-by-country entries, but also a few essays on important themes.

Kirkendall, Richard S., ed. *The Harry S. Truman Encyclopedia.* Boston: G. K. Hall, 1989.

Includes a brief introduction and chronology and three hundred signed articles covering different aspects of Truman's career. The single longest article, at four and a half printed pages, is on the Cold War.

Kutler, Stanley I., ed. *Encyclopedia of the Vietnam War.* New York: Scribner's, 1996.

Contains some 560 articles ranging in length from fifty to five thousand words dealing with every aspect of the Vietnam War. The book also includes ten interpretive essays on key issues of the war.

Malo, Jean-Jacques, and Tony Williams, eds. *Vietnam War Films: Over 600 features, Made-for-TV, Pilot, and Short Movies, 1939–1992, from the United States, Vietnam, Belgium, Australia, Hong Kong, Great Britain, and Other Countries.* Jefferson, N.C.: McFarland & Company, 1994.

Two essays introduce the volume: "Southeast Asia and the French Cinema" and "The War and Vietnamese Films." This volume also contains photos and a bibliography.

Parrish, Thomas. *The Cold War Encyclopedia*. New York: Henry Holt and Company, 1996.

This volume is divided into two parts: an A–Z encyclopedia with hundreds of entries and a lengthy (114 pages) narrative chronology.

Sandler, Stanley, ed. *The Korean War: An Encyclopedia*. New York: Garland, 1995.

Contains 140 articles ranging in length from one to several pages; covers different aspects of the war. There also are biographies of leading figures. Sandler, a military historian, includes an extensive bibliography.

Schwartz, Richard Alan. *The Cold War Reference Guide: A General History and Annotated Chronology*. Jefferson, N.C.: McFarland & Company, 1996.

An overview of the Cold War intended for readers with little or no knowledge of the subject. There also are short biographies of major figures.

Summers, Harry G. Jr. *Korean War Almanac*. New York: Facts on File, 1990.

Colonel Summers is a decorated veteran of the Korean and Vietnam wars. This volume is divided into three parts: the first is an assessment of the historical and geographical realities that shaped the war, the second a detailed chronology of events, and the third a collection of 375 articles on different aspect of the war.

Primary-Source Collections

"Back From the Brink: Cuban Missile Crisis Correspondence Between John F. Kennedy and Nikita S. Khrushchev." *Problems of Communism*, Special Edition, Spring 1992, Vol. XLI.

Contains twenty-five texts of communications sent between October 22 and December 14, 1962. This edition also contains commentaries by Arthur Schlesinger Jr., Feodor Burlatsky, William Taubman, Vladislav M. Zubok, and Philip Bremen.

Bartlett, Ruhl Jacob, and David F. Long. *A Documentary History of United States Foreign Relations*, vol. 2, *The Mid-1890s to 1979*. Washington, D.C.: University Press of America, 1980.

The comprehensive collection of documents and readings. The first volume, *Record of American Diplomacy*, was published in 1948.

Chang, Lawrence, and Peter Kornbluh. *The Cuban Missile Crisis, 1962*. New York: Norton, 1992.

A National Security Archives Reader (see the section on Cold War Projects and Archives), this volume contains more than eighty formerly top-secret presidential, CIA, and Pentagon documents obtained by the National Security Archives.

Daniels, Robert V., ed. *A Documentary History of Communism and the World: From Revolution to Collapse.* Hanover, N.H.: University Press of New England, 1994.

An extensive collection of key documents on international communism and Soviet foreign policy. The earliest documents date from 1914, just before the Bolshevik Revolution, and the latest from 1992, just after the collapse of the Soviet Union.

Faas, Horst, and Tim Page, eds. *Requiem.* New York: Random House, 1997.

According to its title page, this book technically is by the photographers who died in Vietnam and Indochina. Of the three hundred journalists who died covering the wars in Vietnam between 1945 and 1975, at least 135 were photographers. This volume includes photos taken by journalists from almost a dozen countries, including North Vietnamese and Vietcong combat photographers. The editors point out that while photos taken from the South Vietnamese side depicted anything the photographers saw, those taken from the Communist side depicted the North Vietnamese and Viet Cong forces in a positive light only, thereby illustrating the difference between the uses of journalism to expose the truth and promote propaganda.

Freedman, Lawrence, ed. *Europe Transformed: Documents on the End of the Cold War.* New York: St. Martin's Press, 1990.

The editor provides a short introduction. Documents are arranged by topic: Establishment of the Post War System (1949–1963), Fruits of Détente (1970–1984), and Arms Control (1986–1990), for example.

Jensen, Kenneth M., ed. *Origins of the Cold War: The Novikov, Kennan, and Roberts "Long Telegrams" of 1946.* Washington D.C.: United States Institute of Peace, 1991.

During 1946 the Soviet ambassador in Washington (Novikov), the U.S. chargé d'affaires in Moscow (Kennan), and British chargé d'affaires in Moscow (Roberts) sent lengthy telegrams to their respective foreign ministers. (Roberts actually sent three.) The parallels between Roberts's and Kennan's views regarding Soviet intentions are striking. Novikov's telegram illustrates how Soviet officials viewed the world through a Marxist prism and, like the other two, is indicative of the hardening of views taking place during the critical year of 1946. An extraordinary insight into the origins of the Cold War. Novikov's telegram was only recently discovered in the Soviet archives and appears for the first time in English in this volume.

Kornbluh, Peter, and Malcolm Byrne. *The Iran Contra Scandal: The Declassified History.* New York: Norton, 1993.

A National Security Archives Reader (see the section on Cold War Projects and Archives), this volume contains more than a hundred documents obtained by the National Security Archives that deal with policy decisions, covert operations, and the subsequent cover-up.

LaFeber, Walter, ed. *The Origins of the Cold War, 1941–1947: A Historical Problem with Interpretations and Documents.* New York: John Wiley, 1971.

Thomas A. Bailey and Gar Alperovitz provide introductory essays debating the origins of the Cold War. Forty-six documents follow.

May, Ernest R., and Philip D. Zelikow, eds. *The Kennedy Tapes: Inside the White House During the Cuban Missile Crisis.* Cambridge: Belknap Press/Harvard University Press, 1997.

The transcripts of the secret recordings President Kennedy made of his meetings with the special executive committee (Ex Comm) that he formed to deal with the Cuban Missile Crisis. The editors provide connecting text based on other documents (such as personal notes, minutes of meetings, and memoirs) for Ex Comm sessions that were not recorded.

Mokoena, Kenneth. *South Africa and the United States: The Declassified History.* New York: Norton, 1994.

A National Security Archives Reader (see the section on Cold War Projects and Archives), this volume contains more than 350 pages of documents obtained by the National Security Archive on U.S. policy decisions, internal debates, and sensitive negotiations that guided U.S. actions toward southern Africa.

Public Papers of the Presidents of the United States. Washington D.C.: U.S. Government Printing Office, 1960– .

Volumes containing the public speeches and statements of the presidents are published annually. Indexes for each volume are published under the title *Cumulative Indexes to the Public Papers of the Presidents of the United States.*

Remington, Robin Alison, ed. *Winter in Prague: Documents on Czech Communism in Crisis.* Cambridge: MIT Press, 1969.

This volume contains seventy-two documents that cover the Czech reforms, the Soviet reasons for the invasion, and the reaction of the world Communist community.

Siracusa, Joseph M., ed. *The American Diplomatic Revolution: A Documentary History of the Cold War, 1941–1947.* Port Washington, N.Y.: Kennikat Press, 1977.

Fifty documents from Roosevelt's dealings with the Soviet Union to the beginning of the Marshall Plan.

The State Department Policy Planning Staff Papers, 1947–1949. New York: Garland Publishing, 1983.

A three-volume set of documents useful to historians of the early Cold War years.

United States Arms Control and Disarmament Agency. *Arms Control and Disarma-*

ment Agreements: Texts and the History of Negotiations. Washington, D.C.: U.S. Government Printing Office, 1982.

A useful volume that includes the texts of all agreements through 1982.

U.S. Department of State. *Foreign Relations of the United States.* Washington, D.C.: U.S. Government Printing Office, 1861– .

The goal of this ever-growing collection, according to statute, is to provide a "thorough, accurate, and reliable record of major United States foreign policy decisions and significant United States diplomatic actions." Documents must be published within thirty years. They are now available up to 1968. The most important single source of documents regarding American foreign policy.

Zinner, Paul, ed. *National Communism and Popular Revolt in Eastern Europe: Documents on Events in Poland and Hungary, February-November 1956.* New York: Columbia University Press, 1956.

A collection of speeches, party resolutions, editorials, and other documents describing the events that led up to each upheaval what transpired as a result.

Journals, Projects/Archives, and Presidential Libraries

Journals

Cold War International History Project Bulletin. Washington. D.C.: Woodrow Wilson International Center for Scholars, 1992– .

A remarkable new journal born as a result of the end of the Cold War and the accessibility of previously unavailable documents from Soviet and other Communist bloc archives. It contains recently released documents and articles based on those documents. This is the best single source for the most up-to-date research on the Cold War.

Department of State Bulletin. Washington, D.C.: Office of Public Communications, Bureau of Public Affairs, 1939–1989.

This monthly journal presented the U.S. government viewpoint on foreign policy issues. Its post–Cold War name (since 1989) is the *U.S. Department of State Dispatch*.

Diplomatic History. Wilmington: Del.: Scholarly Resources, 1977– .

The journal of the Society of Historians of American Foreign Relations. Has published many seminal articles by academics since it was founded. Also publishes book reviews.

Foreign Affairs. New York: Council on Foreign Relations, 1922– .

Probably the most influential American foreign-policy journal. This is where George Kennan published his "X" article on containment in 1947. Many seminal articles by academics, government officials from various countries, and other specialists have appeared in this quarterly since then. Also publishes book reviews.

Foreign Policy. Washington, D.C.: Carnegie Endowment for International Peace, 1970/71.

Another major journal that publishes articles by both academic and nonacademic specialists, including government officials. Includes book reviews.

International Affairs. Moscow: All-Union Society (*Zanniye*).

During the Cold War this was the organ of the Soviet foreign ministry. During Eduard Shevardnadze's tenure as Soviet foreign minister the journal became a forum for a far more open discussion of previously restricted topics. It now reflects the outlook of the Russian foreign ministry. Also printed in Russian and French editions.

International Affairs. London: Royal Institute of International Affairs. 1922– .

A long-established British journal.

International History Review. Burnaby, B.C.: Simon Fraser University, 1979– .

A Canadian journal. Also publishes book reviews.

International Security. Cambridge: MIT Press, 1976– .

Sponsored by the Center for Science and International Affairs, Harvard University.

Journal of American History. Bloomington, Ind.: Organization of American Historians, 1964– .

Publishes on all aspects of American history, including foreign affairs.

The National Interest. New York: National Affairs, Inc., 1985– .

Publishes on a variety of issues, including foreign affairs. The point of view tends to be traditional or postrevisionist.

Problems of Communism. Washington, D.C.: Document Studies Section, International Information Administration, 1952–1992.

Published a variety of analytical articles on the Soviet Union and other Communist nations. Discontinued in mid-1992, shortly after the dissolution of the Soviet Union. Subsequently revived as *Problems of Post-Communism*.

Projects and Archives

The Cold War International History Project.

The Cold War International History project was established in 1991 at the Woodrow Wilson International Center for Scholars in Washington, D.C. Its goal is to support the release of historical documents by all sides in the Cold War and to disseminate the information and perspectives on the history of the Cold War that emerge as a result of the release of documents from previously inaccessible archives in the former Communist bloc. The CWIHP publishes the *Cold War International History Project Bulletin* as well as individual working papers on aspects of the Cold War. See the website section for more information.

National Security Archive.

The National Security Archive is a nongovernmental, nonprofit library and publisher of declassified documents located at George Washington University in Washington,

D.C. Using the Freedom of Information Act, it has obtained and published tens of thousands of documents related to the Cold War. The archive already has published books on the Cuban Missile Crisis, the Iran-Contra Affair, and U.S. policy toward South Africa (see Primary-Source Collections). It also has published twelve enormous collections of documents on microfiche: *Afghanistan: The Making of U.S. Policy, 1973–1990* (more than two thousand documents), *The Berlin Crisis* (almost three thousand documents), *The Cuban Missile Crisis, 1962* (more than fifteen thousand pages of documents), *El Salvador: The Making of U.S. Policy, 1977–1984* (more than twenty-seven thousand pages of documents), *Iran: The Making of U.S. Policy, 1977–1980* (more than fourteen thousand pages of documents), *The Iran-Contra Affair: The Making of a Scandal, 1982–1988, Nicaragua: The Making of U.S. Policy, 1978–1990* (more than three thousand documents), *The Philippines: U.S. Policy During the Marcos Years, 1965–1986, South Africa: The Making of U.S. Policy, 1962–1989* (more than two thousand documents), *The U.S. Intelligence Community: Organization, Operations, and Management, 1947–1989, U.S. Military Uses of Space, 1945–1991, U.S. Nuclear Non-Proliferation Policy, 1945–1991.* See the website section for more information.

Presidential Libraries

Dwight D. Eisenhower Library, Abilene, KS 67410; tel. 1 (913) 263–4751.
Gerald R. Ford Library, 1000 Beal Avenue, Ann Arbor, MI 48109; tel. 1 (313) 668–2341.
Lyndon Baines Johnson Library, 2313 Red River Street, Austin, TX 78705; tel. 1 (512) 482–5137.
John Fitzgerald Kennedy Library, Columbia Point, Boston, MA 02125; tel. 1 (617) 929–4500.
Richard M. Nixon Library, 18001 Yorba Linda Blvd., Yorba Linda, CA 92686; tel. 1 (714) 993–5075.
Harry S. Truman Library, Independence, MO 64050; tel. 1 (816) 833–1400.

SECTION V

Electronic Resources

Websites

The following websites are online as of the date of publication of this volume. Because the World Wide Web is an unstable and constantly changing environment, these websites may go offline or change addresses without warning. The latest editions of several Web browsers allow automatic searching for updated website addresses. It is still a good idea to run periodic keyword searches for these and other sites, using an engine like Alta Vista or HotBot.

Central Intelligence Agency
http://www.odci.gov/cia/ciahome.html

This website has information about the CIA, its publications, and other topics. First access Publications, then go to the Factbook on Intelligence. From there you can download useful reports such as *The Genesis of the CIA* and *Key Events in the CIA's History*. Other valuable categories on the home page are Public Affairs and Other Intelligence Community Links.

Chronology of Russian History
www.bucknell.edu/departments/russian

This website is located at Bucknell University. After accessing this page, go to "chronology." It covers Russian history from the ninth century onward and includes a section on the Soviet period. It also includes an up-to-date section on the post-Soviet period.

Cold War Forum and Cold War Project
http://hibo.no/asf/Cold-War/about.html

This website is based in Norway. The information currently available is in the Cold War Forum section. It includes an article by Geir Lundestad, "Why Was There a Cold War?"

Cold War Hot Links
http://www.stmartin.edu/~Edprice/cold.war.html

The home page contains links to several dozen other sets of resources. They are of various types and of varying quality and reliability. Some are institutions such as the Rand

Corporation or the CIA. Others are archives, exhibits, or serious research projects. Some are valuable resources, such as the "Cold War Policies, 1945–1991," put together by other resource groups. Many, however, are home pages or exhibits politically tilted toward the left.

Cold War International History Project
http://www.cwihp.si.edu/

The CWIHP was established at the Woodrow Wilson International Center for Scholars in Washington, D.C. Its goal is to disseminate documents from the archives of former Communist states that are only now becoming available. You can access the *Cold War International History Project Bulletin* and other resources through this excellent website. Unless otherwise noted, information at this website can be freely downloaded, searched, copied, cited, and distributed.

East View Publications, Inc., World . . . and other former Soviet Republics
http://www.eastview.com

This website provides some extremely valuable resources on the post-Soviet republics since 1991. However, it also provides links to other websites, such as the Library of Congress Soviet Archives Exhibit, that are very useful for studying the Cold War.

H-Net Reviews
http://www.h-net.msu.edur/reviews/

H-Net is sponsored by the National Endowment for the Humanities and is based at Michigan State University. This site allows you to connect to a huge list of books and articles (choose Reviews by List). At that point, it is a good idea to narrow things down with a keyword search, such as "cold war," which on one occasion turned up twenty-six book reviews.

Korean War Project
http://biz.onramp.net.~Ehbarker

This website was set up by Hal Barker, the son of a Korean War veteran, a photojournalist and writer, and the founder of the Korean War Veterans Memorial Trust Fund. The material available includes an overview of the war, a bibliography (under "Bookstore"), and a "North Korean Travelogue."

Library of Congress
http://www.loc.gov.homepage/lchp.html

Go to the Exhibitions home page. From there you can access Revelations from the Russian Archives (http://lcweb.loc.gov/exhibits/archives/intro.html). There are two "floors" to this exhibit. The first is "Internal Workings of the Soviet System." The second is "The Soviet Union and the United States," which includes an overview of their relationship during the Cold War. Each display contains images of documents from the Soviet archives. You can click on them to get a full-size original. Hanging next to most displays is a translation, which you can access by clicking a small icon. This exhibition also is called the Library of Congress Soviet Archives Exhibit (http://www.ncsa.uiuc.edu/SDG/Experimental/soviet.exhibit/entrance.html#tour). You also can access an exhibit called For European Recovery: The Fiftieth Anniversary of the Marshall Plan (http://loc.gov/exhibits/marshall/) from the exhibits home page of the Library of Congress.

Loyola Homepage on Strategic Intelligence
http://loyola.ed/dept/politics.intel.html

This website is based at Loyola College in Maryland. It provides links to dozens of websites associated with intelligence activities.

The National Security Archive Home Page

The National Security Archive is an independent nongovernmental research institute and library located on the campus of George Washington University. It collects and publishes declassified documents acquired under the Freedom of Information Act. (See the section on Cold War Projects and Archives.) Aside from finding out about the Archive's publications, you can download valuable reports from this website. For example, material available on the Cuban Missile Crisis includes a short introduction, chronology, glossary, and more. This is one of the very best websites on the Cold War.

Rand Corporation Home Page
http://www.rand.org/

This website has information about the Rand Corporation and materials based on Rand's current research. Bibliographies and reports related to Rand's research are available.

USD History Department Home Page
http://ac.acusd.edu/History/

One of the best websites on the Cold War for high school and undergraduate students. Go to the course HIST 177 H.S. Diplomatic History. There you will find very informative resources such as Cold War Policies, which is divided into topics such as "Negotiation 1945," "Demonstrations 1946," "Containment 1947–1949," "Espionage," "Kitchen Debate," and more. There is also a resources list that contains a link to "Books and Film and CD-ROMs."

U.S. Diplomatic History Resources Index
http://www-scf.usc.edu/~Esarantak/stuff.html

This website is based at the University of Southern California. It has a comprehensive A to Z listing of resources available on the World Wide Web. Especially useful are the links to archives, including those of the Presidential libraries.

Washington Post Superpower Summits Archive
http://www.washingtonpost.com/wp-srv/inatl/longterm/summit/archive/archive.html

This website covers every superpower summit from 1959 to 1995. It provides original *Post* articles and photos from the newspaper's archives for each summit.

CD-ROMs/Microfiche

Chronicle of the 20th Century (1995)

This disc contains the text of the book *Chronicle of the 20th Century*, plus a great deal of additional information. It contains a month-by-month guide to the twentieth century, photos and archival video footage, and entries for every day of the century. Published by Dorling Kindersley (New York City) for Mac and Windows.

Day After Trinity (1995)

This disc expands on Jon Else's documentary film *Day After Trinity*, a chronicle of the life and times of nuclear scientist J. Robert Oppenheimer, who directed the Los Alamos Laboratory, where the first atomic bombs were built. This CD-ROM includes the entire film, a dossier from the top-secret files of the Manhattan Project, and other materials. Published by Voyager (Burlington, Vermont) for Mac and Windows.

National Security Archive Index on CD-ROM (1994)

The National Security Archive, in cooperation with Chadwyck-Healy Publishing Company, has produced a three-volume set of document collections on microfiche called "The Making of U.S. Policy." (For details on contents see the listing for the National Security Archive in Section IV.) There is a printed index guide for each microfiche collection. These guides have been brought together on this CD-ROM. It provides detailed descriptions of 35,789 documents that make up the twelve collections; a chronology database that enables users to display detailed chronologies of events covered in the collections; a glossary that provides a quick reference to individuals, events, organizations, specialized terms, and acronyms; and a bibliography database that provides background information on major government documents, books, and articles used in the development of the collections. The index allows the user to search across all collections and to track the role of individuals and organizations across the full span of the Cold War. Published by Chadwick-Healy (Alexandria, Virginia) for DOS.

Public Papers of the Presidents—Harry S. Truman (1996)

Contains eight volumes from the U.S. Government Printing Office. The materials include public messages, speeches, and statements of the President. Published by H-Bar (Oakman, Alabama) for Windows. Distributed by WAE (Clarkston, Washington).

Public Papers of the Presidents—Dwight D. Eisenhower (1996)

Contains eight volumes, as above. Published by H-Bar (Oakman, Alabama) for Windows. Distributed by WAE (Clarkston, Washington).

Seven Days in August (1993)

Contains photos, art, audio, and text from *Time* magazine sources related to the Berlin Crisis of August 1961. Includes a round-table discussion between Soviet and American political figures regarding the pressures both sides faced when the Wall was first built. Published by Time Warner Interactive (New York) for Mac and DOS.

Time Almanac of the 20th Century (1994)

This disc contains more than two thousand articles, five hundred photographs, and forty minutes of video. The top stories of each decade are illustrated by video and photo essays. It includes every "Man of the Year" cover story since 1927. Published by Compact Publications (Washington, D.C.) for Windows. Distributed by WAE (Clarkston, Washington).

USA Wars: Korea (1994)

Along with a wide range of materials on the history of the war, this disc includes a full-length audio of interviews with Korean War veterans. Published by Quanta Press (Minneapolis) for Mac and Windows. Distributed by WAE (Clarkston, Washington).

USA Wars: Vietnam (1994)

This is a vast collection of documents, photos, books, tables, articles, bibliographies, and more covering the history of the Vietnam War. One of its sections covers the Vietnam War Memorial in Washington, D.C. The text selections range from a few pages to book length. Published by Quanta Press (Minneapolis) for Mac and Windows. Distributed by WAE (Clarkston, Washington).

War in Vietnam: A Multimedia Chronicle (1995)

This disc features nearly eight hundred photographs, an hour of original CBS News video, and more than a thousand articles from the *New York Times*. It includes biographical essays and photos, information on the weaponry used in the war, thirty-five maps, and a database on the Vietnam War Memorial in Washington, D.C. Published by Macmillan Digital (New York) for Mac and Windows.

Wings: Korea to Vietnam (1995)

This disc contains information on five hundred aircraft of all types that flew during Cold War era. It includes interactive base tours, war reports with video, photos, animation, and much more. Published by Discovery Multimedia (Bethesda, Maryland) for Mac and Windows 95.

Films and Novels

The films and novels listed in this section have been selected as examples of the range of material that appeared during the Cold War. Some of them, such as the novel *The Spy Who Came in From the Cold* or the feature film *Platoon*, have genuine artistic merit. Others, such as the novel *The Ugly American* or the film *My Son John*, now appear dated and deeply flawed. They are listed here because they reveal something about the atmosphere and attitudes in the United States at the time of their release. Of course, they only tell a part of the story; most Americans, even in 1952, the year *My Son John* came out, when Senator Joseph McCarthy was at the peak of his influence, were not as obsessed with Communism as is the character played by Helen Hayes. They were much more concerned with the problems of their daily lives than with subversion from within. Still, it says something about the United States in the early 1950s that *My Son John* was made at all and that many Americans went to see it. It is, for example, hard to imagine *My Son John*'s being made during the 1970s and 1980s. It is just as hard to imagine *Apocalypse Now*, an antiwar film that appeared in 1979, being made in 1952. Whether we are entertained or not as we watch these films, they teach us something important about what the United States was like when Americans were going to the movie theaters to see them.

The same is true for documentary films. Some of the documentary films included here remain instructive; others tell us more about the thinking of the people who made them than about the topic they cover.

For more on Cold War films see Nora Sayre, *Running Time: The Films of the Cold War* (1982). For discussions of films and literature see Stephen J. Whitfield, *The Culture of the Cold War* (1991) and Fred Inglis, *The Cruel Peace: Everyday Life in the Cold War* (1991), which views its subject matter from a staunchly left-of-center position.

Films

FEATURE FILMS

Advise and Consent (1962). 139 minutes. Dir. Otto Preminger. Stars: Henry Fonda, Don Murray, Charles Laughton, Walter Pidgeon.

Based on the Allen Drury novel, a drama about Senate confirmation of a controversial nominee for secretary of state who advocates a more friendly approach to the Soviet Union. The nominee (Henry Fonda) flirted briefly with Communism as a young man. He finds that long after he rejected Communism, his youthful experimentation has come back to haunt him, just as similar activities came back to haunt many Americans during the late 1940s and 1950s. The film shows both conservatives and liberals as having virtues and flaws, and views their conflict in shades of gray rather than black and white.

Apocalypse Now (1979). 153 minutes. Dir. Francis Ford Coppola. Stars: Martin Sheen, Marlon Brando, Robert Duvall.

Loosely based on Joseph Conrad's *Heart of Darkness*, this antiwar film is one of the grimmest cinematic depictions of the Vietnam War. It accuses the United States of committing terrible excesses during the war.

The Bedford Incident (1965). 102 minutes. Dir. James B. Harris. Stars: Richard Widmark, Sidney Poitier.

A U.S. submarine under the command of a fanatical anti-Communist pursues a Soviet sub into international waters until battle is joined and both ships are destroyed, thereby suggesting that nuclear war could be triggered by chance.

Big Jim McLain (1952). 90 minutes. Dir. Edward Ludwig. Stars: John Wayne, James Arness.

A pro-House Un-American Activities Committee (HUAC) film in which a zealous FBI agent tracks down a Communist spy ring operating in Hawaii. One message of the film is that Communist Party leaders are utterly ruthless and willing to sacrifice their underlings, while the burden of toeing the "party line" drives ordinary members to drink or depression.

Born on the Fourth of July (1989). 145 minutes. Dir. Oliver Stone. Stars: Tom Cruise, Willem Dafoe.

The true story of Ron Kovic, who enlisted in the marines to fight in Vietnam and returned home paralyzed from the chest down. A searing critique of the war and the leaders who took the United States into it. Stone himself is a Vietnam veteran.

The Bridges at Toko-Ri (1954). 103 minutes. Dir. Mark Robson. Stars: William Holden, Grace Kelly, Frederick March.

A war-weary World War II veteran is recalled to service as a fighter pilot in the Korean War. Based on James Michener's best seller, this film depicts the heroism of the pilots who flew the dangerous missions over North Korea and the frustrations many of them felt at having to fight the so-called forgotten war.

The Day After (1983). 120 minutes. Dir. Nicholas Meyer. Stars: Jason Robards, JoBeth Williams.

The story of the catastrophic aftereffects of a nuclear attack on the United States. Set in Lawrence, Kansas, it is perhaps the most controversial made-for-television movie of its time.

The Day the Earth Stood Still (1951). 92 minutes. Dir. Robert Wise. Stars: Michael Rennie, Patricia Neal.

The story of a visitor from outer space (Rennie) who warns that our planet's international conflicts have become a threat to the entire universe because of the development of nuclear weapons. This warning, from a liberal perspective, about the dangers of nuclear war was an unusual theme during the early 1950s. Another science fiction film that made a similar point was *It Came From Outer Space* (1953).

The Deer Hunter (1978). 183 minutes. Dir. Michael Cimino. Stars: Robert DeNiro, John Cazale, John Savage, Meryl Streep, Christopher Walken.

A chronicle of Vietnam-era young Pennsylvania steelworkers: their lives before, during, and after their service in Vietnam. The film is an affirmation of traditional American working-class values. Its heroes are the patriotic young Americans who fought in Vietnam. Its heavies are the cynical politicians who led the United States into a disastrous war and the brutal Communist enemy the American soldiers fought in Vietnam.

Dr. Strangelove, Or How I Learned to Stop Worrying and Love the Bomb. (1964). 93 minutes. Dir. Stanley Kubrick. Stars: Peter Sellers, Sterling Hayden, George C. Scott.

Sellers plays three roles in this film, including the mad Dr. Strangelove. A classic black comedy about a psychotic general who launches a nuclear war that threatens to destroy the world, the film mocks anti-Communism, Soviet and American political leaders, and the American military establishment. Based on the book *Red Alert* by Peter George.

Fail-Safe (1964). 111 minutes. Dir. Sidney Lumet. Stars: Henry Fonda, Walter Matthau.

A computer malfunction triggers events that threaten to ignite a nuclear war. A critique from the liberal point of view of the American military. A similar viewpoint can be seen in *Dr. Strangelove* and *Seven Days in May*. In *Fail-Safe*, an unauthorized American nuclear attack destroys Moscow. To avoid an all-out nuclear war, the American president (Fonda) must agree to destroy New York City to compensate the Soviets for what happened to Moscow.

Full Metal Jacket (1987). 117 minutes. Dir. Stanley Kubrick. Stars: Matthew Modine, Adam Baldwin, Lee Ermey.

This film follows a group of marines from their basic training in the United States to bloody battle in the 1968 Tet Offensive. The frustrating combat the marines face, as they are picked off one by one by a hidden sniper, serves as a metaphor for the futility of the American experience in Vietnam. Based on *The Short Timers* by Gustav Hasford.

The Green Berets (1968). 141 minutes. Dirs. John Wayne and Ray Kellogg. Stars: John Wayne, David Janssen.

One of the few films of the 1960s and '70s that is strongly supportive of the U.S. war effort. It follows the exploits of an elite Special Forces unit in Vietnam. This highly successful film (it still does well as a video rental) was Wayne's patriotic response to the antiwar movement in the United States.

High Noon (1952). 84 minutes. Dir. Fred Zimmermann. Stars: Gary Cooper, Grace Kelly.

A Western set in a town called Hadleyville that fearfully awaits the return of a gang of outlaws whose leader has promised to murder the local marshal. The screenplay is by Carl Foreman, an ex-Communist who quit the Party in 1942. Foreman said the movie was a metaphor: Hadleyville is Hollywood and the outlaws are the House Un-American Activities Committee (HUAC). *High Noon* is considered by many to be the best Western ever made. It was criticized by John Wayne, who considered it anti-American.

I Married a Communist (1950). 73 minutes. Dir. Robert Stevenson. Stars: Laraine Day, Robert Ryan.

A superpatriotic film about a murderous Communist who blackmails a shipping director. Later retitled *Woman on Pier 13*. The Communist supposedly was based on Harry Bridges, the leader of the International Longshoremen's and Warehousemen's Union, who, in fact, opposed racketeering on the West Coast.

I Was a Communist for the FBI (1951). 83 minutes. Dir. Gordon Douglas. Stars: Frank Lovejoy, Dorothy Hart.

Supposedly based on the true story of Matthew Cvetic, who told his story of doing undercover work for J. Edgar Hoover and the FBI to writers at *The Saturday Evening Post*. It portrays Communist Party members as hypocrites who enjoy a luxurious banquet complete with caviar. Despite being largely fiction, the film won an Academy Award for best documentary. It also gave birth to a radio series in 1952 starring Dana Andrews.

Invasion of the Body Snatchers (1956). 80 minutes. Dir. Don Siegel. Stars: Kevin McCarthy, Dana Wynter.

A classic horror/science-fiction film in which people of a small town are replace by duplicates hatched from alien "pods." This was viewed by many as a metaphor for Communist subversion.

Iron Curtain (1948). 87 minutes. Dir. William Wellman. Stars: Dana Andrews, Gene Tierney.

An anti-Communist film said to be based on the true story of Igor Gouzenko, a Soviet code clerk who tried to defect to the West with secret documents. Filmed on location in Canada. Retitled *Behind the Iron Curtain*. Films from the late 1940s and early 1950s with similar themes include *The Red Danube*, in which a ballerina is pursued by Russian agents (1949; 119 minutes; dir. George Sidney; stars: Walter Pidgeon, Ethel Barrymore, Peter Lawford) and *The Steel Fist*, which portrays an escape from an Iron Curtain country (1952; 73 minutes; dir. Wesley Barry; stars: Roddy McDowall, Kristine Miller).

The Manchurian Candidate (1962). 126 minutes. Dir. John Frankenheimer. Stars: Frank Sinatra, Lawrence Harvey, Janet Leigh, Angela Lansbury.

Based on Richard Condon's 1959 novel, this film has been called the "most sophisticated film of the Cold War." An American soldier is brainwashed while a prisoner of war in North Korea to follow any order, including one to kill, when presented with a certain sign. He is part of a Communist plot to take over the presidency of the United States. The film, which was a critical success, also attacks McCarthyism.

MASH (1970). 116 minutes. Dir. Robert Altman. Stars: Donald Sutherland, Elliot Gould, Robert Duvall.

The adventures of three surgeons assigned to a mobile army surgical hospital (MASH) during the Korean War, although the film and the Richard Hooker series of novels on which it is based reflect liberal attitudes toward the Vietnam War. This black comedy and antiwar film spawned a TV series that lasted for nearly a decade.

My Son John (1952). 122 minutes. Dir. Leo McCarey. Stars: Helen Hayes, Robert Walker.

A loyal mother suspects her son of being a Communist spy. She turns him over to the FBI with the words, "Take him away. He has to be punished." One of the most militant anti-Communist films of the early Cold War era. A British film from the early Cold War era with a similar theme was *Conspirator* (1949; 85 minutes; dir. Victor Saville; stars: Robert Taylor, Elizabeth Taylor), in which a woman finds out that her husband is a Communist agent.

The North Star (1943). 105 minutes. Dir. Lewis Milestone. Stars: Anne Baxter, Dana Andrews.

Made during World War II, this film praises Russian resistance to the Nazis. Interestingly, neither Russia nor Communism is ever mentioned: the viewer must deduce the locale on the basis of costumes and sets. The film was subsequently edited down to eighty-two minutes to deemphasize the positive qualities of Russians and was retitled *Armored Attack*, a development that reflected the rising anti-Communist sentiment of the postwar era. Screenplay by Lillian Hellman.

On the Beach (1959). 133 minutes. Dir. Stanley Kramer. Stars: Gregory Peck, Ava Gardner, Fred Astaire.

A small group of survivors of a nuclear war between the superpowers try to live normal lives as they wait in Australia for the inevitable end when radiation from the war reaches them. One of the first films to try to picture what the world would be like after a nuclear war.

On the Waterfront (1954). 108 minutes. Dir. Elia Kazan. Stars: Marlon Brando, Eva Marie Saint, Rod Steiger, Lee J. Cobb.

A movie about corrupt trade-union bosses. The decision of the film's hero to testify against them is the heroic step necessary to break the grip of a corrupt union on the longshoremen. The film has been seen as Kazan's defense of his naming of Communists and fellow travelers during his testimony before the House Un-American Activities Committee (HUAC).

Pickup on South Street (1953). 80 minutes. Dir. Samuel Fuller. Stars: Richard Widmark, Jean Peters.

Communists steal microfilm to give the Soviets the atomic bomb. They are portrayed as more violent and immoral than gangsters, who at least have their own code of honor.

Platoon (1986). 120 minutes. Dir. Oliver Stone. Stars: Tom Berenger, Willem Dafoe, Charlie Sheen.

The main character is based on writer-director Stone himself. Considered by many to be an extraordinarily realistic portrayal about what American soldiers on the front line in Vietnam endured. A film that tried to do the same, 1950s style, for Americans who fought during the Korean War was *Pork Chop Hill* (1959; 97 minutes; dir. Louis Milestone; stars: Gregory Peck, Harry Guardino).

Red Dawn (1984). 114 minutes. Dir. John Milius. Stars: Patrick Swayze, C. Thomas Howell, Lea Thompson.

Small-town teens turn to guerrilla warfare against invading Communists. The film suggests that at least some of the old 1950s fear of the Soviet Union still existed in the 1980s, but it is among the last of the movies to depict a Soviet takeover of all or part of the United States. Another film of the same vintage is *Invasion U.S.A.* (1985; 107 minutes; dir. Joseph Zito; stars: Chuck Norris, Richard Lynch), in which action hero Norris singlehandedly defeats an onslaught of Soviet and Latin American terrorists.

Red Menace (1949). 87 minutes. Dir. R. G. Springsteen. Stars: Robert Rockwell, Hanne Axman.

A war veteran is duped by Communists. This film, which is generally considered McCarthyesque propaganda, was filmed in a quasi-documentary style, complete with a voice-over narration, to lend it more authority.

Salt of the Earth (1954). 94 minutes. Dir. Herbert Biberman. Stars: Juan Chacon, Rosaura Revueltas.

A graphic film about a strike by Mexican-American mineworkers led by a Communist-dominated union expelled by the CIO. The makers of the film, including blacklisted director Biberman, blacklisted screenwriter Michael Wilson, and blacklisted producer Paul Jarrico, held left-wing views. The production of the film faced obstacles at every stage, including the deportation of Revueltas to Mexico as an illegal alien, the refusal of the International Alliance of Theatrical Workers to allow its members to work on the film, the refusal of technicians and film labs to work on sound and film development, and the refusal of theaters to show the film once it was finally finished.

Seven Days in May (1964). 118 minutes. Dir. John Frankenheimer. Stars: Burt Lancaster, Kirk Douglas, Ava Gardner.

The story of an attempted coup led by military men opposed to attempts to improve relations with the Soviet Union. From the novel by Fletcher Knebel and Charles W. Bailey III. The film was supported by the Kennedy administration, which offered to vacate the White House for a weekend if the director wanted to film there.

The Spy Who Came in From the Cold (1965). 112 minutes. Dir. Martin Ritt. Stars: Richard Burton, Claire Bloom, Oskar Werner.

A first-rate dramatic film based on John Le Carré's acclaimed novel. (See Novels section for further details.)

The War Game (1967). 47 minutes. Dir. Peter Watkins.

A graphic and chilling film, shot in black and white and in documentary style, about the aftermath of a nuclear war as experienced by people in southeast England. Watkins made the film for the BBC and the British Film Institute, but it was deemed so upsetting that British national television refused to show it. Eventually it was shown in theaters. The film reflected the antinuclear sentiment in Britain that grew enormously after the 1962 Cuban Missile Crisis.

DOCUMENTARY FILMS

Eisenhower (1993). 150 minutes. PBS.

Part II, "Statesman," covers Eisenhower's presidency. Aired as part of *The American Experience*, a public television series. Produced by Austin Hoyt and Adrianna Bosch.

The Fall of the Berlin Wall (1990). 49 minutes. Dir. Peter Claus Schmidt.

A comprehensive history of the Berlin Wall, including its construction, the successful and failed escapes, and its destruction. One of the producers is Germany's Studio Hamburg.

Frontline: Captive in El Salvador (1985). 58 minutes. PBS.

Examines America's involvement in El Salvador, who benefits from U.S. support, and to what extent the United States is in control of the situation in El Salvador.

Frontline: War on Nicaragua (1986). 60 minutes. PBS.

Examines U.S. policy in Nicaragua and how American foreign policy is made. Accuses the Reagan administration of deception and draws a comparison between the Iran-Contra affair under Reagan with Lyndon Johnson's problems in Vietnam.

Hollywood on Trial (1976). 90 minutes. Dir. David Helperin Jr.

Narrated by John Huston, this film is about the Hollywood Ten, a group of writers and directors who refused to cooperate with HUAC. There are appearances by Ronald Reagan, Otto Preminger, Zero Mostel, and others.

The Hungarian Uprising: 1956 (1993). 30 minutes.

Covers the uprising and its aftermath.

Inside the Soviet Union: Before Gorbachev—From Stalin to Brezhnev (1990). 50 minutes.

Celebrates the sixtieth anniversary of the October Revolution and chronicles Soviet history from Moscow's point of view. Produced by the Society for Cultural Relations, US/USSR, a nonprofit group ostensibly established by Soviet and American citizens after World War II. The actual shooting was done by Soviet filmmakers under supervision of the Soviet government. In short, a Soviet propaganda film.

The McCarthy Years, With Walter Cronkite (1992). 113 minutes. CBS.

A series of reports in which broadcaster Edward R. Murrow stood up to McCarthy and his witch-hunt tactics.

Messengers From Moscow (1995). Series, 52 minutes each. Dir. Daniel Wolf.

A series produced by the BBC and WNET. The film titles are *The Struggle for Europe*, *The East Is Red*, *Fires From the Third World*, and *The Center Collapses*. They examine the crucial confrontations of the Cold War as seen through the eyes of key Communist Party participants and include information gleaned from previously closed Kremlin archives, eyewitness accounts, and rare footage from private sources. The evidence supports the thesis that the Soviet Union was expansionistic, not defensive, after World War II and that containment was a necessary response to deter Stalin.

The Rise and Fall of Mikhail Gorbachev (1991). 60 minutes. PBS.

Chronicles the career of the last leader of the Soviet Union.

Video From Russia: The People Speak (1984). 30 minutes. Dir. Dimitri Devyatkin.

An American film crew shot this film in the Soviet Union without official permission, speaking with people of all ages from several cities.

Vietnam: Chronicle of a War (1981). 89 minutes. CBS Fox.

The film clips are drawn from CBS archives. Narrated by Walter Cronkite.

Vietnam: A Television History (1983). 13 episodes, 60 minutes each. PBS.

This series, the most comprehensive made for television on the Vietnam War, chronicles the war from 1946 to the American withdrawal in 1973 and the collapse of the Saigon regime in 1975. One program deals with legacies, including the fates of American veterans and Vietnamese refugees. The programs are available on seven videotapes.

War and Peace in the Nuclear Age (1989).12 episodes, 60 minutes each. PBS.

A series of twelve films, each dealing with a different period or topic of the nuclear age: *Dawn, The Weapons of Choice, A Bigger Bang for the Buck* (on the hydrogen bomb), *Europe Goes Nuclear, At the Brink* (the Cuban Missile Crisis), *One Step Forward* (détente), *Haves and Have-Nots* (nuclear proliferation), *Carter's New World, Zero Hour* (Europe in the 1970s and 1980s, when NATO sought to place new missiles there), *Missile Experimental* (on new missile technology), *Reagan's Shield* (on SDI), and *Visions of War and Peace*.

Propaganda Films

Anarchy U.S.A. (1966). 78 minutes.

An anti-Communist, anti-civil rights propaganda film in which newsreel footage is used to supposedly reveal methods Communists used to take over China, Cuba, and Algeria and demonstrate that civil rights activists are using the same tactics.

Atomic Attack.

A propaganda film that depicts an ordinary American family trying to cope with the aftermath of an nuclear attack on a nearby city. Shown on the television program *Motorola TV Playhouse* on CBS.

The Atomic Cafe (1982). 88 minutes. Dirs. Kevin Rafferty, Jayne Loader, Pierce Rafferty.

Making use of film clips from the 1940s and 1950s, this film illustrates, and debunks, the government campaign to reduce American concerns about nuclear war. It shows suburban families in their bomb shelters, scenes from army training films, and people being evacuated from prospective nuclear testing sites.

Communist Blueprint for Conquest, Communist Weapons of Allure, Communist Target Youth (1955 and 1956). 103 minutes.

These propaganda films, whose titles are self-explanatory, were originally produced by the Department of Defense and the Armed Forces Information Agency.

Face to Face With Communism. 26 minutes.

A propaganda film that is a fictional account of the seizure of an American town by Communists.

Hearts and Minds (1974). 112 minutes. Dir. Peter Davis.

An examination, but an unbalanced one, of America's policy in Vietnam. The aim is to denounce the war and put much of the blame for it on American culture. Overwhelmingly sympathetic to those who opposed the war and bitterly critical of those who supported it.

Red Nightmare (1953). 30 minutes.

In this propaganda film, an average American is rejected by his family after Communists take over his town. Stars Jack Webb.

Why Vietnam (1965). 32 minutes.

A defense of U.S. policy in Vietnam, placing it within the tradition of America's commitment to help people retain their sovereignty.

NOVELS

Aksenov, Vasili P. *The Island of Crimea.* New York: Random House, 1983.

A fantasy about a politically independent Crimea that satirizes the corruption and decadence of Soviet society.

Clancy, Tom. *Red Storm Rising.* New York: Putnam, 1986.

After one of its largest oil refineries is destroyed by Muslim terrorists, the Soviet Union, beset by an oil shortage, decides to seize the Persian Gulf. One theme of this book is how war can be set in motion by human frailties, at which point the machines of war take on a life of their own. Clancy is also the author of *The Hunt for the Red October* (1984), a thriller about an attempt by a Soviet nuclear submarine to defect to the West.

Doctorow, E. L. *The Book of Daniel.* New York: Modern Library, 1971.

A fictional account of the Rosenberg spy case, as supposedly told by one of their children. The book looks back at the events in question from the vantage point of 1967.

Forsyth, Frederick. *The Fourth Protocol.* New York: Viking, 1984.

A thriller about a Soviet plan to control Britain and destroy NATO by swaying the British election. The Soviet plan is to detonate a small nuclear device near an American military base in Britain and thereby boost antinuclear sentiment.

Greene, Graham. *The Quiet American.* New York: Viking, 1956.

A searing critique of American activities in Vietnam. Some reviewers accused Greene, an Englishman, of being anti-American. At the same time, Greene's warnings about the problems that the United States would face in Vietnam were prescient.

Kundera, Milan. *The Unbearable Lightness of Being*. New York: Harper & Row, 1984.

Set in Czechoslovakia after the Soviet invasion of 1968, Kundera's highly praised book explores the emptiness of life under Communism and how it deadens the minds of the population.

Le Carré, John. *The Spy Who Came in From the Cold*. New York: Coward McCann, 1964.

Alec Leamas, a British secret agent, can no longer endure the amoral world he lives in, where the ends of combating Communism are used to justify the most ruthless means. He has decided he has had enough and will retire, or "come in," after one more assignment. The book was an enormous success and is considered one of the classic statements about the dilemmas associated with waging the Cold War. British author Le Carré's story also was highly successful as a film (see Feature Films section). His other books include *Tinker, Tailor, Soldier, Spy* (1975), *Smiley's People* (1978), and *A Perfect Spy* (1986).

Lederer, William Julius, and Eugene L. Burdick. *The Ugly American*. New York: Norton, 1958.

A harsh critique of American foreign service officers in Southeast Asia, who blunder because they lack knowledge of the language and culture of the region. The point of the book is that the United States must improve the quality of its representatives in order to be successful.

O'Brien, Tim. *The Things They Carried*. Boston: Houghton Mifflin, 1990.

A well-received collection of linked stories about American soldiers in Vietnam that is about both the Vietnam experience and the nature of writing about war.

Smith, Martin Cruz. *Gorky Park*. New York: Random House, 1981.

A Soviet police inspector, facing official obstruction by the Soviet establishment, tries to solve the mystery of three mutilated bodies found in Moscow's Gorky Park with the help of an American police officer, whose brother is one of the victims. The book critiques aspects of both Soviet and American life.

Updike, John. *The Coup*. New York: Random House, 1978.

Set in the fictional African country of Kush, Updike's novel chronicles the efforts of an American-educated dictator committed to revolutionary socialism to preserve his power.

APPENDIX

The Costs of the Cold War

U.S. Foreign Economic and Military Aid Programs, 1946–1990
(in millions of dollars)

PERIOD OR YEAR	TOTAL	ECONOMIC AID	MILITARY AID
1946–1952	41,661	31,116	10,545
1951–1961	43,358	24,053	19,305
1962–1969	50,524	33,392	16,862
1970–1979	66,714	29,602	38,812
1980–1984	62,107	40,460	21,647
1970	6,568	3,676	2,892
1971	7,838	3,442	4,396
1972	9,021	3,940	5,080
1973	9,472	4,117	5,356
1974	8,510	3,906	4,604
1975	6,916	4,908	2,009
1976	6,612	3,878	2,535
1977	7,784	5,594	2,190
1978	9,014	6,661	2,353
1979	13,845	7,120	6,725
1980	9,695	7,573	2,122
1981	10,550	7,305	3,245
1982	12,234	8,129	4,195
1983	14,202	8,603	5,599
1984	15,524	9,038	6,486
1985	18,128	12,327	5,801
1986	16,739	10,900	5,839
1987	14,488	9,386	5,102
1988	13,792	8,961	4,831
1989	14,868	9,860	4,828
1990	15,727	10,834	4,893
TOTAL	373,326	232,173	141,152

Approximately 76 percent of all economic aid was in grants; the remainder was in loans. About 71 percent of all military aid was in grants. About 62 percent of all aid was economic aid.

Source: U.S. Agency for International Development, *U.S. Overseas Loans and Grants and Assistance from International Organizations*, annual reports.

Department of Defense Manpower, 1950–1990
(in thousands)

YEAR	TOTAL	ARMY	NAVY	MARINE CORPS	AIR FORCE
1950	1459	593	381	74	411
1955	2935	1109	661	205	950
1960	2475	873	617	171	815
1961	2483	859	626	177	821
1962	2806	1066	664	191	884
1963	2699	976	664	190	869
1964	2686	973	111	190	857
1965	2654	969	112	190	825
1966	3092	1200	743	262	887
1967	3375	1442	750	285	897
1968	3546	1570	764	307	905
1969	3458	1512	774	310	862
1970	3065	1323	691	260	791
1971	2713	1124	622	121	755
1972	2322	811	587	198	726
1973	2252	801	564	196	691
1974	2162	783	546	189	644
1975	2128	784	535	196	613
1976	2082	779	525	192	585
1977	2075	782	530	192	571
1978	2062	772	530	191	570
1979	2027	759	523	185	559
1980	2051	777	527	188	558
1981	2083	781	540	191	570
1982	2109	780	553	192	583
1983	2123	780	558	194	592
1984	2138	780	565	196	597
1985	2151	781	571	198	602
1986	2169	781	581	199	608
1987	2174	781	587	200	607
1988	2138	772	593	197	576
1989	2130	770	593	197	571
1990	2044	732	579	197	535

Source: U.S. Department of Defense, *Selected Manpower Statistics*, annual reports.

U.S. Military Sales Deliveries to Foreign Governments by Country, 1950–1990
(in millions of dollars)

COUNTRY	1950–1986	1987	1988	1989	1990
TOTAL	113,810	11,114	9,195	7,385	9040
AUSTRALIA	3,703	589	850	583	381
BELGIUM	1,869	27	185	136	156
CANADA	2,022	127	212	144	193
CHINA, TAIWAN	3,239	366	484	353	460
DENMARK	1,066	62	149	93	38
EGYPT	4,112	962	498	441	573
EL SALVADOR	348	76	93	87	58
FRANCE	649	99	37	36	109
GERMANY	8,228	315	382	359	480
GREECE	2,010	79	129	137	114
INDONESIA	293	23	32	187	18
ISRAEL	9,138	1,230	754	230	151
ITALY	1,003	71	62	62	61
JAPAN	2,421	235	212	166	220
JORDAN	1,474	50	75	60	42
KUWAIT	884	58	41	46	52
MOROCCO	721	42	74	32	41
NETHERLANDS	2,973	417	327	391	381
NORWAY	1,531	83	117	95	117
PAKISTAN	1,654	134	139	175	575
PHILIPPINES	252	32	69	72	62
PORTUGAL	191	24	15	32	72
SAUDI ARABIA	32,245	3,324	1,327	986	1,152
SINGAPORE	492	143	191	37	47
SOUTH KOREA	3,089	344	326	316	328
SPAIN	1,376	822	637	658	403
SUDAN	245	26	24	30	—
THAILAND	1,410	95	291	211	175
TUNISIA	385	44	20	25	32
TURKEY	2,108	277	699	619	720
UNITED KINGDOM	4,774	205	180	131	205
VENEZUELA	686	50	27	13	20

Source: U.S. Defense Security Agency, *Foreign Military Sales, Foreign Military Construction Sales, and Military Assistance Facts*, annual reports.

INDEX

Abel, Rudolf, 190

ABM. *See* missiles, antiballistic

Acheson, Dean G., 99–100, 232–33, 311, 315

The Acting President (Gates, Schieffer), 79

Adams, Sherman, 311

Adenauer, Konrad, 100–101, 185

Afghanistan, 5, 46, 78–79, 83, 126, 128, 165, 199, 208; Soviet invasion of, 61, 75–76, 82, 105–6, 109, 161, 196

Africa, 3, 40, 43, 152, 190, 294–95; *see also* individual countries

Agnew, Spiro, 121

airlift, Berlin, 30, 102; *see also* Berlin Blockade

Albania, 86, 179

Algeria, 113

Allende, Salvador, 194

All Fall Down: America's Fateful Encounter With Iran (Sick), 73

Alliance for Progress program (Kennedy), 139

Allied Control Council, 160

Allies, 18, 20, 48

Alperovitz, Gar, 19

Ambrose, Stephen E., 11, 38, 66

America, Russia, and the Cold War, 1945–1966 (LaFeber), 11

America and Russia in a Changing World (Harriman), 130

An American Ordeal: The Antiwar Movement of the Vietnam Era (DeBenedetti), 59

American postwar foreign policy, 12

America's Half-Century: United States Foreign Policy in the Cold War and After (McCormick), 54

America's Longest War: The United States and Vietnam, 1950–1975 (Herring), 53

Ames, Aldrich, 120

Anatomy of a War: Vietnam, the United States, and the Modern Historical Experience (Kolko), 54

Andropov, Yuri, 77

Anglo-Iranian oil company, nationalization of, 45

Angola, 60, 71, 122

antiwar movement, 58–59, 137, 177, 192, 335; *see also* Vietnam War

apartheid, 108

Approaching Vietnam: From World War II Through Dienbienphu (Gardner), 54

Arab-Israeli wars, 69–70, 144, 154, 164

Arab world, 42, 154

Arbenz, Jacobo, 45, 187

arms control, 158–59, 176, 269–75; Bush and, 85, 87; Reagan and, 78, 84; Soviet Union and, 80, 127

arms limitation treaties, 5, 66, 87, 135, 166

arms race, 5, 64